# Economic Growth, Income Distribution and Poverty Reduction in Contemporary China

**Shujie Yao**

RoutledgeCurzon
Taylor & Francis Group
LONDON AND NEW YORK

First published 2005
by RoutledgeCurzon
2 Park Square, Milton Park, Abingdon, Oxon OX14 4RN

Simultaneously published in the USA and Canada
by RoutledgeCurzon
270 Madison Ave, New York, NY 10016

*RoutledgeCurzon is an imprint of the Taylor & Francis Group*

Typeset in Times by
Keystroke, Jacaranda Lodge, Wolverhampton
Printed and bound in Great Britain by
Antony Rowe, Chippenham, Wiltshire

*British Library Cataloguing in Publication Data*
A catalogue record for this book is available from the British Library

*Library of Congress Cataloging in Publication Data*
A catalog record for this book has been requested

ISBN 0–415–33196–X

# Contents

# Figures

# Tables

# Preface

China has experienced 26 years of rapid economic growth at the time of writing this preface. It seems that the momentum of growth is continuing and there is optimism that it can be sustained for at least another 20 years of high growth.

In 2003, China became the fourth largest exporter in the world and the largest recipient of foreign capital inflows. Measured in nominal dollars, per capita GDP surpassed a milestone level of 1,000, a level that Deng Xiao Ping wished to achieve by 2010 when he highlighted his vision of industrialising China in the early 1980s. Measured in PPP dollars, China was well ahead of Japan and ranked number two in the world in terms of total GDP. In a sense, China has established itself as one of the world's economic superpowers, alongside the US, Japan and the European Union. It is the world's largest producer of basic products, including grains, meats, cotton lint, peanuts, rapeseed, fruits, steel, coal, cement, chemical fertilizers and television. In 2003, China produced more steel and steel products than the combined output of the world's two largest economies, US and Japan.

In the meantime, both rural and urban per capita incomes have more than quadrupled over a quarter century. There is no doubt that people's living standards have improved enormously and the majority of the Chinese population have never had such prosperity before, in more than 5,000 years of civilisation. In the countryside, the problem of hunger and destitution prevailed in every corner of the country before economic reforms, but is now confined to an absolute minority. In the cities, many people have started to buy their own houses and cars, which would have been unheard of 15 years ago. The pace of change is unbelievable. About ten years ago, few people dared to think of car ownership or of having a holiday in a foreign country. Today, millions of people have bought, or are queuing, to buy a car. China will soon become one of the world's largest car manufacturers and consumers. Car ownership is predicted to increase by 25–35 per cent per annum in the next few years, which is a net increase of one million units each year. No other country in the world can exceed China in its growth of car and housing ownership. No other developing country in the world has made such an impact on the global economy as has China over the last quarter century.

In recent years, almost all the world's largest 500 multinational corporations (MNCs) have sought business opportunities in China. Some large companies, including the world's largest mining company, BPH Billion, have to rely on the booming Chinese economy to maintain their growth of profitability. VW has now produced more cars in China than in its home country, Germany. In the past, many large car manufacturers were reluctant to enter the Chinese market, but now, almost every big name has its own manufacturing plant in China. A recent successful venture is Honda Guangzhou. It was built based on the plant of a failing joint venture between Guangzhou and Peugeot. After being taken over by Honda, Guangzhou suddenly has become the most popular place for people to buy a car. People have to wait for more than four months to have their cars delivered, even when the quota for a car was worth 40,000 yuan in early 2004. There were similar scenes in the rush to buy Japanese colour television sets in the 1980s and early 1990s, when the quota for a TV set was worth up to 2,000 yuan.

High growth and improving prosperity do not mean that China will necessarily become an economic superpower, continuing its growth and prosperity until it catches up with the industrialised world. In fact, China has not been fully industrialised and, measured on a per capita basis, it is still a poor country. Increased prosperity has led to a highly polarised and fragmented nation: the rural and urban populations have been further divided, the regions have been driven apart, the rich and poor have become entrenched, party and government officials have become more corrupt than at any other time in China's 5,000 year history, and a chronically poor class has been created who have little prospect of escaping poverty, leading to more and more violence and crime.

China's fundamental problem is its unfair income distribution system following the economic reforms. High growth has not been fairly distributed to all the people. This reflects Deng's initial strategy of letting some people and some regions develop and prosper first before being followed by the rest of the people and the other regions. Deng succeeded in fulfilling the first half of his development strategy, through the opening up of the special economic zones and the coastal cities, the encouragement of private enterprises, and allowing party officials and their offspring to set up businesses and seek economic and political rents. However, he died before the second half of his strategy could be realised, that is, enabling the disadvantaged people and regions to catch up with the first-rich. Unfortunately, the third generation of party leadership who took over from Deng has failed to reduce inequality. Instead, income polarisation increased even further and the disadvantaged groups have become more marginalised. In the urban sector, up to 40 million SOE workers have been made redundant from their jobs, many of whom have become trapped in poverty. In the rural sector, up to 200 million peasants are unemployed or underemployed, and about 100 million peasants moved out of their villages to seek jobs in the cities or in the rural areas of southern China. These two groups of disadvantaged people account for about 15–20 per cent of the total population, or about 200 million people, but the government has never recognised this number and continues to publish figures of some 30–40 million people living in poverty.

The scale of inequality can be illustrated by looking at some stark comparisons. It is reported that the wealth of the richest 500 Chinese is equivalent to the combined net incomes of 900 million peasants for two years. The cost of one single meal offered to a high ranking party official could be as much as the average annual net income of ten rural people. The average monthly income of a Beijing worker from the formal section is as much as the total annual income of a construction worker coming from the countryside. In China, prostitution was almost eliminated by Chairman Mao Zedong. Today, no one knows the exact number of young rural girls employed as sex workers for the rich urban class and government officials, but most people know that every star hotel in China has sex workers. In Beijing, Guangzhou, Shanghai, Shenzhen and many other large cities in China, there are numerous sex night clubs. Even in the small towns and cities, sex services have been the main stimulus for local businesses. The pervasive growth of prostitution is the most obvious proof of income polarisation. On the one hand, poor girls have no opportunities to earn money other than selling themselves cheaply. On the other hand, the rich class has become so rich that they can easily afford to buy sex regularly.

Income polarisation is fuelled by the massive scale of corruption and rent seeking of party and state officials. It is also accelerated by the many loopholes of law and order throughout the country under economic reforms. The biggest scandal of party officials under Chairman Mao was Liu Qingshan and Zhang Zhishan, governor and party chief of Tianjin in the 1950s. They embezzled about 1.6 million RMB, for which they both received the death penalty from Mao. Today, no one knows how many party and state officials have embezzled similar amounts of money, but most people know that there are employees in almost every government department and in local government who have managed to make huge sums of money. The chance of being caught by the legal system is probably one in one thousand, but once caught, the total sums found to have been embezzled is often nothing but astonishing. China's biggest case of corruption and tax evasion is the Yuanhua incident in Xiamen, one of the four special economic zones set up by Deng in the early 1980s. The total sum of illegal money was around 70 billion yuan. Over 20 people were sentenced to death and over 100 people were jailed. However, it is believed that there are many bigger fish who have slipped the net because they are too large to be caught by China's legal system. The biggest criminal of the incident, Mr Lai Chanxing, is still at large in Canada, enjoying a lavish life style. Over the last ten years, more than ten people of minister and sub-minister status have been executed. In each case, the total sum of money was as high as 100 million yuan, but no one knows how much money has been transferred overseas or to relatives and close friends at home.

Legal loopholes have led to some cases that involved enormous sums of money being stolen from the state. The latest case involves an accountant of the State Natural Science Foundation. He stole over 12 million yuan and misused over 210 million yuan of state funds. The head of the Bank of China in the Kaiping city of Guangdong stole all the money in that city branch of the bank, totalling 360 million US dollars (equivalent to 2.95 billion yuan).

Many of the richest Chinese people are property developers. They colluded with bank chiefs and local government officials. The developers usually bribe government officials to sell land at low prices and bank managers to lend them money to

buy land and build houses. They then sell houses and take the money for themselves, but refuse to pay back their bank loans. As most banks are state-owned, if
they cannot recover their loans, the state will bale them out. It is reported that
China's largest four state banks, Bank of China, Bank of Industry and Commerce,
Bank of Construction and Bank of Agriculture have accumulated non-performing
loans (NPL) of up to quite a few thousand billion yuan, which equals 30–40 per
cent of their total loans. In early 2004, the Chinese government decided to use
$45 billion of foreign exchange reserves out of the total $403 billion to prepare for
the privatisation and stock listing of two large state banks: the Bank of China and
the China Construction Bank. Before this, the state had already paid over 1500
billion yuan to write off their NPLs.

Why have the state banks accumulated NPLs totalling such a large sum of money?
Why is the government prepared to pay so much money to write off the NPLs?
Obviously, the government wants to get rid of the huge burden carried by the state
banks and make them independent and responsible for their own losses and profits
in the future. Another explanation is that many of the NPLs have become the
private assets of corrupt government officials, who have fled the country, or have
transferred their money abroad. No one knows how many high ranking officials
are in exile with huge sums of money and how many of their children are studying overseas to help their parents transfer money out of the country. China is a
large recipient of foreign capital, but in the meantime, it is also a large loser
of capital to other countries through illegal transfers and money laundering. In the
end, whether China receives or sends out capital, all the benefits have accrued to
the very few rich and the vast majority of people, especially the farmers are the net
losers. Although they are hard working, they continue to live on a low income,
trapped in poverty. Their daughters may find themselves having to become sex
workers or be employed in sweat shops, while their brothers face life on the
construction sites of distant towns and cities with miserable pay and working
conditions.

Rising inequality has led to social disorder and a rising crime rate. Recently there
have been a number of shocking cases which have been exacerbated by inequality.
A man killed over 60 people, including many whole families, before he was
brought to justice. Large scale bank robberies have taken place in many big cities.
Some people have paid large sums of money that they can ill afford to snake-heads
in order to escape the country. There have been many cases of desperate misery.
Over 20 people died on the east coast of England in April 2004 where they have
been working almost as slaves, earning only £1 per day. Over 60 people suffocated
to death in the back of a lorry travelling from the Netherlands to England through
the English Channel two years earlier. If China's fast growth had benefited all the
people, including the poor, then these people would not have risked their own lives
in a foreign country. If all the people had good job opportunities at home, they
would not have become prostitutes, or bank robbers or suffered the profound mental
disorders which result in their becoming mass murders. Many rural migrants
working in the cities have to be separated from their wives for months on end. They
have become the so-called 'no sex' group in China. Their only relief is watching

pornographic movies. Those that cannot control their sex drives are in danger of becoming sexual predators as they do not earn enough money to buy sex like the urban rich.

Income inequality is measurable. The Gini index was typically 0.20 to 0.22 respectively for the rural and urban population in the late 1970s and early 1980s when China was one of the most egalitarian countries in the world. By the mid-1990s, the Gini index was as high as 0.38, and China started to become one of the less egalitarian countries. By the late 1990s up to the first half of 2004, the Gini coefficient in rural China was as high as 0.46 and is still rising. Since all empirical evidence has shown that income distribution has become ever polarised, China is now probably one of the least egalitarian economies in the world today.

In the developing world, there are two distinct types of development model. One is represented by Taiwan, South Korea, Hong Kong, Singapore and Malaysia. Like China, these countries have experienced similar high growth for a prolonged period of time. However, they have also been successful in preventing inequality from rising. As a result, industrialisation and urbanisation has led to a significant reduction and eventual elimination of poverty. Social and political order has also improved over time. In Taiwan and South Korea, there has been some successful democratic movement, allowing people to participate in politics and policy making. Although Hong Kong is a special administrative area of China, its residents enjoy much more freedom and choice than their cousins on mainland China. The other model is represented by Brazil, Argentina, Mexico and South Africa. Although these countries are classified as middle-income countries and are industrialised, they all have a skewed income distribution system, leading to the marginalisation of a significant proportion of the population which lives in absolute poverty.

Although all the Chinese people and Deng Xiaoping were hoping that China would follow the development path of the first group of economies, especially South Korea and Taiwan, in reality, China has been driven unintentionally towards the model of the second group of countries. It can be predicted that China will become another Mexico or Brazil after a few more decades in terms of per capita GDP and in terms of income inequality. There is little prospect that China will become rich and have an equal income distribution as in South Korea and Taiwan, unless the development path is fundamentally modified to become radically pro-poor from now on. Some recent developments of government policy in favour of the western parts of the country and current efforts to help the rural areas and agriculture are encouraging signs. However, such initiatives may be too late, too little and too insincere so that the long term trend of growing inequality cannot be arrested and reversed.

The critical question is 'can China do it?' Based on the recent history and the institutions in place, one cannot be optimistic at this particular point of time. However, if China were to be another Mexico or Brazil, or even South Africa, Deng's original strategy would be at best half-successful, and at worst, China might enter some unforeseen civil unrest before it reaches its final goal of modernisation, urbanisation and industrialisation.

The intention of this book is not to be pessimistic about China's future, but to study the development experiences over the last half century, paying special attention to the rapid growth and social changes in the reform period. It aims to identify the factors that have contributed to China's fast economic growth. In the meantime, it also discusses the main issues of concern for the sustainability of economic growth. I have two main arguments in this book. First, rapid growth has changed China's image as the most populous and one of the poorest nations in the world. China has in effect become one of the main economic powers in the global economy. Second, economic growth must benefit all the people and should not be geared towards skewed income distribution which results in the disadvantaged groups becoming permanently disadvantaged. What I argue here is common prosperity for all, not for some. If China becomes a rich nation measured in per capita GDP in about 30 or 40 years, it should become one the world can admire, such as Japan, South Korea or Taiwan, but not like Brazil and Mexico where a large proportion of the people live in poverty despite the high levels of per capita GDP.

The book is structured as follows. It contains eleven chapters. Chapter 1 is an introduction. It reviews the history of economic development in China since 1949 when the People's Republic was established. It also highlights the central issues of economic growth, income distribution and poverty, suggesting that high growth is a pre-condition for common prosperity, but without a fair income distribution, it is very difficult to eradicate poverty. In this book, poverty is defined as absolute poverty, not as relative poverty. Absolute poverty means that the poverty line is the minimum income level for people to have enough food for survival with a minimum level of non-food expenses. Relative poverty is a comparative definition of poverty for a particular economy. For example, it is reported that there are 3 to 3.5 million children in the UK living in poverty. The poverty in the UK is defined as relative poverty, which is different from the poverty definition for China in this book.

Chapter 2 describes the economic performance of contemporary China from 1949. It is divided into two main sub-periods: pre-reform and reform periods. It explains the successes and failures of pre-reform China. In that period, economic growth rate was high, but people's living standards improved slowly, especially in the rural sector, where the vast majority of people lived in poverty up to 1978. This chapter also discusses the reasons why economic reforms have brought about high growth in the national economy and better living standards for the people. Some problems are created under economic reforms. The main problems are rising inequality, corruption and unbalanced regional development.

Chapter 3 focuses on the performance and problems of agriculture and rural development. In terms of GDP structure, agriculture accounts for a small and rapidly declining share. In terms of employment, agriculture is still the biggest sector for labour and the vast majority of people still live in the countryside. This implies that the living standards of the rural people must be relatively low. However, as government policy has been consistently biased towards the urban and industrial sector, the urban–rural income gap increased, rather than declined under economic reforms. In the pre-reform period, agriculture was neglected and exploited because the government had to use direct and indirect agricultural taxation for urban and industrial development. Within agriculture and the rural sector, there were some irrational policies which were detrimental to production diversification and productivity growth. In the reform period, urban biased policy continued. Peasants have been allowed to move to work in the towns and cities, but they are subject to numerous restrictions and disadvantages. It is impossible for rural migrants to enjoy similar employment rights, let alone the many kinds of state benefits given to urban residents. In reality, rural migrants are used as slavery workers to build the towns and cities but they are denied the benefits of being a formal citizen. They created 'residual values' which are entirely retained for the urban population. The deserted hometowns are short of skilled and able labour, leading to geographical adversity and depression of local agricultural production and rural development. Slow agricultural and rural development is the main reason for urban–rural inequality and rural poverty.

Chapter 4 discusses the relationship between openness and economic performance. China follows the successful example of the Asian NIEs through openness, export-promotion, active integration with the global economy and foreign direct investments (FDIs). It builds an augmented production function to prove that openness, represented by international trade and FDI, has a positive impact on economic growth. The success of China is also due to population control, education and improvement in infrastructure.

Chapter 5 is a methodological chapter. It presents a simple method for calculating and decomposing the inequality index, or Gini coefficient. The entire process can be done in a spreadsheet, but the procedure can be easily translated into a computer programme as well. The methodology is useful for the rest of the book when further calculation of Gini coefficients is required.

Chapter 6 uses some empirical data and the procedure of calculating and decomposing the Gini coefficients developed in Chapter 5 to calculate the inequality between the rural and urban sectors, using a number of economic variables, including GDP, personal incomes and consumption for the reform period. China is divided into three main economic regions: east, central and west. As a result, inequality can be studied on provincial level data. It is concluded that there is a clear urban–rural divide and that there is regional inequality in China under economic reform.

Regional inequality is due to unbalanced regional economic development. Chapter 7 develops an economic model to show that China is diverging into three distinct economic clubs: east, central and west. The main explanation as to why there exist such clubs is that the poor region cannot catch up with the rich region because the spill-over effects from the growth centre (east) to the west diminishes as distance increases. 'Distance' can be regarded as physical distance, but it can also be regarded as non-physical distance, which is usually caused by the lack of good policy and institutions. Human capital and transportation are two important factors that can be developed and mobilised to shorten the non-physical distance between east and west.

Inequality in China is multi-dimensional, including urban–rural inequality, regional inequality and inequality within the rural or urban sector. Chapter 8 uses data for a couple of provinces to study the different aspects of inequality. Apart from analysing the inequality between different population classes, inequality itself can be broken down into income sources. In the rural sector, total income is divided into agriculture and non-agriculture incomes. Non-agriculture refers mainly to rural township and village enterprises (TVEs). It is the non-agricultural income that has caused more inequality within the rural community. This explains why regions with a good TVE sector tend to be much more prosperous than those without. The TVE activities are mainly concentrated in the east so that the eastern provinces are much more prosperous than the western provinces. In the urban sector, income can be divided into time wages, non-time wages, non-wages, tax and transfer incomes. It is the non-wage component that caused more inequality among the urban population. Hence urban reforms that have led to market liberation and ownership diversification is the main reason for rising urban inequality.

Following Chapter 8, the next chapter uses more comprehensive and up-to-date data to study the issues of inequality and poverty in more depth. The main concern of Chapter 9 is to understand how inequality affects poverty reduction. It gives a comprehensive estimation of both urban and rural poverty and concludes that poverty could have been eliminated if income inequality had not risen so quickly. The most effective way of reducing poverty is income growth, but this can easily be offset by the negative effect of rising inequality. This is what has happened in China in the later years of economic reforms.

Urban unemployment and poverty is a relatively new issue in China. Even before economic reforms, urban unemployment and poverty was not a main issue as urban people were heavily protected by the state. Since 1996, China has laid off up to 40 million SOE workers. Some of them have found alternative employment, but many of them have to rely on state pensions and benefits. This is a big issue in China as SOE workers are politically much more powerful than rural people. They can easily cause urban unrest if they live in poverty for too long. Chapter 10 uses a case study to understand the linkage between SOE unemployment and urban poverty. It is found that a large proportion of the laid-off households had both husband and wife laid off at the same time. This group of people are the most vulnerable to poverty. The chance of such families being trapped in poverty was as high as 60 per cent, as compared to less than 5 per cent of the entire urban population. Some further qualitative analyses are also conducted relating to the labour market and poverty situation of laid-off workers' families.

In the literature, most people argue that rural to urban migration is an effective way of escaping poverty. Chapter 11 challenges this by developing a migratory model to understand the motivation and to quantify the effects of various factors on the migration decision. It then argues that migration is probably not an effective way of escaping poverty in rural China for various reasons. First, there are too many people who want to migrate and the towns and cities cannot generate enough jobs for so many migrants. Second, migrant workers earn only a fraction of the income that is earned by a formal urban worker for the same kind of work. Third, since the educated and young people move out of the poor areas, the production in these areas has been depressed, leading to more backwardness and poverty.

Massive migration in China is caused by the huge urban–rural earning differential and highly unbalanced regional development. Migration is not just from rural to urban areas, but from the poor to the most prosperous rural areas. Migration is not a cure, but an outcome of poverty and income disparity. To reduce migration and poverty, a more balanced regional development strategy should be adopted and effectively implemented. More importantly, more jobs and income generating activities should be created in the rural areas, particularly in the backward rural areas. Migration should be regulated to allow rural people to settle down in towns and cities and enjoy the same citizen rights once they become formal residents.

# Acknowledgements

A few chapters of this book draw heavily from the published materials produced by myself and my co-authors, Zongyi Zhang and Zhongmin Wu. I am grateful to the publishers Elsevier, North Holland, John Wiley, Frank Cass and my co-authors for the use of some of the materials. A number of chapters were also made possible because of financial support by the British Academy (Chapter 10), the Department for International Development (UK) (Chapter 9), and the Asian Development Bank (Chapter 9). The Ministry of Agriculture and the Chinese Academy of Social Sciences (CASS) and the National Bureau of Statistics (China) provided some valuable household survey data which made the calculation of poverty lines and poverty head counts possible.

In the process of writing this book, I had direct and indirect assistance from various people, including Ajit Bhalla, Donald Hay, Scott Rozelle, Linxiu Zhang, Liwei Zhu, Zongyi Zhang, Zhongmin Wu, Richard Harris, S. Yitzhaki, Peter Nolan, Peter Sowden, Justin Lin, Xiaobo Zhang, John Knight, Lina Song, Shi Li and John Bonin. I am grateful for their help and comments in one or some parts of this book.

In the process of writing this book, I have to spend hundreds of hours away from home. I would like to thank my wife, Xiaowen Zheng, and my children, Joseph, Julia and Tina for their support. My parents, Tongban Yao and Caoqing Yao have given me consistent support and encouragement. I would like to express my deep love and gratitude to them.

# Abbreviations

| | |
|---|---|
| ADB | Asian Development Bank |
| APEC | Asian and Pacific Economic Cooperation |
| CAP | Common Agricultural Policy |
| CASS | Chinese Academy of Social Sciences |
| CCPCC | Chinese Communist Party Central Committee |
| CES | Constant elasticity of substitution |
| CMP | Cost minimisation problem |
| DFID | Department for International Development |
| DPD | Dynamic panel data estimation |
| EU | European Union |
| FDI | Foreign direct investment |
| FIE | Foreign invested enterprise |
| GDP | Gross domestic product |
| GNI | Gross national income |
| GNP | Gross national product |
| HRS | Household responsibility system |
| IPO | Initial public offering |
| MNC | Multi-national corporation |
| MOA | Ministry of Agriculture |
| NBS | National Bureau of Statistics |
| NIE | Newly industrialised economy |
| NPL | Non-performing loan |
| OECD | Organisation for Economic Cooperation and Development |
| OLS | Ordinary least squares |
| PBC | People's Bank of China |
| PLA | People's Liberation Army |
| PMP | Profit maximisation problem |
| PPP | Purchasing power parity |
| PRC | People's Republic of China |
| RMB | Renminbi, also known as the yuan |
| SARS | Severe acute respiratory syndrome |
| SOE | State-owned enterprise |
| TVE | Township and village enterprise |
| WTO | World Trade Organisation |

# 1 Introduction

## 1.1 A brief history of contemporary China

The twentieth century was probably the most turbulent but fascinating period of China's history of civilisation which spans more than 5,000 years. The country first underwent a tumultuous end to the dynastic and feudalistic system, when the last emperor, Pu Yi, was first forced to move to the hometown of Qing Dynasty, the Manzhouli in northeast China, and was then removed from power altogether by the republican movement, led by Dr Sun Zhongshan, founder of the Republic of China. The seeds of the total collapse of the dynastic system were planted during the second half of the nineteenth century when Britain successfully launched two opium wars on China and signed a number of unfair bilateral treaties, including that to rent Hong Kong Islands for 150 years.

For more than 60 years, from the mid-nineteenth century to 1911, China experienced a humiliating history of a semi-colonial and semi-feudal system, where the populace, the vast majority of whom were petty farmers, were oppressed by the corrupt officials of the Qing Dynasty, invaders from the west and Japan, and the landlords. The period from 1911 to 1937 witnessed numerous civil strikes which held together a heavily wounded society caught between the two main political parties, the Nationalist and the Communist. During the Second World War, China was occupied by the Japanese, whose slaughter of more than 300,000 people in Nanjing angered the entire nation, leading to an unusual coalition between the two otherwise hostile parties against the invaders. The victory of the anti-Japanese war in 1945 became an opportunity for the two parties to eliminate each other. In the end, the Communists won the three years long civil war and the Nationalists, led by Chiang Kai-shek, retreated to Taiwan in 1948. Since then, China has been separated by a narrow water strip of about 30–50 miles, guarded by America's 7th Fleet of Battleships in the Pacific Ocean.

The year 1949 was the most significant turning point in China's contemporary history, which had the following features. First, it was a genuine beginning of a republic system in which the fortunes of people's lives were not determined by one single person, the emperor, but by a large political party, which by now had a membership of over 66 million. Second, the country was free of external suppression from western imperial powers. Third, the Communist party redistributed land almost equally to all rural families, stripping off the ownership once and for all from the land-owning classes.

China's most influential political figure was Chairman Mao, who led the Communist Party from the mid-1930s to its grand victory over the Nationalist Party in 1949. He continued his leadership until he died in 1976. Mao was famous for his tireless attempts to modernise China in his own way, rooted in his feudalistic family background. He launched the land reform in 1949–52 to distribute land equally to all rural households. There had been no other world leader who had been able to do exactly the same thing in such a large country. The effect of land reform on China's economic progress was immense and permanent. Even now after over 25 years of economic reforms, China still retains almost the same system of land ownership and usufruct, as it was over 50 years ago.

Land reform was to give everyone a chance to move out of poverty. To this end, Mao was successful and he should be heralded for his courage, ability and deep concern for the poor. In the early years of Mao's leadership, one of his chief ambitions was to rebuild China into a world power again after over 100 years of humiliation, hunger and disease. He wanted to show to the world that the Chinese people were a great people and that China could catch up with the United Kingdom and the US in decades. Although Mao was right in his thought, his tactical approach to economic development was flawed due to his misunderstanding of human nature: its selfishness. He advocated Lei Feng as a model of selflessness to be followed by the whole nation, based on the naïve assumption that collectivisation was the best form of economic organisation to quickly change China from a poverty-stricken nation to a world class power. Hence, the years following the land reforms saw collectivisation, culminating in the People's Commune, in which many hundreds of households pooled their resources together to produce a restricted set of agricultural products, particularly cereals and cotton. In the cities, state investments were concentrated in the state-owned enterprises (SOEs) after private firms were involuntarily merged or taken over by the state from 1956. Private enterprises were prohibited, since they were regarded as an ownership form which did not fit in well with the socialist ideology of economic development and construction.

The People's Commune faced a tremendous setback in the first three years of the movement. Poor weather and disastrous crops from late 1958 triggered China's largest famine and loss of life in the following three years (Lin, 1992; Chang and Wen, 1997; Yao, 1999a). It was estimated that 18.5 million people died, and there were 30.1 million fewer births over the famine period (Yao, 1999a). To rectify the situation, Mao asked Liu Shaoqi, Deng Xiaoping, Chen Yun and a number of other senior officials to implement a recovery programme. One key element of the recovery programme was an institutional reform consisting of two main policies. One was to modify the commune system so that a three-tier ownership and operational structure was created, that is, the commune, the production brigade and the team, the other was a household responsibility system in the production team. In a sense, decision making became significantly less centralised under the new system, and agricultural production started to recover from 1962. The famine was over by the end of 1962, and by 1965 grain output had fully recovered to its pre-famine level.

Mao's second important political movement was the Cultural Revolution, which was launched shortly after the country recovered from the famine crisis. During the Cultural Revolution, Liu, Deng and Chen were prosecuted for their recovery policies implemented during 1962–5, as Mao accused them of following the capitalist road by introducing the household responsibility system. The Cultural Revolution started in 1966 and ended with the death of Mao in 1976. The whole decade of the Cultural Revolution had brought the Chinese economy to a total stagnation thereby subjecting the vast majority of the rural people to absolute poverty. The higher education system was also seriously affected because formal university entry examination was abolished and all the universities were forced to recruit students from workers, peasants and soldiers who were selected without clear academic criteria.

In retrospect, Mao's political life was full of vicious political movements to remove his political contenders, because of his single-minded determination to make China powerful through collectivisation and common prosperity. The outcome, however, was totally different from what had been intended. China managed to create and maintain a highly egalitarian society, although there was an apparent division between the urban and rural populations. The Gini coefficient among the urban residents was typically around 0.20, and that among the rural population was around 0.22 throughout most of the pre-reform era. However, income equality was brought about at a high price; the whole country was poor despite tremendous growth in industrial output and a structural change in the national economy. By 1978, 80 per cent of the population still lived in the rural areas, and 70 per cent of the labour force was agriculture-based. Officially, the government stated that 270 million of the rural population lived in absolute poverty in 1978, but an unofficial estimate shows that at least 75 per cent of the rural population, or about 600 million were absolutely poor (Yao, 2000).

Contemporary China scholars and researchers would regard the pre-reform period 1949–78 to be a disastrous period in modern Chinese history. This is true if the performance in that period is compared with the spectacular growth in the post-reform era. However, if it is compared to the pre-liberation period from the later half of the nineteenth century until 1949, China had made a significant advance not only in industrial and agricultural output, but also in health and education.

According to Peter Nolan (2003),

> from the mid-1950s, when the collectivisation of agriculture was accomplished and industrial planning implemented, through to the mid-1970s, China made enormous progress in many key aspects of social and economic development. The growth rate of national product was faster than in most developing countries. . . . In normal times, the mass of the people enjoyed a high degree of livelihood security. Most impressive of all, the country achieved enormous advances in health and education. For many economists, the key indicators of

development are 'basic needs' in nutrition, health and education. By the mid-1970s, China's levels of infant mortality and child death rates had fallen to exceptionally low levels compared with other developing countries. Infant mortality had fallen to just 71 per thousand compared with 124 per thousand in low income countries (excluding Indian and China) and 81 per thousand in middle-income countries. Life expectancy at birth, arguably the most important single indicator of development, had risen from 36 years pre-1949 to 71 years in 1981, an extraordinary achievement (Nolan, 1995: 49). The system also provided a high degree of security, drastically reducing the age-old fear of an unforeseen personal, natural or economic disaster that was the reality for every farm family and for a large fraction of the urban workforce in pre-Revolutionary China.

## 1.2  Comparison of economic performance in modern China

China's achievements in the pre-reform era were heralded by numerous Western scholars as evidence that equal distribution of income could help the poor countries to achieve high levels of life quality and social development.

The most fundamental problem of the pre-reform period was not growth, but inefficiency. Over 50 per cent of state investments were concentrated in heavy industries, which generated limited employment. China's failure in this period was probably the very low level of allocative efficiency and the inability of the state industries to create jobs. In other words, China failed to exploit its comparative advantage through developing the labour intensive industrial sectors. As a result, industrial growth was high but the market was short of consumer goods and agricultural products. To finance the development of capital-intensive industries, the state had to impose high levels of taxes on agriculture through direct land tax and indirect taxes using the so-called price scissors, which paid low prices to agricultural goods and charged high prices for rural consumer goods and agricultural production materials. As a result, output growth in agriculture did not lead to improvement in farm income. By 1978, per capita rural income was only 134 yuan per annum, which was $78.8 given an exchange rate of 1/1.7 in 1978, or only $0.21 per day, just over one-fifth of the international poverty line of $1 per day defined by the World Bank. Even if income was calculated in PPP terms, it would be still significantly less than $1 per day. Using the most conservative measurement of a poverty line, it was estimated that at least 75 per cent of the rural population, or about 600 million rural people lived in absolute poverty in 1978. This level of poverty was significantly greater than the official and World Bank estimates which shows 30 per cent of the rural population, or 270 million rural people were absolutely poor in 1978, compared to around 190 million in 1957 (Nolan, 1995).

Institutional economists, including some writers like Justin Lin, Peter Nolan and Nicholas Lardy, argued that the most disturbing outcomes of the pre-reform policies were a severe erosion of work incentives and frequent disruptions to the production schedules and plans by political events. Furthermore, numerous ill-conceived capital construction projects, notably the 'backyard iron and steel campaign', and the heavy industrial projects in the third-front areas (inland and remote from the coast), caused an immense waste of scarce resources, which were largely tapped from agriculture and the rural sector.

Although Mao made many mistakes in his economic policy, he could still be regarded as the pre-eminent political figure in twentieth-century China. In hindsight, Mao left China with many valuable achievements: equal distribution of land, greatly improved standards of general health and basic education, a society with limited levels of corruption, a country free of many deadly diseases, a people with a strong spiritual belief, a comprehensive industrial production system, and an effective agricultural production infrastructure, especially the irrigation system. All these achievements were the foundation of a spectacular economic growth in the post-Mao period from 1978, led by China's second towering political figure of the twentieth century, Deng Xiaoping. For the sake of academic debate it may be attractive to emphasise the achievements of the Maoist period. Indeed, many aspects of the Maoist period are worthy of study. However, it is not a development path to which China is likely to return, nor would many Chinese people wish it to.

Economic reforms started from 1978 after the Gang of Four was brought to justice and Deng Xiaoping resumed his political leadership within the Party. Deng was a fascinating and controversial political leader in the Communist Party history. During wartime, he was a great hero, party leader, army political commissar and commander. He worked closely with many army generals, especially General Liu Bochen. During the civil war from 1946–9 against the Nationalist Party Army, Liu was commander and Deng was political commissar of the Third Field Battle Force of the People's Liberation Army (PLA). When people said the Liu-Deng Army, they meant the Third Field Battle Force, which was probably the most powerful fighting regiment of the PLA. Deng's biggest contribution during the civil war was when he became general commander of a special forefront force to cross the Changjiang River in order to take control of south China from the Nationalist Party Army after the grand victory of the famous Three Big Battles of Liaoning-Shenyang, Beijing-Tianjin and Huaihai.

Deng became a senior party official after 1949 and worked as a deputy to Premier Zhou Enlai. At the end of the great famine, Deng worked with Liu Shaoqi and Chen Yun to help the country recover from the disastrous famine, but along with the others, he fell victim to Mao's political struggle at the beginning of the Cultural Revolution. Deng disappeared to a remote village in Jiangxi Province until 1973 when he was called back by Mao to help run the country. From 1966 to 1972, China abolished the closed-book examination tradition throughout the country from primary to higher education. In 1973, soon after Deng came to power again, he resumed the examination system at the primary and secondary education levels. Henceforward, entry from junior high school to senior high school was through examination competition. Deng also encouraged farmers to retain their private plots of land and relaxed the restriction on rural and urban free markets. However, shortly after Zhou died in early 1976, the Gang of Four forced Deng out of politics through the order of Mao, who was very frail and sick but clear-headed enough to keep Deng's party membership, which was crucial for him to be restored to power one year later.

In July 1977, Deng was restored to power during the Third Plenum of the Tenth National Congress of the Chinese Communist Party Central Committee (CCPCC). On 10 August 1977, he became deputy chairman of the CCPCC and deputy chairman of the Military Committee of the CCPCC during the First Plenum of the Eleventh National Congress of the CCPCC. In March 1978, Deng became chairman of the Chinese People's Political Consultative Congress. In 1981, he became chairman of the Military Committee of CCPCC. Deng was never the chairman of the CCPCC itself, which was the number one position of the party and the country, but he was de facto the most influential figure within the party and the People's Congress. It was him who should be credited with the success of China's economic reforms. He was famous for his own proverb, 'A cat is a good cat as long as it can catch mice, it does not matter whether it is black or white.' He used this proverb indirectly to criticise Mao's rigid philosophy that socialism must be based on public ownership, that the bigger the enterprise the better, and his emphasis on self-reliance, and his closed-door policy. To break the deadlock of Mao's doctrines and his legendary influence on people's thinking, Deng launched a nationwide study campaign to debate that 'truth must come from practice', not from a prescribed teaching and narrowly defined socialism offered by Marxism, Leninism and the thoughts of Mao Zedong. Deng advocated that as long as China was to become rich, as long as people's living standards were to be significantly improved, it did not matter if the country did not maintain dominant state ownership, total equality, or the principle of self-reliance and of maintaining a closed door to international competition.

The easiest place for reform, however, was the countryside and agriculture, for various reasons. First, almost all the poor people lived in the countryside, depending on crop farming for their living, the cities and industries being heavily protected and subsidised by the state. Hence, there were strong incentives for farmers to participate in the reform programme. In fact, many production teams in south China had secretly (and illegally) carried out some forms of production responsibility and free (black) market activities. The official reform policy was just to legalise what some had been doing for years and encouraged all production teams to sign production contracts with individual households. Second, Deng had some experiences gained from the recovery period of 1962–5 when he was a member of the leading team in the economic recovery programme. The essence of the recovery programme in the early 1960s was the so-called 'three freedoms and one contract', meaning free local markets, free production decisions by production teams, self-responsibility for losses and profits, and household production contract responsibility. The 'three freedoms and one contract' became the reform package to be implemented throughout China from 1978. From 1979, the first political directive issued each year by the CCPCC was all about agricultural and rural reform. By 1983, the household production responsibility system was implemented throughout the whole country.

Apart from institutional reforms, the price system was also changed. From the second half of 1979, the prices of many agricultural products, particularly grains, were raised so that state procurement prices moved close to free market prices, providing significant financial incentives for farmers to raise production. Grain output rose from 300 million tons in 1978 to over 400 million tons in 1984. Per capita farm incomes rose dramatically by almost 15 per cent per year over the same period, which was probably the golden epoch of rural China, not only for the reform period, but also for the entire Chinese history of many thousand years. It was in this period that rural hunger and malnutrition were finally eliminated in the vast majority of the Chinese rural areas. The incidence of poverty was brought down from 75 per cent to about 7.3 per cent; the total number of rural poor declined from 600 million to less than 58 million using a low and official poverty line (Yao, 2000). In fact, the incidence of rural poverty reached its lowest point in 1984 over the entire reform period from 1978 up to today. This remarkable achievement set a cornerstone in the history of rural development not only in China, but also in the world. The initial success of agricultural reform was remarkable and unanticipated, even Deng Xiaoping himself said that he could not believe that the reforms could lead to such an improvement on people's living standards and agricultural productivity.

Urban and industrial reforms followed in the footsteps of agricultural reforms, starting from the early 1980s. Urban reforms were focused on the state-owned industrial sector, which was renounced for its inefficiency and loss-making, nurtured by the lack of property rights and soft budget constraints. Since SOEs could not be easily privatised, similar reform measures like those implemented in agriculture were used to reform SOEs, particularly the production responsibility and contract system. The wages system was also reformed as bonus payments were introduced to stimulate production incentives among workers. To tackle the principal–agent problem, a compromise measure was the director's responsibility, which specified that the party secretary of each enterprise would not interfere with production decisions, which should be the sole responsibility of the director, whose promotion and reward would be closely related to firm performance. The profit system was replaced with a taxation system so that firms would no longer deliver all their profits to the state, but could retain part of the profit after taxation. Retained profits could be used for bonus payments, capital investment, pension and other social benefits given to employees.

Various reform measures implemented in the 1980s appeared to have had some effect as far as production incentives were concerned but they failed to fundamentally solve the problem of SOEs (Hay *et al.*, 1994; Groves *et al.*, 1994; and Yao, 1997c). They continued to make huge losses and retained profits always involved an intensive bargaining process between individual firms and their higher authorities. This was because the market was not competitive, as input and product prices were heavily distorted by government policies. Firms were responsible for the employees' pensions, housing, healthcare and the education of their children. Such a social burden implied that SOEs could not compete with non-state firms, which did not exist prior to reforms, but were encouraged to compete with the state economy after reforms. Non-state enterprises, particularly the rural township and village enterprises (TVEs) and foreign invested enterprises (FIEs) had the advantage of employing cheap labourers from the countryside without making any commitment to their job security and social benefits. Newly established firms and foreign invested firms were also given tax reduction and exemption in the first three to five years.

Due to the ineffectiveness of various reform measures tried out throughout the 1980s, the government started to contemplate some more radical reforms in the 1990s. The first radical reform was the privatisation of some small and medium-sized enterprises while the large ones continued to be state-owned. Many loss-making small and medium enterprises were allowed to become bankrupt, or be taken over or merged with non-state firms, or even sold to foreign companies. Large-scale enterprises were allowed to form joint-stock companies, or joint ventures with both domestic and foreign firms. The joint-stock companies and joint ventures were made possible because the Shanghai Stock Exchange was opened in December 1990 and the Shenzhen Stock Exchange in July 1991, and because foreign firms were allowed to invest in China.

Foreign direct investment was allowed right from the beginning of industrial reform in the early 1980s, but it was highly restricted until 1992 when Deng Xaioping made his famous tour to south China. During his tour he talked to local party officials that 'we should move more quickly in domestic reforms, and be braver and more open to the outside world'. From 1993, flow of foreign capital rocketed, and by 1996, China became the largest recipient of foreign direct investment in the developing world and the second largest recipient in the world, second only to the US. Despite the Asian Financial Crisis during 1997–8, China continued to attract large inflows of foreign capital, and by 2002, became the world largest recipient, surpassing the US. The accumulative stock of direct foreign investments was $501 billion in 2003 (*People's Daily*, 2004: 15 January).

Foreign investment has played a key role in stimulating China's exports. International trade has been one of the most important stimuli of economic growth over the reform period. In 1978, China ranked 23 in the world for its trade volumes, by 2002, China became the sixth largest exporter and the seventh largest in total exports and imports. In 2003, China became the fourth largest exporter of the world, with a trade volume of $851 billion (*People's Daily*, 2004: 12 January). The composition of China's exports has changed from that dominated by agricultural commodities and raw materials to that dominated by manufacturing goods. The share of manufacturing goods rose from less than 50 per cent in 1980 to more than 90 per cent in 2002. The contribution of foreign invested firms to China's exports increased from nothing to over 50 per cent by 2002 (Yao, 2003). In recent years, China, especially in the Pearl River Delta and the Changjiang River Delta, has become the world's largest manufacturing base of many industrial goods, including colour television sets, computers, and other electronic appliances. In the early 1980s, over 90 per cent of TV sets sold in China were Japanese brands. Nowadays, over 90 per cent of TV sets sold are Chinese brands. In the first five months of 2003, China exported 770,000 colour TV sets for a value of more than $80 million (*People's Daily*, 2003: 4 July).

Economic reform in China has been an evolutional process, following Deng's 'white and black cat theory', and his pragmatic, gradual approach to reforms, and featuring the 'groping stones to cross the river' approach. This was because there was no example of how to transform a centrally-planned economy into a market-oriented system in world development history, especially when it involved such a large, diverse, and poverty-stricken country like China. When Mr Gorbachev was to reform the former USSR, he opted for a big bang approach, that is, he abandoned the whole planned economy system through a one-off privatisation programme and destroyed the communist party for democracy, as he thought it was the only way forward for the former USSR. The sad result was that the country was split into numerous independent states and the economy suffered many years of consecutive decline. In sharp contrast, Deng's 'groping stones to cross the river' approach worked extremely well in China while the basic political structure and the communist party were kept intact.

From 1978 and in the following quarter century, China has created an un-debatable economic miracle in world development history. The first and most significant achievement was in the agricultural sector from the late 1970s to 1984 when agricultural output jumped enormously and the vast majority of the farming population solved the problem of 'wen and bao', that is, enough food to eat and enough clothing to keep warmth, which was the most fundamental problem in China for many thousand years. China's second most important achievement is the rapid development of rural township and village enterprises (TVEs). From 1949 to 1978, over 90 per cent of state investments were concentrated on the SOEs located in the urban areas, and little investment was made in the rural and agricultural sector. A significant proportion of state revenue was taken from the rural sector through direct and indirect taxation. However, large investments in SOEs failed to create enough jobs so that surplus agricultural labour could not be absorbed into industrial production, although industrial output rose enormously over the period 1949–78. Agriculture's contribution to gross domestic product (GDP) declined from over 80 per cent in the early 1950s to only 28 per cent in 1978, while industry's contribution to GDP rose from less than 10 per cent to 50 per cent over the same period. This significant shift in output structure was not matched by a similar shift in employment structure. By 1978, over 80 per cent of the total population still lived in the countryside and 70 per cent of the total labour force was still in agriculture. It was estimated that about 200 to 300 million agricultural labourers were either unemployed, or under-unemployed. There was no chance that China would be able to solve the rural employment problem through industrialisation in the cities and concentration on SOEs, but Mao did not even allow the rural areas to develop sideline production and cash crops, let alone rural industries and services. Hence another important contribution of Deng was that he encouraged farmers to set up their own non-farm enterprises as well as allowing them to produce cash crops and engage in sideline production. The rural free markets were also allowed to open for the exchange of agricultural goods and services.

Small-scale TVEs existed in the late 1970s but they did not make any significant contribution to the local economies and employment prior to economic reforms.

Only from the mid-1980s when they were officially encouraged did they grow explosively. The decade 1985–95 was the golden decade of TVEs, whose gross industrial output rose by over 20 per cent per year. Total employment increased from 70 million to over 136 million (Yao and Liu, 1998), which was significantly greater than the total employment of the entire SOE sector. TVEs also made a significant contribution to state tax revenue and national exports. Over one-third of state revenue and 40 per cent of national exports come from TVEs today.

In the reform period, China also made significant advances in science, technology and education. Nowadays, China has become one of the most important countries making contributions to basic science research, although it still lags far behind the key players like the US, Germany, Japan, the UK and France. In education, the most significant progress has been in higher education. In 1982, only 0.6 per cent of the Chinese people received higher education, but in 2000, this share rose six-fold to 3.6 per cent. China is also one of the few developing countries which has made significant progress in reducing illiteracy among the population. The illiteracy rate was 23 per cent in 1982, but by 2000, it was down to only 7 per cent. In hindsight, China's explosive economic growth would not have been possible without the great enhancement and accumulation of human capital, which is probably the most obvious disadvantage of many other comparable developing countries in Asia and Africa, or even in Latin America.

Apart from the gradual institutional reforms and significant advance in education and technological progress, the other main features of China's reforms were its close engagement with the world economy, which included not only the massive inflows of foreign direct investments and the highly aggressive export push strategy, but also its ability to reform and maintain a stable foreign exchange market. The domestic currency was initially overvalued but it was gradually depreciated and made convertible in current account transactions through a single exchange rate from the dual-track regime in January 1994. It was then maintained at a very stable level against the US dollar, but kept unconvertible with capital account transactions. This gradual and pragmatic approach on managing the foreign exchange market not only enabled China to attract huge inflows of foreign capital and stimulate external trade, but also saved China from contagion during the 1997–8 Asian Financial Crisis that crippled Thailand, South Korea, Indonesia, Malaysia, and badly hurt Hong Kong, Singapore, Taiwan and the Philippines.

The main achievements of economic reforms in China can be highlighted in the following areas.

### *Fast and sustainable economic growth for over a quarter century and the momentum of growth is continuing today*

From 1978 to 2001, GDP per capital in current prices rose from 379 to 7,543 yuan, or by 500 per cent in real terms at an average annual growth rate of 8.1 per cent (NBS, 2002). China maintained a high rate of growth even in the period of the Asian Financial Crisis, and continued its momentum when the entire world was subject to a significant slowdown after the 9/11 event in 2001 and the second Gulf

War in Iraq in April 2003. In early 2003, China, Hong Kong and Taiwan endured an unanticipated disaster caused by the spread of a severe acute respiratory syndrome (SARS) which killed a few hundreds and infected many thousands in a short span of time, especially in Beijing and Guangdong. Despite the SARS scare, China was able to manage the crisis and maintain a high growth rate of 9.1 per cent in GDP and 35 per cent in international trade (*People's Daily*, 2004: 12 and 21 January). China's impressive ability is demonstrated by its quick reaction to the SARS crisis, and the building of a large, sophisticated and state-of-the-arts hospital, the Little Tan Mountain Hospital in the outskirts of Beijing, to house almost all the SARS patients in Beijing in only eight days. All the doctors and nurses were selected from the eight large military districts of the People's Liberation Army (PLA) throughout the country. It is probably true that there is no other country in the world, including the US and the UK, which is able to build such a modern hospital and mobilise so many resources in such a short time.

### China has become one of the largest producers of many manufacturing products in the world

In 2001, China was the world's biggest producer of cereals (453 million tons), cotton (5.3 million tons), meat (63.3 million tons), peanuts (14.4 million tons), rapeseed (11.3 million tons), fruit (66.6 million tons), fish (43.8 million tons), steel (151 million tons), coal (1.1 billion tons), cement (661 million tons), fertilisers (33.8 million tons), television sets (40.9 million sets); and the second largest producer of electricity (1.48 trillion kwh), chemical fibres (8.4 million tons) and cotton cloth (29 billion metres) (NBS, 2002).

In the past 15 years, China has built 19,437 kilometres of motorways. The longest motorway is called Tong-Shan, which starts from Tongjiang County in Heilongjiang on the border of Russia to Shanya City in the southern end of Hainan Island, with a total length of 5,700 kilometres and a total investment of 570 billion yuan. In early 2003, the entire motorway was completed on the land and the remaining parts will be large bridges and cross-sea and cross-channel construction. China has the largest number of fixed-line telephone and mobile phone users and is now the fourth largest manufacturer of automobiles after the US, Japan and Germany, surpassing France, the UK, Italy and South Korea.

### People's living standards have improved significantly

From 1978 to 2001, real income per capita in the countryside rose more than five times, and in the cities more than four times. In nominal terms, per capita rural incomes rose from 133 yuan to 2,366 yuan, and per capita urban income from 343 yuan to 6,859.6 yuan (NBS, 2002). In the past, it was difficult for rural households to buy bicycles, radios and watches, and almost impossible to think of buying TV sets, video recorders and washing machines. Nowadays, many of these durable consumer goods are easily affordable for the vast majority of rural households, especially in the more prosperous eastern provinces. Many households have started buying motor cycles and motor vehicles. In the cities, there have been an increasing number of households that are able to buy motor cars, particularly in the large cities like Beijing, Guangzhou, and Shenzhen. In 1985, there were only 19,300 private cars in the whole country, by 2001, there were 4.7 million, and in Beijing alone there were over 550,000 private cars, as there were in Guangdong, and in Hebei, there were 410,000 cars. Car ownership is still expanding rapidly among the largest cities at more than 30 per cent per year.

The most important improvement in living standards is probably in housing. Per capita gross living space increased enormously in the countryside, from 14.7 m$^2$ in 1985 to 25.7 m$^2$ in 2001. In the cities, not only the living space has increased, the quality of housing has also improved significantly. Per capita gross living space rose from 10 m$^2$ in 1985 to 21 m$^2$ in 2001 (NBS, 2002). In the past, housing was exclusively allocated by the state, or through the work units. Today, housing has been largely commercialised, either entirely through the market, or through work units and employees partnership.

### *Significant progress in urbanisation and industrialisation*

China could be regarded as a newly industrialised nation if it were to be judged on its economic structure. Agriculture's share in GDP declined from 28 per cent in 1978 to only 15 per cent in 2001. This structure is not dissimilar to many middle-income countries, and close to the poorest nations in the European Union. However, the employment structure shows that China is still a very agrarian economy. The share of agricultural labour was 50 per cent in 2001, although it had declined significantly from 70 per cent in 1978. China is one of the very few countries in the world, which has such a high agricultural labour share. The share of agricultural labour is typically less than 5 per cent in the industrialised economies such as the US (2.6 per cent), the UK (1.5), Japan (5.1 per cent), and Australia (4.9). Only some of the poorest developing countries have a share of agricultural labour close to 50 per cent, such as Pakistan (47.3 per cent) and the Philippines (39.1 per cent). Thailand (48.5 per cent) and Romania (41.8 per cent) also have a high share of agricultural labour (NBS, 2002).

The level of urbanisation in China is still low by international standards, especially when it is compared to countries with a similar economic structure. The share of rural population in the total population declined by 20 percentage points from 82 per cent in 1978 to 62 per cent in 2001. In 2001, China had 662 cities, 166 of them had a population of over one million. Due to the sheer size of the population, urbanisation in China cannot rely on expanding or establishing super large metropolitan cities, but should depend on the organic growth of rural towns, and the commercialisation of villages. Although there has been a tremendous progress in rural industrialisation and urbanisation in the past two decades, rural development has experienced a critical slowdown since the mid-1990s.

### *Integration with the world economy*

China's integration with the world economy is manifested by its ability to attract foreign capital and to expand international trade. The integration process culminated in its entry into the World Trade Organisation (WTO) in December 2001. With WTO membership, China will face many challenges as well as opportunities. On the positive side, China will be able to exploit further its comparative advantage in exporting labour-intensive manufacturing goods to the industrialised world, especially the US, EU and Japan without being subject to regular review on the most favourable trading nation status as it was in the past by the US. China will also have to re-organise its industrial structure and make domestic firms, particularly the SOEs, even more efficient and competitive. On the negative side, however, China will face a number of short-term painful adjustments, and some of the economic sectors may suffer as a result if they cannot react quickly to the new environment. The most vulnerable sectors may include agriculture, financial institutions as well as the high-tech and capital intensive industries like automobiles.

### *Significant social progress*

China's social progress can be reflected in the following areas: reduction of rural poverty, an increase in education levels and the quality of healthcare.

## 1.3 Future prospects

The remarkable achievements of China in the last quarter century are undeniably clear, but the next question is whether China can maintain its growth in the new century so that it can become a truly world economic superpower. In absolute terms and measured in official foreign exchange rate, China was the seventh largest economy in the world in 2002 after the US, Japan, Germany, the UK, France and Italy. China's GDP was about $1.3 trillion, compared to $1.7 trillion for the UK. However, if GDP were measured in PPP dollars, China's GDP would be $5.2 trillion, which would be about half that of the US and one and a half that of Japan's. Hence, the most optimistic estimate suggests that China is now the second largest economy in the world. However, on a per capita basis, China is still one of the poorest nations in the world even if its GDP is measured in PPP dollars. This implies that China will have a long, long way to become a rich nation comparable to the industrialised world.

### *Growth constraints and challenges ahead*

In world development history, it is relatively easy for a poor country to grow faster than a rich country due to the law of diminishing marginal return on capital. However, not all the relatively poor countries can converge with the relatively richer economies. China has been able to reduce its gaps with the industrialised economies in the past two and a half decades, but many other developing countries have failed to do so. The real question is whether China can maintain its growth momentum and reduce its gap with the rich nations even further and faster.

Unfortunately, development history also suggests that once a poor country becomes relatively better off after a long period of growth, it will be increasingly difficult to maintain the same rate of growth. The second half of the 1990s saw this happen in China. From 1980 to 1996, China was able to achieve a two-digit growth rate, but since 1997, the growth rate has been hovering between 7 and 8.5 per cent. In the first three years of the twenty-first century, China is one of the world best performers, but it has found it hard to achieve a growth rate of 8 per cent without resorting to deficit financing.

If we look at the deficit situation, China ran a large deficit in the crisis period of the Great Leap. It then ran into deficit again during economic reforms. Before 1999, the budget deficit was less than 2 per cent of GDP and 10 per cent of revenue, and after 1999, the deficit was more than 2 per cent (2.9 per cent in 2002) and over 15 per cent of revenue. In terms of the percentage of GDP, the deficit is not unacceptably high, but there are two main worries in the budgetary situation. First, the deficit runs continuously and rises by year. This did not happen in the pre-reform period. Second, the deficits in the last 3–4 years are high, and if this trend continues, China may run into long-term crisis.

The slowdown of economic growth may be due to an adverse world economic environment, but it may be more a reflection of the lack of dynamism within the domestic economy to achieve the same rate of growth sustained from the mid-1980s to mid-1990s.

China has a number of critical problems and potential dangers that may hamper the prospect of high and sustainable growth. The biggest problem is income distribution and rising inequality. Prior to economic reform, China was undoubtedly one of the most egalitarian countries in the world, with the Gini coefficient of around 0.20 among both the rural and urban populations. Inequality existed largely due to the segregation of two politically and economically heterogeneous sub-population groups: urban and rural. In 1978, the urban–rural per capita income ratio was about 2.4, but dropped to 1.7 in 1984 and rose again since then (Yao, 2000). Although egalitarian, pre-reform China was not a desirable model as the whole population was poor.

To move the majority of the Chinese out of poverty, Deng was right to let some people and some regions become rich first at the beginning of reforms as an incentive to promote productivity growth. Hence, economic construction was highly concentrated in four special economic zones in Shenzhen, Shantou, Zhuhai and Xiamen in the early 1980s and then spread to fourteen coastal cities and Hainan Island. Some people also became rich because they were able to seize the market opportunities. The first market opportunity was the development of private enterprises and free markets in the early 1980s. A typical example was that of the farmers in Wenzhou of Zhejiang Province who became prosperous because they were able to specialise in some lucrative rural non-farm production and service activities. The first wave of rich Chinese was the so-called private entrepreneurs in the town and villages, and later in the cities.

The second opportunity was the opening of the Shanghai and Shenzhen Stock Exchanges. Only the most profitable SOEs were allowed to be listed in the stock exchanges, and through the seriously under-valued IPO (initial public offering) and insider information, many people were able to make huge profits and become extremely rich in a very short period of time.

The third opportunity was the privatisation of housing and the construction boom of private housing from the mid-1990s. In addition, China also launched numerous public capital investment projects throughout the country. Property developers, bankers and party officials colluded with each other to seize these large investment projects and make huge profits from them. Construction projects were financed by bank loans at low interest rates. Only people who were able to borrow bank credits and secure land were able to build houses, and only the party officials in charge of banks and land were able to determine who were to get access to bank credits and land. Hence, China was open to an unlimited sea of rent-seeking activities and corruption as well as business opportunities. After the construction projects were completed, many people would have become very wealthy. If the projects turned out to be unprofitable and went bankrupt, the banks would be unable to recoup their loans, which then became non-performing. It is estimated that the proportion of NPLs (non-performing loans) in China's four largest commercial banks, the Industrial and Commercial Bank, the Bank of China, the Construction Bank and the Agricultural Bank, was at least 20 per cent of the total loans. Some suggest this proportion could be as high as 30–50 per cent. In other words, up to 5,000 billion yuan of bank loans could be non-performing, and a large proportion of the NPLs must have been eroded into pockets of private individuals. NPLs alone would account for the recently acquired wealth of thousands of rich businessmen and party officials. In under ten years, China has seen the rise of numerous rich people with private personal assets of over 10 million, 100 million, or even multi-billion yuan.

In the 1990s and right into the new century, China has experienced explosive economic growth, but at the same time, national wealth has become highly concentrated in the urban sector, especially in the hands of the rich class, consisting mainly of party officials, private businessmen, relatives of party officials, highly paid professionals, such as university professors, lawyers and doctors. The rest of the population has also become much better off than before, but there is a significant proportion of the population, especially the laid-off SOE workers, and the majority of the peasantry which has not benefited from the growth. As a result, income inequality keeps on rising all the time.

### *Inequality in China*

In China income inequality is multi-dimensional, including urban–rural inequality, inter-regional inequality and within region inequality. Urban–rural inequality is a long legacy inherited from the Mao's era, when rural people were prohibited from moving to the cities, and when agriculture was heavily taxed to support urban and industrial development. Fast agricultural growth from 1978 to 1984 was the best period for the rural population, when urban–rural inequality was brought down to its lowest level from 1949. However, the golden age for the rural population ended abruptly in 1985, and from then on, rural people have been left behind by their urban counterparts, although they have been allowed to migrate to the cities.

Most development economists would think that by allowing rural–urban migration, the gap between urban and rural incomes would eventually be eliminated. This, however, has not worked and may well never work in China for a variety of reasons.

First, China still maintains the strict residency registration system and rural migrants are not given any right to obtain an urban citizenship. As a result, they do not have access to any of the social, healthcare and education services in the cities. In addition, rural migrants can only engage in low-paid and arduous jobs, which are generally unwanted by the formal urban residents. According to some columnists, a typical young female migrant working in Shengzhen is paid about 400–500 yuan per month, living in a crowded room shared by six to eight similar aged girls from possibly the same region in one of the inland provinces such as Hunan, Sichuan, Guizhou, Anhui or Jiangxi. A senior manager from Hong Kong, or Taiwan, working in the same factory as the young girls may have a salary up to 50,000 yuan per month, which is 100 times the average wage of the girls. These young females have to support their families back home, but the wage was not really enough for their own expenses. In such an unequal environment, it is not surprising that some of the young girls resort to having secret affairs with their bosses, and many of them become 'night club' three-accompanies girls (who seal their services to men in three different ways: eating, drinking and sleeping with them), and some even become prostitutes. A recent informal survey shows that a full-time street girl in Shengzhen can earn up to 200 yuan per day, and many can earn up to 1,000 yuan per day, which is twice as much as their normal monthly salary. However, little is known about how much these young girls, most of them are less than 20 years old, have suffered by becoming street prostitutes, or the secret lovers of the Hong Kong and Taiwanese businessmen.

Second, China has a rural population of 900 million and a surplus labour of about 150 to 200 million who need to be transferred out of agriculture. Although there are about 60 million migrants each year, the vast majority of them do not have a permanent job, and do not stay in the cities for more than six months in a year. Due to the recent radical reform of the SOEs, up to 40 million SOE workers have been made redundant. The top priority of local governments is to find alternative jobs for the retrenched workers, hence there is a fierce competition for jobs between rural migrants and laid-off workers. In other words, the cities do not have enough capacity to absorb so many rural labourers.

Third, China has maintained an urban-biased policy since 1949 and this policy has been particularly obvious since the mid-1990s. State investments are highly skewed towards the urban economy. Although the rural population accounts for over 60 per cent of the total population and agriculture accounts for 50 per cent of the total labour force, state investments in agriculture have been consistently less than 5 per cent. China has a huge bank deposit of over 9 trillion yuan in 2002 from both the urban and rural households, but little money has been lent back to the rural sector. During the Sixteenth National Congress of the CCPCC held at the end of 2002, one of the most important issues considered by the Congress was the so-called 'three-nongs' problem. Nong in Chinese can be peasant, rural or agriculture as all these words, once translated into Chinese, start with a word 'Nong'. So why is the 'three-nongs' is a big issue? Obviously, the peasants have been vastly disadvantaged in terms of income growth and many peasants (up to 200 million depending on how a poverty line is drawn) are still living in absolute poverty after 25 years of phenomenal economic growth in the country. Rural development has slowed down for various reasons. The TVE sector has experienced a significant slowdown since the mid-1990s and has ceased to become the growth engine of the rural economy. Rural healthcare and education have become increasingly more expensive and many households are easily subject to poverty, either because someone in the family suddenly falls ill, or parents cannot afford to pay for their children's schooling. Agricultural production is slowing down. Grain output reached its peak of 512 million tons in 1998, but has declined to about 450 million tons in recent years. Agricultural prices are so low that farmers, especially those on the eastern coast, have found agricultural production a burden, rather than a profit-making enterprise. Their plight has now been exacerbated because they are unable to find enough off-farm jobs to supplement their incomes and are unable to move to the cities. The accession to WTO may open up some opportunities for agricultural exports, but it is more likely that it will depress domestic agriculture in the short and medium terms, as China will not be allowed to heavily subsidise farming.

The second dimension of inequality is inter-regional. Regional inequality among the rural population and the urban population has increased significantly over the past 25 years. The richest provinces are concentrated in the eastern coast and the poorest provinces in the west. The World Bank (1997) estimates that over one half of China's total inequality measured by the Gini coefficient is due to inter-provincial inequality. Yao and Liu (1998) shows that over three-quarters of inter-provincial inequality is due to income differences among three geo-economic zones, east, central and west. The latest estimation by Yao *et al.* (2003) shows that rural China may have 100–200 million rural poor, but a large proportion of them are concentrated in a few very poor provinces in the west. The Gini coefficient for the rural population has increased from about 0.20 (Yao and Liu, 1998) in 1978 to 0.45 in recent years (MOA, 2002). The ratio of per capita incomes between the richest province and the poorest province rose from 2.80 (Shanghai/Guizhou) in 1985 to 4.16 (Shanghai/Guizhou) in 2001 (NBS, 2002).

Inequality among the urban population also increased over time. On the one hand, people are impressed by the rich urban class to buy luxurious motor cars and huge residential houses, to send their children to the US and UK for higher education or even primary and secondary education. There are tens of thousands of Chinese students coming to study in the UK, right from nursery to PhD levels. Many parents are able to pay about 200,000 yuan per year to finance their children's education from high school upwards. One brand-named motor car like BMW,

1967W, or Mercedes may cost over one million yuan. On the other hand, China has laid off millions of SOE workers. In a recent survey in Tianjin and Guangzhou, among the households with laid-off workers, 50 per cent of them had two workers (husband and wife) laid off. If both husband and wife are laid off and neither of them finds alternative employment, the likelihood for that household to live in poverty is 67 per cent, this is in sharp contrast to the national urban poverty rate of less than 5 per cent (Yao, 2003). In China, urban inequality is also largely caused by inter-regional inequality. The ratio of per capita income between the richest province (Guangdong) and the poorest province (Qinghai) was 3.5 in 1998 (Yao *et al.*, 2003).

The last dimension of inequality in China is that of marginalisation: inequality within the same region. Even in the most prosperous regions, poverty may be prevalent, and low income households are marginalised due to the lack of an established social security system. For example, Guangdong is the richest province in China and its per capita GDP measured in PPP is close to that of a middle-income country, but it still has a large number of absolute poor in both the cities and the countryside.

### Poverty

Agricultural reform during 1978–84 significantly reduced the level of rural poverty but the trend was brought to a halt from 1985 up to the early 1990s. By 1998, China still had up to 200 million people living in absolute poverty based on various estimates by different authors, although official data always showed less than 4 million rural poor. In the 1980s and 1990s, the government aimed to eliminate poverty by 2000, and hence official publications in numerous official newspapers had to reflect the gradual decline in the total number of rural poor. In reality, official publications are mostly untrustworthy. For instance, the *People's Daily* reports that the number of rural poor was only 26 million in 2000, declining from 270 million in 1978 (*People's Daily*, 2000b). In early 2003, shortly after the Sixteenth National Congress of the CCPCC, China's new premier, Wen Jiabao, told a news conference that China had about 3.5 million rural poor, but that if a relatively higher poverty line based on the international standard was used, the figure would be 85 million. This is the first time that a high ranking Chinese official has admitted such a high incidence of rural poverty.

There have been few studies on urban poverty, because, as the World Bank has rightly pointed out, poverty in China was exclusively a rural phenomenon prior to economic reforms, because urban residents were heavily protected both in terms of their job security and the many social benefits available to them, which were unavailable to the farmers. Recent reforms have had two important effects on the urban population. First, job security is not guaranteed. Loss-making SOEs were allowed to become bankrupt and to lay off workers. Second, rural people were allowed to move to the cities to compete for jobs. These two developments not only imply that urban workers are subject to unemployment, but the retrenched workers have found it more and more difficult to secure a second job because numerous rural migrants would take on any job available at low wages which are unacceptable even to the laid-off workers.

In recent years, two types of urban people have been most vulnerable to poverty, the laid-off workers and rural migrants. Official statistics only collects income data for urban residents, not for rural migrants. Based on official statistics, China had up to 5 million urban poor in 1998, but the actual number could be significantly higher if rural migrants living in the cities were included.

Urban poverty is a new phenomenon in China as it is a by-product of the most recent reforms. Although the scale and depth of urban poverty is not comparable to rural poverty, the former could cause far more damage to China's social and political stability as the urban people are more organised and concentrated around the power base of the party and the state. For the rural people, as long as the majority has enough food to eat, they can hardly cause any damage to social stability. However, if China were to become an economic superpower, it is important that absolute poverty, whether it is urban or rural, is eliminated. This is why the principal goal of the Sixteenth National Congress of the CCPCC was to make China into a Xiaokang society in an all round way. Xiaokang in Chinese means that an average Chinese will not only have enough to eat and wear, but also enjoys a lifestyle typical of a middle-income economy.

## 1.4 Conclusion

After a quarter century of rapid economic growth, China has started to shake the world. It has become one of the largest trading countries in the world, the most popular destination of foreign direct investment, the largest producer of many important industrial and agricultural products such as steel and cereals. In PPP terms, China is about 50 per cent bigger than Japan, becoming the second largest economy in the world. Measured in nominal exchange rate, China is the seventh largest. As the economy continues to expand rapidly, China will surpass Italy, France and the UK in about ten years' time, and Germany in about 20 to 30 years.

However, as China is the most populous country in the world and its population accounts for over one-fifth of the world's total, it is still a very poor nation in terms of income per capita. On the other hand, the government and people are anxious to make China one of the most powerful economies in the world. This means that it will have to maintain a high rate of economic growth in the coming decades. One critical challenge is whether China is able to maintain the same growth in the future as it had done in the past. Although the answer to this question is not clear-cut, it is almost certain that China, for various reasons, will have more challenges ahead to face.

The first reason is that it is unlikely that high rate of growth can be repeated for another 20 to 30 years, purely because of the law of diminishing marginal return on capital. Although China is still in the Lewis phase of development with unlimited reserves of cheap labour, labour costs have gone up rapidly in the urban industrial sector. The expansion of economy has been largely due to the intensive use of both labour and capital in the past. In the future, return on capital will inevitably decline as the economy moves away from labour-intensive industries (e.g. textiles and food processing) towards the capital- and technology-intensive industries (e.g. computers, electrical appliances and automobiles).

The second reason is that China has accumulated many problems over the last 25 years despite its recent history of remarkably improved economic performance. One problem is ever-rising income inequality, which is multi-dimensional, and hence extremely difficult to resolve. Another problem is the high level of corruption. Although Deng Xiaoping has been proved right to let some people become rich first as an incentive to boost productivity, the problem is that many of the rich Chinese have accumulated their wealth through corruption.

In theory, corruption is unavoidable in a rapidly developing economy where the legal, social and political systems have numerous loopholes, but there are good examples in the world showing that it can be effectively contained for the sake of long-term development and common prosperity. Hong Kong, Singapore, Taiwan and South Korea are such examples; economic growth has been among the best of the world but corruption has been contained to a low level. Of course, corrupt officials in China may find excuses for their behaviour by arguing that many other countries, such as Brazil, Argentina, Indonesia, India, Russia and Pakistan are also very corrupt. However, if one looks at some of the most corrupt countries in the world, it is fairly obvious that such countries have little chance of becoming an economic superpower. Indonesia's prosperity was brought to end when the Asian Financial Crisis hit the country hard in 1997–8, followed by the downfall of the country's dictator and the most corrupt head of state, Mr Suharto. Argentina suffered a wholesale bankruptcy after the country was hit by a wave of consecutive economic crises. GDP per capita in Pakistan was significantly higher than China's in the 1970s, but now, it is only 60 per cent of China's (World Bank, 2002). According to the World Bank, over 30 per cent of the population in Pakistan have less than $1 per day (an international poverty line), compared to 17 per cent in China in 2000 (World Bank, 2002). GDP per capita in Brazil is four times as high as in China, but it still has over 9 per cent of its population living in poverty with less than $1 per day.

If China is going towards the direction of rampant corruption and skewed income distribution, it is easy to conclude that it is unlikely to become a world superpower. At best, China will become another Brazil in 20 to 30 years' time, and at the worst, China will become another Indonesia or Argentina. This is not, however, the ambition of the government and the people. Hence, if China wants to become a world superpower, one important condition is that corruption must be contained and the trend of rising inequality must be reversed.

Another problem is poverty. Although on average, per capita income has risen enormously, a large number of people are still living in absolute poverty. The types of poverty and its geographical and sociological distribution means that poverty will not easily be eliminated in China, as it is closely linked to corruption and income inequality.

The discussion in this chapter boils down to three important issues in China: growth, income inequality and poverty. These three issues hence become the focus of this book. In the rest of this book, I will deal with these issues in great detail to help readers to understand China much better. For academic interest, researchers will have a better understanding of how China is likely to progress in the new century. For policy makers, this book will point out some fundamental issues that need to be addressed if China is to become the next economic superpower.

# 2 Economic performance in contemporary China

## An overall assessment

## 2.1 Introduction

In this book, the history of contemporary China refers to the period from 1949, when the People's Republic was founded, up to today. In this period, there are two clear episodes of economic development. The first episode was from 1949 to 1978, which is also referred to the pre-reform period, during which China was led or highly influenced by Mao Zedong. The second episode was from 1978 onwards. This period is referred to as the reform period, or the post-Mao period, during which China was led or highly influenced by Deng Xiaoping. Deng has been considered to be the principal architect of economic reforms. All other political leaders have mainly followed his reform philosophy and strategy. The pre-reform period is Mao's and the post-reform period is Deng's if the history of contemporary China is divided by means of who led and/or dominantly influenced the country.

The pre-reform period can be divided into a few sub-periods, including land reform (1949–52), the initial stage of socialist construction (1953–7), the Great Leap Forward movement (1958–61), the recovery period (1962–5), the Cultural Revolution (1966–76), and a transition period after the Cultural Revolution (1976–8).

The pre-reform period had the following main features. First, China transformed the feudalistic system dominated by private ownership to a socialist system dominated by collectivisation and the People's Commune. Second, there were numerous political movements, some of which were closely linked to the transformation from a feudalistic to a socialist system (land reform and the Great Leap Forward), but some of which were associated with the personal characteristics of Mao, whose philosophy of political control was by means of struggle. Third, economic development was important, but Mao always tried to achieve economic goals through political means.

The reform period rectified the mistakes made by Mao. Development according to the law of economics has been the principal guide for Deng's reforms. First, collectivisation was abandoned in agriculture and production responsibility was introduced to transform state industries. Second, private enterprises and foreign firms were encouraged to create competition and improve efficiency of resource allocation. Third, import substitution and self-reliance were replaced by export push and openness so that foreign technologies and the best international management and organisation practices were introduced into China. Finally, various reform methods have been implemented gradually, usually through the trial-and-error, or 'groping stones to cross the river' approach.

The outcomes of economic performance between the two periods are distinctively different. In the pre-reform period, tremendous growth and industrial structural change took place, but China remained essentially agrarian and people's living standards improved only marginally. At the end of the period, the vast majority of rural people did not have enough food to eat or enough clothing to keep warm. In other words, the majority of the rural population was absolutely poor. In the cities, although residents were not hungry, there were acute shortages of daily necessities and the state-owned enterprises were not only making huge losses, but also unable to absorb the surplus labour released from agriculture.

The reform period has been heralded as a time when China's economic miracle was created. Fast economic growth took place first in the countryside and then in the cities. Real per capita GDP increased by over 8 per cent per year for 25 years, achieving the best performing record in world development history. People's living standards improved enormously, and the vast majority of rural people were lifted out of poverty. There has been no shortage of supply of any commodities in both the countryside and the urban areas and commodity prices have been highly stabilised. In the meantime, China has been opened to the outside world for both trade and direct foreign investments. Significant progress has also been made in the areas of science and technology, education and healthcare.

The biggest problems in the reform period have been rising inequality and the difficulties of eliminating poverty, rampant corruption and environmental pollution. These problems will pose significant threats and dangers to China's future growth and prosperity. If these problems are not resolved properly, the tremendous economic achievements over the last 25 years may be jeopardised and China will find it increasingly more difficult to modernise its economy without enduring social and political instability.

In this chapter, I will discuss the economic performance, problems and lessons to be learnt for both the pre-reform and reform periods. The purpose of this chapter is to provide a background for the other chapters of the book.

## 2.2 Economic development and problems in the pre-reform period

During the pre-reform period China's economic achievement was very impressive but it had some obvious limitations and problems. When the PRC was established in 1949, China was not only the most populous nation, but also one of the poorest countries in the world. With 22 per cent of the world's population living on 5 per cent of its arable land, China faced a conflict between population growth and economic development, a problem unlike any confronted by any other developing country (Riskin, 1987). However, China shifted rapidly away from agriculture towards industry with agriculture's share in gross domestic product (GDP) falling from 57 to 28 per cent during the pre-reform period (Nolan and Dong, 1990). Apart from the three years of the Great Famine (1959–61), people's living standards were generally much higher than during the pre-1949 period. Measured by constant 1990 prices, per capita GDP in China in 1977 was over 2.5 times that in 1952, rising from 246 to 625 yuan and growing annually at the average rate of 3.81 per cent (NBS, 1999b, author's calculation). These figures put China at the top among the low-income countries in growth performance.

One important feature of the Chinese economy in the pre-reform period was that prices were stable under a centrally-planned and tightly controlled environment. The general retail price rose only 0.76 per cent per annum. However, consumption growth did not keep up with GDP growth. The growth rate of consumption was 2.18 per cent. The growth rate in rural areas was only 1.67 per cent per annum. The growth rate of consumption in urban areas was much higher at 3.02 per cent per annum, but it was still lower than GDP growth (NBS, 1999b, author's calculation). These figures imply that households did not fully enjoy the fruits of economic growth, especially the rural households, under the economic policies of high capital accumulation (investment). The growth difference of consumption between rural areas and urban areas under the urban-biased policy created a big rural/urban disparity, which persists up to the present.

Before the founding of the PRC, the Chinese economy was seriously damaged during the Sino-Japanese War (1937–45) and the following Civil War (1946–9). After the founding of the PRC, China entered a three-year economic rehabilitation period: the land reform period. During this period, the government focused on economic recovery after the wars. In agriculture, land reform was carried out throughout the country. Land ownership was taken by the state but land was divided into plots to be used by individual farmers. Landlords and rich peasants were prosecuted for exploiting the landless before the revolution. By 1952, agricultural land was largely distributed to farmers according to household size. The land reform stimulated production incentives among the poor and semi-poor peasants and within three years, agricultural production resumed the pre-war levels. In retrospect, land reform in China was probably the most radical institutional change in its 5,000 years of civilisation. The reform could have set a solid foundation for economic development and industrialisation; but in what followed China entered a rough development path.

After land reform, China adopted a Soviet-style planning model for long-term economic development. The first plan, or the First Five-Year Plan, covered the period 1953–7 and was designed to build 694 specific large-scale industrial construction projects, especially 156 Soviet-aided projects. During this period, the government completed socialist transformation in both industry and agriculture, that is, the change from private ownership to joint state–private ownership in industry and the introduction of producer cooperatives in agriculture. The national economy developed well in this period. Agricultural output increased by 28.7 per cent and industrial production by 2.28 times in real terms (NBS, 1999b, author's calculation).

The First Five-Year Plan period (1953–7) was probably the most prosperous sub-period in pre-reform China. During this time, people, especially the rural population, enjoyed a level of prosperity that had not been experienced before and was not repeated until after the Cultural Revolution ended in 1976.

However, the People's Commune movement and the Great Leap Forward movement (1958–61) interrupted the smooth economic development. The communes were designed as both production units and local governments, and charged with undertaking the affairs of industry, agriculture, trade, education and the military. The People's Commune movement tried to transform China quickly from a socialist system to a communist system. The Chinese government hoped that the economy could jump to a higher level in a short time. This was the thinking behind the Great Leap Forward movement which attempted to achieve high economic growth based mainly on massive labour inputs without a change in the traditional methods of production. The policies of the Great Leap Forward and the People's Commune Movement led to chaos in the economy and society. Due to three consecutive years of poor weather and misinformed policies, agricultural output declined by 27.3 per cent and industrial output by 50 per cent from 1958 to 1961 (NBS, 1999b, author's calculation).

The Great Leap Forward movement and the People's Commune were the most disastrous political and economic events in modern Chinese history. Due to the great success of land reform and the achievements of the First Five-Year Plan, Mao was very anxious to modernise China as quickly as possible. He advocated that China could catch up with Britain in 15 years and the United States in 20 years from 1958. When the Great Leap began, an inevitable but ridiculous response spread throughout the country. Low level cadres reported inflated output figures to their superiors, who, in turn, inflated the figures and reported them to their higher level authorities. When the figures came to the central government and Mao himself, they were probably inflated many times. For example, in 1958 when grain output was roughly at the same level as in 1957 (200 million tons), the inflated official statistics reported that China was having a bumper crop and grain output rose by more than 50 per cent in one year. Based on the false information, Mao asked all peasants to eat in the Commune Kitchens as much as they could possibly eat. All the national resources were then mobilised to produce iron and steel, the two key materials representing industrialisation and modernisation in the eyes of Mao. People were asked to give up anything made of metal to the local backyard steel makers, who used furnaces usually built with a few clay bricks.

The Great Leap reached its peak in 1959, but China's grain output dropped by 30 million tons in that year. Ironically, the government was not aware of the serious situation and official statistics still reported another bumper crop for the country, achieving a record high output level. By mid-1958, many parts of the country were effectively in famine, but China was still exporting large amounts of grain to pay for its external debts. Grain exports continued in 1960, although grain output dropped by another 27 million tons. Hundreds of thousands of people started to die of hunger and acute malnutrition from early 1960, and by the end of 1961 over 13 million people had starved to death. The country also sustained a loss of over 30 million potential births (Yao, 1999a).

The failure of the Great Leap Forward and the great famine in 1959–61 forced the government to reconsider and adjust its economic policies. The following three years from 1963 to 1965 were used as a readjustment period for the recovery of the national economy from the disaster. Four guidelines, namely adjustment, consolidation, enrichment and elevation, were drawn up and implemented quickly in this period. The adjustment put agricultural development as the first priority to eliminate famine. The consolidation emphasised changing authorities and functions in both commune and industry management to clear the chaos caused by the People's Commune movement and the Great Leap Forward. The enrichment focused on strengthening the links among different economic units. The elevation led to the shift of attention from increasing gross output to improving quality and product variety. The recovery policies were effective and successful. In this period, real agricultural output rose by 36.9 per cent and industrial output by 64.2 per cent (NBS, 1999b, author's calculation). By 1965, grain output had again reached the level recorded in 1957 (195 million tons), although the famine was effectively over by the end of 1962, when grain exports were halted and imports were used to alleviate food shortages. Low level authorities were asked by the central government not to inflate statistical figures and a strict surveillance system of food security was established.

The policies implemented in the recovery period were mainly articulated by Liu Shaoqi, who was once president of China and first deputy chairman of the Communist Party. Liu's close reform allies included Deng Xiaoping and Chen Yun in the central government and the governor of Guangdong, Tao Zhu. The main policies were to allow farmers to make their own decisions, to be responsible for their losses and to allow free rural markets. The Commune was subdivided into three administrative levels: the commune, the production brigade and the production team. In eastern Guangdong, for example, a typical commune had about 20 production brigades and 100 villages; each village had five to ten production teams; and each team had 30 to 50 households. The Commune was effectively a local government in charge of all the production teams and brigades. There were also schools, clinics, hospitals and small factories in each commune. The county party committee appointed the party secretary of the commune. The commune secretary was regarded as a state cadre and earned a wage, which was given and determined by the state. Leaders at the brigade and team levels were selected from local farmers, hence they did not enjoy the status of state cadreship and did not earn a cash-based wages. Their incomes were linked to the production performance of the brigades and the teams. As a result, they had good incentives to improve productivity in the brigades and teams under their leadership. In the recovery period, as production was also contracted to individual households, production incentives were motivated not only at the (brigade) team level, but also at the household level.

However, the beginning of the Cultural Revolution in 1966 brought China into a new round of economic depression. Despite the political nature of the Cultural

Revolution, the normal production activities were severely interfered with by the political struggles since the politicians only cared about revolution rather than production. Per capita GDP declined by 14.1 per cent, and industrial output by 18.1 per cent in real terms from 1966 to 1968. In addition, the Cultural Revolution led to chaos in both the economy and society. In the early 1970s, China tried to improve its economic relationship with the Western countries in order to achieve modernisation in industry, agriculture, science and technology and defence. However, the Cultural Revolution continued and extended during this period and the country largely failed to achieve its ambitious goal.

Although the Cultural Revolution was largely motivated by Mao's political need to remove his rivals, particularly Liu Shaoqi, from power, the political movement had a clear goal of economic development. The strategy was to build a comprehensive heavy industrial base so that the country would be able to produce anything that would be required for modernising the economy. Resources were mobilised, mainly from agriculture and the rural economy, to establish large and capital intensive manufacturing enterprises. For security reasons, the large state-owned enterprises (SOEs) were spread out in all parts of the country, with a heavy concentration in the third front (the remote and mountainous areas, which were not easily targeted by Western imperials). The biggest and most famous manufacturing establishments included the First, Second and Third Automobile Plants in Changchun of Jilin Province in northeast China, Shiyang in Hubei of central China and Nanjing in Jiangsu of eastern China. There were also a few large steel makers, including Anshan Steel Company in Liaoning, Wuhan Steel Company in Hubei and Baotao Steel Company in Inner Mongolia. Apart from the Second Automobile Plant in Shiyang, all the above-named large SOEs were supported with Soviet technologies and managerial styles. Products were first introduced in the late 1950s and the same technologies were used for more than 20 years. Such companies absorbed huge investment resources from the state but they created a limited number of jobs. Their profits were acquired not through competition but through state subsidies or using their monopolistic position in a highly regulated system.

The pre-reform strategy was not only featured with the overemphasis of heavy industries, the country was also isolated from the outside world. There were limited import and export activities. Foreign investment was totally prohibited. Exports mainly consisted of raw materials and agricultural products; imports were largely capital equipment to support the domestic industrial drive. This strategy, however, worked quite well in terms of industrial production. In 1952, the economy was predominantly agrarian as industries accounted for only 20.6 per cent of the total GDP. Over the period 1952–78, total industrial GDP grew by 11.5 per cent per year in real terms. By 1978, industry's share in GDP rose to 48.3 per cent.

Fast industrial growth was impressive, but it was not matched by agricultural growth. Over the same period, real agricultural output (value-added) grew by only 2.15 per cent per year. As a result, agriculture's share in GDP declined sharply from 50 per cent to 28.2 per cent. The growth in agricultural output hardly matched the growth in population, which was 2.08 per cent per year over the same period.

One direct implication was that people's consumption levels were not improved significantly for over 25 years, as detailed below.

China's industrial development strategy led to a fundamental change in the output structure of the economic sectors, but it failed to transform the employment structure. The share of agricultural employment in the national total declined from 83.6 per cent to 70.6 per cent. This reduction in employment share was substantially less than the reduction in agriculture's GDP share in the national economy. This implied that rural labour could not be transferred out of agriculture for the whole period. The total employment in agriculture actually rose from 182 million in 1952 to 307 million in 1978, or by 2 per cent per year. Many studies in the most recent literature suggest that a large proportion of the rural labour force was effectively unemployed or underemployed.

Agricultural labour force rose by an average of 2 per cent per annum, which was close to the average growth rate of agricultural value-added, implying that output per farmer increased by only 0.15 per cent. Given the accumulation of agricultural investments, there was hardly any total factor productivity growth. Economic development and fast industrial expansion in the pre-reform period failed to change the agrarian nature of rural China in two important aspects. First, agricultural productivity was more or less unchanged. Second, the employment structure by sector was similar to that of the poorest economies in the world.

Even in the industrial sector, there was a fundamental problem because production was too much focused on heavy industry. In 1952, heavy industry accounted for one-third of the total industrial output value, and light industry accounted for the other two-thirds. By 1978, heavy industry accounted for 57 per cent of the total industrial output value, while light industry accounted for only 43 per cent. As the light industries were relatively more labour-intensive and produced goods for final consumption, the decline in light industries led to a chronic and acute shortage of consumer goods. Hundreds of items of daily necessity, such as soaps, matches, clothing, gasoline, cooking oil, sugar, bicycles, radios and watches were in short supply. On the other hand, there were huge quantities of heavy industrial products, including steel and machinery, which did not find their markets. Such products were produced according to a central plan, not the need of the market. In 1978, it was estimated that at least a quarter of the total steel production was stored in warehouses where it rusted away.

*Table 2.1*  Some main indicators before economic reform

|  | As % of national total | | Average annual growth % |
|---|---|---|---|
|  | *1952* | *1978* | *1952–78* |
| Industry GDP | 20.6 | 48.3 | 11.51 |
| Agriculture GDP | 50.0 | 28.2 | 2.15 |
| Industry employment | 7.2 | 17.2 | 6.29 |
| Agriculture employment | 83.6 | 70.6 | 2.00 |

Sources: NBS, 1999b; NBS, 2002.

Due to unbalanced development within the industrial sector, there were a few strange features in the national economy. On the one hand, the government was proud of its success in raising industrial output, but on the other hand, people felt not only poor, but also let down by the system as they faced shortages of goods throughout the year.

Another problem in industry was that SOEs dominated the sector. Private enterprises were prohibited. Business people were labelled with anti-socialism and prosecuted if they attempted to set up private firms. Even collective enterprises were greatly discouraged.

There were two fundamental defects in industrial policy. First, competition was suffocated in a tightly controlled and centrally-planned system. SOEs were given a plan at the beginning of the year to produce a prescribed set of goods. Once these goods were produced, they would be bought and sold by the state commercial department at given prices. As a result, firms did not have any pressure or incentive to produce more than what they were asked to. They also lacked incentives to innovate and improve product quality or design. For example, the model of the famous truck, the Jiefang Truck, produced by the First Automobile Plant, assumed the same design and technology for over 30 years since its first model was built in the late 1950s. Second, workers' incentives were low. As wage payment was not directly linked to firm performance and individual efforts, workers did not work hard and many of them shirked while on duty. The same salary scale was applied to all kinds of factories throughout all parts of the country. There was no need for workers to work hard and be innovative. As along as one was given a job, that job would become an iron bowl for the rest of his/her life. If a firm made a loss, the state would write it off. If the firm made a profit, the profit would be delivered to the state. As a result, the whole industrial system was highly inefficient. Firms were making profits according to the distorted prices set by the state, which were offset by losses made by other firms. For example, a coal mine was making a loss simply because the price of coal was set too low. A steel factory was making a profit simply because steel price was set too high. The distorted price system made the monitoring of enterprise performance virtually impossible. A simple solution to bypass the high cost of monitoring was for the state to treat all enterprises as a big operational unit under its control. But what could be used to bail out the state if all firms were inefficient? In China, unfortunately, the answer was agriculture and the rural population.

For a long period of time, agriculture and the rural population were used as hostage by the state to support the urban sector and industries. The state collected taxes from agriculture in two different forms: direct and indirect agricultural taxes. Direct tax was basically land tax and was paid in kind, which was large initially but declined over time as a proportion of agricultural production. In 1978, for example, direct agricultural tax accounted for less than 5 per cent of the total agricultural output value. Indirect tax was the most important tax levied on the rural economy. Agricultural products, mainly grain, cotton and others, were given low procurement prices. Farmers had to deliver a certain proportion of agricultural products, particularly and most importantly grain, to the state at prices that were less than the average cost of production. For example, the state procurement price of unprocessed rice in Guangdong was only 0.196 yuan per kg in 1978, whilst one kg of chemical fertilisers (the effective contents of which is nitrogen) would cost farmers more than 4 yuan. The famous scissors effect came from the fact that farmers were charged higher prices for production materials, including fertilisers, pesticides and farm machinery, and paid low prices for their products. Due to the scissors effect, the majority of Chinese farmers were living in absolute poverty year after year. Hunger and malnutrition prevailed even in a bumper year, but became significantly worse if there was a crop failure.

The government set the procurement quota at the beginning of the harvest season irrespective of the actual final harvest. In a bumper year, farmers might have enough food to eat for the whole season after delivering the quota to the state. However, agricultural production was subject to many kinds of natural disasters and crops often failed. If the crop failed, the state quota still had to be delivered, but the government might give back some of the quota if the crop was really bad.

Apart from delivering cheap grain to the state, farmers were often forced to sell all kinds of farm products, including pork, eggs, chickens and ducks to the state at low prices in exchange for coupons of rationed consumer goods such as soap, fertilisers, matches, cloth and cooking oils. In the mid-1970s, for example, farmers raised pigs and chickens but were unable to eat pork and eggs, whilst the urban residents who did not raise pigs and chickens were able to eat pork and eggs. The open discrimination against rural people was probably unprecedented in world history, but unfortunately, such discrimination has lasted up to today as will be clearer in the rest of this book.

China's agricultural policy in the pre-reform era was largely a failing one, not so much because agriculture had to bear the cost of both an inefficient indus-trialisation programme and urban development, but because the government intervened with every aspect of rural life.

Government intervention had some positive results though, particularly in the areas of irrigation, basic healthcare and primary education. There was no doubt that China achieved high levels of healthcare and primary education and had estab-lished an efficient irrigation and drainage system. Such achievements were mainly realised through mobilising cheap labour from the countryside itself, although the state provided some essential financial and managerial support. For example, the barefoot doctor system was probably the most cost-effective healthcare system in the world, with all the barefoot doctors being selected from the farming community and trained by local hospitals. Primary education was also achieved at a low cost, as a large proportion of teachers were farmers themselves and paid in kind, instead of cash. Teachers' pay was directly linked to the level of harvest of production teams. Thanks to the low-cost system of primary education and healthcare, rural China was able to achieve long life expectancy and good literacy rates despite the very low level of income per capita.

The significant improvement in the irrigation system was due to the construction of numerous small-scale reservoirs and a water system. Irrigation was an essential element of productivity improvement in agriculture. In 1952, only 20 million hectares, or 18 per cent of the total cultivated areas, were irrigated. By 1978, the irrigated areas rose to 45 million hectares. China had only 5 per cent of the world's arable land, but its population accounted for 22 per cent of the world's total. As population grew by about 2 per cent per year, agricultural output had to grow more than 2 per cent so that per capita agricultural output could increase. China was able to increase agricultural output by 2.15 per cent per year during 1952–78, which was low compared to the post-reform era, but it was significant in the sense that such a growth was realised with a declining area of arable land. Due to industrialisation and urbanisation, the total area of cultivated land declined from 108 million hectares in 1952 to 99 million hectares in 1978. Hence, increased agricultural output was achieved through raising land productivity year after year. For example, over the period 1952–78, China's grain output increased from 164 million tons to 305 million tons, or a rise of 86 per cent, which was realised despite a reduction in grain crop area by over 2 per cent (NBS, 1999b).

The negative aspects of government intervention were also clear, particularly when a production decision was centrally made by the state, or by the local government. A number of examples would suffice to prove that many government policies were irrational. One such example was that in the People's Commune, where farmers were not allowed to sell any agricultural products to the markets. In fact, during the Cultural Revolution, the rural local markets were declared illegal. Another example was that rural non-farm enterprises were also considered illegal, particularly if they were run by private individuals. In the most revolutionary years, school students were asked to see and criticise the 'wrong-doing' of private businessmen who 'illegally' produced some non-agricultural products, such as scissors, knives, baskets and bricks for sale. Private businessmen and traders were frequently prosecuted and their workshops were closed down. One further example was that even in crop farming, farmers would not be allowed to produce cash crops if they did not plant enough areas for grain crops. As grain had a strategic importance for the livelihood of people and the food security of the country, there was a strict production quota system in place. Every production team in every locality had to plant a minimum area of grain crops. Only after the quota was fulfilled did the commune authority allow production teams to produce cash crops.

In retrospect, if we examine China's industry and agriculture policies at the same time, it is easy to find that Mao had a special model in his mind for developing the Chinese economy. His objective was to build China into a world economic and political superpower. But in his mind, the only constraint for him to achieve the objective of his model was the lack of key industrial and agricultural goods. Also in his mind, the key industrial good was steel and the key agricultural good was grain. If China were able to increase steel and grain output, then China would be able to catch up with the most advanced capitalist economies such as the US and the UK.

In Mao's view, he also thought that China could grow faster than any industrialised economy in the world because socialism was a far more superior social and political system than capitalism for economic development and construction. The key features of socialism were state-ownership and central planning. State owner-ship could mobilise resources more easily and quickly than private ownership. This was the first advantage of socialism. The second advantage of socialism was central planning. Mao believed that central planning could guide all kinds of production activities according to a pre-designed growth model. Hence socialism could avoid the vast waste of resources caused by the boom-and-bust business cycles typical in a free-market system.

Mao also believed that socialism had a third advantage over capitalism in the sense that workers were the masters, not the slaves of management. As workers were the masters of firms, they would have the strongest incentives to work hard and make a contribution, or even sacrifice, to socialist construction. Moreover, under state ownership, because the owners of firms were the state, socialism could then avoid the exploitation of workers by the capitalists. As a result, workers would be able to enjoy common prosperity and the country would be able to eliminate inequality and poverty.

Mao's economic development model would be perfect if all his assumptions were correct. In practice, he managed to apply his model throughout the country rather 'effectively' according to his thought. Industrial development was focused on steel production and its related heavy industries. Agricultural development was focused on grain production. As China lacked the initial source of capital, agri-culture was used as a resource base to support industrial development, mainly in the form of cheap products. It was amazing that China was able to sustain this development model for over 20 years. Unfortunately, by the end of the Cultural Revolution, Mao's pre-set objectives were largely unrealised. Although physical outputs such as steel and grain rose rapidly and the economic structure had changed with a much bigger industrial sector, people's living conditions did not improve significantly, particularly in the rural areas. The third advantage of socialism, absolute equality, was realised, but it came with a heavy price, that is, equality with common poverty, instead of equality with common prosperity.

Most China scholars are puzzled by a number of paradoxes in pre-reform China. The first paradox was that high growth in industry did not lead to an industrialised economy as the vast majority of the labour force still depended on agriculture. The second paradox was that rapid growth in industrial and agricultural output did not lead to a genuine improvement in people's living standards. The average annual growth of real GDP was 6.4 per cent from 1952 to 1978. Such a high rate of growth would compare favourably to any other country in the world over the same period. However, the annual growth rates of real consumption per capita increased by only 1.8 per cent for the rural population and 3.1 per cent for the urban population. The growth rate of real consumption, particularly for the rural population, was sub-stantially less than the growth rate of real GDP per capita. One possible explanation was that much of the GDP growth was wasted. Another possible explanation was that GDP growth was largely based on investments and labour inputs, instead of productivity growth. The average annual growth rates of labour and investments were 2.7 per cent and 9.1 per cent, respectively. If the elasticities of labour and capital were assumed to be 0.5 each, that would leave a small residual, or 0.5 per cent per year, accounting for productivity growth. As the population growth rate was also high at 2 per cent, it was not surprising that people's living standards did not improve significantly. By 1978, the vast majority of the rural population was living in absolute poverty despite a long period of decent economic growth.

To sum up, China's economic development in the pre-reform period showed major characteristics of instability. Development policies and plans were interrupted frequently by many damaging political movements. While the overall record of growth was good compared with that of many other low-income countries, it was disappointing compared with that of the newly industrialised economies in southeast Asia, particularly South Korea, Singapore, Hong Kong, Taiwan.

Part of the explanation lies in China's development policies and strategies, which resulted in low productivity in industry and agriculture, inefficiency in resource distribution, an imbalance between investment and consumption, and an unbalanced economic structure between heavy and light industries (Dong, 1980; Nolan and Ash, 1995). Prybyla (1985) concluded that China's economy in the late 1970s suffered serious quality problems, including:

- chronic shortage of wanted goods, including both consumer and producer goods;
- massive waste, including mis-allocation of resources and inefficient use of resources in production and distribution;
- backwardness of technology, including stagnation of research, development, innovation and diffusion of modern technology;
- breakdown of incentive system, including deficient incentives to labour, management and entrepreneurship.

However, the main reason was due to the many political struggles, especially the Great Leap Forward (1958–61) and the Cultural Revolution (1966–76), which depressed production incentives. As a result, the economy failed to perform up to its full potential (Lardy, 1983).

## 2.3 Economic development under reforms

The death of Mao and the downfall of the Gang of Four created a historic opportunity for the party leadership to choose a new direction for economic development. The transitional period from 1976 when Mao died to 1978 was a period of uncertainty as to where China should go. On the one hand, Hua Guofeng, Mao's hand-picked successor, did not have the ability to control the party leadership and had no idea of how China should move forward after an entire decade of political chaos caused by the Cultural Revolution.

What Hua could do was to persuade the country to stick to what Mao said before he passed away. Hence China should carry on with whatever policies Mao implemented under his own leadership. This, however, was not acceptable to the other leaders in the central government, and directly contradictory to what people actually needed. In other words, China needed to be reformed. The old system could not continue without subjecting the country to a total collapse.

The central issue of reform was to break away from Mao's doctrines of socialist development and the definition of socialism should also be re-defined. The traditional definition was state-ownership and central planning. To change the definition, non-state ownership, especially private ownership should be encouraged. Central planning should be combined with or substituted by market forces for guiding production and resource allocation. The ultimate goal was, however, the improvement of people's living standards and the modernisation of the economy.

Obviously, Hua was not the right person to lead China in this new direction and none of the other people in power had the ability to lead the country, either. Hence, most people turned their eyes to Deng Xiaoping for leadership, as Deng had the right qualities and experiences. Deng was re-called to Beijing in 1977 and restored his political power as deputy chairman of the Communist Party. The Third Plenum of the Eleventh Party Congress supported his reform proposals and China entered a totally new episode of economic development.

Generally speaking, economic reforms can be divided into four stages, the rural reform (1978–84), the urban reform (1985–8), the slowdown of economic reforms (1989–91), and the macroeconomic structural reform after 1992.

There were two main reasons why economic reforms in China started from the agricultural sector. First, agriculture was not dominated by state-ownership. It was organised under the so-called three tiers of ownership: commune, production brigade and production team. Land and other resources were collectively owned, instead of state-owned. Farmers were not paid with cash but according to the accumulated work points made during the production season and their reward was based on the level of harvest. The state did not have any obligation to protect farmers if there was a crop failure.

This organisation and ownership structure implied that farmers had little resistance to accepting privatisation and risk-taking if they were allowed to retain more products for their effort. Hence, the so-called household responsibility allowed farmers to retain whatever was left after their delivery of crops to the state. In the earlier years of reform, the only resistance to the household production responsibility was from the local cadres, especially at the commune level. The commune cadres were not sure whether it was right for a socialist country to de-collectivise. They were also afraid of losing their power if farmers were allowed to make their own production decisions. However, the pressure for reforms was high as farmers had suffered enough under the commune system and production incentives were very low. In addition, Deng Xiaoping advocated his cat theory, that is, 'a cat is a good cat as along as it can catch mice, and it does not matter if the cat is black or white'. In other words, Deng told people not to worry about Mao's definition of collective socialism. Communes and production teams should be allowed to implement household production responsibility if such a responsibility could raise productivity and farm incomes.

By contrast, it was difficult for China to reform the industry and urban sector as it was predominately state owned. Urban workers were paid with a regular salary and were heavily protected by a complicated system of state subsidies and all kinds of benefits which were denied to the peasants. Urban reforms were impossible to be implemented without severe resistance from both managers and workers.

The second reason why reforms started from the countryside was due to the fact that the vast majority of peasants lived in absolute poverty even after almost three decades of socialist revolution and construction. If the Party failed to reduce rural poverty, China would have no chance of being modernised. In addition, the rural sector would be unable to support urban and industrial development if all the people were too poor. Hence, the need to reform agriculture and raise agricultural productivity was important not only for reducing rural poverty, but also for accumulating more resources for urban development.

The rural reform consisted of both policy and institutional changes, Riskin (1987) suggested that rural and agricultural reforms comprised several distinct aspects:

- substantial increases in procurement prices of agricultural products
- increased autonomy for decision-making to the rural collectives
- the change of policy from emphasising forced local self-sufficiency in grain to encouraging diversification and specialisation
- decollectivisation of decision-making and organisation.

The focus of rural reform was the household production responsibility. Before reforms, farmers were organised within a production team. They worked collectively for all the production tasks right from field preparation to crop harvest. They earned work points every day. The team leader assessed and assigned work points to individual team members on a daily basis. Households could also earn work points through selling manual fertilisers to the team. At the end of the harvest season, the total work points of each household and the whole team would be calculated by the team accountant. The harvest was then translated into monetary income. After deducting the cost of production, the net revenue was then divided by the total number of work points to derive their unit value. The total value of work points for each household was then calculated. Households used their earned work point value to buy agricultural produce from the team. In south China, for example, the main agricultural produce was rice, which was the main crop, and teams were forced by the commune to produce rice for sale to the state as well as for self-consumption. After delivering a given quota of rice to the state, the remaining part of the total output was used for self-consumption and seeds. The amount that was available for distribution to households would be distributed based on two main criteria: population and work points. This implied that every team member would be allocated a certain amount of rice irrespective of sex, age and work point contribution, although a certain proportion of retained rice was allocated to work points. Hence, if a household did not earn any work points, it would be entitled to the first stage of distribution, but if a household had work points, it would be entitled to the distribution based on both family size and work points.

   Distribution at the team level was quite fair and open. The team leader had limited power to influence the distribution. However, the amount of product that could be distributed to households depended on the level of harvest as well as on the quota that had to be delivered to the state. The state quota included both agricultural tax and forced procurement at low prices. Agricultural tax was low, consisting of 3–5 per cent of total production, but forced procurement was large, accounting for 30–50 per cent of total production. The procurement price was set low and kept more or less unchanged for many years. For example, the procurement price of unprocessed rice in Guangdong was 0.196 yuan per kg. Such a price was usually less than the cost of production. Hence, forced procurement represented an implicit tax on agriculture. Another problem of forced procurement was that it was fixed at the beginning of the production season. State quota had to be fulfilled whatever the final level of harvest. If there was a crop failure, the team had little to distribute to households after fulfilling the state quota. The state might give back some, or all, of its quota if the harvest was really poor.

   Within the production team, although the distribution was fair and open, team members might not have enough incentives to work to their best potential. This institutional issue was fully discussed by Lin (1988). The key issue was that agricultural production tasks could not be correctly assessed until the final harvest and it was almost impossible for the team leader to monitor the real efforts of team members on a daily basis. Another problem was that agricultural production was highly seasonal. In some periods of the year, there were few activities, but during the planting and harvesting seasons, there was too much work in a relatively short period of time. If farmers did not work extremely hard during those seasons, the final output would be severely affected. Under the team system, it was almost impossible to ask all team members to work hard without shirking. For example, the harvesting season of early rice in Guangdong usually coincided with the monsoon season. If a typhoon was predicted to arrive in five days, all the rice had to be harvested within five days. Otherwise, the crop would be destroyed. Once the rice was harvested, it had to be dried using a limited area of drying surface in the open air. The drying process might take seven to ten days uninterrupted. However, downpours of rain often interrupted the process. A lot of labour was required to move the rice to and from the warehouse to the drying area. If rain continued for a few days, the rice was in danger of fermenting in the warehouse.

   The household responsibility system solved many of the problems of the production team discussed above. The team allocated a piece of land to each household. It also asked each household to deliver a certain amount of output to the state through the team. Each household became an independent management unit. It had the maximum incentive to save cost and raise productivity, because the more it produced, the more it could retain for self-consumption. Household members would perform every task to the best of their ability during the entire process of production. In the off-peak season, farmers saved time to do off-farm work without any restrictions or penalties being imposed by the team. In the peak season, household members would work extremely hard to harvest their crops in good time and store rice inside their own houses for drying if the weather was poor.

Alongside the household responsibility system, the state also implemented a number of policies to stimulate agricultural production and increase farm incomes. Such policies included the successive increases in state procurement prices of cereals in 1979, legalisation of rural free markets, the legalisation of off-farm production and more freedom given to farmers for diversifying production away from staple food crops to cash crops.

As markets developed and incomes improved, household savings grew rapidly, workers were encouraged to specialise in various sideline productions ranging from forestry to fishery and to develop township and village enterprises (TVEs). The share of TVEs in China's GDP rose from almost nothing in 1978 to 13 per cent in 1985 and to 28 per cent in 1998 (MOA, 1999; NBS, 1999b).

The success of agricultural reforms was manifested by the rapid increase of grain production from 1978 to 1984. In six years, total grain output rose by 108 million tons from 300 to 408 million tons. The same amount of increase took more than two decades in the pre-reform period. Over the same period, real per capita rural income rose by about 15 per cent per annum, or more than doubled in six years (Yao, 1994). The gross output of farming, forestry, animal husbandry and fishery grew at an annual rate of 7.59 per cent in the period 1978–84 (NBS, 1999b; author's calculation), compared to 2 per cent in the pre-reform period.

Following the tremendous success of rural reforms, China launched its large-scale reform in the industrial sector in 1984 although urban reform was carried out piecemeal before 1985.

The urban reforms covered both the production management and distribution systems, focusing on the expansion of enterprise autonomy and the reduction of the government within-plan allocations. The main steps included:

- The state leased out many small state-owned enterprises (SOEs) to collectives or individuals.
- The 'factory director's responsibility system' was introduced to reduce the level of unwanted political interference by party secretaries.
- Enterprise autonomy was expanded. The command system was gradually replaced by a free market system.
- Local governments were granted considerable authority over budgetary revenues and expenditures. The practice of budgeting all fixed and circulating capital free of charge (soft budget) was gradually replaced by the use of repayable bank loans bearing interests (hard budget).
- An experimental shareholding system was set up to allow the state and enterprise workers to own its assets and care for its economic well-being. The state, enterprises and individuals were permitted to invest in companies through the purchase of shares.
- A contract labour system was introduced, aimed at breaking the 'iron rice bowl' (life-long secure jobs) in SOEs.

(Riskin, 1987; Perkins, 1988; Zhang, 2000)

The expansion of enterprise autonomy not only freed enterprises from the past control of the state administration (i.e. the separation between government administration and enterprise management) but also gave enterprises the right to share profits and control issues in operational management. With reduction of the government within-plan allocations, markets were gradually introduced for trading inputs and outputs. The practice of budgeting all fixed and circulating capital free of charge was replaced by the use of repayable bank loans bearing interest. By abolishing the monopoly power of governmental agencies in some areas, competition was introduced and the prices of various industrial products were allowed to change with a limitation. In this stage, the Chinese economy gradually became a two-track system, with a part of the system running under the traditional planning mechanism and the other part operating under the newly established market mechanism. Reforms had been pursued in areas such as salaries, housing, public utilities, medical care and social welfare. Despite some negative side effects, the urban reforms are successful. The GDP for industry grew at an annual rate of 14.04 per cent in real terms from 1984 to 1988 (NBS, 1999b, author's calculation). Measured in 1990 constant prices, per capita GDP in China increased by more than six times from 1978 to 1999, rising from 659 yuan to 4,203 yuan, or by 9.22 per cent per annum (NBS, 2000).

The progress of the economic reforms slowed down during the period of 1989–91 due to the different views on economic reforms, problems associated with economic growth and modernisation (inflation, over-investment, budgetary deficits and corruption) and the incident of Tiananmen Square.

Economic reforms were driven again and accelerated after Deng Xiaoping's southern tour in the spring of 1992. During that trip, Deng appealed for economic development to be accelerated and opened up, and claimed 'only development is the real truth'. In October 1992, the Fourteenth National Congress of the Party endorsed Deng's views and called for the establishment of a 'socialist market economy'. The goal of establishing a socialist market economy was adopted in China's constitution during the first session of the Eighth National People's Congress in March 1993. Since then, the economic reforms were broadened and deepened to macroeconomic areas including the reforms of the fiscal and monetary system. Major reforms in 1990s are:

- reforming the exchange rate system (allowing RMB to be devalued without formal government action);
- adjusting the fiscal system (introducing a new tax assignment system that separates central and local taxation authorities);
- reforming the bank system (establishing an effective central banking system and a profit-making commercial banking system);
- opening the stock markets in Shanghai and Shenzhen;
- deepening state-owned enterprises reform to improve the efficiency of state enterprises;
- adopting systems of accounting, laws on property rights and patent protection;
- reforming the social security system;

- reforming the services sector;
- accelerating housing reforms.

(Bhalla, 1995; Liou, 1998)

In addition to domestic reforms, China also adopted an open policy for international trade and investment. It changed from a self-reliance and import substitution development strategy to an export promotion strategy. In the meantime, foreign investments were allowed to enter China to transform its inefficient industrial sector and improve competition and technologies. In theory and practice, China's open policy has proved to play an important role in economic growth under economic reforms. The reforms referred to policy changes that resulted in decentralisation and marketisation, the opening up related to policy changes that integrated China into the world economy. The adoption of the open-door policy indicated a change of China's economic development philosophy and principles. In the pre-reform period, China implemented a self-reliance development policy, which emphasised the utilisation of domestic resources (labour, capital, and land). Under the open-door policy, China returned to the World Bank and IMF and borrowed from these institutions and foreign governments, and encouraged foreign investment from joint ventures to wholly owned foreign-investment firms (Riskin, 1987; Gao, 1996; Liou, 1998). China's open policy culminated in December 2001 when it was allowed to join the World Trade Organisation (WTO) more than twenty years after the first application.

Before 1978, China's foreign trade was centralised at the national level and was conducted by 12 state-owned foreign trade corporations (FTCs). Along with economic reforms, the FTCs were gradually given greater autonomy and made more accountable for their operations. The management of the trade system was also decentralised from the central government to the provincial governments. By the late 1980s the number of FTCs had soared to more than 5,000. Moreover, large state-owned enterprises and foreign-funded enterprises were also given the right to export on their account (Lardy, 1992). Foreign trade increased from $1.94 billion in 1952 to $20.64 in 1978, to $360.63 billion in 1998 (NBS, 2000), which ranked China, excluding Hong Kong, the tenth largest trading nation in the world, rising from the twenty-third place in 1978. The latest statistics show that China will break the record of international trade to a new level of $851 billion in 2003, representing an annual growth of 37 per cent from the previous year (*People's Daily*, 2004: 12 January, p. 1). China's ranking in international trade has been up-lifted year after year. In 2002, China was considered to rank number 6 in the world. In November 2003, the Financial Times reports that with a 40 per cent annual growth rate China will surpass Japan to become the world's third largest importer, behind only Germany and the US. It also reports that China generated a trade surplus of $6 billion in October 2003 alone. The US also blames China for generating a trade surplus of $100 billion in 2002.

Aside from the changes in the foreign trade system, more and more areas were opened up to attract foreign investment. The opening of cities and areas took a well-planned and sequential process as shown below:

- four special economic zones (SEZs), Shenzhen, Zhuhai, Shantou and Xiamen, in 1979;
- 14 open coastal cities, from Dalian in the north to Beihai in the south, in 1984;
- three deltaic areas, Yangtze River, Pear River and Minjiang River, in 1985;
- Liaodong Peninsula and Shandong Peninsula in 1987;
- Hainan Island as an independent and open province in 1988;
- Shanghai Pudong New Zone in 1990.

In addition to the initial decision by the central government, many provincial governments and the local governments issued their own preferential policies for foreign investment. By the mid-1993, over 1,800 special zones at and above the county level had emerged (Liou, 1998; Zhang, 2000). Most of the open areas are concentrated along the eastern coastal region, reflecting a shift of development strategy from the balanced approach in the pre-reform period to a coastal-biased policy since 1978.

The development of the SEZs is crucial to China's economic reforms in general and to the open-door policy in particular. The Chinese government used the SEZs to serve as experimental units for testing policy measures in the economic structural reform and as a school for learning the value and rules of the market system. Local governments in the SEZs have the authority to make investment decisions that are outside the state plan and are allowed to provide preferential policies to attract foreign investors. The preferential policies included the lower tax rates, tax holidays, and exemptions of import licenses and custom duties on imports of machinery and equipment as well as on their exports. Following the success of economic development in SEZs, which benefited from foreign investment, management, technology, skills and equipment and the increase of foreign trade, many policies were developed and implemented nationally later. The trial-and-error approach in a gradual manner is a key character of the Chinese economic reforms.

## 2.4  Half a century of economic performance: an overview

Since the founding of the People's Republic, China went through over half a century of socialist construction and industrialisation. China is one of the few surviving 'socialist' countries in the world as all the former socialist countries in eastern Europe have changed to a non-socialist system. However, the actual economic system in China today is very different from that of half a century ago. A traditional definition of socialism contained three key elements distinctively different from capitalism: public (state) ownership, communist leadership who represent the peasants and workers, and distribution according to labour not capital. In China today, apart from communist leadership, public ownership has been substituted with a multi-ownership system where private enterprises have been and will be greatly encouraged, state ownership has been modified to become shareholding companies, distribution by labour has been changed to distribution by both labour and capital. Even the remaining element of communist leadership has changed its nature, as the communist party has ceased to only represent the poor, but to represent both rich and poor. In addition, many communist party members and leaders themselves have become rich and super rich. The new China is considered to be 'socialism with a Chinese character', which was used by Deng Xiaoping in order to reform China without upsetting the old communist guards who were used to Mao's doctrines of socialism and public ownership.

Whether socialism with a Chinese character is a good thing or not, the reality is that China today is very different from a quarter century ago, and fundamentally different from half a century ago. As mentioned in the previous chapter, China had suffered more than a century of civil wars, imperial invasion, poverty, diseases and destitution before 1949. The founding of the People's Republic set a cornerstone for a new history of China in the sense that it was free from any external imperial powers. Although there were mistakes by Mao, he had made a tremendous contribution to China as one of the most powerful countries today.

The latest 25 years of reforms have transformed China from a poverty stricken nation into a relatively modernised one as well as being one of the fastest growing economies in the world. The recent successful launch (15 October 2003) of a manned spacecraft, Shengzhou 5, has not only shocked the world, but also encouraged all Chinese people to gain further confidence in the foreseeable future to come. China is now number 3 in the world in terms of space technology although it is still far behind the US and Russia.

However, China is a newly industrialising country and is still enjoying the fastest economic growth rate among all countries. Despite the SARS (severe acute respiratory syndrome) outbreak in early 2003, China achieved a 9.1 per cent GDP growth in 2003 (*People's Daily*, 2004: 21 January), a 37 per cent growth in foreign trade to reach a new record of $851 billion (*People's Daily*, 2004: 12 January). People are becoming richer and richer and continue to save large sums of money for investment. In the first nine months of 2003, private bank deposits rose by 1.4 trillion yuan, making cumulative deposits break the 10 trillion yuan mark for the first time. China's foreign exchange reserves at the end of September 2003 reached a record high of $383.9 billion, rising by 48.4 per cent from the previous year (*People's Daily*, 2003: 18 October, p. 1). In most developing countries, local currencies are usually overvalued due to shortage of foreign exchanges. In China, the opposite occurs, as China's main trading partners, including the US and Japan have been trying to persuade China to raise the value of the yuan.

The latest statistics show that China is now the biggest producer of many key agricultural and industrial products, including steel, cement, electricity, colour TV sets, chemical fertilisers, personal computers, cloth, coal, cereals, fish and meats. The total output of steel in China will be more than 200 million tons, which will be equal to the combined production of the US and Japan, the second and third largest steel producers in the world. China has also become one of the largest car producers, after the US, Japan, Germany and France. It will soon surpass France to become the fourth largest car producer in the next couple of years. In another twenty years' time, China may also challenge the US and Japan to become the world's largest car manufacturer, as it has done in steel and electricity production.

The booming Chinese economy can also be reflected by the unforeseen expansion in education, both domestic and overseas. Fifteen years ago few Chinese parents could afford to send their children to study overseas. Today, many universities in the US, UK, Canada, Japan and Australia have to rely on recruiting Chinese students as one of their main financial sources. In the UK, for example, the total number of Chinese students has reached 125,000 in 2003 and is still expanding exponentially. In the late 1980s, the total number of Chinese students studying in UK universities was less than 10,000 (private information from the Chinese Embassy in London).

There is no doubt that China has created an economic miracle in world development history although it is still a poor country measured on per capita terms. The so-called China miracle is due to the very simple fact that it has sustained a high and continuing growth for more than half a century in the most populous nation of the world. Although many economies in Asia, including Japan, South Korea, Hong Kong, Singapore, Taiwan have been industrialised in the twentieth century, the combined population of all these economies is substantially less than that of China. In addition, China used to contain the vast majority of the world's people living in poverty, but due to its continuing high growth, the incidence of poverty in China has been greatly reduced. Such a reduction in the level of poverty implies that China has made a significant contribution to the well-being of mankind on the earth and set a good example for other similar poor countries to develop their own economies. The latest development in India and Vietnam, for example, is a good indication that poor countries can achieve high economic growth if they adopt similar open and liberalised policies.

If we compare the achievements of China itself between the pre-reform and post-reform periods, we can also see how policy changes can lead to very different development results. Table 2.2 summarises some key economic indicators for China. The table uses 1952, instead of 1949 as the first year for two reasons. First, the period 1949–52 was a recovery period after the founding of the People's Republic, if 1949 were used as the first year of comparison, it could lead to upward biased estimates of growth. Second, many economic data and activities were unavailable in 1949. The turning point year was in 1978 for the pre-reform and reform periods. The last year of comparison is 2001, which is the latest year that comprehensive data are available at the time of writing this book.

Of the 48 years from 1952 to 2001, 25 were in the pre-reform period and 23 were in the reform period. The two periods had roughly the same length for comparison. At the most aggregate level, total GDP grew by 7.8 per cent on an annual basis, or by 36 times for the entire 48 year period. This would be a remarkable achievement if it were compared to any other country in the world in the same period. However, the average growth rate disguises a significant difference between the two sub-periods. The average annual growth rate in the reform period was 3.0 percentage points higher than the pre-reform period. In the meantime, the annual rate of population growth was much lower in the reform period than in the pre-reform (1.2 per cent versus 2.1 per cent). As a result, the growth rate of GDP per capita in the reform period was almost twice as high as in the pre-reform period (8.2 per cent versus 4.3 per cent).

High growth in GDP led to high growth in real consumption per capita, particularly in the reform period. Real per capita consumption rose 7.1 per cent on an annual basis in the reform period, compared to 2.3 per cent in the pre-reform period. However, it is also noted that real per capita consumption in the urban sector rose by more than 0.6 percentage points than in the rural sector for the entire 48 year period. This is an issue of importance which will be discussed in detail in the rest of this book.

The prosperity of the Chinese population in the reform period can be best described by the amount of private bank deposits by both the rural and urban residents. In 1978, the total deposit was only 21 billion yuan, by 2001, it was 7.4 trillion yuan, and by September 2003, it had surpassed the 10 trillion yuan mark, reaching 10.1 trillion yuan (*People's Daily*, 2003: 18 October, p. 1). This tremendous accumulation of personal wealth is the result as well as the foundation of China's fast economic growth.

Another indicator of prosperity is the phenomenal growth of key agricultural and industrial products. Despite a rapid growth in the pre-reform period, the growth in the reform period became more impressive. For instance, China produced no television sets before the early 1980s, but by 2001, it had produced more than 40 million. The average annual growth rate of the physical production of key industrial goods such as electricity, steel, cement and fertilisers has now been above the two-digit level for about half a century.

The booming development of telecommunications in China is almost unmatched by any other country in the world. In 1949, only 300,000 households had a telephone line. After economic reforms, the telecommunications industry experienced a phenomenal growth. The total number of telephone lines rose from 1.9 million in 1978 to 100 million in 1998. In the following five years, from 1998 to September 2003, the total number of telephone lines rose to over 500 million. Of these, there were 255 million landlines and 247 million mobile phones. Less than ten years ago, the biggest bottleneck of economic development in China was transportation and telecommunications. Today, China has the largest telecommunication market in the world. China also has the second longest motorway system after the United States. The longest motorway in China is from Tongjiang in Heilongjian to Sanya in Hainan, with a total length of 5,500 kilometres.

In recent years, some China experts have cast doubt on the reliability of China's GDP statistics (Rawski, 2001). However, if one observes the improvements in people's incomes, the growth of physical products, the pace of infrastructure development such as the Three Gorges Dam, the national network of motorways, the exponential expansion in information and telecommunication industries, the intense activities of international trade and foreign direct investments, one should not be so pessimistic about China's official statistics. In my own view, the Chinese publications of official statistics have been improved over the years and are now the best available sources of statistical information for research in China.

Even in agricultural production, despite the gradual decline of the area of arable land, the physical outputs of most key agricultural products grew steadily over time. Grain output broke the 400 million record in 1984, and the 500 million tons record by the mid-1990s. Due to subdued domestic demand and stagnant prices, grain output was deliberately adjusted downwards through reducing the cropping areas from the late 1990s. The development of grain production in China also proved that some Western scholars had failed to understand China's production abilities. Lester R. Brown (1995) predicted that no one in the world would be able to feed the Chinese population. The last decade of development has shown that China is more than capable of feeding its own population. It was the first time in China's history that farmers have deliberately reduced the level of grain production for almost a decade so far.

The slowdown of grain production has been over-compensated for by the fast growth in the production of livestock products, fishery and forestry. From 1978 to 2001, the annual growth rate of meat products was 9.1 per cent and that of fishery products 10.2 per cent. As the value of meat and fish is much higher than that of grain, China has managed to raise agricultural productivity through diversification away from crop farming to animal husbandry and fishery. As a result, the production structure in agriculture has been changed from that dominated by cropping (mainly cereal cropping) to that featured heavily with non-cropping activities. The share of crop farming in total agricultural output declined from 80 per cent in 1978 to only 55.2 per cent by 2001, while the share of forestry, animal husbandry and fishery rose from less than 20 per cent to about 45 per cent. The deepening of agricultural structure change, coupled with the rapid development of township and village enterprises have been two important driving forces for the rapid transformation of rural China. The pre-reform rural countryside was dominated by subsistence crop farming and a primitive level of rural industrialisation. The post-reform rural areas, particularly in the eastern parts of the country, have enjoyed a long period of industrialisation and urbanisation, which is not commonly observed in most parts of the developing world.

In the pre-reform period, the level of urbanisation was low. From 1952 to 1978, urban population as a share of the total population rose from 12.4 per cent to only 17.9 per cent, or a rise of 5.5 percentage points for exactly one quarter of a century. The pace of urbanisation was rapid from 1978 onwards. By 2001, the urban population share rose to 37.7 per cent, or a rise of about 20 percentage points in 23 years. In terms of employment, the transformation was even more obvious. The share of agricultural employment in total employment declined by 13 percentage points from 1952 to 1978, and by another 20 percentage points from 1978 to 2001. By 2001, agricultural employment accounted for half of the national employment.

Despite the significant changes in the population and employment structures, the speed of such structural changes has not been comparable to the change in the output structure. Agriculture's share in national GDP declined from 50 per cent in 1952 to 28 per cent in 1978 and then to 15 per cent in 2001. This level of agriculture's share in GDP suggests that China is in effect an industrialised economy, but the levels of urbanisation and agricultural employment imply that China is still in the Lewis stage of economic development. In other words, China still has abundant surplus agricultural labour to be transferred out to the more productive non-agricultural sectors. This is a challenge as well as an opportunity for the future development of the Chinese economy. The challenge is that China still needs to create a huge number of non-farm jobs every year for the next few decades. The opportunity is that China will still be able to grow faster than the industrialised countries because of its bottomless sea of cheap labour.

## 2.5 Conclusion

This chapter studies the development policies of China for two different sub-periods from 1949. It can be summarised that policies in the pre-reform period had the following features.

### *Central planning and state ownership*

This meant that production and management were highly centralised and enterprises were largely state-owned in the industrial and urban sector. In the rural sector, collectivisation and the commune were the dominant organisation structure, although from 1962 onwards, the formal commune was substituted with the so-called three-tier ownership, i.e. commune, production brigade and production team.

### *Import substitution and self-reliance*

The country was largely close to the outside world. There was no FDI and trade activities were restricted to the very basic needs of the country for its development of heavy industries.

### *Capital-intensive instead of labour-intensive industries*

Industrial development was focused on capital-intensive (heavy) industries. This development strategy did not exploit the comparative advantage of the country. China's comparative advantage was its cheap labour, which was largely confined to agricultural production. Even in the agricultural sector, little attention was paid to diversification. Crop farming was the main rural activity to support a low-price food system in the urban sector.

### *Irrational policies and political struggles*

Many policies were irrational in the sense that they were inconsistent with human or economic nature. Many assumptions on economic policies were unrealistic. The Great Leap Forward movement and the Cultural Revolution were two major political events that damaged the Chinese economy and people's lives severely. The great famine during 1959–61 led to a direct loss of about 13 million lives and a reduced number of births of more than 30 million. After the Cultural Revolution in 1976, the vast majority of the Chinese peasants were suffering from hunger and malnutrition. In other words, the vast majority of the rural population was living in absolute poverty.

*Table 2.2* Key economic indicators of contemporary China, 1952–2001

| Key indicators | Unit | 1952 | 1978 | 2001 | Annual growth rate % | | |
|---|---|---|---|---|---|---|---|
| | | | | | 1952–78 | 1978–01 | 1952–01 |
| 1 Population | M | 575.0 | 963.0 | 1276.0 | 2.1 | 1.2 | 1.7 |
| Urban | % | 12.4 | 17.9 | 37.7 | 1.5 | 3.3 | 2.3 |
| Rural | % | 87.6 | 82.1 | 62.3 | -0.3 | -1.2 | -0.7 |
| 2 Employment | M | 207.0 | 402.0 | 730.0 | 2.7 | 2.6 | 2.7 |
| Agriculture | % | 83.6 | 70.6 | 50.0 | -0.7 | -1.5 | -1.1 |
| Industry | % | 7.2 | 17.2 | 22.3 | 3.5 | 1.2 | 2.4 |
| Services | % | 9.2 | 12.2 | 27.7 | 1.1 | 3.6 | 2.3 |
| 3 GDP current prices | Bn yuan | 68.0 | 362.0 | 9593.0 | 6.9 | 15.3 | 10.9 |
| Agriculture | % | 50.0 | 28.2 | 15.2 | -2.3 | -2.6 | -2.4 |
| Industry | % | 20.6 | 48.3 | 51.2 | 3.5 | 0.2 | 1.9 |
| Services | % | 29.4 | 23.5 | 33.6 | -0.9 | 1.6 | 0.3 |
| 4 Real GDP index | % | 100.0 | 471.4 | 3740.9 | 6.4 | 9.4 | 7.8 |
| 5 General price index | % | 100.0 | 121.6 | 424.5 | 0.8 | 5.6 | 3.1 |
| 6 Consumer price index | % | 100.0 | 125.3 | 583.5 | 0.9 | 6.9 | 3.7 |
| 7 Real consumption/head index | % | 100.0 | 178.0 | 863.4 | 2.3 | 7.1 | 4.6 |
| Rural | % | 100.0 | 158.0 | 699.2 | 1.8 | 6.7 | 4.0 |
| Urban | % | 100.0 | 217.0 | 912.2 | 3.1 | 6.4 | 4.6 |
| 8 Bank deposits | Bn yuan | 0.9 | 21.0 | 7376.2 | 13.4 | 29.0 | 20.7 |
| 9 Structure of agricultural output | % | 100.0 | 100.0 | 100.0 | 100.0 | 100.0 | 100.0 |
| Farming | % | 85.9 | 80.0 | 55.2 | -0.3 | -1.6 | -0.9 |
| Forestry | % | 1.6 | 3.4 | 3.6 | 3.1 | 0.2 | 1.7 |
| Animal husbandry | % | 11.2 | 15.0 | 30.4 | 1.2 | 3.1 | 2.1 |
| Fishery | % | 1.3 | 1.6 | 10.8 | 0.8 | 8.6 | 4.5 |

*Table 2.2* continued

| 10 Key agricultural/industrial products | | | | | | | |
|---|---|---|---|---|---|---|---|
| Grain | M ton | 164.0 | 305.0 | 453.0 | 2.5 | 1.7 | 2.1 |
| Meat products | M ton | 3.4 | 8.6 | 63.3 | 3.8 | 9.1 | 6.3 |
| Fish | M ton | 1.7 | 4.7 | 43.8 | 4.2 | 10.2 | 7.0 |
| Cloth | Bn metre | 3.8 | 11.0 | 29.0 | 4.3 | 4.3 | 4.3 |
| Colour TV sets | M set | 0.0 | 0.0 | 40.9 | – | – | – |
| Coal | M ton | 66.0 | 620.0 | 1161.0 | 9.4 | 2.8 | 6.2 |
| Electricity | Bn kwh | 7.3 | 256.6 | 1480.8 | 15.3 | 7.9 | 11.7 |
| Steel | M ton | 1.4 | 31.8 | 151.6 | 13.5 | 7.0 | 10.3 |
| Cement | M ton | 2.9 | 65.2 | 661.0 | 13.3 | 10.6 | 12.0 |
| Fertiliser | M ton | 0.0 | 8.7 | 33.8 | 24.0 | 6.1 | 15.1 |
| Vehicles | 1000 | 0.0 | 149.1 | 2342.0 | – | 12.7 | – |
| 11 Foreign trade | $bn | 1.9 | 20.6 | 509.8 | 10.0 | 15.0 | 12.4 |
| Exports | $bn | 0.8 | 9.7 | 266.2 | 10.8 | 15.3 | 12.8 |
| Imports | $bn | 1.1 | 10.9 | 243.6 | 9.4 | 14.6 | 11.9 |
| 12 Exchange rates | Yuan/$ | 3.4 | 1.7 | 8.3 | -2.7 | 7.1 | 1.9 |
| 13 Actually used FDI | $bn | 0.0 | 0.2 | 46.9 | – | 26.8 | – |
| 14 Telephone lines* | M | 0.3 | 1.9 | 502.0 | 6.8 | 25.0 | 15.0 |

Sources: NBS, 1999b; NBS (2002). Data on telephone lines is from *People's Daily*, 24 October 2003, p. 1.

Notes: FDI = foreign direct investments, KWH = kilowatt hour. (*) Data for telephone are for the years of 1949, 1978 and 2003. The figure in 2003 was by the end of September 2003. Of the total number of phones, 255 million are landlines and 247 are mobile phones.

By contrast, economic policies in the reform period have the following features.

### Export promotion and globalisation

Exports have become an important impetus of economic growth and international cooperation. China opens its door much more widely than any other transition and developing economy in the world. China became the largest FDI recipient among the developing world. Its ranking in international trade moved from number 23 to number 6 in 2002. It will soon become one of the top four trading partners in the world. Japan and the US have become aware that China is now their main competitor in international trade. Every year, China has managed to generate a huge surplus from its trading activities with these two trading superpowers. Over the last two years, Japan and US have been trying hard to persuade China to appreciate its yuan in order to reduce its trade surplus.

### Labour-intensive industries, urbanisation and industrialisation

Compared to the pre-reform period, China has been trying to increase the level of urbanisation and industrialisation. The development of township and village enterprises, especially in the eastern coastal areas, is the key to rural industrialisation. Hundreds of small towns in Guangdong, Zhejiang, Jiangsu, Shangdong and Fujian have become major industrial cities. Even in the inland areas, the former small county towns have become prosperous industrial centres. In addition, millions of farmers have been allowed to move to the local cities and settle down there as formal urban residents. The share of rural population and the share of agricultural labour have declined much faster in the reform period than in the pre-reform period.

The prosperity of the rural economy and the rapid change in the employment and industrial structure have been due to the shift of industry policy to emphasise the development of labour-intensive industries which have exploited China's comparative advantages. In the past two decades, China has emerged to become one of the world's most important producers of labour-intensive manufacturing products, ranging from toys and clothing to colour TV and motor vehicles.

### Rational policies and social stability

One important factor for China's success under economic reforms has been social stability for more than a quarter century. As mentioned in Chapter 1, China suffered more than 100 years of wars and imperial invasions before 1949. The pre-reform period was also full of internal struggles and political movements. In a sense, the reform period is the most peaceful era in China's modern history. This period also coincided with the end of the cold war in the world, which meant that China has enjoyed the most favourable external environment as well.

Domestically, China learnt from its past mistakes of political struggles and the leadership under Deng emphasised economic development, the prosperity of the people and social stability. Although the Tiananmen Square incidence in 1989 caused some trouble throughout the country, the government managed to control the country's political situation afterwards and regained the respect of the Chinese people and the world community. The fast development and rapid accumulation of people's wealth in the 1990s proved that social stability was key to China's economic success. The fourth generation of the communist leadership under President Hu Jingtao has won widespread support by the Chinese people. Despite many problems facing the new leadership, it is believed that China's social stability will continue in the following decades. Hence, China will continue its modernisation and industrialisation drive as it did in the last two and a half decades.

However, China's future success may not be guaranteed as many new problems have been created during the process of economic reforms.

Before ending this chapter, it is important to list the key problems facing China today.

### *Weak agricultural base and a relatively poor rural population*

This problem is referred by the Chinese leadership as the three-nongs problem. The three nongs refers to peasants, rural area and agriculture. Economic growth has led to rising urban–rural disparity and agriculture has been used to support the urban and industrialisation drive again since 1984. Rural income stagnated from 1985 to 1994. Agricultural production slowed down from the mid-1980s. Lack of investments means that agricultural productivity cannot increase as fast as it did in the earlier years of reform during 1978–84.

In recent years, the development of TVEs has also slowed down and stopped to absorb more labour released from agriculture. Rural–urban migration has been active but this process cannot continue indefinitely, especially when urban industries are laying off millions of SOE workers. Hence, the transfer of agricultural labour to non-farm or urban activities is still a slow and painful process.

### *Industrial reforms*

The SOE sector has been and still is the biggest problem in China. Despite the recent wholesale redundancies of SOE workers, the efficiency of this sector is still a problem. Reform in the banking sector is slow and the problem of non-performing loans is the biggest issue in China's financial system. After joining the WTO, China has a limited period of time to reform its highly inefficient and corrupt banking system.

### *Inequality and poverty*

Inequality and poverty come hand-in-hand. Despite the phenomenal growth and the rapid accumulation of personal wealth, China still has a huge number of people living in absolute poverty. More importantly, the government always fails to recognise the true scale of poverty in the country. In one year, it says there are so many people living in poverty. In another year, it can publish another set of figures. The publication of poverty incidence is far too sensitive for the government to say the truth. It makes the task of identifying and reducing poverty particularly difficult. However, the government has to recognise that the existence of poverty cannot be underestimated for two reasons. First, poverty can trigger unrest and threaten social stability. As has already been seen, social stability has been one of the key factors to China's economic success. If China could not continue to maintain social stability due to rising inequality and poverty, then the government would jeopardise its long term ambition to make China an economic superpower by the middle of this century. Second, the government has a moral obligation to eliminate poverty after such a long period of economic growth. It is shameful in the sense that per capita GDP has risen more than six times over the last 25 years and China still has over 100 million peasants and over 20 million urban residents living in absolute poverty.

The incidence of poverty and the difficulty of alleviating poverty has been due to rising inequality. In China, inequality is multi-dimensional, including rural–urban inequality, inter-regional inequality, within-regional inequality caused by marginalisation.

Inequality is also caused by corruption. It needs to stress that many communist party leaders have abused their powers and used loopholes in the laws and institutions for rent-seeking activities. The types of corruption are numerous as China's economic activities become more and more complex. Economic success has provided increasing opportunities for corrupt officials to make political rents. The government has set up many institutions design to control corruption, but a recent report shows that out of the total corruption cases investigated, over 40 per cent involved the anti-corruption officials.

Both Jiang Zhemin and Hu Jiangtao have warned the party officials that the future of the party and the state could be jeopardised by the widespread corruption if it were not effectively controlled. The problem is that many corruption practices have been accepted as 'legalised' or 'semi-legalised', and the chance of being caught is still very small. However, corruption is not unique to China. It happens everywhere in the world, particularly in the transition economies such as those in Russia, India, Pakistan, Brazil, Indonesia and Argentina. The extent of corruption in China may not be the worst in the world, but if China fails to control corruption, there is little prospect for China to reduce inequality and eliminate poverty. These are the two important issues of research in this book.

# 3 Agricultural and rural development

## 3.1 Introduction

The CCPCC issued its first document of 2004: 'Chinese Communist Party Central Committee and the State Council's opinion on some policies to improve peasant incomes' (*People's Daily*, 2004: 10 February). This was the first such document issued by the CCPCC since 1949 about how to improve farm incomes. It was also the second time that the CCPCC issued the first document of the year on agriculture since 1978. The first time had been during 1982–6, when it issued the first document of the year for five consecutive years to boost agricultural production and rural development. Since 1985, peasants, agriculture and rural areas have been largely neglected and disadvantaged due to the continuation of urban-biased policy.

The first document of 2004 hence signifies the seriousness of the problems surrounding urban–rural inequality and the weakening of agricultural and rural development in China, even though China has been heralded for achieving high growth for more than a quarter century.

The *People's Daily* (2004: 10 February) summarises a few key problems regarding stagnant farm incomes and the poor state of agriculture and rural development:

- From 1997 to 2003, per capita farm income rose by half the rate of per capita urban income. In 2003, per capita rural income was only 2622 yuan, compared with per capita urban income of 8500 yuan.
- Urban–rural per capita income ratio rose from 2.47 to 3.24 from 1997 to 2003.
- It is more difficult for grain growing farmers to increase their incomes. As a result, grain output has declined in recent years. In 2003, grain output was only 430.6 million tons, down by 26.4 million tons, or 5.8 per cent from 2002, or down by 82 million tons from the peak level of 512 million tons achieved in 1998.
- In 2003, there were 99 million rural people working outside their home towns, up by 5 million from 2002.

In the first document of 2004, the CCPCC aims to allocate 150 billion yuan to support agricultural and rural development, up by 30 billion yuan from the previous year. It also aims to reduce agricultural tax rate from the present level of 8.4 per cent of agricultural gross output value to 2.4 per cent by 2009, implying that the central government has to give up 40 billion yuan of agricultural tax revenue each year by 2009.

The first document of 2004 is seen as the second most serious CCPCC action to tackle the 'three-nongs' problem (the problem of peasant, agriculture and rural areas) since economic reforms started in 1978. Not only does it reflect the dire situation in rural China, it also suggests that China cannot continue its development policy without encountering the agricultural and rural problems, as it had done in previous decades.

China was predominantly an agrarian economy when the People's Republic was established in 1949. Agricultural population accounted for 83 per cent of the nation's total of 542 million and agricultural output accounted for over 50 per cent of GDP.

However, Mao's ambition was to quickly industrialise the economy based on resources transferred from agricultural production through direct and indirect taxation and a tightly controlled population registration system to ban rural people from migrating into cities.

The urban biased policy had led to slow growth in agricultural productivity and income under Mao's leadership, such a policy continued into the reform period up to today. Apart from the earlier years of reform from 1978 to 1984, agriculture and the rural population have been disadvantaged by state development policy throughout the modern Chinese history. This has led to a number of undesirable consequences in the economy even after over 25 years of high growth since economic reforms. First, urban–rural income inequality persists and rises over time despite Mao's ambition to eliminate the 'three differences' inherited from the old society.[1] Second, the slow down of agricultural and rural development can have a negative impact on urban and industrial development due to the weakening of forward and backward linkages from agriculture to the non-agricultural sectors. Third, slow agricultural and rural development is the main reason for rural poverty which is a key concern for social and political stability.

In short, agricultural and rural development is still an important issue in China for its future prosperity. The problems of rural areas, agriculture and peasants are closely linked to sustainable economic growth, income distribution and poverty reduction. The rest of this chapter provides some basic information on agricultural and rural development in the pre-reform period, discusses the contributions of agriculture to the national economy, and examines the prospects and constraints on agricultural and rural development under economic reforms. The information provided in this chapter will be useful in understanding the key issues of income inequality and poverty in China.

## 3.2 Agricultural and rural development in the pre-reform period

Economic development between 1949 and 1978 can be divided into two different sub-periods. The first sub-period of 1949–57 includes Land Reforms and the First Five-Year Plan. Industrial and agricultural production increased rapidly and people's living standards were greatly improved. The second sub-period includes the Great Leap Forward movement and the Cultural Revolution. The Great Leap Forward movement (1958–62) was characterised by the 'Three Red Flags': the People's Commune, Agriculture Learning from Dazhai and Industry Learning from Daqing. The movement resulted in the most devastating famine in Chinese history. The so-called Three Difficult Years of 1959–61 saw millions of people starve to death. All economic indicators had significantly negative growth rates. The re-adjustment period of 1963–5 restored the economy but it was followed by the Cultural Revolution from 1966 up to 1978. The Cultural Revolution resulted in the longest period of political turmoil and economic stagnation since 1949.

### 3.2.1 Agricultural performance

Economic development in China accelerated rapidly after the civil war. By 1952 the economy had almost recovered to the pre-war peak level. Real national income more than quadrupled between 1953 and 1978, registering an annual growth rate of 5.68 per cent. This was in marked contrast to the first half of the twentieth century, when there was no sustained per capita growth (Perkins, 1988; Lardy, 1983).

Dramatic growth was accompanied by far-reaching changes in the structure of the national economy. The share of national income originating in industry rose from 20 per cent in 1952 to nearly 50 per cent in 1978, whilst agriculture's share shrank from 58 per cent to less than 33 per cent. Paradoxically, although the pace of growth and structure of output changed dramatically since 1949, the composition of employment (and the population) remained predominantly agrarian. Although official data on the urban population is based on a changing definition and thus must be used with caution, China's development during the pre-reform period was nonetheless accompanied by an unusually slow pace of urbanisation and a structural change in employment.

Between 1953 and 1978 the labour force almost doubled to 401.5 million. However, agriculture absorbed almost two-thirds of that increase, and its share of employment only shrank from about 83 per cent to 71 per cent of the total. The sharply declining trend in the product share of agriculture was accompanied by an unusually small reduction in its share of the total labour force. Consequently, in terms of production structure China resembled a relatively industrialised country, although its employment structure was similar to that of some of the world's least developed economies.

Regarding employment, a substantial proportion of the workforce was under-employed in the rural areas. During the Cultural Revolution, all farmers were strictly confined to crop production. They were not allowed to take up any jobs in the urban areas or to diversify production activities in their own communities. Sideline production, high value-added crops and livestock production were restricted to a minimum. All these factors resulted in an enormous waste of labour resources and the stagnation of farm incomes.

The contradiction between the structure of output and the composition of the labour force raised several major issues for understanding Chinese economic development in the pre-reform period. First, whereas industrial production and national income grew rapidly, the living standard of the peasantry stagnated, or even declined, between 1957 and 1978 (Table 3.1).

Second, agricultural growth was highly unstable, particularly during the Great Leap Forward movement (1958–62) and the Cultural Revolution (1966–78). Whilst industrial output between 1953 and 1978 grew at an annual rate of 10.7 per cent, agriculture grew at only 2.7 per cent and cereal output at only 2.4 per cent (Ministry of Agriculture, 1991). Since population growth averaged 2.0 per cent over this period, the margin for improvement in food consumption was rather modest for an economy in which per capita gross domestic product in constant prices tripled. Indeed, although China's industrial growth accelerated tremendously during the whole pre-reform period, it appeared that agricultural growth did little more than keep pace with the expansion of population.

One may argue that the slow pace of agricultural development in that period was explained primarily by China's land shortage. Whilst China's population grew by two-thirds between 1952 and the late 1970s, the area of arable land shrank by more than 10 per cent. Land reclamation programmes between 1957 and 1977 brought an additional 17 million hectares into cultivation, but was more than offset by 27 million hectares of arable land used for building roads, housing, factories and so on. Arable land per agricultural worker also declined by half between the early 1950s and the late 1970s. Whilst the man/land ratio was growing in virtually every developing country in Asia since the 1940s, increased pressure of population on the land was most intense in China (Lardy, 1983). Under conditions of unchanging agricultural technology, increased population on fixed or even decreasing land area can be expected, via the inexorable law of diminishing returns, to produce successively smaller increments of agricultural output. However, from the experience of the First Five-Year Plan and the adjustment period between 1962 and 1965 after the disastrous Great Leap Forward, as well as the experience of the post-Mao period

*Table 3.1* Per capita peasant income, 1956–78 (yuan)[a]

| Year | 1956 | 1960 | 1965 | 1977 | 1978 |
|---|---|---|---|---|---|
| Current price | 43.1 | 41.3 | 52.3 | 65.5 | 74.7 |
| Constant price | 45.5 | – | 41.3 | 47.5 | 52.7 |

Source: Ministry of Agriculture, 1989.

Note: a  The income only includes collective distribution.

after 1978, Chinese agriculture could have developed much more rapidly if the policies had been appropriate.

### 3.2.2 Investment strategy

The state allocated extremely modest investments either directly to agriculture or to the branches of industry that produced modern inputs for agricultural production. Moreover, the state's high indirect agricultural taxation (through low prices and mandatory procurement of grains and other crops) greatly curtailed reinvestment of internal resources within the farm sector. As a result, farm assets per agricultural worker remained extremely low. Thus the poor performance of agriculture may have been the consequence of an agricultural policy that tended to be myopic and extractive rather than developmental. Underinvestment in the mid-1960s when the pace of technical change in agriculture increased provided an example. Investment in agriculture was reduced just when its rate of return was rising due to new opportunities provided by new seed varieties, particularly rice. Skewed investment allocations increased the share of investment in industry, where the rate of return was lower than agriculture and declining. That distortion of investment allocation reduced the rate of growth of the economy below what could have been achieved.

Heavy industry was assigned almost 50 per cent of the total basic construction investment over the period 1953–78, whereas the share of investment in agriculture was only 12 per cent, and that in light industry was only 5.5 per cent.

Whilst such a strategy might make sense over a short period (such as the First Five-Year Plan) to establish a basic industrial infrastructure, pursued over the long term it was highly detrimental to agriculture and rural development and encouraged waste and inefficiency in state industries.

Although the absolute numbers employed in industry and construction rose impressively, from 17.2 millions in 1952 to 70.7 millions in 1978, the structure of employment was not transformed. Heavy industry developed in its own way, ignoring the real market demand for its products. Consequently, huge amounts of various products were permanently held in warehouses, whereas the market was short of agricultural products and other consumer goods produced by the light industrial sector, which depended largely on the farming sector for its inputs. Furthermore, a considerable amount of surplus agricultural labour (which was estimated to be more than 100 million farmers in 1978) could not be absorbed into the industrial sector which had already found it difficult to absorb the unemployed people in the cities and towns.

The outcome of such an industrialisation strategy was as follows: capital per worker grew rapidly over the long term, rising more than nine-fold from 1957 to 1978, while the number of industrial workers rose less than three-fold. The value of fixed assets per worker was vastly greater in industry than in agriculture. Chinese data report an annual average real growth of industrial output of about 9–10 per cent from 1957 to 1979, but at an increasing capital cost: in the state industrial sector the gross value of industrial output per 100 yuan of fixed assets (original value) fell from 138 yuan in 1957 to 98 yuan in 1965 and still stood at only 105 yuan in 1975 (*Chinese Economic Yearbook*, 1982: Section 6.18).

To implement the heavy-industry oriented policy, the state had to supply the cities (industry) with enough food procured from the farming sector and set strict regulations on migration from the countryside to the urban areas. The resource transfer including food from the countryside took two major forms. The first was through direct agricultural taxation. This was relatively severe originally, but remained fixed in absolute terms so that its share in total farm income fell steadily. Agricultural tax fell from 13 per cent of net income, or 9.5 per cent of gross income, of the basic accounting units in 1958 to 4.3 per cent of net income, or 2.9 per cent of gross income in 1981 (NBS, 1986). The second was through indirect agricultural taxation in the form of low prices and mandatory state procurement of grain and other agricultural commodities. Since free marketing in rural areas was strictly regulated, official data on free market prices were not available for that period. However, as far as grain is concerned, free market prices used to be twice or three times as high as the state procurement prices paid to farmers. Even in 1980, when the procurement prices of grain had been greatly raised and free markets were de-regulated, free market prices were still much higher than the procurement prices. According to the World Bank, the net loss of farm revenue on mandatory grain sales was estimated to be 23 billion yuan in 1988 (World Bank, 1991: 18), equivalent to 26 yuan per rural inhabitant and about 5 per cent of average rural per capita income in 1988. It has to be pointed out that resource transfer in the pre-reform period must have been far more severe in relative terms as the gap between state procurement prices and free market prices must have been much smaller in 1988 than in the pre-reform period.

In the pre-reform period, state procurement prices hardly covered the material costs of production. By delivering their surplus to the state, farmers were stripped off any possible cash incomes to improve their living standards and increase production capacity. The remaining part of the total output was usually not enough for self-consumption. As a result, malnutrition and hunger were widespread throughout the countryside.

In principle, the compulsory procurement quota was set against the level of total production and the basic requirement for self-consumption. In reality, the level of basic requirement was often treated as a residual after a fixed amount of quota. In addition, total state procurement was often raised by the so-called 'above-quota' procurement if harvests were bumper. However, if harvests were poor, state quotas were not usually adjusted downwards to allow more retention for self-consumption. In the most revolutionary years, production teams were even 'educated' by the commune leaders to deliver much more than the quotas to the state through political praise, as a result, team members suffered much more severely. The revolutionary spirit was vividly demonstrated by the modern opera of 'Praise in the Dragon River' (Long Jiang Song) in the mid-1970s in which farmers were highly praised by delivering grains to the state.

The burden on farmers was not limited to compulsory delivery and low procurement prices. Excessive quality control and delayed payments for their products delivered to the procurement stations incurred invisible costs. In Guangdong, for instance, the most difficult task for rice farmers was to meet the quality requirement of grain delivered to the procurement stations. In many areas, farmers had to carry their grain for a distance of 3 to 10 kilometres to the stations. If the grain could not meet the quality standards, which were often arbitrary and far too high, they had to carry the grain back and wait for later delivery. This tedious process of procurement incurred enormous labour cost which was fully borne by the production teams.

Because of the constraints of arable land as mentioned above, farmers had to raise yield by applying more and more current inputs such as fertilisers, insecticides and labour. As state procurement prices did not offer sufficient returns, farmers often found it un-affordable to buy these inputs due to the lack of cash income and rural credit. This created a vicious circle: low price leading to low income, low income leading to low inputs, and low inputs leading to low production. Consequently, the income and living standards of the peasantry remained unchanged or increased modestly for over two decades from 1956 to 1978 (Table 3.1).

Unfortunately, state extractions of grain and oils from the countryside at below-market prices did not lead directly to large state profits. The state commercial system incurred growing financial losses on the purchase and resale of grain and edible vegetable oils. The purchase of grain from the peasantry at low prices nonetheless contributed a transfer from agriculture to other sectors of the economy, since maintaining low prices for basic food in urban areas was a central component of the state wage policy. After 1956 labour productivity in the state industrial sector rose at an average annual rate of almost 3 per cent, yet the state held real wages constant or declining for more than two decades. The combination of rising productivity and constant or even declining real wages allowed the profits of state-managed enterprises to soar from 11.4 to 49.3 billion yuan between 1959 and 1977 (Yao, 1994). The fiscal system channelled most enterprise profits directly to the state budget. A constant or declining real wage strategy, however, was predicated partly on the continuous provision of basic foodstuffs to workers at low, fixed nominal prices. By 1961–2 this policy required state subsidies for the commercial sector. But over time, the real cost of the subsidy was held down by extracting grain from the countryside at low prices.

### 3.2.3 Self-sufficiency and comparative advantage

State intervention in agriculture was not limited to reducing its share of investment or extracting resources, especially grain and vegetable oils. State policy frequently inhibited the efficient use of the modest resources remaining within agriculture. Policy-makers tended to undervalue the law of value and the role of marketing. Periodic efforts were made to reduce specialisation in production and marketing of agricultural products.

From 1949 through 1957 regions with resource endowments, which gave them a comparative advantage in animal husbandry or in the cultivation of economic crops, were encouraged to specialise. The state encouraged specialisation not only through price and credit incentives, but also through the supply of staple foods to producers of economic crops. Prior to 1958 this supply was achieved through a combination of public and private marketing. Between 1953 and 1963 almost half of all grain collected by the state, through taxes and procurement, was resold in rural areas.

After 1965, specialised production was abandoned in favour of a policy of local foodgrain self-sufficiency. Rural areas were still allowed to produce economic crops or raise animals, but only after they had achieved basic food self-sufficiency.

The policy of local self-sufficiency was not simply exhortative but it was also reinforced by other powerful policy instruments. First, the state reduced the share of foodgrain that it purchased or collected in taxes. In 1966, before the self-sufficiency policy was effectively underway, state procurement and taxes had surpassed the average of the First Five-Year Plan and as a share of output were equal to the 25 per cent average of 1956 and 1957. In the following decade procurement and taxes grew extremely slowly and in 1976 through to 1978 averaged less than 48 million tons, up less than 10 per cent compared to 1966. Since grain production had increased by over a third, the share of output distributed directly by the state through the Ministry of Food declined from about 25 per cent to 20 per cent. Moreover, the comparison of procurement prices and taxes in 1976–8 with those in 1956–7 understated the decline in marketing because private grain sales in the 1950s and presumably in the first half of the 1960s averaged several million tons per year, adding several percentage points to the share of foodgrain output that was 'marketed', whereas private grain sales from 1966 through to 1978 officially were prohibited and probably quite small. Marketed output declined from 30 per cent during the First Five-Year Plan to 20 per cent in 1976–8.

Not only was the share of grains procured by the state in 1977 and 1978 substantially smaller than that during the First Five-Year Plan, the quantity of grain resold to the agricultural population grew only by a third between 1957 and 1977/8 while the agricultural labour force over the same period grew almost 70 per cent. Since the total quantity of marketed grain reflected largely the degree of urbanisation, the quantity of grain sold to peasants was a more accurate reflection of the extent to which marketing policy facilitated specialised production.

Interprovincial transfers of grain, an important component of the policy of the 1950s facilitating specialisation, were also curtailed substantially. By 1978 provincial exports had declined to less than 1.5 per cent of production compared to 4.7 per cent in 1953–6 and 2.8 per cent in 1965 (Lardy, 1983). If grains, predominantly rice and soybeans, destined for international markets were excluded from interprovincial transfers, the decline was even more dramatic – to 0.1 per cent in 1978 compared to 3.4 per cent in 1953–6 and 1.5 per cent in 1965.

Agricultural tax policy reinforced grain self-sufficiency. During the 1950s there had been a gradual tendency to allow the payment of agricultural tax in cash or crops other than grain, thus drawing peasants into specialised commercial crop production. Peasants in cotton-producing areas delivered cotton rather than grain to meet their tax obligation. In 1955, 8 per cent of the agricultural tax was paid in cotton, a significant share for a crop that occupied only about 4 per cent of sown area. By the 1960s and well into the 1970s the state was more insistent on payment in grain. That posed a significant additional constraint on producing units since the agricultural tax in the mid-1970s amounted to about 13 million tons, almost one-third of all grain procurement by the state. Since grain could not usually be purchased on rural markets, it was necessary for all regions to grow grain to meet their own demands.

The pattern of growth after 1965 reflected the grain self-sufficiency policy and the declining profitability of commercial crop production. In the years 1966 through 1970 grain output increased at an average annual rate of 4.5 per cent, while non-grain crops and animals, except for tea, grew at lower rates: cotton 1.7 per cent, oilseed crops 0.6 per cent, sugarcane 0.1 per cent sugarbeet 1.2 per cent, live pigs 2.3 per cent, aquatic products 1.3 per cent, and tea 6.2 per cent (Ministry of Agriculture, 1991). The consequence of attempted self-sufficiency was declining allocative efficiency within agriculture and declining per capita consumption of many non-cereal foods.

Increased inefficiency was most evident in regions of northwest China which had a significant comparative advantage in the production of meat and other animal products. By the late 1960s these regions were forced to devote increased resources to grain production. Pasture lands were brought under grain production despite the lack of water resources adequate for growing field crops and the high probability of increased wind erosion. In many cases grain yields achieved on these lands were less than a tenth of the national average and were obtained only at the expense of reduced production of high-value animal products.

Pursuit of increased grain production was not limited to predominantly pastoral regions but extended to areas previously specialising in non-grain crops, such as peanuts, oil-bearing seeds, cotton and other economic crops. Consequently the area sown to these crops in regions with a significant comparative advantage was reduced.

Increased inefficiency, however, was not confined to regions that were grain deficient. While some regions were initially more than self-sufficient in grain, reduced opportunities to purchase non-grain crops from other regions led these grain-surplus regions to increase the share of their land allocated to producing cash crops. Because the yields of these crops were relatively low, that reallocation reduced efficiency.

### 3.2.4 Institutional changes

Although he recognised agriculture as a major market for industrial goods and seemed to support, at least in official statements, a policy of concurrent growth, Mao Zedong sought to achieve agricultural growth primarily through organisational changes and to accelerate industrial development through a high level of state investment expenditures, financed largely through direct and indirect taxes on agriculture. He argued that the revolution in production relations could accelerate the expansion of production forces.

Organisational changes were considered necessary for building China as a modern advanced socialist country. The central issue of organisational changes was to establish a system of public ownership. In the agricultural sector, the state tried to abandon private ownership of land and other major means of production. Following the land reform, peasants were immediately forced to set up mutual-aid organisations. In 1952, 40 per cent of the country's total peasant households belonged to mutual aid teams, and in 1954 they increased to 58 per cent. Simultaneously with the swift growth of the mutual-aid teams, peasants were persuaded to organise 'semi-socialist' agricultural producers' cooperatives characterised by the pooling of land as shares and a single management. In 1952 there were only about 3,600 agricultural producers' cooperatives, but they grew rapidly because they were considered to be more socialist. By the first half of 1955 their number increased to 670,000, embracing some 17 million households. In July 1955 Mao Zedong delivered his report 'The Question of Agricultural Cooperation'. Based on this report the Central Committee of the Chinese Communist Party adopted the 'Decision on the Question of Agricultural Cooperation' in October of the same year. Under the inspiration of these documents, a high tide of socialist cooperation on a magnificent scale appeared in the second half of 1955. By 1956 the organisation of agricultural cooperation was in the main complete in China. By the end of 1956, 120 million peasant households, or 96 per cent of all the peasant households in China had joined cooperatives. More than 100 million of them or 88 per cent, joined the advanced agricultural producers' cooperatives (NBS, 1960).

The leadership expected that such radical institutional changes in the rural areas would pave the way for rapid growth in the rural economy. Presumably due to the socialist enthusiasm induced by land reforms and due to the emphasis on the roles of marketing, agricultural production increased rapidly during the First Five-Year Plan (1953–7). The success in this period, therefore, encouraged Mao Zedong to accelerate the process of socialism through the establishment of the People's communes.

Beginning in the summer of 1958, in the short space of a few months more than 740,000 agricultural cooperatives were merged and reorganised into over 26,000 large-scale People's Communes in which industry, agriculture, trade, education and military affairs were combined and government administration and commune management were merged. The communes embraced 120 million peasant households, or over 99 per cent of the total peasant households of all the nationalities in China (NBS, 1960).

After the establishment of the people's communes in 1958, the peasants in the communes had to work under the supervision of the head of the commune. The state also practised forced procurement and distribution of some major crops such as grain, cotton and oil-bearing crops. Furthermore, the reward of individuals was not directly linked to their efforts. Everybody, regardless of his/her contribution to the commune's production, received the same reward. This system vastly discouraged the individual's incentive to work. Moreover, since the state's compulsory procurement quota of agricultural products, especially grain, cotton and pigs was based on the previous production level or even on the plan target, the more the peasants produced, the more they had to deliver to the state. As a result, the communes refused to raise production because they could not benefit correspondingly. Consequently, although the state put much more emphasis on the production of grain as discussed above, the real performance was very disappointing. Foodgrain output declined dramatically after 1958. Accelerated by natural disasters, grain production reached its nadir in 1960 since 1949. The production of grain declined by 28 per cent in 1960 compared to 1958. It was not until 1965 that total production recovered to the level of 1957. Per capita consumption declined even more. In 1960, per capita consumption decreased by 19.5 per cent compared to 1957. Because the urban population (non-agricultural population including those state employees working in the rural areas) was guaranteed by the state with adequate amounts of grain and oils, per capita consumption in the countryside was much lower, especially for the poor areas in Western China. Acute shortage of food in the late 1950s and early 1960s developed into the most devastating famine in China's history. The extent of destruction caused by this disaster was reflected in both the low fertility and high death rate over the Three Difficult Years of 1959–61, when over 13 million people died of hunger and malnutrition.

In 1962, some Party leaders (Lui Shaoqi, Deng Xiaoping, Chen Yun etc.) came to realise the serious situation in the rural areas and persuaded the government to lift the restrictions over the people's communes. Consequently, the single commune accounting unit was changed into the so-called 'system of three-level ownership (namely, the commune, the production brigade and the production team) with the production team as the basic accounting unit.'

The system of household contract production was introduced. The private plot, which was abandoned in the Great Leap Forward, was re-introduced and enlarged. Farmers were also allowed to trade their surplus products in the free markets after meeting the state procurement quota. Indeed, these methods were highly effective. Both the communes and the peasants were encouraged by the policies. Consequently, production soared again. By 1965 agriculture output recovered to the level in 1957. Unfortunately, Mao Zedong denied the achievements and the policies of this adjustment period. He still insisted on his programme of 'high-level socialism'. He launched the Great Cultural Revolution simply to punish the leaders who implemented the adjustment policies. His strategy as exposed between 1966 and 1976, was to develop socialism through highly organised collectivisation.

Beginning in 1966, the private plots were greatly reduced, and in some regions were totally abolished. The rural free markets were again considered 'capitalist' and closed. Those who traded their surplus products in the 'black markets' were severely punished both economically and politically. Moreover, surplus labourers in the countryside were not allowed to take part in any activities in the urban areas. The production of sideline activities, cash crops and livestock was strictly controlled. Anybody who attempted to produce more than a certain amount of this production set by the commune (state) would be severely punished. The state, represented by the commune, not only dictated tp peasants what they must produce but when and how to produce it. Since most of the commune leaders, who were state-salary employees, were incompetent in farming, their behaviour, usually corresponding to their superiors, was frequently irrational.

Political pressure and the irrational economic behaviour of the Party leaders greatly suppressed the incentives and the freedom of the Chinese peasantry. The management structure of the people's commune unnecessarily increased the cost of production. It also made it impossible to monitor the performance of individual team members in the production process. Experiences indicated that farmers worked hard throughout the year but about half of their income had to be deducted to cover the overheads of the commune, the production brigade and the production team. In a poor year, when the harvest of crops was low, team members might have no income at all after fulfilling tax and overhead obligations. The outcome of the policies was the modest pace of agricultural development and stagnating living standards of the peasantry for more than two decades.

## 3.3 Agriculture's role in China's economic development

Agriculture's role in economic development has been debated based on two different views. The first view argues that agriculture only plays a passive role as a major source of resources for the development of industry and other non-agricultural sectors. This is reflected in the dualistic model developed in Lewis and others (Lewis, 1954; Hirschman, 1958; Fei and Ranis, 1964). In a typical dualistic model, agriculture provides materials, capital and labour for the rest of the economy (forward linkage effects). It suggests that as industrial sector is more productive than agriculture, resources should be transferred from the latter to the former in order to modernise the economy and raise total national output.

The second view not only confirms the forward linkage effects of agriculture but also emphasises its backward linkage effects to other sectors of the economy. In other words, agriculture not only provides materials, capital and labour but also a huge market for the non-agricultural sectors. This view is reflected in Kuznets (1964), Mellor and Lele (1973), Hazell and Roell (1983), and many others.

The contribution of agricultural growth to economic development varies significantly from country to country and from one time period to another within the same economy. For example, in an industrialised country where agriculture has a very small share in GDP, the role of agriculture may not be important. In a developing economy where agriculture is usually a major production sector and accounts for a large proportion of GDP, the role of agriculture is crucial.

Within the same economy, agriculture's contribution to economic development tends to change over time. For example, it plays a relatively more important role when the economy is predominantly agrarian. As the economy grows, the share of agricultural output in GDP and the share of rural population in total population tends to decline gradually over time. Consequently, the contribution of agriculture to the national economy becomes less and less important. Almost all the industrialised nations had gone through this stage of structural transformation. In the developing world, however, this structural change did not take place until the 1950s and the pace of transformation varies significantly in different economies.

Due to unrealistic ambition and poor foresight, most governments of the developing world have been trying to industrialise their economies at so high a speed that agricultural growth is suffocated, resulting in low efficiency in industries and poor performance of the entire economy. In many countries, real outcomes contradict the initial policy objectives. The philosophy behind the industry-biased strategy is essentially based on the first view on agriculture's role presented above.

China provides a good example of this strategy. Before economic reforms, the government over-emphasised the development of capital-intensive industries at the expense of agriculture, light industry and services. The industrialisation strategy resulted in poor agricultural production and low efficiency of the state-industrial sector. With better price and marketing incentives as well as institutional reform, especially the dismantling of the commune system, China has achieved better agricultural growth and industrial efficiency since 1978. One important reason for China's success during economic reforms and openness is that policies are designed to adjust the unbalanced development structure between agriculture and industry and to encourage farm production. On the one hand, the prices of many agricultural products were raised a few times to increase the return to agricultural production. In the late 1980s, some products such as vegetables and livestock products were allowed to be marketed freely in the local markets. On the other hand, the rigid administrative control imposed by the former commune system was scrapped to give farmers more freedom and choice in production and marketing.

China has experienced many economic cycles of booms and busts but it is interesting to note that most boom years were positively related to more favourable agricultural policies whereas all the poor years were negatively related to poor agricultural performance. Although economic growth has not been entirely determined by agricultural production, the Chinese experience indicates that agriculture has been the most important driving force of the economy since 1949 even though the share of agricultural output in national income has been declining sharply over time.

In this section, the assessment of agriculture's role follows the conventional approach by dividing the contributions of agriculture into four different categories and examines these contributions in the Chinese economy since 1949. The four contributions proposed by Kuznets (1964) and discussed in Ghatak and Ingersent (1984) include (1) product contribution or the forward linkage effect; (2) market contribution or backward linkage effect; (3) factor contribution or inter-sectoral transfers; and (4) foreign exchange contribution.

### 3.3.1 Main contributions of agriculture to economic growth

#### (a) Product contribution

Product contribution is usually measured by the size of agriculture in the national economy. By definition, the importance of agriculture declined steadily over time. In the early 1950s, agriculture accounted for 50 per cent of GDP, but by 1978 it accounted for 28 per cent. Agriculture's share in GDP remained stable for over 12 years from 1978 to 1990 due to its rapid growth in the earlier years of economic reform. However, as state policies shifted away from rural to urban development, its share declined sharply in the 1990s. By 2003, it was less than 15 per cent (Table 3.2).

There are two main reasons for a declining share of agriculture in national income. One is the inevitable trend of economic development which requires a higher growth rate of non-agricultural sectors than agriculture dictated by the Engel's law.

The Engel's law states that as personal disposal income grows as a result of economic development, consumers tend to spend a lower proportion of incremental income on agricultural products. In China, the Engel's law is verified by the very low income elasticities of food demand. For example, the income elasticities of cereals are close to zero or negative although the demands for animal products are more elastic (Table 3.3).

Another reason for slow agricultural growth is government policy which has been discriminating against agriculture and the rural population. Before economic reforms, farmers were forced to deliver grains and other agricultural products to the state at very low prices. For example, the procurement prices of grains paid to farmers were less than half of the market prices before 1978 (Lardy, 1983; and Yao, 1994). Market liberalisation, price reform and other policy measures more

*Table 3.2* GDP and sectoral structure in selected years

| Year | GDP at current price (bn yuan) | Sectoral structure of GDP (%) | | |
|------|------|------|------|------|
| | | Agriculture | Industry | Services |
| 1952 | 68 | 50.0 | 20.6 | 29.4 |
| 1978 | 362 | 28.2 | 48.3 | 23.5 |
| 1990 | 1855 | 27.1 | 41.6 | 31.3 |
| 2003 | 11669 | 14.8 | 52.9 | 32.3 |

Sources: NBS (CSYB, Chinese edition) various issues for 1952, 1978 and 1990; *People's Daily*, 21 January 2004 for 2003.

*Table 3.3* Income elasticities of demand for agricultural products, 1988 and 1952–88

| Agricultural products | Urban | | Rural | |
|------|------|------|------|------|
| | Time series | Cross section | Time series | Cross section |
| Cereals | −0.20 | −0.33 | −0.06 | 0.15 |
| Pork/beef/mutton | 0.34 | 0.57 | 0.73 | 0.26 |
| Poultry | 1.66 | 0.93 | 1.48 | 2.16 |
| Eggs | 0.52 | 0.58 | 1.06 | 1.66 |
| Fish | 0.04 | 0.59 | 0.89 | 4.54 |

Sources: NBS, 1989 (CSYB) household income and expenditure data. Estimates: World Bank 1991: 12.

Note: Significant differences between the time-series and cross-sectional results suggest that the estimates are very crude. They have to be interpreted with caution.

favourable to agriculture since 1978 have stimulated faster agricultural growth. As a result, the declining rate of agriculture's share in national income was reduced to 0.02 per cent per annum during 1978–90 from 1.9 per cent before 1978. This is a potent explanation of how government policies can affect agricultural growth.

Although the share of agricultural output in GDP tends to decline because of the Engel's law and government policy biased against agriculture, it is important not to overlook the critical importance of product contribution of domestic agriculture to economic growth. More importantly, it needs to be stressed that government policies deliberately designed to achieve unbalanced development against agriculture can result in overall poor performance of the entire economy. The comparison of economic performance between the pre-reform and reform periods of the Chinese economy potently supports this argument. It is noticable that economic performance was very poor in the pre-reform period when agriculture was squeezed hard (through explicit and implicit taxation) to support industrial development. In addition, the institutional framework under the commune and a whole set of other political and economic policies (e.g. grain self-sufficiency for every locality and the suppression of commercial activities in the rural areas) had helped to suffocate agriculture. The more favourable policies for agriculture in the reform period have achieved better performance not only in agriculture but also in the rest of the economy even though the bias against agriculture in the reform period still persists (Yao, 1994; Bhalla, 1990).

The importance of agriculture's product contribution is not only by the provision of food and other agricultural products for a huge population but also because it provides a huge amount of raw materials for industrial production. In addition, although agriculture's share in GDP is now less than 15 per cent, over two-thirds of the total population and half of the workforce still earn their living directly through agriculture.

In the early 1950s, over 60 per cent of the total industrial production was agriculture-based. Although the dependency of industrial production on agriculture declined over time, by 1992, two-thirds of light industrial output, or 30 per cent of the total industrial production still relied on agriculture for raw materials. Even by 2002, 23.8 per cent of the total industrial output was based on agriculture and its related activities (Table 3.4).

### (b) Market contribution

Market contribution refers to the demand by agriculture for different inputs, such as fertilisers, insecticides, machinery, electricity, and transportation and to the farmers' consumption effects on the rest of the economy. Agricultural demand for industrial inputs was accelerated by the increasing constraints of arable land and crop area. Per capita arable land and crop area declined respectively at 2.08 per cent and 1.69 per cent per year between 1953 and 1989 (Yao, 1994).

Despite the acute shortage of land, China managed to achieve significant growth of per capita agricultural output, especially during the reform period. Per capita grain output increased by 0.44 per cent during 1953–78 and by 1.56 per cent during

*Table 3.4* Output values of agriculture-based industries and their shares in total industrial output values (current prices)

| Year | Gross output value of agriculture-based industries (bn yuan) | As % of gross light industrial output values | As % of gross industrial output values |
|------|------|------|------|
| 1952 | 19.5 | 86.7 | 55.9 |
| 1960 | 40.5 | 74.0 | 24.7 |
| 1965 | 50.5 | 69.8 | 36.0 |
| 1970 | 70.7 | 73.6 | 34.0 |
| 1975 | 96.3 | 70.0 | 30.8 |
| 1980 | 163.9 | 71.0 | 33.5 |
| 1985 | 283.2 | 69.3 | 32.3 |
| 1990 | 611.9 | 69.7 | 32.7 |
| 1991 | 700.0 | 68.4 | 31.7 |
| 1992 | 827.9 | 67.8 | 29.9 |
| 2002 | 2636.5 | 60.8 | 23.8 |

Sources: Ministry of Agriculture (Planning Bureau), 1989: 52–3, 60–1 for 1952–85; NBS, 1991 (CSYB): 399 for 1990, 1992; 411 for 1991, 1993; 417 for 1992; NBS, 2003 (CSYB): 465–6 for 2002.

1978–89 per year. Total grain output in 1998 reached a record high of 512 million tons (NBS, 2003). Then, due to subdued domestic demand, for the first time in China's modern history it deliberately reduced grain production. By 2002, grain output was down to 457 million tons. The dramatic change in grain output shows that China has the ability to grow enough food for its large population. Grain is no longer a big concern of Chinese agriculture. This is largely due to its technological progress and significant improvement in land productivity.

To compensate for the slow growth in grain demand, meat, vegetable, fish, cooking oils and other food products have grown enormously during the reform period. Both meat and fish production increased by about 10 per cent per year for the entire reform period. Meat output rose almost eight-fold and fish over nine-fold from 1978 to 2001 (Table 3.5). The rapid growth in meat and fish production implies that people's living standards have been greatly improved and the dietary pattern has been fundamentally transformed from that dominated by cereal to that by non-cereal, high-value and high-quality food.

Sustainable growth has been achieved through steady improvements in land productivity. Increased land productivity, however, has relied on increased use of industrial products, such as fertilisers, insecticides, farm machinery and equipment and electricity. This suggests that an increasing share of agricultural output value is accounted for by the non-farm sectors. For example, grain yield increased by almost three times from 1,155 kg/hectare in 1950 to 4,342 kg/hectare in 1992, to 4,885 kg/hectare in 2002. But the use of fertilisers increased by more than 260 times from 0.75 kg/hectare to 281 kg/hectare over the same period. After over 50 years of development, agricultural land became well irrigated and agricultural production well mechanised (Table 3.6). Irrigation and mechanisation involved large amount of industrial inputs into agriculture, creating a strong backward linkage effect driving the rapid development of agro-industries.

*Table 3.5* Output of key agricultural products

| Year | Grain (m tons) | Meat (m tons) | Fish (m tons) |
|---|---|---|---|
| 1952 | 164.00 | 3.40 | 1.70 |
| 1978 | 305.00 | 8.60 | 4.70 |
| 2002 | 457.00 | 65.90 | 45.60 |
| Growth 1952–78 (%) | 2.51 | 3.78 | 4.19 |
| Growth 1978–2002 (%) | 1.73 | 9.07 | 10.23 |
| Growth 1952–2002 (%) | 2.14 | 6.28 | 7.04 |

Sources: NBS (50 years) and NBS (various issues).

Note: Growth is the average annual growth rate of the concerned periods.

*Table 3.6* Fertiliser use, irrigation and mechanisation indices

| Year | Grain yield (kg/ha) | Fertiliser application (kg/ha) | Irrigated area/arable land | Tractor-plough area/arable land |
|---|---|---|---|---|
| 1950 | 1155 | 0.75 | 0.09 | 0.00 |
| 1960 | 1170 | 4.50 | 0.27 | 0.02 |
| 1965 | 1635 | 13.50 | 0.32 | 0.15 |
| 1970 | 2010 | 24.75 | 0.35 | 0.18 |
| 1975 | 2355 | 36.00 | 0.43 | 0.33 |
| 1980 | 2745 | 87.00 | 0.45 | 0.41 |
| 1985 | 3480 | 123.60 | 0.45 | 0.36 |
| 1989 | 3690 | 160.86 | 0.47 | 0.45 |
| 1992 | 4342 | 196.63 | 0.51 | 0.54 |
| 2002 | 4885 | 280.62 | 0.55 | 0.60 |

Sources: 1950–86: Ministry of Agriculture (Planning Bureau), 1989; 1987–9: Ministry of Agriculture (*Statistical Materials of Chinese Agriculture*, various issues); 1992: NBS, 1993, 2003 (CSYB): 332, 349, 359 and 371. Irrigation and tractor-plough area in 2002 are personally estimated.

Note: Fertiliser use is calculated as effective contents per hectare of crop area.

Farmers' income is largely determined by the rate of agricultural growth. As farmers' income grows, they are able to buy more consumer goods produced by agriculture and non-agricultural sectors.

This consumption effect has been widely recognised. Mellor (1976), Mellor and Lele (1973) and Hazell and Roell (1983), in particular, have called attention to the potential power of agricultural consumption linkages. Hirschman's (1958) assessment on agriculture as a low-linkage, underpowered engine of growth erred because it neglected these important consumption linkages.

As China is still basically agrarian and 70 per cent of the total population is living in the countryside, the rural community is inevitably a dominant market for many domestically produced consumer goods.

Economic reforms have brought about a sustainable and significant increase in farmers' incomes. As rural incomes grow, farmers are spending a higher proportion of incremental expenditure on manufacturing products. For instance, many traditional durable goods, such as TV sets, watches and bicycles have a limited market in the urban areas, but they have a very strong and expanding market in the countryside (Nolan, 1991).

### (c) Factor contribution

There are two basic factors: capital and labour, which can be provided by agriculture to the national economy.

Capital transfers from agriculture took place mainly in the form of indirect agricultural taxes through forced procurement of agricultural products at below market prices. The Ministry of Agriculture estimated that about 70–80 per cent of total state revenue was from taxing agriculture in the 1950s. Although the share of state revenue from agriculture declined over time, by the mid-1980s, about half of the state revenue still relied on agriculture (Table 3.7).

Tax revenue from agriculture in Table 3.7 does not include taxes collected from the rural township and village enterprises (TVEs), a new and dynamic production force since economic reforms. If these were included, it would add 4.2 billion yuan in 1978 and 36.5 billion yuan in 1989, or 4.2 per cent and 13.4 per cent of the total state tax revenues (Yao, 1994). In other words, the total rural-to-urban capital transfers were much greater than the agriculture to the non-agricultural sectors.

A logical industrialisation process should benefit from capital transfers and increased use of cheap agricultural labour. In China, however, industrial develop-ment in the pre-reform period did not use much labour from agriculture although

*Table 3.7* Capital transfers from agriculture (bn yuan)[a]

|  | Total transfers[b] | As % of state budget | State subsidy to agriculture[c] | Net transfer |
|---|---|---|---|---|
| 1957 | 22.1 | 71 | – | – |
| 1965 | 35.8 | 76 | – | – |
| 1971 | 38.4 | 52 | – | – |
| 1978 | 44.2 | 39 | – | – |
| 1984 | 67.7 | – | – | – |
| 1986 | 89.4 | – | – | – |
| 1987 | 104.5 | – | – | – |
| 1988 | 130.2 | – | – | – |
| 1953–85 | 680.0 | – | – | – |
| 1978–85 | 481.5 | 47.5 | 224.9 | 176.8 |

Source: Ministry of Agriculture (Research Centre of Economic Policy), 1991: 139–41 and 159.

Notes: (a) Values are calculated at current prices. (b) Calculated according to the 'scissors difference' and the volumes of trade between agricultural and non-agricultural sectors (for more explanation, see note 2). (c) State subsidies to agriculture include state investment in agriculture, input subsidies and all the other possible subsidies to agriculture and the rural areas. (d) Most agricultural taxes are in the form of indirect taxation by paying farmers at below market prices for their products and charging them at above market prices for inputs and consumer goods. The main beneficiaries are urban industries and consumers.

rural-to-urban migration since 1979 has been substantial. Farmers were largely excluded from the industrialisation process although they had contributed almost all the accumulated capital assets of the state industries. This was an inevitable outcome of the state industrial policy characterised by high capital intensity and urban bias.

There were two undesirable consequences of this development strategy. First, labour could not be quickly transferred from agriculture to other industries, leading to agricultural labout being severely under-utilised and unproductive. Second, industrial labour was highly expensive as enterprises had to employ only the urban workers who were entitled to various state subsidies. However, high labour costs had to be entirely borne by the enterprises. As a result, domestic industrial goods were not competitive internationally and required heavy protection from the state.

Significant labour transfers from agriculture to other industries and non-farm enterprises were possible during economic reforms. However, such transfers were confined to within the rural economy. This was characterised by the dramatic development of TVEs. Obviously the development of agriculture and non-agricultural enterprises in the rural areas has been mutually beneficial. One great advantage of TVEs over the state-owned industrial sector is that the former have substantially benefited from using cheap labour released from agriculture. The state sector has 'selfishly' excluded farmers from participation but it has had to bear the inevitable consequences: low profitability and low growth, and eventually self-destruction as competition from the collective and private sectors, particularly from TVEs, intensifies over time.

The most recent reform on SOEs has led to the redundancy of about 40 million workers. Urban industrialisation has increasingly been dependent on workers with rural residency, or the so-called peasant workers who work in the cities but are not entitled to urban citizenship, a phenomenon unique in China. It is estimated that as many as 80 million such peasant workers are employed in the cities. This number is now greater than the total workforce of SOEs (Lu Xieyi, 2003). Peasant workers provide cheap labour for the rapid expansion of China's urban economy over the past 25 years of economic reforms. According to the National Bureau of Statistics, the total urban employment was 232 million people in 2000, of which SOEs accounted for 81 million and collective enterprises another 15 million. In 2002, there were 95 million peasant workers employed in the urban areas, implying that the number of peasant workers was almost equal to the combined employment of SOEs and collective enterprises. In some industries, such as construction, building materials, mining, textiles, garments and toys, over 80 per cent of the workforce were peasant workers.

Peasant workers are discriminated against in the cities in various ways. They are paid a fraction of what a normal urban worker would be paid for exactly the same kind of work. In Shenzhen, the Shenzhen Labour Bureau reported that in 1995, the average monthly wage for Shenzhen workers was 2,500 yuan, but it was only 800 yuan for workers without a Shenzhen residency. On 21 January 2004, the Chinese New Year eve, when President Hu Jingtao visited a peasant household in a village close to Shijiazhuang, the capital city of Hubei Province near Beijing, a young farmer told him that he made 3,000 yuan over seven months in Beijing as a construction worker (*People's Daily*, 2004: 21 January). In Beijing, the average monthly wages was 2,010 yuan in 2003, and the average monthly wage in the finance and insurance sector was 4,602 yuan (NBS, 2003, and personal estimates based on the actual data in 2002). The official wages do not include all kinds of extra benefits and subsidies as well as grey incomes. If all the non-official wage incomes were included, the actual wages would be about 50 per cent higher. This means that the average monthly gross income per worker in Beijing is equivalent to one year's income of this young farmer working in Beijing. The wage gap between an ordinary migrant worker and an ordinary citizen could be as large as seven to twelve times. In fact, the young farmer's income would be hardly enough for food and housing if he were to live a normal urban life like the people of Beijing. In other words, he would be considered to be living in absolute poverty even if he used all his earning to live in Beijing without sending any money back home.

Moreover, peasant workers are subject to all kind of abuses. They have to do the most arduous, dirtiest and dangerous jobs in the urban areas. In each of China's largest and richest cities of Beijing, Shanghai and Guangzhou, there are over 3 million peasant workers doing all kinds of hard work. They work seven days a week and over 12 hours per day but get a minimum salary which is hardly enough for their own living without also supporting their families back home. However, when these cities report their GDP each year, these peasant workers are excluded from the official statistics. This is how Beijing, Shanghai, Guangzhou and Shenzhou can grow so fast and become so prosperous for so many years and the momentum of growth is still continuing. It is obvious that resource transfers from rural to urban areas have taken a new form. Instead of taxing agriculture, the government created an environment to suck in tens of millions of young peasant workers into towns and cities and squeeze their blood and sweat, or Marx's so-called residual values, to sustain high industrial growth and maintain high living standards for government officials and registered urban citizens, leading to huge and ever rising urban–rural income inequality, an issue to be focused on later in this book. Peasant workers in the cities and their families back in the countryside still remain very poor. President Hu must be aware of this huge urban–rural divide and the misery of farm life. This was why he chose to make and eat dumplings with a poor peasant family on the eve of the Chinese New Year.

*(d) Foreign exchange contribution*

Agricultural exports had been a dominant source of foreign exchange earnings in China up to the 1990s. In the 1950s, they accounted for more than 80 per cent of total foreign exchange earnings. Although by the 1980s their dominant position was gradually supplemented by manufacturing goods, they still contributed about 40–45 per cent of the total national exports in the early 1990s (Table 3.8). As imports of agricultural goods and related products (e.g. chemical fertilisers) are much smaller than agricultural exports, the agricultural sector has been a large net foreign exchange earner. From the late 1990s, the share of agricultural exports in

*Table 3.8* External trade of agricultural products (bn US$ and %)

| Year | Exports | | Imports | | Export–imports:(1)–(2) | |
|------|---------|---|---------|---|---------|---|
| | Value (1) | As % of national total | Value (2) | As % of national total | Value (3) | As % of total national imports |
| 1953 | 0.83 | 81.60 | – | – | – | – |
| 1960 | 1.36 | 73.30 | – | – | – | – |
| 1965 | 1.54 | 69.10 | – | – | – | – |
| 1970 | 1.68 | 74.40 | – | – | – | – |
| 1975 | 4.41 | 60.70 | – | – | – | – |
| 1980 | 8.82 | 48.66 | 6.76 | 33.75 | 2.06 | 10.29 |
| 1985 | 11.99 | 43.84 | 8.23 | 19.48 | 3.76 | 8.90 |
| 1989 | 23.88 | 45.45 | 15.31 | 25.89 | 8.57 | 14.49 |
| 1990 | 24.50 | 39.45 | 13.93 | 26.12 | 10.56 | 19.80 |
| 1991 | 28.12 | 39.15 | 15.64 | 24.52 | 12.48 | 19.57 |
| 1992 | 37.02 | 43.55 | 22.83 | 28.32 | 14.19 | 17.61 |
| 2002 | 20.01 | 6.10 | 7.25 | 2.46 | 12.76 | 4.32 |

Sources: Ministry of Agriculture (Planning Bureau), 1989: 517–19 for 1953–80. NBS, 1991: 618–19; 1992: 630–31; 1993: 636–7; 2003.

Notes: (a) Data for 1953–80 are provided by the import–export departments. Data after 1980 are provided by the customs. These two sources of data may not be consistent. (b) Imports and exports under agriculture include two categories: (i) agricultural primary products: foods and processed foods (e.g. live animals, livestock products, fishery products, vegetables, tea and coffee), beverage and tobacco products, industrial raw materials (e.g. leather and cotton) and others (e.g. animal feeds and unclassified live animals); and (ii) agriculture-based light industrial products: cotton yards, clothing and other related textile products for exports; fertilisers, clothing and other related textile products for imports. (c) All the import and export values are calculated at current prices in US dollars.

total exports has been declining sharply due to the extraordinary growth in international trade, particularly after China joined the WTO in December 2001. In 2002, for example, the share of agricultural exports was reduced to 6.1 per cent from its peak of 44 per cent a decade ago. However, agricultural exports still generated $13 billion of net exports for the Chinese economy in that year.

## 3.4 Prospects and constraints on agricultural development in the new century

China has achieved high economic growth for more than a quarter century. In the last 25 years, real per capita gross domestic product (GDP) more than quadrupled. Real per capita urban and rural incomes increased in a similar order. By 1998, China became the world's largest producer of many industrial and agricultural products, including crude steel, coal, cement, chemical fertilisers, TV sets, cereals, meat, fish, cotton lint, groundnuts, rapeseeds and fruits (NBS, 1999c, pp.876–8). In the meantime, the Chinese economy has become highly integrated with the world economy. It has been the largest recipient of foreign direct investments (FDI) in the developing world since 1996. Starting from a low level, total accumulative

FDI inflows rose rapidly from $1.8 billion in 1983 to $305.9 billion by 1999 (NBS, 2000: 604). The latest statistics shows that the economy is entering another run of high growth even though there was a breakout of SARS in the first few months of 2003. GDP rocketed by 9.1 per cent and FDI reached an all time high at $53.5 billion, making a total stock of $501.47 billion (*People's Daily*, 2004: 15 January).

In 1978, China was the twenty-third largest trading nation in the world and by 2001 it had become the ninth largest, excluding Hong Kong and Macau. In 2002, it was the sixth largest and by 2003, it was the fourth largest. If China continues this rate of growth, it will soon surpass Japan and Germany to become the second largest exporter of the world. In most industrialised countries, numerous consumer goods are now mostly made in China. The country has become more and more the manufacturing centre of the world. The value of total imports and exports rose from $20.6 billion in 1978 to $360.6 billion in 1999 (NBS, 2000: 588). In 2003, the total trade volume reached $851.2 billion, rising by 37.1 per cent over 2002, which was the fastest growth since 1980. Both exports and imports surpassed $400 billion, with a net surplus of $25.5 billion. The volume of bi-lateral trade with each of the three largest trading partners, Japan, US and EU, all surpassed the $100 billion landmark (*People's Daily*, 2004: 12 January).

While most parts of the world have been experiencing a slowdown or recession since 1999, China's GDP continues to grow at more than 7 per cent per year and the country continues to expand exports and absorb foreign capital. By 2000, China's gross national product (GNP) ranks number seven in the world in nominal dollars, but it ranks number two if it is calculated in the purchasing power parity (PPP) terms. China's GNP measured in PPP was $4,966 billion, which was 48 per cent greater than Japan's, the third largest economy in the world (World Bank, 2002).

Apart from rapid economic growth and openness, China has made significant progress in many other areas, including education, health and poverty reduction. In education, the number of students enrolled in higher education increased from 0.86 million in 1978 to 4.13 million by 1999 (NBS, 1984: 483; NBS, 2000: 651). The number of students enrolled in secondary schools rose from 6.64 million to 8.01 million over the same period (NBS, 1984: 483; NBS, 2000: 651). The illiteracy rate for young people aged 15–24 was reduced from 10 per cent in 1980 to 3 per cent in 1997 (World Bank, 1999). Over the same period, the illiteracy rate for this age group was reduced from 47 per cent to 32 per cent in the low-income countries and from 11 per cent to 5 per cent in the middle income countries. In health, the child mortality rate (age 1–5) was reduced from 167 to 151 per thousand in China from 1980 to 1997. In the same period, the same mortality rate was reduced from 320 to 265 in the low-income countries and from 195 to 168 in the middle income countries (World Bank, 1999). In poverty reduction, the official statistics shows that the total number of rural poverty has been reduced from 270 million in 1978 to less than 30 million by 2000. Although most unofficial estimates are much greater than the official statistics on poverty head counts, no one doubts that the level of poverty in rural China has been substantially reduced and that

China has contributed greatly to the world efforts in reducing human poverty on the earth.

In many respects, China's achievements in the past decades are miraculous in world development history. Only a few countries in the world have been able to maintain such high growth for so long a period of time. China has over 5,000 years of civilisation, but it is only the economic development of this reform period that has fundamentally changed the world's most populous nation from a poverty and disease stricken country to such a prosperous, dynamic and rapidly industrialising economy.

Despite the great success, economic development in China has not been without serious problems, particularly in the rural sector. The main concerns of the rural economy are many but the following are the most important ones:

- relatively low growth of rural incomes compared to urban incomes
- rising income inequality and the increased difficulty in fighting against poverty
- rural surplus labour and constraints on the development of township and village enterprises (TVEs)
- environment
- poor social services
- challenges of WTO accession
- poor local government and excessive taxes.

### 3.4.1 Relatively low income growth in the rural sector

As discussed previously, China has undergone a prolonged period of rapid economic growth. The structure of the national economy has also changed dramatically. Agriculture's share in GDP declined from 28.1 per cent to 14.2 per cent from 1978 to 2003. Industry's share in GDP rose from 48.2 per cent to 52.9 per cent and the share of the services sector increased from 23.7 per cent to 32.3 per cent over the same period. The structure of the national economy in 2003 makes China look much like an industrialised country. The share of agriculture in GDP was similar to that of Japan in 1960. However, if we look at the change in the employment structure, a different picture emerges. Agriculture's share in total national employment was 50 per cent in 2003. Although it had declined significantly from 70.5 per cent in 1978, the share of agricultural employment makes China still look much like a developing economy. In other words, China's employment structure is still predominantly agrarian. This has an implication on rural development and farm income. Some recent studies indicate that China has 270 million surplus rural workers and only 130 million of them work in TVEs. Hence, it implies that China needs to find another 140 million non-farm jobs for the rural population, a task that will not be completed for some decades to come. In 2003, China created only 8.5 million new urban jobs but 4 million were taken by laid-off SOE workers. When urban school leavers and university graduates were taken into account, there were few jobs left for rural migrant workers (*People's Daily*, 2004: 20 January).

China started its economic reforms from the countryside in 1978. The first phase of economic reforms achieved remarkable results (Lin, 1988; Johnson, 1988). Agricultural output increased dramatically and real per capital income rose by almost 15 per cent per annum from 1978 to 1984 (Yao, 2000). Over this period, the per capita urban–rural income gap was also reduced significantly. For example, the urban–rural per capita consumption ratio was reduced from 2.9 to 2.3 (Figure 3.1).

However, the relatively high growth in rural income was short-lived and the state biased policy against the rural population regained its momentum from 1985 when large-scale industrial reforms began. In retrospect, the government was using the success of rural reform to subsidise the heavy cost of restructuring the urban economy. As a result, the prices of agricultural products were reduced in real terms. In the meantime, the prices of agricultural inputs rose (Yao, 1994). Yao (2000) estimates that real per capita income in rural China rose by a mere 0.7 per cent per annum from 1985 to 1991, while real per capita urban income rose sharply by 2.7 per cent. In 2003, per capita urban income was 8,500 yuan, rising by 9.3 per cent; rural per capita income was 2,622 yuan, rising by only 4.3 per cent, which was achieved because the central government had tried for so many years to raise rural income (*People's Daily*, 2004: 21 January). The extreme polarisation between the rural and urban population has now shamelessly accepted as a norm by central and local governments. It seems impossible to reverse this inequality trend based on the present institutional setting, despite the awareness of the new generation of government led by a people-centred party secretary and head of state, Hu Jingtao.

The relative slow growth of urban income during 1978–84 was compensated for by the much higher growth in the later period. Consequently, the urban–rural income gap widened again. By 1995, the urban–rural per capita consumption ratio surpassed its peak level in 1978, reaching a higher new peak at 3.5 (Figure 3.1). Even in 1999 after a few years of the government's efforts to support agricultural and rural development, the urban–rural consumption ratio was still as high as 3.3. The extent of urban–rural inequality in China is unmatched by the majority of

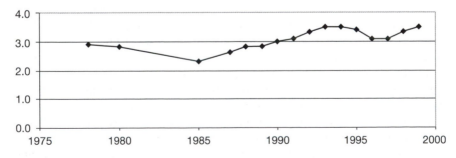

*Figure 3.1* Urban–rural per capita consumption ratio, 1978–99.

Source: NBS, 2000: 70.

countries in the world. According to Yang and Zhou (1996), the average urban–rural income ratio was only 1.5 for a sample of 36 countries and few countries have a ratio of more than 2.0. To a great extent, the discrimination of state policy against agriculture and the rural population is more a political than an economic issue, although one may argue that the central government has been constrained by the difficulties of reforming SOEs. However, one may argue that it is the existence of the SOEs and their low efficiency that reflect both the embedded interests of corrupt government officials and the necessary mechanism of the party and the state to hold on to their control over the national economy. It is therefore a political issue that makes economic development in rural China particularly difficult and complex.

To explore this issue further, we need to have a more careful study of the change of the employment structure in both the urban and rural sectors. Before economic reforms started in 1978, China used over 90 per cent of state revenue to develop the SOE sector, by 1978, this sector employed 74.5 million workers, rising from 15.8 million in 1952. In the meantime, the national labour force was 401.5 million, rising from 207.3 million in 1952 (NBS, 2000: 118). In other words, the increase in the employment of SOEs was only 30 per cent of the increase of the country's new labour. The rest of the increased labour had to be absorbed by the rural economy. Because the government did not allow the development of rural non-farm industries before 1978, the increased labour force was confined to the traditional agricultural sector. This explained why China failed to transform its economy and raise people's incomes despite the tremendous investments in SOEs, which thrived and expanded because of state subsidies and protection (Grove *et al.*, 1994; Hay *et al.*, 1994; Perkins, 1994; and Yao, 1997c).

The reform period has a number of important changes. First, SOEs have been subject to various kinds of reforms and restructuring in order to improve efficiency. Second, the urban economy was allowed to be diversified into all kinds of ownership and the traditional socialist doctrine of monotonic state ownership was abandoned. Third, the rural economy was allowed to develop the township and village enterprises, private enterprises and self-employment. Over 20 years of constant changes, the employment structure in 1999 became highly diversified (Table 3.8).

The share of SOE employment in total urban employment declined sharply from 57 per cent in 1996 to 38 per cent in 1999, and to 29 per cent in 2002, a loss of 40.8 million workers over 6 years. The share of collectively owned enterprises also declined sharply, with a net loss of 19 million workers. The employment in the new ownership firms, including private enterprises, foreign-owned or joint venture firms and self-employed firms rose from zero in 1978 to 55.6 million in 1996 and expanded to 165 million in 2002, accounting for two-thirds of the total urban employment. A similar picture of employment in the rural sector also emerged. The most spectacular change is the emergence of the TVE sector, rural private firms and self-employed enterprises. In 1978, TVEs accounted for only 9.2 per cent of the total rural employment, by 2002, the share rose to 27 per cent. In

*Table 3.9* Changes of employment structure in China, 1978 and 1999 (million)

|      | China | Urban | Of which | | | Rural | Of which | | |
|------|-------|-------|------|------|------|-------|------|------|------|
|      |       |       | SOE | COE | OTE |       | TVE | ONE | AGR |
| 1978 | 401.5 | 95.1  | 74.5 | 20.5 | 0.0 | 306.4 | 28.3 | 0.0 | 278.1 |
| 1996 | 688.5 | 198.2 | 112.4 | 30.2 | 55.6 | 490.4 | 135.1 | 38.6 | 316.7 |
| 1999 | 713.9 | 224.1 | 85.7 | 17.1 | 121.3 | 489.8 | 127.0 | 48.0 | 314.8 |
| 2002 | 737.4 | 247.8 | 71.6 | 11.2 | 165.0 | 489.6 | 132.9 | 38.8 | 318.1 |

Sources: NBS, 2000: 118–19; NBS, 2003: 126–7.

Notes: SOE  state-owned enterprises, COE  urban collectively owned enterprises, OTE  other forms of enterprises, including urban private firms, foreign joint ventures, foreign-owned firms and self-employed firms. TVE  rural township and village enterprises, ONE  other rural non-farm enterprises, including rural private firms and self-employed firms, AGR  agriculture.

addition, the other forms of non-farm employment rose from nothing in 1978 to 38.8 million, or almost 8 per cent of the total rural employment.

The changes in the employment structure at both the national and sectoral levels signify a great step towards industrialisation and urbanisation, but what is wrong with the changes and how are they reflected by the slow progress in rural development and agricultural incomes? The fundamental problem is that the rural sector was left entirely to itself without any government support. If we look at the structural changes in rural employment, we can find the following evidence. First, the absolute number in agricultural employment did not decline over 24 years, instead, it increased by almost 40 million. As agricultural productivity and income are generally much lower than any other form of employment, the majority of the rural population are still dependent on low income employment. Second, the transfer of surplus agricultural labour has been largely due to the increase in TVE employment. In other words, rural people find their employment in rural industries, which are less productive and generate lower incomes than urban enterprises. As a result, TVE workers earn much less than their urban counterparts. In recent years, rural people are allowed to seek employment in the cities as the state regulation on urban to rural migration has become less restrictive. However, even when rural migrants working in the cities, they are generally engaged in the low-pay activities in the urban economy. As mentioned earlier in this chapter, peasant workers are subject to all kinds of hardship. They are paid a fraction of what their urban counterparts would be paid and are denied any of the benefits that are available to urban citizens. Most peasant workers are young and educated. Once they become old, sick or injured, they are sent back to their home towns. A survey in Shenzhen shows that the vast majority of female peasant workers are between 18 to 35 years of age. They help the cities to construct numerous buildings, to produce goods for exports and pay direct and indirect taxes to municipality governments, but they are separated from their relatives living in the countryside. The poor home towns are deprived of young and able people and have little prospects of being modernised and becoming prosperous. Such an unfair employment and migration system has been blamed for exaggerating the ever rising urban–rural divide, instead of mitigating it as most classical theorists might expect as a result of rural–urban migration.

Putting all these factors together, it is not difficult to understand that the population in China is clearly divided into two heterogeneous groups: urban and rural. In all aspects, the rural people are all engaged in low-pay activities and the urban people are in the high-pay ones, which forces the urban–rural income gap to rise. Without letting a large number of rural workers engage in the urban formal sectors and enjoy the same rights as urban workers, there is little chance for the rural people to catch up with their urban counterparts in terms of income. This trend continues despite the recent reforms that have led to millions of SOE retrenched workers, who are still highly protected and looked after by the state.

### 3.4.2 Rising inequality and the difficulty in reducing rural poverty

In China, inequality is multi-dimensional, including urban–rural inequality, inter-regional inequality and inequality within the same region. We have discussed urban–rural inequality in the above section. According to the World Bank (1997), urban–rural inequality explains about one third of the total inequality in China in 1995 and one half of the increase in inequality from 1985 to 1995. China was considered to be a very egalitarian economy in the world before 1978. The World Bank (1997) reports that China's Gini coefficient rose from 0.288 in the 1980s to 0.388 in the 1990s. Further estimates by Yao *et al.* (2004) show that the Gini coefficient rose further in the late 1990s (see below).

Another important dimension of inequality is inter-regional inequality. Inter-regional inequality is much greater in the rural areas than in the urban areas. Before economic reforms, rural China was also a very egalitarian society. The Gini co-efficient was only 0.212 in 1978 (MOA, 1991; Yao and Liu, 1998). With economic reforms, inequality increased significantly over time. By 1994, the rural Gini co-efficient was 0.32 (MOA, 1991; Yao and Liu, 1998). Further estimates by Yao *et al.* (2004) show that the rural Gini coefficient rose to 0.36 in 1996 and 0.42 in 1998. Yao and Liu (1998) also show that over 50 per cent of the total rural inequality was explained by inter-provincial inequality. In 1999, for example, rural per capita net income was 5409.1 yuan in Shanghai, the highest income province (city), but it was only 1309.5 yuan in Tibet, the lowest income region. The income ratio between the richest region and the poorest region was 4.13. Furthermore, the income gaps increased significantly over time. For instance, per capita income ratio between rural Shanghai and Tibet was only 2.28 in 1985.

In China, most of the poor regions are concentrated in the western parts of the country and the richest provinces are concentrated along the eastern coast. The regional divergence, instead of convergence, in per capita income has been explained by Yao and Zhang (2001a) because of the lack of trickledown effects from the growth centres in the east to the remote and mountainous regions in the west. However, the rising income gap is also explained by government policy, which encouraged some regions and some people to get rich first in the first phase of reforms. The preferable policies given to the east was in fact at the expense of slow progress in the inland areas, which were permanently disadvantaged despite the later efforts by the central government to boost development in western China. The last dimension of rural inequality is the rising inequality within each region. In other words, even the rich provinces will have many low-income people.

Due to rising income inequality between regions and rising inequality within each region, it has become difficult to fight against poverty in rural China. Yao (2000) estimates that the majority of poverty reduction in rural China took place in the period 1978–84, when the poverty head count was reduced by over two-thirds. After 1985, however, the number of rural poor increased and it was not until the early 1990s that it started to decline again. This happened despite a continuous increase in average per capita income. According to the Chinese official estimate, the number of rural poor was less than 30 million. However, many independent researchers have shown that the number of rural poor could range from 100 to 280 million (Yao *et al.*, 2004; Stiglitz, 2002). Although there is no doubt that rural poverty has been reduced significantly since economic reforms started in 1978, the incidence of poverty in rural China still remains high and the task of reducing poverty further has been greatly constrained by rising inequality. It is worth noting that China's rural poverty prevails not only in a few regions of natural adversity, but also in the most prosperous provinces, such as Guangdong, Shanghai and Jinagsu. The relative spatial concentration of poverty corresponds to Carl Riskin's (1994) ecological model, which supposes that poverty is concentrated in a few regions of great natural adversity. The prevalence of poverty in the prosperous areas (or normal regions in Riskin's terms) corresponds to Riskin's second model – the socioeconomic model, which describes how poor people are marginalised in a normal region. In terms of poverty alleviation, it is easy to target the poor if they are confined to a particular area of natural adversity. However, it is far more difficult and costly to target the poor if they are scattered far apart in prosperous areas.

### 3.4.3  *Rural surplus labour and constraints on the development of TVEs*

The most effective way to reduce poverty is through income growth, which in turn, depends on how agricultural surplus labour can be transferred out of agriculture. Many informal estimates suggest that China may still have 100 to 150 million surplus agricultural labourers. There are two alternative ways that labour can be transferred out of agriculture: migration and employment in rural non-farm enterprises. The latest official statistics shows that there are more than 30 million rural migrants working in the cities although the actual number of rural to urban migrants could be higher than 100 million (Wu and Yao, 2002; *China Economic Information*, 2004). The increase in rural to urban migration has been possible because the government has relaxed its control policy and because the urban economy has been able to absorb non-urban residents. However, the majority of rural migrants working in the cities are temporary workers who do not have a permanent residency right.

The most noticeable and admirable development of the Chinese economy in the past decades must be the emergence of the TVE sector. Although TVE development is important in other developing countries, its role in the Chinese economy has been fundamental for the following reasons. First, TVEs have become one of the most important economic sectors (along with the state-owned enterprises and agriculture) in the Chinese economy in terms of their contribution to GDP. Second, unlike the state-owned industries, the development of TVEs does not require investment from the government. Third, TVEs are the most important employers of surplus agricultural workers. Fourth, TVEs have become an increasingly important source of rural incomes and national exports (Yao and Liu, 1996). However, the development of TVEs itself has some important limitations when it is expected to transform rural China from an agrarian society into a dynamic, prosperous and industrialised community. First, the majority of TVEs have a limited technical capacity and human resources to become internationally competitive companies. Most of them are processing industries using local cheap materials and low or unskilled labour. Second, the development of TVEs has been highly uneven across regions. TVE activities are largely concentrated in the prosperous regions in the eastern coast. Many western provinces have limited TVE activities, which is the main reason why such regions have low rural incomes. Third, the development of TVEs has not been fully supported by the government in terms of investments, credit provision and the like. As mentioned previously, the majority of state investments have been concentrated in SOEs and little funds have been allocated to facilitate the development in rural industries and infrastructure. The only advantages that TVEs have over their urban counterparts are low labour costs and autonomy of management. Such advantages were important in the early stage of development but became less significant over time as labour costs rose and competition increased from other forms of enterprises, especially the foreign-owned firms and joint ventures.

The constraints on the development of TVEs are manifested by the recent struggle of the sector in terms of output and employment growth. Employment in TVEs was only 28.3 millions in 1978 and expanded rapidly to 135.1 millions in 1996. After 1997, TVEs were unable to increase employment. Total employment was reduced to only 127 million by 1999. This is more than a setback in the development of TVEs, it suggests that TVEs have faced significant constraints as to how many people they can employ and still remain competitive with other sectors of the economy. There are a number of concerns over the future development of TVEs: the upgrading of technology, the challenge in domestic and international competition, the capacity to absorb more and more labour released from the agricultural sector, the ability to generate more incomes for the rural population, and the development in the disadvantaged inland provinces. In all respects, the development of TVEs needs assistance from both the central and regional governments. However, due to the legacy of state discrimination against agriculture and the rural sector and the difficulty in reforming the urban economy, there is serious doubt that the government will be able to deliver the required support to all these needs. As a result, the future of TVE development remains rather uncertain and pessimistic.

### 3.4.4 The environment

Most available literature has focused on the success of economic growth and little attention has been paid to how the environment has been affected by the rapid growth of economic activities. There is no doubt that economic growth in the past decades has come about with a heavy cost to the natural environment. At the national level, there are a number of worrying signs. The number of natural calamities, such as droughts, floods and sandstorms, has been on the increase. In 1998, the flooding in central China lasted for over one month causing huge damage to a number of provinces along the Youngtze River (Changjiang). In 2001, a severe sandstorm hit north China, in particular Beijing, which lasted for more than two weeks. This has caused concern that the Chinese government will commit billions of yuan to protect the city before it holds the 2008 Olympics Games. In 2002, another flooding caused huge damage to half the territory of Hunan province. At the local level, the damage to the air, soil and water systems in most parts of rural China is obvious and permanent. At the village level, for example, most water streams are heavily polluted or even blocked by mud and dirt. This is because agricultural production has become more and more dependent on chemical fertilisers and pesticides. In the past, organic fertilisers, such as night soil and household waste were used as fertilisers. Since economic reforms, most of the night soil and household waste have been dumped into streams without any regulation or control. Air pollution is another problem, resulting from the mushrooming TVEs. In Guangdong, for example, when travelling from Guangzhou to Shengzhen in 2002, one could see thousands of chimneys smoking along the Guangzhou–Shengzhen highway. These smoking chimneys belong to the hundreds of TVEs producing cement, bricks and tiles in the rural communities. There is no doubt that the chimneys have brought about huge economic wealth to the local peasants but they must also have added tremendous toxic pollution to the air. Similar pollution can be observed everywhere in the rest of Guangdong and many other provinces in China, although the extent of pollution may vary in different areas.

China is now the biggest producer of traditional (and the most polluting) industrial products. In 2003, it produced over 200 million tons of steel, 215 million tons of steel products, 760 million tons of cement, 1.4 billion tons of coal. It is predicted that the total output of steel will rise by another 30 million tons, that of cement by 90 million tons and that of coal by 50 million tons in 2004. These products are among the most polluting industrial goods but they are desperately needed for China to maintain its high growth rate of GDP (*China Economic Information*, 2004). China has also become one of the world's largest producers of TV sets and other electronic appliances. Motor cars have become one of the most wanted goods in China. Almost all of the world's largest car manufacturers have set up joint ventures in China, making China one of the most important car producers in the world. In 2003, the total sales of motor vehicles were 4.3 million units, rising by 1.1 million units from the previous year. It is predicted that total sales and production of vehicles will rise by at least one million units each year in the next four to five years (*China Economic Information*, 2004). Rising car ownership is a sign of economic prosperity, but it also creates congestion and pollution. In Beijing, for example, it is estimated that the direct cost of congestion is about six billion yuan per year. China will soon rival the USA in terms of car ownership and pollution. The consequence on global warming is beyond doubt one of the biggest challenges not only for China itself but also for the entire world.

Environmental pollution and the deterioration of people's quality of life raise serious questions as to whether China can continue to develop its economy as it has done in the past. In the countryside in particular, there is even more concern as to how TVEs are to be further developed without causing more damage to the living environment for human beings. The issue of sustainable growth remains a real challenge to the Chinese people and government in the new century.

### 3.4.5 *Challenge of WTO accession*

China joined the WTO in December 2001. Accession to WTO may have both positive and negative effects on the national economy. On the positive side, it may help China to accelerate its integration with the global economy and makes domestic firms more competitive in the world market. The effects on different sectors of the economy may differ greatly, but it is likely that the agricultural sector may have to bear the burden of WTO accession more unfairly compared to the rest of the economy. In future, there will be fewer or no subsidies for agricultural production. Despite little evidence of agricultural subsidies at present, the general rule of economic development suggests that agriculture is the most vulnerable sector in terms of international competition when a country becomes highly industrialised. The fact that the European Union has to use about half of its budget to support the Common Agricultural Policy (CAP) and that Japanese rice producers need huge subsidies to survive imply that agriculture in China, too, will become increasingly unattractive without government support. Even at its present level, agricultural production is the least income-enhancing activity in rural China. If agricultural terms of trade have to deteriorate after WTO accession, more and more agricultural workers will have to move out of agriculture and find alternative employment in the TVEs, or move to the cities. As discussed previously, as the cities have a limited capacity to absorb rural migrants and the development of TVEs has faced severe constraints, the prospects for any further labour transfer from agriculture remain highly pessimistic and challenging. It is most likely that the accession of WTO will make things worse in the countryside before it makes them better in the future. It is also likely that WTO accession will have a negative effect on the income growth of the peasantry in China.

In short, we have discussed a number of issues relating to the rural economy in China. We have deliberately avoided discussing the linkage between the rural and the urban sectors except when we need to compare the income levels. However, it needs to be stressed that most of China's development problems are still primarily agricultural and rural problems. This is because the rural population accounts for about 70 per cent of the country's population, and because the rural people are still disadvantaged in many aspects. In recent years, there has been evidence of rising urban poverty, but many studies show that poverty is still primarily a rural problem in China.

The most fundamental problem of economic reform is that it has failed to reduce urban–rural income inequality. Instead, such inequality has increased. The reduction of urban–rural inequality was one of the three most important social and economic development objectives of the Communist Party. However, since the Communist Party has changed its nature although it still keeps the same name, it is not surprising that China has been going on its way to become one of the most unfair and unequal economies on earth. This is reflected by the state policy to continue its support to the urban economy at the expense of the rural population. Hence, urbanisation and industrialisation in rural areas has been largely achieved by the farmers themselves without government support. Instead, the rural local people have to bear the entire cost of the vast and expanding political machine at and below the county level governments. Not only are farm incomes low, the peasants are also subject to unlimited exploitation and the corruption of the township and village officials whose salaries and corrupt lifestyles have to be supported by imposing numerous local taxes and duties on the rural residents.

When rural migrants work in the cities, they can only do the most unwanted jobs left over by their urban counterparts. They do not enjoy the same benefits enjoyed by legal residents. They have to travel to the cities and are subject to levies for the permits they require to work in the cities. They are separated from relatives and live alone in the poor areas of the cities and suffer from loneliness and distress.

## 3.5 Conclusion

This chapter discusses the experiences of agricultural and rural development in China. Agriculture's role in the national economy has declined sharply due to its low share in GDP. However, the large majority of population is still living in the countryside and about half of the labour force is still engaged in agriculture.

The paradox between a profound change in economic structure and a predominant agricultural labour force is the consequence of state urban biased policy, which was practised by Mao but carried forward into the reform period.

In the pre-reform period, farm income hardly grew due to excessive resource transfer from the rural to the urban economy and irrational policies under the commune system. Economic reforms brought about six years (1978–84) of dramatic agricultural productivity and rural income growth, but such prosperity was short-lived. Later economic reform was again focused on the urban and industrial sector. The continuation of urban biased policy, corruption and the legacy of rural–urban separation are the main reasons for the ever rising urban–rural divide, making poverty reduction increasingly more difficult. China has changed from a very egalitarian society to one of the world's most unequal nations as a result of economic reforms.

Resource transfer from rural to urban sectors took the form of direct and indirect agricultural taxes in the pre-reform period and lasted to the late 1980s. From the 1990s, resource transfer has taken a different form, that is, the sheer exploitation of peasant workers working in the cities. Agriculture has been neglected in many ways: low investment, unfair terms of trade, and deprivation of able labour which has been sucked into cities because of the enormous urban–rural wage gap.

China's problems of unfair income distribution and poverty lie in the problems of agriculture, peasants and rural areas, or the so-called 'three-nongs' problem. This problem is so serious that the CCPCC has now issued its first document of 2004 attempting to make some radical changes. Particular measures will include the following:

- more financial support from the central budget to agricultural and rural development;
- gradual reduction of agricultural tax from 8.4 per cent to 2.4 per cent from 2004 to 2009;
- special support will be given to grain growing farmers to stop the decline of grain production.

However, nothing has been mentioned on institutional reforms. At present, agricultural land is owned by villages and village cadres can sell land to support their salary and administrative cost. Empirical observation in Guangdong show that local government officials are highly corrupt in a number of aspects, including selling collective land for their own benefits and charging illegal fees on farmers. If institutions are not reformed, farmers will continue to suffer and the fundamental problems cannot be resolved.

# 4 Openness and economic performance

## 4.1 Introduction

The remarkable economic growth in China over the last quarter century has been due to Deng's policy on economic reforms, but it is further explained by China's development strategy which changed from a close-door to an open-door orientation. China's open-door policy was imitated from the successful experiences of the four Asian tiger economies of Hong Kong, Taiwan, Singapore and South Korea. The four tigers are regarded as the first tier of newly industrialised economies (NIEs) in Asia. Some latecomers, particularly Malaysia and Thailand are considered to be the second tier of NIEs. China, followed closely by Thailand and Malaysia, has been trying to imitate the model set by the first-tier NIEs. In many respects, China has successfully copied their policies: openness featured with FDI, export push, high domestic investment and accumulation of human capital.

The Asian financial crisis in 1997–8 led most people to ponder whether the high growth in Southeast Asia was a bubble and could not be heralded as a successful model of economic development. However, the aftermath of the crisis suggests that all these countries, except Indonesia, have recovered very well and continue to perform as strongly as before. The strong performance of China and South Korea in particular, and the resilience of Hong Kong, Taiwan and Singapore since 1998 have shown solid evidence that China and the Asian tigers are still among the best performing economies in the world. Hence, there is no doubt that the development experiences of these countries, particularly their open-door development strategy should be a good model of development.

China has moved and will continue to move further in that direction, especially after joining the WTO. This chapter summarises the key elements of openness and uses an empirical model to prove that openness has helped China to catch up with the Asian NIEs.

## 4.2 Economic performance and openness: a brief review

According to the latest statistics (Table 4.1), China is classified as a middle-income economy by the World Bank, but it is still a poor country compared to the first-tier NIEs. In 2000, for example, China's per capita gross national income (GNI) in nominal terms was $840, which was only 3.2 per cent of Hong Kong's, or 16.3 per cent of the world average. Even in PPP terms, China's per capita GNI was only 15.3 per cent of Hong Kong's and 53.6 per cent of the world average. However, China shares a number of common features with the NIEs in terms of openness, investments in physical and human capital, and to some extent, strong governance. These features have made China and the NIEs different from many of the low-income countries in Africa, Latin America and South Asia.

The annual growth rate of per capita GNP ranged from 4.1 per cent in Malaysia to 7.5 per cent in Taiwan during 1965–97 (Table 4.2). This is in sharp contrast to the world's average of 1.4 per cent. Over the reform period after 1978, China's economic growth was almost unmatched by any other economy in the world. Its gross domestic product (GDP) more than quadrupled in 20 years (1978–95). Real per capita disposable income more than tripled in the cities and almost quadrupled in the countryside (Yao, 2000). From 1994, China has become the second largest recipient of foreign direct investment (FDI) after the USA (Nolan and Wang, 2000). The latest figures show that China became the world's fourth largest trading (and exporting) economy in 2003, moving from the twenty-third in 1978 (*People's Daily*, 2004: 12 January). Due to the Asian economic crisis, China's exports plummeted in late 1998 and early 1999, but recovered strongly from mid-1999. Overall, total exports in 1999 reached a record high of $194.9 billion, up 6.1 per cent from 1998, imports were $165.7 billion, up 18.2 per cent. By 2003, the volume of trade reached $851 billion, rising by 37 per cent from the previous year.

*Table 4.1* Main economic indicators of selected economies in 2000

| Countries | Population (million) | Nominal GNI/head (US$) | PPP-GNI/head (US$) |
|---|---|---|---|
| China | 1,261 | 840 | 3,940 |
| Hong Kong | 7 | 25,950 | 25,660 |
| Indonesia | 210 | 570 | 2,840 |
| Japan | 127 | 34,210 | 26,460 |
| Korea, Rep | 47 | 8,910 | 17,340 |
| Malaysia | 23 | 3,380 | 8,360 |
| Singapore | 4 | 24,740 | 24,970 |
| Taiwan* | 22 | 12,333 | 12,333 |
| Thailand | 61 | 2,010 | 6,330 |
| Low income | 2,459 | 420 | 1,990 |
| Middle income | 2,693 | 1,970 | 5,650 |
| High income | 903 | 27,510 | 27,450 |
| World | 6,054 | 5,150 | 7,350 |

Sources: World Bank, 2000: 12–14. Data for Taiwan is from NBS, 2000: 854.

Notes: * Figure for Taiwan is GNP/head in 1998. PPP-GNI is gross national income converted to international dollars using purchasing power parity rates. An international dollar has the same purchasing power over GNI as a US dollar in the United States. Low Income ($785 or less), middle income ($785–$9,655), high income ($9,656 or more). GNP gross national product, GNI gross national income.

*Table 4.2* Economic and population growth in selected economies

|  | GNP/head annual growth 1965–97 (%) | Population annual growth 1965–97 (%) |
|---|---|---|
| China | 6.8 | 1.7 |
| Hong Kong | 5.7 | 1.8 |
| Indonesia | 4.8 | 2.0 |
| Japan | 3.6 | 0.8 |
| Korea | 6.7 | 1.5 |
| Malaysia | 4.1 | 2.6 |
| Singapore | 6.3 | 1.9 |
| Taiwan | 7.5 | n.a. |
| Thailand | 5.1 | 2.1 |
| Low income | 1.4 | 2.4 |
| Middle income | 2.2 | 1.7 |
| High income | 2.3 | 0.8 |
| World | 1.4 | 1.8 |

Sources: The United Nations, 1997 for Taiwan. World Bank, 1999: 24–6, for all the other economies.

High economic growth in China and the NIEs has been associated with and enhanced by relatively slow population growth. In the NIEs, low population growth reflected the general negative trend of women's fertility as per capita income rises over time. In China, it has been induced by a stringent family planning policy, which restricted each urban family to have only one child and each rural family to have two children.

China's family planning policy may not be popular among its populace and may have some undesirable long-term consequences, but the actual outcome of birth control has a number of advantages. First, it has helped to improve the average living standards of the population given a certain level of economic activity. Second, it has reduced the pressure on employment and the natural environment. Third, it has helped enhance human capital accumulation as more resources can be allocated to education and healthcare.

High economic growth in China and the NIEs has led to a significant reduction in the level of poverty. Poverty reduction in the NIEs was much more significant than in some large Latin American and South Asian countries during the 1970s and 1980s. In China, more than 75 per cent of the rural population lived in poverty in 1978. This proportion rapidly declined to less than 13 per cent by 1996 (Table 4.3).

The most common features of China and the NIEs for their economic success are high rates of savings, export push and investments in physical and human capital. High saving rates may reflect the traditional culture of the Chinese and the East Asian people rather than a result of government policy. This traditional culture has been extremely helpful for capital accumulation and education in the developing economies. All the NIEs had a savings/GDP ratio of more than 30 per

*Table 4.3* Changes in poverty incidence

| Economies | Period | Percentage of population below poverty line | |
|---|---|---|---|
| | | *First year* | *Last year* |
| Indonesia | 1972–82 | 58 | 17 |
| Malaysia | 1973–87 | 37 | 14 |
| Singapore | 1972–82 | 31 | 10 |
| Thailand | 1962–86 | 59 | 26 |
| China (rural) | 1978–96 | 75 | 6.7–13 |
| Brazil | 1960–80 | 50 | 21 |
| Colombia | 1971–88 | 41 | 25 |
| Costa Rica | 1971–86 | 45 | 24 |
| India | 1972–83 | 54 | 43 |
| Morocco | 1970–84 | 43 | 34 |
| Pakistan | 1962–84 | 54 | 23 |
| Sri Lanka | 1963–82 | 37 | 27 |

Sources: World Bank, 1993: Table 1.1, p. 33 for all countries except China, and Yao, 2000 for rural China.

Notes: This table uses economy-specific poverty lines. Official or commonly used poverty lines are used. In other cases the poverty line is 30 per cent of mean income or expenditure. The poverty line is measured in PPP dollar terms at about $300–$700 a year in 1985 except for Malaysia ($1420) and Singapore ($860). Apart from Malaysia, China, Costa Rica and Sri Lanka, measures for entries are per capita incomes. The measures of entries for other countries are per capita expenditures. The data for China is just for the rural population as few urban people are considered to be poor.

cent. In Singapore and China, the saving rate is as high as 40–50 per cent, compared favourably to 22 per cent of the world average and 17 per cent in the low-income economies (Table 4.4). In some sub-Saharan African countries, the saving rate is negligible. Needless to say, saving is a prerequisite for domestic investments, which in turn, is an important factor for positive economic growth. In 1965–97, most NIEs and China maintained an average annual growth rate of 7.7 per cent to 10.9 per cent in physical investments, compared to 3.9 per cent in the low income economies and 3.2 per cent of the world average.

The endogenous growth theory suggests that investment in human capital is as important as physical investment. Accumulation of human capital is reflected in a number of areas, particularly in health and education. Improvement of people's health has led to a significant increase in life expectancy and a large reduction in child and infant mortality. In China and the NIEs, life expectancy is significantly higher, and child mortality lower than in the low-income economies (Table 4.5). In education, the campaign to popularise primary and secondary school education has been highly successful. By 1997, almost all Chinese children were able to receive primary education and over 70 per cent (rising from 46 per cent in 1980) of the relevant aged children were able to receive secondary education. In the low-income economies, the gross enrolment rate in secondary school was only 43 per cent in the same year (World Bank, 1999: 78–80). The popularisation of primary and secondary education in China and the NIEs led to a significant reduction in

*Table 4.4* Investments and savings

|  | *Investment annual growth 1965–97 %* | *Savings as % of GDP 1997* |
|---|---|---|
| China | 10.9 | 42.7 |
| Hong Kong | 7.7 | 30.6 |
| Indonesia | 9.2 | 30.6 |
| Japan | 4.7 | 30.5 |
| Korea | 12.4 | 34.2 |
| Malaysia | 10.1 | 44.4 |
| Singapore | 9.6 | 51.2 |
| Thailand | 9.0 | 35.7 |
| Low income | 3.9 | 17.0 |
| Middle income | 2.1 | 26.2 |
| High income | 3.1 | 21.4 |
| World | 3.2 | 22.2 |

Source: World Bank, 1999: 174–6.

adult illiteracy. Young-aged population illiteracy was almost eliminated in Korea and Singapore by the late 1990s. It was reduced to 1–3 per cent of the relevant age population in China and other NIEs. This is in contrast to 32 per cent in the low-income economies.

*Table 4.5* Investments in human capital

|  | *Life expectancy at birth (years)* | | *Child mortality (age 1–5), deaths/1000* | | *Illiteracy rate (age 15–24) as %* | |
|---|---|---|---|---|---|---|
|  | *1980* | *1997* | *1980* | *1997* | *1980* | *1997* |
| China | 67 | 70 | 167 | 151 | 10 | 3 |
| Hong Kong | 74 | 79 | 118 | 83 | 4 | 1 |
| Indonesia | 55 | 65 | 238 | 214 | 11 | 3 |
| Japan | 76 | 80 | 100 | 73 | 0 | 0 |
| Korea | 67 | 72 | 272 | 103 | 0 | 0 |
| Malaysia | 67 | 72 | 190 | 151 | 12 | 3 |
| Singapore | 71 | 76 | 157 | 102 | 3 | 1 |
| Thailand | 64 | 69 | 245 | 171 | 4 | 2 |
| Low income | 52 | 59 | 320 | 265 | 47 | 32 |
| Middle income | 65 | 69 | 195 | 168 | 11 | 5 |
| High income | 74 | 77 | 143 | 100 | 0 | 0 |
| World | 63 | 67 | 218 | 167 | 24 | 16 |

Sources: World Bank, 1999: 110–12 (life expectancy and child mortality), 78–80 (illiteracy rate amongst young people).

Another common feature of China and the NIEs is their integration with the global economy. This is reflected in their export-push development strategy and the absorption of foreign capital. Hong Kong and Singapore are the most open economies measured by the trade/GDP ratio. The volume of trade is two to three times that of PPP-GDP. The trade/GDP ratios are also high in other NIEs, ranging from 16.9 per cent in Thailand to 90 per cent in Malaysia. These ratios are significantly higher than the average ratio of the low-income economies (Table 4.6).

*Table 4.6* Integration with the world economy

| | Trade in goods as % of PPP-GDP | | FDI inflows as % of PPP-GDP | | FDI inflows, current prices ($bn) | |
|---|---|---|---|---|---|---|
| | *1987* | *1997* | *1987* | *1997* | *1990* | *1997* |
| China | 6.8 | 8.5 | 0.2 | 1.2 | 3.5 | 44.2 |
| Hong Kong | 125.0 | 250.4 | – | – | – | – |
| Indonesia | 11.1 | 13.7 | 0.1 | 0.7 | 1.1 | 4.7 |
| Japan | 20.8 | 25.0 | 1.2 | 1.0 | 1.8 | 3.2 |
| Korea | 36.6 | 44.9 | 0.5 | 1.2 | 0.8 | 2.8 |
| Malaysia | 49.4 | 90.0 | 0.7 | 2.9 | 2.3 | 5.1 |
| Singapore | 200.7 | 290.7 | 10.0 | 14.3 | 5.6 | 8.6 |
| Thailand | 16.9 | 29.7 | 0.4 | 1.0 | 2.4 | 3.8 |
| Low income | 7.0 | 8.4 | 0.1 | 0.3 | 1.1 | 10.6 |
| Middle income | 10.3 | 18.6 | 0.3 | 1.4 | 22.6 | 150.0 |
| High income | 27.4 | 38.7 | 2.2 | 3.1 | 167.0 | 233.9 |
| World | 20.6 | 29.6 | 1.5 | 2.4 | 192.7 | 394.5 |

Sources: World Bank, 1999: 324–6 (trade and FDI).

In terms of international trade, China is still far less open than the NIEs. In 1997, for example, the trade/PPP-GDP ratio was only 8.5 per cent. However, the figures in Table 4.6 may understate China's openness in two respects. First, because China is a large country, it is difficult, or impossible to achieve the same level of trade/ GDP ratio as that of the small city economies of Hong Kong and Singapore. Second, the GDP figures are calculated in PPP terms. If they were calculated in nominal terms, the trade/GDP ratio in 1997 would be 31 per cent for China, rising from 8.81 per cent in 1977 (Pomfret, 1997: Table 1). By 2003, the normal trade/GDP ratio reached 60 per cent (personal estimate based on official trade and GDP data).

Another indication of openness is the absorption of foreign capital. In 1978, there was little FDI in China. By 1995, China became the second largest recipient of FDI after the USA. The most rapid growth in FDI was registered in the late 1980s and 1990s. The FDI/PPP-GDP ratio rose six-fold from 0.2 per cent to 1.2 per cent in 1987–97. Total FDI inflows rose almost thirteen-fold from $3.5 billion in 1990 to $44.2 billion by 1997 (Table 4.6). In 1998, China accounted for 28 per

*Table 4.7* Top ten recipients of FDI in the developing world, 1998

|  | FDI ($bn) | As % of total |
|---|---|---|
| All LDCs | 160.0 | 100.0 |
| China | 44.8 | 28.0 |
| Brazil | 25.6 | 16.0 |
| Mexico | 10.7 | 6.7 |
| Argentina | 5.9 | 3.7 |
| Poland | 5.9 | 3.7 |
| Malaysia | 5.3 | 3.3 |
| Chile | 5.3 | 3.3 |
| Thailand | 5.1 | 3.2 |
| Venezuela | 4.0 | 2.5 |
| Russia Fed | 3.2 | 2.0 |
| Rest of world | 44.2 | 27.6 |

Sources: World Bank (1999), *World Development Indicators* (Washington, DC), p. 323.

cent of the total FDI flowing into the developing countries (Table 4.7). China's absorption of foreign capital followed the recent development path of Malaysia, Korea and Singapore. In general, the NIEs and China are much more open to FDI than most of the low-income and middle-income economies over the last three decades.

## 4.3  How does openness affect growth?

### 4.3.1  Growth and openness: an international perspective

One relevant study on the NIEs is by Sengupta and Espana (1994). They use time series data to estimate an augmented Cobb-Douglas production function including export as an explanatory variable for GDP growth. In their sample, there are two NIEs (Korea and Taiwan), three mature industrialised countries (Japan, Germany and Belgium) and one developing economy (the Philippines). The regression results show that in all cases except Japan, export had a positive and significant effect on GDP growth (Table 4.8). Their model does not include FDI and foreign exchange rate, which are particularly important for the Chinese economy under transition. In the next sub-section, we will extend the model to include all these variables for China.

Figure 4.1 shows further evidence on the positive relationship between GDP and export growth. Over the period 1990–5, China achieved the fastest growth in GDP and exports among the APEC (Asian and Pacific Economic Cooperation) members. The NIEs are among the best performers. The mapping of cross-countries' growth shows a clear and positive relationship between GDP and export.

*Table 4.8* Externality effect of exports on growth, 1967–86

| Economies | Intercept | I | I² | L̇ | Ẋ | R² | DW | X/Y (%) |
|---|---|---|---|---|---|---|---|---|
| Korea | −208.9 | 0.151* | n.a. | 0.024* | 0.401* | 0.614 | 1.96 | 30.6 |
| Taiwan | 6.8* | 0.094* | n.a. | 0.050 | 0.438* | 0.933 | 1.56 | 56.7 |
| Japan | −7.7 | 0.615* | −0.384* | 0.119* | 0.116 | 0.690 | 1.98 | 12.9 |
| Belgium | −314.8* | 1.148 | −0.001 | 0.631* | 0.333* | 0.419 | 1.95 | 59.0 |
| Germany (FRG) | −190.0* | 1.651 | −0.003 | 0.028* | 0.610* | 0.447 | 2.44 | 28.3 |
| Philippines | −0.7* | 0.336* | n.a. | 0.001 | 0.389* | 0.407 | 1.52 | 21.6 |

Source: Sengupta and Espana, 1994: Table 4.

Notes: (1) The dependent variable is GDP growth. (2) $I$ and $I^2$ respectively denote investment and its squared term, $\dot{L}$ and $\dot{X}$ respectively labour and export growth, X/Y export/GDP ratio. (3) The '*' sign denotes significance at the 5 per cent level or below.

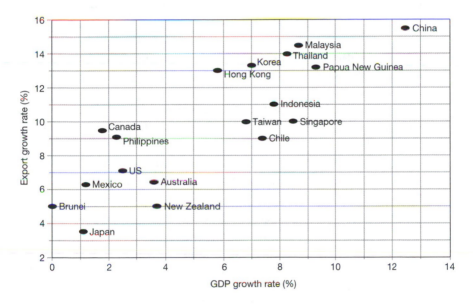

*Figure 4.1* GDP and export growth in APEC economies, 1990–5.

Source: Pan, 1998: Figure 4.9.

Some recent studies on FDI focus on how it is determined but not on how it is linked to economic growth. Liu *et al.* (1997) shows that FDI is determined by GDP growth, international trade, and other variables. Some more descriptive studies (e.g. Chen *et al.*, 1995; Lardy, 1995) suggest that FDI has an important role in China's economic performance, but there have been no studies that quantify the triangular relationship between FDI, export and economic growth. However, in a cross-country study, Pan (1998) finds a positive relationship between the ratios of

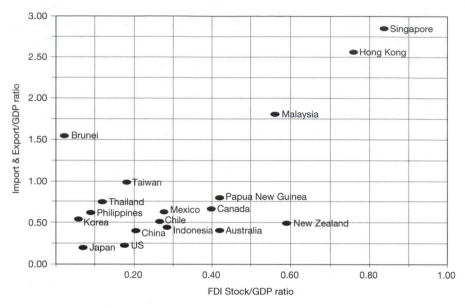

*Figure 4.2* Trade/GDP and FDI/GDP ratios in 1995 in the APEC economies.

Source: Pan, 1998: Figure 4.10.

trade/GDP and FDI/GDP among the APEC economies (Figure 4.2). Three of the
NIEs (Singapore, Hong Kong and Malaysia) had the highest FDI stock/GDP and
trade/GDP ratios.

### 4.3.2 Growth and openness: evidence from the Chinese regions

Before economic reforms, import-substitution and rigid price control were two
major features of China's development strategy. For example, there was little
FDI in as late as 1982, four years after the inception of economic reforms in 1978.
The total amount of FDI was only $0.64 billion in 1983, but increased gradu-
ally thereafter, reaching $4.37 billion by 1991. After Deng's famous tour to South
China in 1992, there was a sudden surge of FDI. The total inflow jumped to $11.3
billion in that year, rising to $27.5 billion in 1993, $33.8 billion in 1994 and $53.5
billion in 2003 (Table 4.9). By the end of 2003, there were 465,277 foreign invested
firms, with a stock of actually used FDI of $501.47 billion (*People's Daily*, 2004:
15 January). It is also worth noting that China itself has become a major investor
in other countries. By 2003, it has invested over $36 billion in 86 different countries,
surpassing South Korea (*People's Daily*, 2004: 28 January).

It is obvious that the history of FDI is much shorter in China than in the NIEs.
In addition, FDI is highly concentrated in a number of provinces along the eastern
coast (Guangdong, Jiangsu, Shanghai, Tianjin, Fujian, Shangdong, Zhejiang,
Hainan, Liaoning and Hebei). In 1995, for example, the eastern region accounted
for over 88 per cent of total FDI, with Guangdong alone accounting for 27 per cent.

Even after a few years of government efforts to promote investments in the western region, the pattern of FDI distribution remained essentially the same in 2002, with the eastern region accounting for 87 per cent and Guangdong 21.5 per cent. Guangdong and Jiangsu received over 40 per cent of total FDI in 2002 (NBS, 2003: 675). One important reason for the skewed distribution of FDI across regions is the early reforms that focused on opening up four special economic zones in Guangdong and Fujian in 1980, fourteen coastal cities in 1984, Hainan Island in 1988 and Shanghai Pudong Development Zone in 1989. Of course, there are fundamental reasons why the coastal cities were selected as open zones. Compared to the inland areas, the coastal regions had a more productive agricultural and industrial basis, a more efficient transportation system, better environmental and human resources, and above all, an easier access to China's largest investors, especially Hong Kong.[1]

China's strategy to open its market for foreign investors has coincided with and is reinforced by its effort to promote exports. Right from the inception of economic reform, China emphasised that foreign invested firms (foreign-owned companies, equity joint ventures and cooperative ventures) must produce a large proportion of their outputs for export. As a result, many foreign invested firms were concentrated in the export processing and manufacturing areas in the special economic zones, the open cities and Hainan Island. This investment strategy produced some spectacular results. First, total exports increased dramatically from only $18.2 billion in 1980 to $194.9 billion by 1999. After joining the WTO in 2001, China's exports rocketed. By 2003, total exports reached $438.4 billion. China's export ranking in the world moved from number 6 in 2001 to number 5 in 2002 and number 4 in 2003. Second, the share of manufactured exports in total exports rose from 49.9 per cent in 1980 to 91.2 per cent by 2002. Rapid expansion of exports and significant change in the export mix resembled the export performance of Korea and Taiwan in the 1960s and 1970s, and of the second-tier NIEs in the 1980s and early 1990s. Third, foreign invested firms played an important role in China's export drive. Their exports were negligible in the first half of 1980s but increased to $46.9 billion, or 31.7 per cent of total exports by 1995 (Table 4.9). By 2002, this share had jumped to 52.2 per cent.

Although China's success in attracting FDI and promoting exports can be explained by many factors, it is important to note that gradual reform in the foreign exchange market had played a critical role. Without devaluing the yuan, it would be impossible to make the Chinese market attractive for foreign investors whose transactions involve frequent exchanges of foreign currencies and the yuan. In the early 1980s when the official exchange rate was substantially lower than the black market rate, foreign investors had little incentive to invest in China.[2]

In the late 1980s, the government established a few official swap markets to facilitate the reallocation of foreign exchange and to maintain a dual exchange rate mechanism. The swap market was an official channel allowing investors to change foreign currencies into yuan at a higher rate than the official exchange rate. It was the first important step of the government to provide incentives to attract FDI and promote exports. As foreign exchange reserves increased rapidly in the early 1990s,

*Table 4.9*  Chinese FDI, exports and structure, 1980–2003

| Year | Actual FDI ($bn) | Total exports ($bn) | Export by foreign invested firms as % of total | Manufactured exports as % of total |
|------|------|------|------|------|
| 1980 | 0.2 | 18.2 | 0.0 | 49.7 |
| 1985 | 2.0 | 27.4 | 1.1 | 49.4 |
| 1986 | 2.2 | 30.9 | 1.6 | 63.6 |
| 1987 | 2.6 | 39.4 | 3.0 | 66.5 |
| 1988 | 3.7 | 47.5 | 5.2 | 69.7 |
| 1989 | 3.8 | 52.5 | 8.3 | 71.3 |
| 1990 | 3.8 | 62.1 | 12.5 | 74.4 |
| 1991 | 4.7 | 71.8 | 16.8 | 77.5 |
| 1992 | 11.3 | 85.0 | 20.4 | 79.9 |
| 1993 | 27.5 | 91.8 | 27.5 | 81.8 |
| 1994 | 33.8 | 121.0 | 28.7 | 83.7 |
| 1995 | 37.7 | 148.8 | 31.7 | 85.6 |
| 1996 | 41.7 | 151.1 | 40.7 | 85.5 |
| 1997 | 44.2 | 182.7 | 40.9 | 86.9 |
| 1998 | 44.8 | 183.7 | 44.0 | 88.8 |
| 1999 | 40.3 | 194.9 | 45.4 | 89.8 |
| 2000 | 40.7 | 249.2 | 47.9 | 89.8 |
| 2001 | 46.9 | 266.1 | 50.1 | 90.1 |
| 2002 | 52.7 | 325.6 | 52.2 | 91.2 |
| 2003 | 53.5 | 438.4 | n.a. | n.a. |

Sources: Lardy, 1995: Tables 1, 6 and 7 and Pomfret, 1997: Tables 2 and 3 for data up to 1995. Data for 1996 and 1997 are derived from NBS, 1998. Data for 1998–9 are from *People's Daily*, 14 March 2000. NBS, 2003 (CSYB): 654, 671, 670.

the dual rate system was abolished in January 1994, as were the swap markets. By then, the yuan had been gradually devalued towards its market equilibrium level (Chou and Shih, 1998: Table 2). The official exchange rate was devalued from 1.68 yuan per dollar in 1978 to 8.321 yuan in 1995, or by almost 400 per cent. In real terms, when adjusted by the US and Chinese consumer price indices, the real exchange rate rose by over 200 per cent in the same period (Table 4.10). Due to China's stability policy and its successful performance in international trade and attraction of FDI, the official exchange rate fluctuated between 8.2–8.4 yuan to one dollar from 1996 up to now.

Turning to the growth theory, China's systematic reforms in the foreign exchange market, its efforts to promote exports and to attract FDI all have the same objective, that is, creating a better environment for economic growth. If we consider economic growth as the core of the model, then output is determined by physical inputs (physical capital and labour), the internal production environment (human capital, transportation, institutions and the like), and the external environment (FDI, export and the foreign exchange mechanism). This economic growth model can be illustrated in Figure 4.3.

Output (GDP) is basically determined by two physical inputs: labour and capital. However, the efficiency of input usage, or economic performance, is further

*Table 4.10* Nominal (official) and real exchange rates of yuan/US$

| Year | Nominal exchange rate | Real exchange rates |
|------|-----------------------|---------------------|
| 1978 | 1.680 | 1.740 |
| 1979 | 1.550 | 1.750 |
| 1980 | 1.500 | 1.820 |
| 1981 | 1.705 | 2.220 |
| 1982 | 1.893 | 2.570 |
| 1983 | 1.976 | 2.730 |
| 1984 | 2.327 | 3.260 |
| 1985 | 2.937 | 3.920 |
| 1986 | 3.453 | 4.430 |
| 1987 | 3.722 | 4.610 |
| 1988 | 3.722 | 4.050 |
| 1989 | 3.766 | 3.650 |
| 1990 | 4.784 | 4.780 |
| 1991 | 5.323 | 5.390 |
| 1992 | 5.515 | 5.460 |
| 1993 | 5.762 | 5.190 |
| 1994 | 8.619 | 6.540 |
| 1995 | 8.321 | 5.660 |
| 2000 | 8.278 | – |
| 2002 | 8.277 | – |
| 1995/1978 | 4.953 | 3.253 |

Sources: NBS, 1996, for the official exchange rates and China's CPI. US Department of Commerce, 1980–96, for the US CPI.

Notes: $RE_t = OE_t (CPI_{US}/CPI_{China})$, $RE$ and $OE$ respectively denote real and official exchange rates, CPI is consumer price index using 1990 as the base year.

determined by two sets of factors: external and internal. The external factors are related to openness, including FDI, export and the foreign exchange mechanism. The internal factors include human capital, infrastructure, location and institutions (e.g. government policy, legal regulations etc.). Economic performance varies significantly across countries due to the variations in both internal and external factors. Some recent cross-countries studies reveal that human capital, saving and population growth are three main variables responsible for inter-country growth differences (Islam, 1995; Sala-i-Martin, 1996).

However, few studies have considered all the internal and external factors in a cross-countries or cross-regions analysis. This may be due to some difficult technical problems, such as multicollinearity and simultaneity, that cannot be reconciled in a single regression model. To overcome these problems, instead of estimating one single equation, we have three regression models (with FDI, Export and GDP as the dependent variables) run in a seemingly unrelated equation system. We also use the dynamic system approach with appropriate instruments in the DPD (dynamic panel data estimation) proposed by Arellano and Bond (1998).

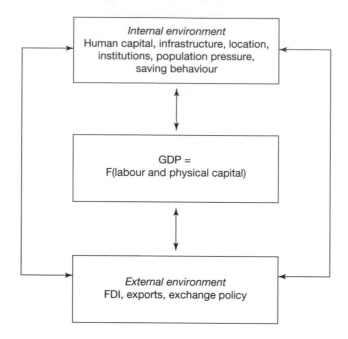

*Figure 4.3* Economic growth and production environment.

Since it is difficult to obtain comparable data for different countries, we use the panel data for the Chinese provinces over the period 1978–95. Each province can be treated as a separate economy because there are significant differences among the provinces regarding the degree of openness and economic performance. The empirical results are presented in Table 4.11. GDP is defined as a function of capital stock, employment, human capital, real exchange rate, FDI, export and transportation. Other variables include a dummy variable representing the eastern economic area (east), a dummy variable representing the unusual economic boom in 1992–5 after Deng's famous tour to South China, and a time trend.

The results suggest that apart from capital and labour, both internal and external factors have a significant impact on GDP. For the external factors, the effects of export and real exchange rate are much stronger than that of FDI. The output elasticity of export is over 0.11, of real exchange rate 0.10, and of FDI less than 0.01. For the internal factors, human capital is more important than transportation and location. The output elasticity of human capital is 0.054. The location effect (east) is insignificant. This may be due to the fact that regional productivity differences have been largely explained by the variations in other external and internal factors. The estimated coefficient on the time trend indicates that the Hicks-neutral technological progress was 1.1 per cent per annum. It reflects a location-invariant macro productivity shock over the data period.

Export is defined as a function of GDP, real exchange rate, location and the lagged dependent variable. The dummy variable for the period 1992–5 is also

*Table 4.11* Regression results based on a panel data of 30 Chinese provinces in 1980–95

| GDP | | | Export | | | | FDI | | |
| --- | --- | --- | --- | --- | --- | --- | --- | --- | --- |
| Xs | βs | t-values | | Xs | βs | t-values | | Xs | βs | t-values |
| Constant | -17.55 | -1.79 | | Constant | -0.783 | -3.19 | | Constant | -3.044 | -4.15 |
| Labour | 0.409 | 12.13 | | GDP | 0.187 | 4.85 | | GDP | 0.165 | 2.33 |
| Capital | 0.472 | 8.85 | | Exchange | 0.141 | 1.91 | | Wages | 0.114 | 0.92 |
| Human | 0.054 | 2.69 | | East | 0.288 | 3.55 | | Exchange | 0.626 | 2.65 |
| Exchange | 0.102 | 9.76 | | D92–95 | 0.256 | 4.55 | | Transport | 0.157 | 1.63 |
| FDI | 0.006 | 1.69 | | Export(-1) | 0.793 | 18.79 | | Human | 0.044 | 0.52 |
| Export | 0.111 | 13.29 | | | | | | East | 0.373 | 3.57 |
| Transport | 0.038 | 1.68 | | | | | | D92–95 | 0.529 | 4.96 |
| East | 0.033 | 0.29 | | | | | | FDI(-1) | 0.798 | 18.93 |
| D92–95 | 0.021 | 2.68 | | | | | | | | |
| Time | 0.011 | 2.01 | | | | | | | | |

Test-statistics (GDP)

| | | |
| --- | --- | --- |
| $R^2 = 0.981$ | | |
| Wald | | p=0.000 |
| Sargan | | p=0.889 |
| M1 | -1.56 | p=0.119 |
| M2 | -0.864 | p=0.388 |

Test-statistics (Export)

| | | |
| --- | --- | --- |
| $R^2 = 0.931$ | | |
| Wald | | p=0.000 |
| Sargan | | n.a. |
| M1 | -1.295 | p=0.195 |
| M2 | 0.718 | p=0.473 |

Test-statistics (FDI)

| | | |
| --- | --- | --- |
| $R^2 = 0.919$ | | |
| Wald | | p=0.000 |
| Sargan | | n.a. |
| M1 | -0.948 | p=0.343 |
| M2 | -0.749 | p=0.454 |

Data sources: NBS, 1996.

Notes: All the variables are in natural logarithms. Values are measured in 1990 constant prices. Detail explanations on data, model specification, estimation techniques, test-statistics are provided in the appendix.

included. All the explanatory variables are significant at the usual 5 per cent level. Referring to the regression results on GDP, it is clear that export and GDP are interdependent. The long-run elasticity of export with respect to GDP is 0.89, suggesting that a 10 per cent rise in GDP will lead to an 8.9 per cent rise in export, holding other conditions unchanged. Real exchange rate is another important factor affecting export. In other words, without reforming the exchange market, China's exports would have been severely disadvantaged.[3] Although the location factor is not significant in the GDP equation, it is significantly associated with export. This indicates that the eastern area is far more export-oriented than the inland provinces, even after all the other factors are controlled for.

FDI is defined as a function of GDP, effective wages (nominal wages adjusted by productivity), real exchange rate, transportation, human capital, location and the lagged dependent variable. The dummy variable for 1992–5 is also included. Like export, FDI is mainly determined by GDP, with a long-run elasticity of 0.825. The real exchange rate also plays an important role in FDI. The location factor is significant, indicating that the eastern area is much more successful in attracting FDI than the rest of the country. The effects of human capital and wages on FDI are positive but not significant, implying that wage differentials across provinces were not a significant concern of foreign investors in the data period. In reality, wage differences may just reflect the variation in labour quality.

The quantitative relationship between GDP and the three factors of openness can be summarised and illustrated in Figure 4.4. In the model, real exchange rate is treated as an exogenous variable. The results suggest that it had a significant and sizeable effect on the three endogenous variables: FDI, export and GDP. It is clear that the gradual devaluation of RMB towards its real equilibrium exchange rate with the US dollar over the data period has been one of the most important factors responsible for China's success in attracting FDI, promoting export, and above all, stimulating economic growth.

FDI and export have a simultaneous relationship with GDP. FDI inflows and export stimulate GDP growth, which, in turn, provides a solid basis for attracting more FDI and export push. Such an interaction among these three economic

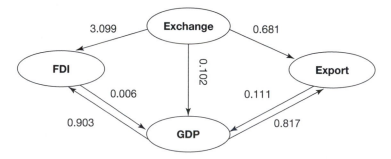

*Figure 4.4* Linkage between openness and output in the Chinese regions, 1980–95.
Source: Table 4.11.
Notes: The values are long-run elasticities. Arrows indicate the direction of impact.

variables formed a virtual circle of openness, growth, more openness and more growth.

## 4.4 Economic crisis and recovery

Only four years after the World Bank published the book *The East Asian Miracle* (World Bank, 1993), all the high performing economies in East Asia were plunged into a deep financial and economic crisis in late 1997 and 1998. The crisis was first triggered by the collapse of the Thai baht and stock market. The contagion soon spread into Malaysia, Indonesia and Korea. All these countries were so severely affected that the International Monetary Fund (IMF) was asked to pump huge sums of money to rescue their economies.[4]

The Asian crisis brought down the world GDP growth from 4.8 per cent in 1997 to just 1.9 per cent in 1998. Japan was already in recession before the crisis, but the crisis hit Japan particularly hard. Its recession contributed to 0.5 percentage points of the decline in world GDP in 1998. Since Japan was the power engine in East Asia, its own recession accelerated the decline of the NIEs. The worst hit economies were Thailand, Indonesia, Malaysia and Korea. In 1998, output fell by 13 per cent in Indonesia, 8 per cent in Thailand, 6.7 per cent in Malaysia and 6.0 per cent in Korea. Even Hong Kong and Singapore were forced into negative growth in 1998. Only Taiwan and China managed to maintain a positive growth, but at a much lower rate than before the crisis (Table 4.12). The scale of crisis was unprecedented in these economies during their recent development history.

In early 1998, the crisis seemed to spread into the already fragile Russian and other eastern European economies. A world-wide economic depression looked imminent as the US and western European stock markets suffered severe losses

*Table 4.12* GDP growth of the NIEs in economic crisis, 1997–9, by quarter

|  | China | Hong Kong | Indonesia | Korea | Maylasia | Singapore | Taiwan | Thailand |
|---|---|---|---|---|---|---|---|---|
| 1997Q1 | 9.4 | 6.1 | 6.6 | 5.4 | 8.2 | 3.8 | 6.8 | −0.4 |
| 1997Q2 | 9.6 | 6.4 | 6.6 | 6.3 | 8.4 | 7.8 | 6.3 | −0.4 |
| 1997Q3 | 8.1 | 5.7 | 6.6 | 6.3 | 7.4 | 10.1 | 6.9 | −0.4 |
| 1997Q4 | 8.2 | 2.7 | 6.6 | 3.9 | 6.9 | 5.6 | 5.9 | −0.4 |
| 1998Q1 | 7.2 | −2.8 | −6.2 | −3.8 | −1.8 | 5.6 | 5.9 | −8.0 |
| 1998Q2 | 6.8 | −5.2 | −16.5 | −6.6 | −6.8 | −1.5 | 5.2 | −8.0 |
| 1998Q3 | 7.6 | −7.1 | −17.4 | −6.8 | −8.6 | −0.7 | 4.7 | −8.0 |
| 1998Q4 | 9.6 | −5.7 | −13.9 | −5.3 | −8.6 | −0.8 | 3.7 | −8.0 |
| 1999Q1 | 8.3 | −3.4 | −10.3 | 4.6 | −1.3 | 1.2 | 4.3 | 0.1 |
| 1999Q2 | 7.1 | 0.7 | 1.8 | 9.8 | 4.1 | 6.7 | 6.5 | 3.5 |
| 1999Q3 | 7.0 | 4.5 | 0.5 | 12.3 | 8.1 | 6.7 | 5.1 | 3.5 |
| 1999Q4 | 6.8 | 8.7 | 5.8 | 12.3 | 10.6 | 7.1 | 6.8 | 7.7 |

Source: *The Economist* (1997–9, various issues), Economic Indicators.

Notes: Average of latest three months compared with average of previous three months. The rates for Thailand in 1997 and 1998, for Indonesia in 1997 are annual rates.

in mid-1998. In the third quarter of 1998, there was a strong speculation that China might have to devalue the RMB to maintain a competitive edge against the NIEs. It also looked as if that the potential collapse of the RMB and the Chinese economy would serve a final blow to trigger a global crisis. Suddenly, China's ability and willingness not to devalue its currency became the centre of world attention. In late 1998, Mr Zhu Rongji, China's premier, promised that China would not devalue the RMB. In early 1999, the central government also ordered the central bank, the People's Bank of China, to issue 100 billion yuan investment bonds to boost its domestic economy in face of a depressing external market. For the first time in over twenty years, China experienced a significant negative growth in exports in late 1998 and early 1999. However, China's effort not to devalue the RMB and its ability to achieve a GDP growth of 7.8 per cent in 1998 played a significant role in easing the crisis in Asia.

During the economic crisis, many economic analysts thought that the Asian miracle might have been over, and the 'bubble' may have burst. Paul Krugman shares the view that Asia's crisis was due to corruption and crony capital (Krugman, 1998). He argues that the failure of the financial system in east Asia was due to excessive investments in risky and low returns (or unprofitable) projects. It is therefore logical to infer that the bubble must burst once bad debts and financial losses accumulated to such a point which even the government cannot bear. Krugman's explanation is valid in the sense that the Asian economies have some fundamental problems in the financial institutions and governments' soft attitudes towards large state enterprises and banks. His hypothesis, however, may not be sufficient to prove the sudden occurrence of a deep crisis. Radelet and Sachs (1998) suggest that there were other important factors responsible for the sudden collapse of Thailand, Malaysia, Indonesia and Korea. It can be argued that two of their explanations are still valid today, (1) panicked reversals in capital flows, and (2) the lack of a legal and regulatory framework to support a liberalised and wide-open financial system in the world market.

Panicked reversals in capital flows were caused by the so-called herd behaviour of domestic depositors and foreign investors: if one decides to withdraw money in anticipation of a crisis, others will follow. The worst hit economies (Thailand, Indonesia, Malaysia and Korea) had the highest short-term debt-to-reserve ratios, which rendered them the most vulnerable to attacks by investors rushing to draw out money in panic. Panicked outflows of capital may be due to the premature opening of domestic financial markets to foreign investors. In Thailand, Indonesia, Malaysia and Korea, new banks and finance companies were allowed to operate without supervision and adequate capitalisation. This financial environment was partly responsible for the capital withdrawals, panic and deep economic contraction that followed. In contrast, Hong Kong, Singapore and Taiwan had a much more mature financial market with a far better monitoring and supervision mechanism than Indonesia, Thailand, Malaysia and Korea. This explained why the former suffered far less during the crisis than the latter.

Like the worst hit economies, China's financial system had similar problems of corruption, crony capital, huge non-performing loans and losses by the state-owned enterprises and banks. However, China was able to escape a similar crisis. In retrospect, it was not because China had a better economic basis than the crisis economies, but because it had a more pragmatic approach to financial market reforms. The Chinese government understood well that it could not entirely open up its financial market for foreign investors given the poor state of its financial institutions and the unpredictable volatility of stock markets. Foreigners were restricted to investing in the B shares in the Shanghai and Shenzheng stock exchanges. The RMB was gradually devalued but it was kept unconvertible in capital account transactions even after a unified exchange rate was introduced in 1994. Moreover, foreign banks and other financial institutions are not allowed to open branches in China without going through a tedious administrative procedure. China's gradual reform and openness in the financial market resembled its gradual reform approach in the real sectors of the economy.

In the middle of the Asian crisis, some observers suggested that Asia's development was somehow a bubble, rather than a miracle, and when the bubble burst, the remarkable achievement of these economies in the past decades would be completely wiped out by the crisis. This view is obviously mistaken. In the past decades, there have been enormous gains in income levels, heath and education. It is precisely the development strategies of export-push, FDI attraction and massive investments in physical and human capital that make these economies strong enough to withstand such an unanticipated shock without total collapsing.

No one was able to predict a deep crisis in Asia before it happened. Equally surprisingly, no one was able to predict a quick recovery. Many observers suggested that it might take many years for the crisis economies to move from negative to positive growth. The latest statistics, however, show that none of the crisis economies suffered more than six consecutive quarters of negative growth. Figure 4.5 (derived from Table 4.12) shows that the quarterly GDP growth rates of the

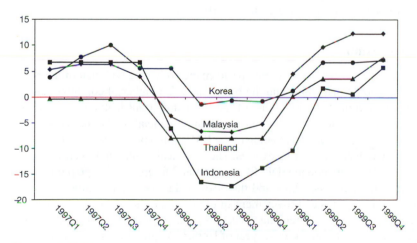

*Figure 4.5* GDP growth rates of crisis economies in Asia, 1997–9.

Source: Table 4.12.

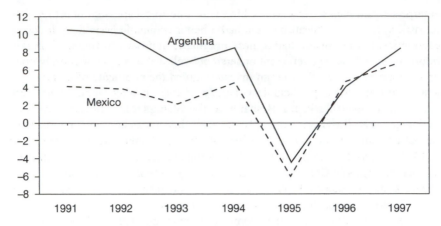

*Figure 4.6* Real GDP growth rates, Argentina and Mexico, 1991–7.

Source: Radelet and Sachs, 1998: Figure 1.

worst hit economies, Indonesia, Thailand, Malaysia and Korea, exhibit a clear V-shape pattern, which is not dissimilar to that experienced by Mexico and Argentina in their crisis years of 1994–6 (Figure 4.6).

In most economies, GDP growth slowed down from the first quarter to the last quarter in 1997. It then plunged into real contraction throughout 1998 (except China and Taiwan, and Singapore in the first quarter), but recovered into the positive territory from the first quarter of 1999 in Thailand and Korea, and from the second quarter of 1999 in all the other crisis economies. By the end of 1999 and early 2000, the recovery trend appeared unstoppable. In the last quarter of 1999, GDP grew 12.3 per cent in Korea, 10.6 per cent in Malaysia, 6.8 per cent in Thailand and 5.8 per cent in Indonesia (Table 4.12). Singapore, Taiwan and China also achieved significant GDP growth.

## 4.5 Conclusion

This chapter compares the economic performance of China with that of the NIEs. There is no doubt that China and the NIEs shared a number of common features in their development strategy. One of the most important features is openness, including the attraction of FDI, export-push and financial market reforms. In the Chinese case, the gradual devaluation of the RMB was a prerequisite for its success in attracting FDI and promoting exports. The empirical results show a clear circular positive relationship among GDP, FDI, export and foreign exchange policy.

Apart from openness, China and the NIEs had some other common features, particularly in savings and investment in physical and human capital. All these economies have achieved tremendous economic and social progress over the past three decades. Apart from the crisis year of 1998, GDP growth has been persistently higher than the world average, people have become far more educated, life expectancy is much higher, infant and child mortality has become much lower. It is precisely this economic and social progress that makes China and the NIEs capable of recovering quickly from the unexpected and devastating crisis of 1997–8.

Of course, China and the NIEs have a number of fundamental economic problems, particularly in the financial markets. Corruption, crony capital, financial repression, and the like, were the main causes for economic instability and periodic depressions. In the NIEs, their efforts to open up the financial market for foreign investors without an effective monitoring and control mechanism on the flows of short-term capital was one major factor responsible for the recent economic crisis. China's pragmatism and gradualism proved to be highly successful in guarding against a similar disaster.

Although China has been successful in terms of economic growth, it has a number of notable weaknesses, including the inefficiency and loss-making of state-owned industries, the debt-ridden financial institutions, corruption and crony capital, uneven regional development, environmental degradation and rising income inequality. These problems may greatly undermine its ability to maintain high economic growth and to avoid any deep economic recession, but the experiences and lessons learned from the crisis economies are useful for its future economic development. One such lesson is that the timing and scale of financial reforms need to be carefully designed. China has joined the World Trade Organisation (WTO), hence it will become more open than before. The real challenges will come from the most vulnerable sectors of the economy: banking, insurance, capital and technological intensive manufacturing, and agriculture. Once China has to open all these sectors for international competition, there is the potential danger that it may not be able to cope with the cyclical shocks that are typical of international capitalism. Some sectors may be so unprofitable that a large number of firms have to be closed down, with thousands of people being made redundant. The stock markets and the financial sectors may have to withstand huge short-term capital flight and international speculation, as it was the case in the NIEs during the 1997–8 crisis.

However, China has to be prepared for such challenges. The main conclusion drawn here is that openness can promote economic growth, but openness may also bear some unforeseen risks. Hence, it is useful to stress the timing, scale and sequencing of reform in the financial and stock markets. China was successful in the past because of gradualism, but this also implies that it still has a long way to go to become a truly open economy which can engage in full-scale competition with the industrialised economies.

# 5 Decomposition of Gini coefficients by population class and income source

## A spreadsheet approach and application

## 5.1 Introduction

A Gini coefficient can be decomposed in two different ways. First, if the total population is divided into a few classes (by sex, by occupation, by region, etc.), the Gini coefficient for the entire population can be decomposed into three components: (a) intra-class component arising from income variations within each of all classes; (b) inter-class component arising from the differentials of mean incomes between classes; and (c) overlapped component arising from the fact that poor people in a high-income class may be worse off than rich people in a low-income one. Second, if per capita income can be divided into several sources for the total population (e.g. wages and non-wage incomes), the Gini coefficient can be decomposed by income source.

In the literature, there are numerous formulae for calculating the Gini coefficient and many methodologies for decomposition. Needless to say, different formulae and methodologies have their own advantages and limitations. One common feature of previous studies is that they use rather cumbersome techniques such as matrix algebra or covariances as their starting point for deriving the Gini. One of the most authoritative studies in matrix algebra is by Pyatt (1976), who uses game theory to derive the Gini coefficient and its decomposition into class components. Pyatt's method is too complicated and rather impractical in empirical analyses. Later studies on decomposition by class (e.g. Cowell, 1980; Shorrocks, 1984) and by income source (e.g. Fei *et al.*, 1978 and 1979; Kakwani, 1980; Pyatt *et al.*, 1980; Shorrocks, 1982) also include cumbersome and/or inaccurate technical sections, as relying on the rank of individuals is neither the most appropriate technique for deriving the Gini nor is it easy to decompose it by both class and income source at the same time. More recent studies by Lerman and Yitzhaki (1984, 1985 and 1989) and Shalit (1985) allow quicker calculations of the Gini but their methods still require cumbersome regressions and do not provide simple decomposition by class. Silber's (Silber, 1989) method provides a more systematic approach for decomposition by both class and income source but he still relies on rather complicated matrix operations.

Although there are numerous formulae for the Gini, they can be classified into two major groups, one relying on matrix operations as exemplified by Pyatt (1976), and the other relying on rank and covariances as exemplified by Pyatt *et al.* (1980). Many authors would agree that matrix algebra is generally more cumbersome than the rank and covariance method. However, most authors who follow the rank and covariance technique have not questioned its critical limitation of being a biased estimator of the Gini when different observations have different frequencies. One exception is found in Lerman and Yitzhaki (1989). They point out that the co-variance formula used by Pyatt *et al.* (1980) is only suitable for individual data (in fact, it is also suitable for evenly grouped data), but a variant of the covariance formula developed by Lerman and Yitzhaki (1989) can be used for evenly grouped data (in fact, it is also suitable for unevenly grouped data). However, Lerman and Yitzhaki's 1989 formula does not provide a simple solution to the decomposition by population class as the covariance cannot be obtained through a simple ordinary least squares (OLS) regression (a detailed explanation is given in Appendix A, see p. 121).

In most empirical studies, economic analysts have to use unevenly grouped data rather than individual or evenly grouped data. For example, household survey data contains households with different sizes. Assigning a rank to each house-hold is equivalent to making an assumption that each household is regarded as one single individual. If this assumption is relaxed, the ranking and covariance formula becomes a biased estimator of the Gini. A similar and more serious problem exists when data contain large groups rather than individual households.

In short, economic analysts may have too many alternative methods to choose from, but they may not find any single one that can perform every task using every kind of data. The objective of this chapter is to present a simple and an accurate estimator of the Gini, to develop a systematic method of decomposition by popu-lation class and income source, and to demonstrate how the methodology can be conveniently applied. All the calculations will be conducted in a logically pro-grammed spreadsheet without using matrix algebra, integration, regression or covariances. The derivation and decomposition of the Gini coefficient become nothing but the sorting and re-sorting of the same spreadsheet. Because the same general formula of the Gini coefficient is used throughout, this methodology is suitable for all kinds of data (individual, evenly and unevenly grouped). Many complicated concepts regarding the Gini and its components are given an intuitive economic interpretation. A household survey data set for Sichuan, China, is used to show, step by step, how the methodology is applied in empirical analyses. The main text and the calculations are presented in the most understandable way so that both theorists and applied economists can easily follow the formulae and calculations without a strong command over mathematics and computer pro-gramming. Of course, the same procedure can be translated into sophisticated computer packages to increase computational efficiency, especially when the data sets are really large (n > 5000). All complicated mathematical proofs are provided in three self-explained appendices.

Using a household survey data for Sichuan province, China, it is shown that the methodology is easy to apply not only for grouped data but also for non-grouped household level data. Furthermore, as the sample is taken from the entire population of Sichuan province, it is possible to derive the inter-class component of the Gini coefficient that measures urban–rural income inequality. This is particularly interesting because, to my best knowledge, there have been no studies on China that analyse urban–rural income inequality this way.

## 5.2 The Gini coefficient and its decomposition by class and income source

### 5.2.1 A simple formula of the Gini coefficient

The Gini coefficient is widely used to measure income inequality between individuals (or households). It can be derived from many alternative formulae, some of which are found in Bhattacharya and Mahalanobis (1967), Rao (1969), Gastwirth (1972), Pyatt (1976), Mookherjee and Shorrocks (1982), Fei *et al.* (1978 and 1979), and Pyatt *et al.* (1980). Most authors arrive at their formulae by calculating the area between the Lorenz curve and the diagonal line of a unit square as shown in Figure 5.1. Only Pyatt introduces the concept of game theory by defining the Gini coefficient as the ratio of the expected gain of a randomly selected individual in the population to the average income of that population (Pyatt, 1976: equation 1). The novelty of Pyatt's formula is that it can be exactly decomposed into three separable components if the population is divided into classes (for more discussion, see Yao and Liu, 1996; and Appendix B, p. 123). Pyatt *et al.* (1980) define the Gini coefficient as a function of the covariance between per capita income and its rank (see Appendix A).

One advantage of the covariance method is that the Gini coefficient can be calculated and decomposed without using matrix algebra (for more discussion see Yao, 1997a). However, it is still a rather cumbersome technique as it involves many rankings, re-rankings of observations and the calculations of many covariances when it is used for decomposition. In addition, the covariance cannot be obtained through a simple OLS regression (Appendix A) when grouped data are analysed. The formula presented below will bypass the use of regression, covariance, ranking and matrix algebra altogether.

If the total population is divided into n income groups (a group can contain just one person, or one household, or many people, or many households), let $w_i$, $m_i$ and $p_i$ represent respectively the income share, per capita mean income and relative population frequency of the $i$-th group ($i = 1, 2, \ldots n$), the Gini coefficient of the whole population can be defined by equation (5.1) which is based on the principle illustrated in Figure 5.1 to calculate the area of 2A (a complete mathematical proof is provided in Appendix A for equation 5.1).

$$G = 1 - 2\sum_{i=1}^{n} B_i = 1 - \sum_{i=1}^{n} p_i(2Q_i - w_i) \tag{5.1}$$

$$Q_i = \sum_{k=1}^{i} w_k, \text{ is cumulative income share up to } i.$$

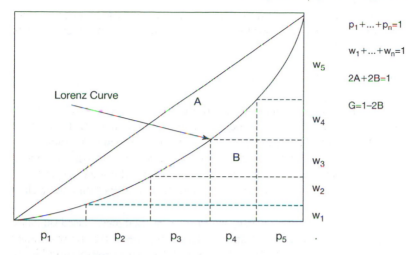

*Figure 5.1* Lorenz curve and Gini coefficient in a unit square.

The sums of $p_i$ and $w_i$ from 1 to $n$ are all equal to unity. Before equation (5.1) is used, $p_i$ and $w_i$ must be so arranged that they strictly follow the ascending order of per capita incomes $(m_i)$.[1]

Equation (5.1) has a number of advantages over other formulae to derive Gini coefficients. First, it can be easily laid out in a spreadsheet as shown in the next section. Second, it can be used to calculate the inter-group, or the inter-class component of the Gini coefficient. Third, it can be easily decomposed into its respective components by population class and income source as discussed below. Thanks to these advantages, it is possible to derive and decompose the Gini coefficient through constructing a logically structured spreadsheet by sorting and re-sorting it according to a specified column containing average per capita incomes (see the examples in section 5.3).

### 5.2.2 Decomposition of the Gini coefficient by population class

A Gini coefficient can be decomposed into three components if the population is divided into a finite number of classes. For example, the population of Sichuan can be divided into the rural and urban sub-populations. Of course, a population can be divided into as many classes as possible by any other social or economic criteria. Each sub-population can also be divided into a number of smaller population classes. As a result, the Gini coefficient can be decomposed more than once if the whole population is divided into classes more than once. As we use data from a household survey in Sichuan, the classification of population is first made by a rural–urban division. The rural and urban sub-populations are then classified by region. As a result, the Gini coefficient is decomposed twice (two tier decomposition). The decomposition is, however, based on exactly the same formula and principle. If one understands the first tier decomposition, one should be able to do the second tier decomposition.

Let $G$ denote the Gini coefficient for the entire population under concern, it can be decomposed into three components: intra-class, inter-class and overlapped as shown in equation (5.2),

$$G = G_A + G_B + G_O \tag{5.2}$$

$G_A$ is the intra-class component of $G$. If there is no income inequality within each of all the classes, $G_A = 0$. $G_B$ is the inter-class component of $G$. If the mean incomes of all classes are identical, $G_B = 0$. $G_O$ is the overlapped component of $G$. If the richest person in any low income class I is not better off than the poorest person in any high income class J, $G_O = 0$. The relative contribution of $G_B$ to $G$ has important implications on inter-class income inequality. If $G_B$ is small, inter-class inequality is small, or vice versa.

Equation (5.2) is due to Pyatt (1976) who uses matrix algebra based on game theory to derive the Gini coefficient and its class components (for more detailed discussion, see Yao and Liu, 1996). The methodology used by Pyatt is highly complicated but it proves that $G$ can be exactly decomposed. After simplifying Pyatt's matrices, I have proved that Pyatt's matrices can be translated into simple equations that are easily apprehended. Equation (5.1) and the following equations are based on my mathematical and computational proofs. Because the principal objective is to present a methodology that can be easily understood and conveniently applied in empirical studies, complicated matrix algebra and mathematical proofs are avoided in the main text but presented in Appendix B.

For convenience, the decomposition procedure to derive the four elements in equation (5.2) is described by the following four steps.

*Step 1*   Use equation (1) to derive $G$.

*Step 2*   $G_B$ can be derived from equation (5.3) which looks similar to equation (5.1).

$$G_B = 1 - 2\sum_{I=1}^{S} B_I = 1 - \sum_{I=1}^{S} P_I (2Q_I - w_I)$$

$$Q_I = \sum_{K=1}^{I} w_K, \text{ is cumulative income share up to } I. \tag{5.3}$$

$S$ denotes the number of population classes, $p_I$ and $w_I$ the population and income share of the $I$-th class ($I = 1, 2, \ldots S$) in the population. The explanation for equation (5.3) is akin to that for equation (5.1). The only difference is the definitions of $p_I$ and $w_I$. To derive $G_B$, all the elements in equation (5.3) must be sorted in an ascending order of class mean incomes $m_I$, such that $m_1 \leq m_2 \leq \ldots \leq m_S$.

*Step 3* $G_A$ can be derived from equation (5.4).

$$G_A = \sum_{I=1}^{S} W_I p_I G_I \tag{5.4}$$

As defined above, $w_I$ and $p_I$ are respectively the income and population shares of class $I$ in the total population. $G_I$ is the Gini coefficient for the $I$ sub-population. There are $S$ Gini coefficients for $S$ classes. The equation for $G_I$ looks identical to equation (5.1) except that the calculation is now focused on a particular sub-population.

*Step 4* $G_O = G - G_A - G_B$.

The computation from steps 1 to 4 does not involve any matrix algebra and can be easily carried out on a spreadsheet. Thus, this decomposition method of $G$ signifies a crucial improvement on Pyatt's method (Appendix B).

It needs to be stressed that $G_O$, $G_A$ and $G_B$ are all non-negative. $G_O$ can be directly obtained from equation (5.1) if all the elements in the equation are sorted by class mean incomes (first key) in an ascending order and by household or group per capita incomes (second key) in an ascending order to obtain a concentration coefficient, denoted as $G'$ throughout this chapter. The difference between $G$ and $G'$ is equal to $G_O$. If the value of $G_O$ is obtained this way, step 2 or step 3 can be avoided to save computation time. The fact that $G_O$ can be derived in two different ways provides an effective checking mechanism in our decomposition method. If the two estimated values of $G_O$ are different, it is a signal that some mistakes have been made in the computation process.

The concept of concentration coefficients (some authors call them pseudo-Gini), and further explanation as to why $G_O$ can be obtained this way are provided after Lemma 1 in the next sub-section.[2] Here it is necessary to emphasise that in the sorting process to obtain $G'$, the first key of sorting must be based on a strict ascending order of class mean incomes so that the class with the lowest mean income is the first group and that with the highest mean income the last group. The second key of sorting must strictly follow an ascending order of per capita incomes so that the poorest household is placed in the first position and the richest household in the last position within each of all classes. If the first key of sorting does not follow the ascending order of class mean incomes, the value of $G'$ will be underestimated, and it may even become negative (see Lemma 1 below). In this case, the difference between $G$ and the biased estimate of $G'$ is not equal to $G_O$.

### 5.2.3 *Decomposition of Gini coefficient by income source*

If per capita income of the $i$-th household, or group, $m_i$ ($i = 1, 2, \ldots n$) is divided into $F$ number of income sources, $G$ in equation (1) can be exactly decomposed into $F$ number of components.

The decomposition method of G into source components is found in Rao (1969) for a case of non-grouped data, i.e. each individual family representing one single income group. Fei *et al.* (1978: Theorem A5) and Pyatt *et al.* (1980) developed a method of decomposition for a case of equal group size, i.e. $p_i = p_j$.

The Pyatt *et al.* (1980) decomposition method has two major limitations. First, it has to calculate many covariances: the covariance between the mean total incomes ($m_i$s) and their rank, the covariances of mean source incomes ($m_{fi}$s, for all $f$) and their ranks, and the covariances of mean source incomes (for all $f$) and the rank of mean total incomes (Pyatt *et al.*, 1980). Although with modern computing technology covariances are easily obtainable, the fact that for each covariance the same income data has to be re-ranked once makes the method unnecessarily complicated. Second, we have proved that their method cannot be applied to calculate and decompose G for unevenly grouped data although it is possible to decompose G when the population is evenly grouped (Lerman and Yitzhaki, 1989; Appendix A). These limitations, however, are easily overcome by the following procedure. One obvious attraction of this method is that it uses exactly the same formula that is used to decompose G by population class (for more detailed discussion, see Yao, 1997a). Again, there is no need to use any matrix algebra or to run any regression. Another attraction is that everything can be done in the same logically structured spreadsheet. Finally, potential biases embodied in the covariance formulae are effortlessly avoided.

Let $G_f$ be the Gini coefficient of source income $f$ ($f = 1, 2, \ldots F$), $C_f$ the concentration ratio of source $f$, $u_f$ and $u$ respectively the means of source income $f$ and total income, $w_f = u_f/u$ the share of source income $f$ in total income, then $G_f$ and $C_f$ can be defined by equation (5.5) with different ordering criteria,

$$C_f = 1 - 2\sum_{i=1}^{n} B_{fi} = 1 - \sum_{i=1}^{n} p_i(2Q_{fi} - w_{fi})$$

$$Q_{fi} = \sum_{k=1}^{i} w_{fk}, \text{ is cumulative income share of source } f \text{ up to } i. \qquad (5.5)$$

where $p_i$ is defined in equation (5.1) as the population share of the $i$-th household in total population. $w_{fi} = p_i m_{fi}/u_f$ is the income share of the $i$-th household in total source income $f$. The sum of $w_{fi}$ over all n households, or groups, is equal to unity. In equation (5.5) $p_i$s and $w_{fi}$s must be sorted according to an ascending order of per capita total incomes $m_i$s, such that $m_1 \le m_2, \ldots \le m_n$, in order to derive $C_f$. To calculate the Gini coefficients of per capita source incomes, denoted by $G_f$ for all $f$, all the elements in (5) have to be re-sorted according to an ascending order of per capita factor incomes, denoted by $m_{fi}$.

With $C_f$s, G can be decomposed into its source components in equation (5.6). To avoid complicated presentation in the main text, the mathematical proof of equation (5.6) is given in Appendix C (p. 126).

$$G = \sum_{f=1}^{F} w_f C_f \tag{5.6}$$

where $F$ is the number of factor incomes and $w_f$ the share of source $f$ in total income. In other words, the Gini coefficient that measures total income inequality is the weighted average of the concentration coefficients of all source incomes.

Intuitively, if $C_f > G$ and if total per capita income remains unchanged, an increase in the income share of source income $f$, or $w_f$, will lead to more income inequality, or vice versa. Thus, the understanding of $C_f$ is important.

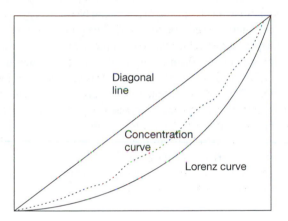

*Figure 5.2* Lorenz and concentration curves.

As mentioned earlier, both $G_f$ and $C_f$ are calculated with the same formula and elements. The only difference is the ordering principle for the elements in equation (5.5). If the ordering of $m_{fi}$ (per capita source income) is exactly the same as that of $m_i$ (per capita total income), then $C_f = G_f$. If the ordering of $m_{fi}$ is different from that of $m_i$, it is easy to prove that $C_f < G_f$. This is because an ascending order of $m_{fi}$ actually minimizes the area under the concentration (Lorenz) curve to calculate $G_f$ (area 2B in Figure 5.1). Thus, a different ordering of $w_{fi}$s and $p_i$s by any other criterion will never yield a concentration curve lying below that for $G_f$ as shown in Figure 5.2 where the solid line lying below the diagonal line is the Lorenz curve and the dotted line is the concentration curve.

If the ordering of $m_i$ is different from that of $m_{fi}$, the concentration curve to calculate $C_f$ must lie above the Lorenz curve to calculate $G_f$ (for similar discussion, also see Fei *et al.*, 1978: Appendix). Therefore, $C_f < G_f$ if the ordering of $m_i$ is different from that of $m_{fi}$. In short, the relationship between $G_f$ and $C_f$ can be described by Lemma 1 below.

*Lemma 1*

$C_f$ can be negative as well as positive but $G_f$ (and $G$) is always non-negative. In the extreme case when the ordering of $m_{fi}$ is totally opposite to that of $m_i$ (the highest $m_i$ corresponds to the lowest $m_{fi}$, etc.), then $C_f = -G_f$. Thus, $C_f$ and $G_f$ have the following relationship:

$$-G_f \leq C_f \leq G_f \tag{5.7}$$

In sub-section 5.2.2, it is mentioned that $G_O$ can be defined as the difference between $G$ and a concentration coefficient, denoted by $G'$, that is derived from resorting all the elements in equation (5.1) by population class (first key) and by per capita incomes $m_i$ (second key) in an ascending order. It can be logically proven if we remember that $G_O$ is a non-negative component of $G$. The condition for non-negativity is easily satisfied. By definition, if the richest people in any income class are not better off than the poorest people in the next higher income class (measured by class mean incomes), the value of $G_O$ is equal to zero. In this case, it is obvious that $G = G'$. On the other hand, if the richest people in some classes are better off than the poorest people in their next higher income classes, $G_O > 0$ and $G > G'$. Finally, re-sorting the elements in equation (5.1) by class in an ascending order of class mean incomes and then by household in an ascending order of per capita incomes effectively excludes the overlapping effect on $G$, the resulting $G'$ must also be non-negative. Hence, $G_O = G - G' \geq 0$. This overlapping effect is reflected by the area between the concentration and the Lorenz curves as shown in Figure 5.2.

## 5.3  An application for Sichuan province in China

### 5.3.1  *Data and the purpose of application*

The principal objective of this section is to show how our methodology works in an empirical analysis. As a result, we only use a household survey data set in 1990 for Sichuan province in China, instead of having a complete case study on income inequality for the whole country. However, as Sichuan is the largest province with a total population of 111.04 million, which is almost 10 per cent of the national population of 1,185.52 million in the sample year, the analysis of income inequality in Sichuan itself will provide an important insight into income inequality in the country.

The most important aspects of income distribution in China include urban–rural inequality and regional inequality. Most previous studies on China (e.g. Griffin and Zhao, 1993; Knight and Song, 1993b; Hussain *et al.*, 1994; Yao, 1997a, 1997b), however, either focus on the urban sector or on the rural population in separation. This is partly because the rural and urban sub-populations are two rather heterogenous classes of people in terms of incomes or partly because the methodology of Gini coefficient decomposition is not well understood by some applied analysts.

However, in order to demonstrate how the Gini coefficient is decomposed to reflect income inequality in different sectors and different groups of the population, this section first merges all the urban and rural households together to derive a Gini coefficient for the entire population. It then decomposes the coefficient into three components: between urban–rural, intra urban–rural, and the overlapped. The Gini coefficients respectively for the urban and rural sectors are then decomposed further. For the Gini coefficient of the urban population, it is decomposed into three components: between regions of the urban population, intra-regional of the urban population, and the overlapped. For the Gini coefficient of the rural population, it is decomposed in the same way into three components. The entire decomposition process is illustrated in Figure 5.3.

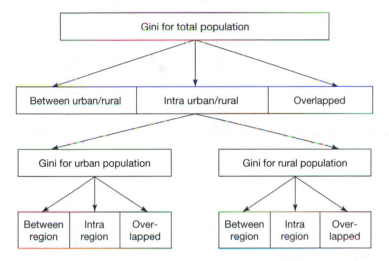

*Figure 5.3* Two-tier decomposition process of Gini coefficients.

As the urban and rural households have different sources of income, the decomposition of Gini coefficients by income source has to be carried out separately for both the Gini coefficient of the urban population and that of the rural population. The data is collected using the stratified simple random sampling technique in order to make the sample as representative as possible for the general situation without significant biases. The household survey was conducted by the National Bureau of Statistics (NBS) via its vast national survey network. The rural data were collected by the NBS rural investigation team and the urban data by the urban investigation team. The household surveys are conducted every year for every province of the country. The income data used in this chapter are calculated as the net incomes per capita for the rural households and disposable incomes per capita for the urban households. Per capita net income of the rural households includes net farm production income and non-farm employment income, which in turn, includes employment income in the state-owned or rural township enterprises and remittances sent by family members or relatives living in distant areas. The per capita income of urban households includes basic wages and non-wage income. The latter includes bonus, income transfers or any other non-wage incomes.

For demonstration purpose, we use the data for Sichuan in 1990 (NBS, 1990).[3] In total 6,624 households (or 27,453 people) were surveyed (Table 5.1). The average household size was 4.4 people in the rural areas and 3.2 people in the urban sector. Per capita income was 1,424 yuan for the urban population compared to just 559 yuan for the rural population. Per capita incomes were calculated on a per

*Table 5.1* Average per capita income by region (yuan/p.a.) in 1990

| Region ID | Region names | Number of households | Population (heads) | Household size | Per capita income |
|-----------|--------------|----------------------|--------------------|----------------|-------------------|
| *I Rural Sichuan* | | | | | |
| 1 | Jintong | 480 | 2048 | 4.3 | 726 |
| 2 | Shuangliu | 598 | 2461 | 4.1 | 668 |
| 3 | Shanglin | 120 | 532 | 4.4 | 515 |
| 4 | Dayu | 80 | 398 | 5.0 | 698 |
| 5 | Qilai | 100 | 387 | 3.9 | 447 |
| 6 | Nantong | 80 | 304 | 3.8 | 874 |
| 22 | Fengdu | 540 | 2249 | 4.2 | 446 |
| 23 | Wulong | 399 | 1772 | 4.4 | 437 |
| 24 | Xiyang | 519 | 2184 | 4.2 | 552 |
| 25 | Ziyang | 300 | 1389 | 4.6 | 449 |
| 26 | Jiangyang | 320 | 1362 | 4.3 | 622 |
| 28 | Rengqiu | 600 | 2555 | 4.3 | 548 |
| 29 | Lezhi | 420 | 1780 | 4.2 | 527 |
| 30 | Yibin | 420 | 1899 | 4.5 | 516 |
| 31 | Guliu | 80 | 368 | 4.6 | 646 |
| 32 | Jiangan | 80 | 423 | 5.3 | 714 |
| 33 | Leshan | 80 | 486 | 6.1 | 588 |
| 34 | Renshuo | 160 | 810 | 5.1 | 463 |
| Rural Sichuan | | 5376 | 23407 | 4.4 | 559 |
| *II Urban Sichuan* | | | | | |
| 1 | Chendu | 156 | 498 | 3.2 | 1782 |
| 2 | Congqing | 234 | 732 | 3.1 | 1548 |
| 3 | Zigong | 78 | 270 | 3.5 | 1551 |
| 4 | Nancong | 78 | 253 | 3.2 | 1469 |
| 5 | Wanxian | 78 | 265 | 3.4 | 1233 |
| 6 | Wenjiang | 78 | 252 | 3.2 | 1374 |
| 7 | Zijiang | 78 | 252 | 3.2 | 1246 |
| 9 | Ermei | 78 | 251 | 3.2 | 1302 |
| 10 | Hanyang | 78 | 245 | 3.1 | 1286 |
| 11 | Xuyong | 78 | 262 | 3.4 | 1059 |
| 12 | Luzhou | 78 | 247 | 3.2 | 1406 |
| 13 | Leshan | 78 | 243 | 3.1 | 1417 |
| 14 | Guangyang | 78 | 276 | 3.5 | 1279 |
| Urban Sichuan | | 1248 | 4046 | 3.2 | 1424 |
| *III All Sichuan* | | 6624 | 27453 | 4.1 | 687 |

Source: NBS, 1990 household surveys.

head basis irrespective of age and sex. This is done so because most Chinese households have similar family structures: two adults and two children in the rural areas, and two adults with one child in the cities. There are some exceptions, of course. For example, some families may not have any children at all and others may have three generations (or even four generations) registered as one single household. However, it is assumed that the household structure factor will not affect our basic conclusion on income distribution.

### 5.3.2 Decomposition of Gini coefficients by population class

By merging all the rural and urban households together and by sorting the data set in an ascending order of per capita income, the Gini coefficient for the whole population can be derived by use of equation (5.1). The spreadsheet layout is demonstrated in Table 5.2 which includes only the first five (the poorest) and the last five (the richest) households of the entire sample of 2,940 households.

Once the sample is separated into two groups, rural and urban, the Gini coefficients of the two groups are calculated in a similar way to Table 5.2. These latter coefficients are used to calculate the intra-group component $G_A$ by use of equation (5.4). The between group component, $G_B$, is obtained by use of equation (5.3). The calculations of $G_A$ and $G_B$ are illustrated and explained in Table 5.3.

*Table 5.2* Gini coefficient for the whole population

| RID (1) | $n_i$ (2) | $p_i$ (3) | $m_i$ (4) | $p_i m_i$ (5) | $w_i$ (6) | $Q_i$ (7) | $p_i(2Q_i - w_i)$ (8) |
|---|---|---|---|---|---|---|---|
| rural | 4 | 1.5E–04 | 51.8 | 8E–03 | 1E–05 | 1.10e–05 | 1.60e–09 |
| rural | 5 | 1.8E–04 | 61.2 | 1E–02 | 2E–05 | 2.72e–05 | 6.96e–09 |
| rural | 3 | 1.1E–04 | 97.7 | 1E–02 | 2E–05 | 4.27e–05 | 7.64e–09 |
| rural | 4 | 1.5E–04 | 111.0 | 2E–02 | 2E–05 | 6.63e–05 | 1.59e–08 |
| rural | 5 | 1.8E–04 | 111.2 | 2E–02 | 3E–05 | 9.58e–05 | 2.95e–08 |
| ...... | | | | ...... | | ...... | |
| | | | There are 6614 other households omitted from this table | | | | |
| ...... | | | | ...... | | ...... | |
| rural | 2 | 7.3E–05 | 3547 | 0.2584 | 0.0004 | 0.9978 | 0.0001 |
| Urban | 2 | 5.7E–05 | 3553 | 0.2019 | 0.0003 | 0.9981 | 0.0001 |
| Urban | 3 | 1.1E–04 | 3563 | 0.4050 | 0.0006 | 0.9987 | 0.0002 |
| Urban | 4 | 1.3E–04 | 3572 | 0.4669 | 0.0007 | 0.9993 | 0.0003 |
| Urban | 3 | 1.1E–04 | 3938 | 0.4475 | 0.0007 | 1.0000 | 0.0002 |
| Total | 27452 | 1.0000 | 4283819 | 686 | 1.0000 | 2170 | 0.6918 |
| | | | | | | $G' = 0.3041$ | $G = 0.3082$ |

Notes: This table only lists the first and last 5 households for illustrative purposes. The meaning of each column is given as follows: (1) area ID; (2) household size; (3) population share of the *i*-th household in total sample, the sum is unity; (4) per capita income by household; (5) population share multiplied by per capita income, the sum is average per capita income of the population; (6) income share of the *i*-th household in gross income of the population, $w_i = p_i m_i / \Sigma p_i m_i$; (7) cumulative income share, the last number is unity; (8) the sum is equal to area 2B in Figure 5.1, the difference between unity and the sum is the Gini coefficient as shown in equation (5.1).

*Table 5.3* Intra- and between group components of Gini coefficient for the whole sample

| RID (1) | $n_I$ (2) | $p_I$ (3) | $m_I$ (4) | $p_I m_I$ (4) | $w_I$ (5) | $Q_I$ (6) | $P_I(2Q_I - w_I)$ (7) | $G_I$ (8) | $p_I w_I G_I$ (9) | (10) |
|---|---|---|---|---|---|---|---|---|---|---|
| Rural | 23407 | 0.853 | 559 | 477 | 0.694 | 0.694 | 0.592 | 0.232 | 0.137 | |
| Urban | 4046 | 0.147 | 1424 | 210 | 0.306 | 1.000 | 0.250 | 0.196 | 0.009 | |
| Sum | 27453 | 1.000 | 1983 | 686 | 1.000 | 1.694 | 0.842 | $G_A = 0.146$ | | |
| | | | | | | | | $G_B = 0.158$ | $G = 0.308$ | |
| | | | | | | | | $G_O = 0.004$ | $G' = 0.304$ | |

Notes: The meaning of each column is given as follows: (1) area ID; (2) rural/urban population; (3) population shares, the sum is unity; (4) group average per capita income; (5) population share multiplied by per capita income, the sum is average per capita income of the population; (6) income shares, $w_I = p_I m_I / \Sigma p_I m_I$. (7) cumulative income share, the last number is unity; (8) the sum is equal to area 2B in Figure 5.1, the difference between unity and the sum is the between-group component of the Gini coefficient in Table 5.2 based on equation (5.3), or $G_B = 0.158$; (9) the rural and urban Gini coefficients are calculated in a similar way as shown in Table 5.2; (10) the sum is the intra-group component of the Gini coefficient in Table 5.2 based on equation (5.4), or $G_A = 0.146$. Finally, $G_O = G - G_A - G_B = G - G'$. $G$, $G$ and $G'$ are all obtained from Table 5.2.

Re-sorting all the observations in Table 5.2 first by class in an ascending order of class mean incomes (so that rural is the first class and urban the second) and then by household in an ascending order of per capita incomes, $G'$ is obtained. The difference between $G$ and $G'$ is the overlapped term $G_O$, or 0.004. For checking purpose, the difference between $G$ and the sum of $G_B$ and $G_A$ must be identical to the difference between $G$ and $G'$.

In the second tier of decomposition, the corresponding Gini coefficients respectively for the rural and urban populations are decomposed into their own components: inter-regional, intra-regional and the overlapped. The calculations of these two Gini coefficients are similar to the principle demonstrated in Table 5.2. The calculations of the inter-regional, intra-regional, $G'$, and the overlapped term for the rural population are provided and explained in Table 5.4. Deriving the same components for the urban Gini coefficient is similar and hence not presented.

The two tier decomposition results by rural–urban division and by region for the rural and urban populations are summarised in Table 5.5.

### 5.3.3 Decomposition of rural–urban Gini coefficients by income source

As the rural and urban sectors do not have the same income sources, it is not possible to decompose the Gini coefficient for the whole population by income source. Instead, the Gini coefficients for both the rural and urban populations are decomposed by their respective sources of income. In the rural sector, total per capita income consists of farm production net income and non-farm income. In the urban sector, per capita income consists of time wages, non-time wages, non-wage income, and tax and transfers.

The principle of decomposition by income source is illustrated in Table 5.6 for the rural Gini coefficient. The decomposition of the urban Gini coefficient is similar

Table 5.4 Intra- and between group components of Gini coefficient for the rural sample

| RID (1) | $n_I$ (2) | $p_I$ (3) | $m_I$ (4) | $p_I m_I$ (5) | $w_I$ (6) | $Q_I$ (7) | $p_I(2Q_I - w_I)$ (8) | $G_I$ (9) | $p_I w_I G_I$ (10) |
|---|---|---|---|---|---|---|---|---|---|
| Wulong | 1772 | 0.0757 | 437 | 33.1 | 0.0591 | 0.0591 | 0.0045 | 0.2349 | 0.0011 |
| Fengdu | 2249 | 0.0961 | 446 | 42.9 | 0.0766 | 0.1357 | 0.0187 | 0.2050 | 0.0015 |
| Qilai | 387 | 0.0165 | 447 | 7.4 | 0.0132 | 0.1490 | 0.0047 | 0.1481 | 0.0000 |
| Ziyang | 1389 | 0.0593 | 449 | 26.6 | 0.0476 | 0.1966 | 0.0205 | 0.1983 | 0.0006 |
| Renshuo | 810 | 0.0346 | 463 | 16.0 | 0.0286 | 0.2252 | 0.0146 | 0.2147 | 0.0002 |
| Shanglin | 532 | 0.0227 | 515 | 11.7 | 0.0209 | 0.2462 | 0.0107 | 0.1827 | 0.0001 |
| Yibin | 1899 | 0.0811 | 516 | 41.9 | 0.0748 | 0.3210 | 0.0460 | 0.1999 | 0.0012 |
| Lezhi | 1780 | 0.0760 | 527 | 40.1 | 0.0716 | 0.3926 | 0.0543 | 0.1940 | 0.0011 |
| Rengqiu | 2555 | 0.1092 | 548 | 59.8 | 0.1069 | 0.4996 | 0.0974 | 0.2081 | 0.0024 |
| Xiyang | 2184 | 0.0933 | 552 | 51.5 | 0.0921 | 0.5916 | 0.1018 | 0.2258 | 0.0019 |
| Leshan | 486 | 0.0208 | 588 | 12.2 | 0.0218 | 0.6135 | 0.0250 | 0.2278 | 0.0001 |
| Jiangyan | 1362 | 0.0582 | 622 | 36.2 | 0.0647 | 0.6782 | 0.0752 | 0.2313 | 0.0009 |
| Guliu | 368 | 0.0157 | 646 | 10.2 | 0.0182 | 0.6963 | 0.0216 | 0.2227 | 0.0001 |
| Shuangli | 2461 | 0.1051 | 668 | 70.2 | 0.1256 | 0.8219 | 0.1596 | 0.1936 | 0.0026 |
| Dayu | 398 | 0.0170 | 698 | 11.9 | 0.0212 | 0.8431 | 0.0283 | 0.2401 | 0.0001 |
| Jiangan | 423 | 0.0181 | 714 | 12.9 | 0.0231 | 0.8662 | 0.0309 | 0.2457 | 0.0001 |
| Jintong | 2048 | 0.0875 | 726 | 63.5 | 0.1136 | 0.9797 | 0.1615 | 0.2209 | 0.0022 |
| Nantong | 304 | 0.0130 | 874 | 11.4 | 0.0203 | 1.0000 | 0.0257 | 0.1715 | 0.0000 |
| Rural Sichuan | 23407 | 1.0000 | 10436 | 559.0 | 1.0000 | 9.3154 | 0.9010 | $G_A=0.0161$ | $G_A=0.2320$ |

$$G_B = 0.0990$$
$$G_O = 0.1169$$

Notes: RID = regional ID. The meaning of each column is given as follows: (1) regional ID; (2) regional population; (3) population shares, the sum is unity; (4) regional average per capita incomes; (5) population share multiplied by per capita income, the sum is average per capita income of the rural population; (6) income shares, $w_I = p_I m_I / \sum p_I m_I$; (7) cumulative income share, the last number is unity; (8) the sum is equal to area 2B in Figure 5.1, the difference between unity and the sum is the inter-regional component of the Gini coefficient based on equation (5.3), or $G_B$ =0.099; (9) the regional Gini coefficients are calculated in a similar way as shown in Table 5.2; (10) the sum is the intra-regional component of the rural Gini coefficient based on equation (5.4), or $G_A$ =0.0161.

*Table 5.5* Summary results of two-tier decomposition

|  | Components of Gini coefficients | | | | Shares in % | | | |
|---|---|---|---|---|---|---|---|---|
|  | $G$ | $G_A$ | $G_B$ | $G_O$ | $G$ | $G_A$ | $G_B$ | $G_O$ |
| All Sichuan | 0.308 | 0.146 | 0.158 | 0.004 | 100.0 | 47.4 | 51.3 | 1.3 |
| Rural Sichuan | 0.232 | 0.016 | 0.099 | 0.117 | 100.0 | 6.9 | 42.7 | 50.4 |
| Urban Sichuan | 0.196 | 0.017 | 0.074 | 0.105 | 100.0 | 8.7 | 37.8 | 53.6 |

Notes: In the first tier decomposition, $G$, $G_A$, $G_B$, and $G_O$ respectively refer to the Gini coefficient for the whole population and its inter-rural/urban, intra-rural/urban and the overlapped components. In the second-tier decomposition, they respectively refer to the Gini coefficient for the rural (or urban) population and its inter-regional, intra-regional and overlapped components.

and hence not presented. The structure of Table 5.6 is similar to that of Table 5.2 except that the former has three income columns, instead of one, i.e. per capita total income, per capita farm production income and per capita non-farm income. The summary results are recorded in the matrix boxed at the right-hand bottom of the table. The first row of the matrix records the rural Gini coefficient (0.232) and its associated concentration ratios for the two source incomes, farm production (0.198) and non-farm (0.463). These three parameters are obtained by use of equations (5.1) and (5.5) when the elements in the table are sorted in an ascending order of per capita total incomes in column (4). With the two concentration ratios and the shares of source incomes in total income, the Gini coefficient can be decomposed into its source components by use of equation (5.6). We then can decide which source income contributes more proportionally than its share in total income towards income inequality (the Gini coefficient). Just for complete information, if all the elements in Table 5.6 is sorted in an ascending order of per capita farm production incomes in column (5), the Gini coefficient of farm production income is obtained as shown in the central element of the boxed matrix (0.233). The explanation refers to equation (5.5). Similarly, if all the elements are sorted in an ascending order of non-farm incomes in column (6), the Gini coefficient of non-farm income is obtained (0.74). It needs to be stressed that the Gini coefficients of the source incomes need not be used when the Gini coefficient of per capita total income is decomposed.

Table 5.7 presents the summary results of the decomposition of both the rural and urban Gini coefficients. In rural Sichuan, traditional income (farm income) was still a predominant source of total income. In the urban sector, traditional income (wage income) was less important. One important finding of the results is that traditional incomes (farm income and wages) are more equally distributed than non-traditional incomes (non-farm and non-wage incomes). As a result, non-farm income accounts for 12.7 per cent of total income but contributes 25.3 per cent of the rural Gini coefficient. In the urban sector, non-wage income accounts for 64.5 per cent of total income but contributes 70.2 per cent of the Gini coefficient. Finally, it is interesting to note that non-time wages, taxation and income transfers all helped reduce income inequality as they contributed negatively to the overall Gini coefficient for the urban population.

*Table 5.6* Decomposition of the rural Gini coefficient by income source

| HID (1) | $n_j$ (2) | $p_j$ (3) | $m_{ti}$ (4) | $m_{ai}$ (5) | $m_{ni}$ (6) | $p_i m_{ti}$ (7) | $p_i m_{ai}$ (8) | $p_i m_{ni}$ (9) | $w_{ti}$ (10) | $w_{ai}$ (11) | $w_{ni}$ (12) | $Q_{ti}$ (13) | $Q_{ai}$ (14) | $Q_{ni}$ (15) | $p_i(2Q_{ti}-w_{ti})$ (16) | $p_i(2Q_{ai}-w_{ai})$ (17) | $p_i(2Q_{ni}-w_{ni})$ (18) |
|---|---|---|---|---|---|---|---|---|---|---|---|---|---|---|---|---|---|
| 2656 | 4 | 2E–04 | 52 | 43 | 9 | 9E–03 | 7E–03 | 1E–03 | 2E–05 | 2E–05 | 2E–05 | 2E–05 | 2E–05 | 2E–05 | 3E–09 | 3E–09 | 4E–09 |
| 2262 | 5 | 2E–04 | 61 | 56 | 5 | 1E–02 | 1E–02 | 1E–03 | 2E–05 | 2E–05 | 1E–05 | 4E–05 | 4E–05 | 4E–05 | 1E–08 | 1E–08 | 1E–08 |
| 2362 | 3 | 1E–04 | 98 | 88 | 9 | 1E–02 | 1E–02 | 1E–03 | 2E–05 | 2E–05 | 2E–05 | 6E–05 | 6E–05 | 5E–05 | 1E–08 | 1E–08 | 1E–08 |
| 2265 | 4 | 2E–04 | 111 | 105 | 6 | 2E–02 | 2E–02 | 1E–03 | 3E–05 | 4E–05 | 1E–05 | 1E–04 | 1E–04 | 7E–05 | 3E–08 | 3E–08 | 2E–08 |
| 1678 | 5 | 2E–04 | 111 | 102 | 9 | 2E–02 | 2E–02 | 2E–03 | 4E–05 | 4E–05 | 3E–05 | 1E–04 | 1E–04 | 9E–05 | 5E–08 | 5E–08 | 3E–08 |

There are 5,379 households but only the first five (poorest) and the last five (richest) are listed in this table. The rest are omitted.

| HID (1) | $n_j$ (2) | $p_j$ (3) | $m_{ti}$ (4) | $m_{ai}$ (5) | $m_{ni}$ (6) | $p_i m_{ti}$ (7) | $p_i m_{ai}$ (8) | $p_i m_{ni}$ (9) | $w_{ti}$ (10) | $w_{ai}$ (11) | $w_{ni}$ (12) | $Q_{ti}$ (13) | $Q_{ai}$ (14) | $Q_{ni}$ (15) | $p_i(2Q_{ti}-w_{ti})$ (16) | $p_i(2Q_{ai}-w_{ai})$ (17) | $p_i(2Q_{ni}-w_{ni})$ (18) |
|---|---|---|---|---|---|---|---|---|---|---|---|---|---|---|---|---|---|
| 5097 | 2 | 9E–05 | 2361 | 594 | 1768 | 0.202 | 0.051 | 0.151 | 0.0004 | 0.0001 | 0.0021 | 0.998 | 0.998 | 0.993 | 0.0002 | 0.0002 | 0.0002 |
| 235 | 4 | 2E–04 | 2390 | 2373 | 17 | 0.408 | 0.405 | 0.003 | 0.0007 | 0.0008 | 0.0000 | 0.998 | 0.999 | 0.993 | 0.0003 | 0.0003 | 0.0003 |
| 542 | 3 | 1E–04 | 2494 | 2211 | 284 | 0.320 | 0.283 | 0.036 | 0.0006 | 0.0006 | 0.0005 | 0.999 | 1.000 | 0.994 | 0.0003 | 0.0003 | 0.0003 |
| 1442 | 2 | 9E–05 | 3257 | 537 | 2720 | 0.278 | 0.046 | 0.232 | 0.0005 | 0.0001 | 0.0033 | 0.999 | 1.000 | 0.997 | 0.0002 | 0.0002 | 0.0002 |
| 108 | 2 | 9E–05 | 3547 | 947 | 2600 | 0.303 | 0.081 | 0.222 | 0.0005 | 0.0002 | 0.0031 | 1.000 | 1.000 | 1.000 | 0.0002 | 0.0002 | 0.0002 |
| Total | 23407 | 1.000 | – | – | – | 559 | 488 | 71 | 1.000 | 1.000 | 1.000 | 2163 | 2254 | 1532 | 0.768 | 0.802 | 0.537 |

(a) Sorted by total per capita income

(b) Sorted by farm per capita income

(c) Sorted by non-farm per capita income

| | (a) | (b) | (c) |
|---|---|---|---|
| $C_{tf} =$ | 0.232 | 0.198 | 0.463 |
| $C_{af} =$ | – | 0.233 | – |
| $C_{nf} =$ | – | – | 0.740 |

Notes: (a) $t$, $a$ and $n$ denote respectively total, farm and non-farm. $C_{tf}$, $C_{af}$, $C_{nf}$ denote respectively the concentration (or Gini) coefficients with respect to income source $f$ ($t$, $a$, and $n$). (b) The letters $m$, $p$, $w$, and $Q$ denote respectively per capita income, population share, income share and cumulative income share. (c) The meaning of each column is explained as follows: (1) household ID, (2) household size, (3) population share of the $i$-th household in the sample population, the sum is unity, (4)–(6) per capita total income, farm production income and non-farm income, (7)–(9) population shares multiplied by per capita incomes, the sums are average per capita total, farm production and non-farm incomes of the sample population, (10)–(12) income shares of the $i$-th household in total, farm production and non-farm incomes, the sums are unity, (13)–(15) the respective cumulative shares in total, farm production and non-farm incomes, (16)–(18) the sums of these columns are used to calculate the area 2B in Figure 5.1, the differences between unity and these sums are the Gini (or concentration) coefficients which are recorded automatically as a matrix in the box located at the right-hand bottom of the table.

*Table 5.7* Decomposition results of rural–urban Gini coefficients by income source

| | Rural Gini coefficient | | | Urban Gini coefficient | | | | |
|---|---|---|---|---|---|---|---|---|
| | Total income | Farm income | Non-farm income | Total income | Time wages | Non-time wages | Non-wage income | Tax and transfer |
| $G_f$ or $C_f$ | 0.232 | 0.198 | 0.463 | 0.196 | 0.166 | −0.250 | 0.213 | 0.144 |
| $u_f$ (yuan) | 559 | 488 | 71 | 1424 | 641 | 10 | 918 | −145 |
| $w_f$ | 1.000 | 0.873 | 0.127 | 1.000 | 0.450 | 0.007 | 0.645 | −0.102 |
| $w_f C_f$ | 0.232 | 0.173 | 0.059 | 0.196 | 0.075 | −0.002 | 0.137 | −0.015 |
| Share in $G$ | 1.000 | 0.745 | 0.253 | 1.000 | 0.382 | −0.009 | 0.702 | −0.075 |

Notes: $G_f$ and $C_f$ are Gini coefficients and concentration ratios, $u_f$ = mean total and source incomes per capita; $w_f$ is the income share of source $f$ in total income.

## 5.4 Conclusion

Many mathematical economists have tried to simplify the calculation and decomposition of the Gini coefficient but as far as I know, none of them has come up with a simple and systematic procedure like the one presented in this chapter. One can always argue that with modern computers, any complicated mathematical formulae will be applicable by any one, but I still argue that the simpler, the better.

Many readers may ask why the Gini coefficient needs to be decomposed and what exactly is the meaning of $G_O$. Using the Sichuan household survey data, it is possible to understand the economic and policy implications of Gini coefficient decomposition and the economic interpretation of $G_O$.

In section 5.3, the decomposition of the Gini coefficient for the whole sample by population class is conducted twice. The first tier decomposition is to reveal the extent to which rural and urban people are divided. This is one of the most important aspects of the Chinese income distribution system. The results suggest that the overall Gini coefficient is quite high (0.308) although the Gini coefficients for the rural or the urban populations are low (0.232 and 0.196). Thus most empirical studies that focus only on the rural population or only on the urban population have greatly understated the overall income inequality in China. Another striking result is that the overlapped component ($G_O$) explains only 1.3 per cent of the Gini coefficient (Table 5.5). This means that very few rich rural households are better off than the poor urban households. In other words, there exists a clear rural–urban separation in the Chinese society as far as personal income is concerned. Although the actual welfare levels between the rural and urban households may not be as different as per capita incomes (e.g. rural households have more children and more housing space), the fact that $G_O$ is almost equal to zero is a striking result.

Contrary to the first tier decomposition, the results of the second tier decomposition suggest that although there are significant inter-regional income inequality, regional division in income distribution is not as acute as rural–urban division. The overlapped component explains 42.7 per cent of rural inequality and 37.8 per cent of urban inequality.

The decomposition of Gini coefficients by income source also has important economic and policy implications. The results in Table 5.7 suggest that after economic reform, non-traditional incomes (non-farm income in the rural areas and non-wages income in the urban sector) had made a significant contribution to per capita total income (12.7 per cent and 64.5 per cent respectively in rural and urban areas). Another finding is that non-traditional incomes were more unequally distributed than traditional incomes, explaining the negative effect of economic reform on income distribution. However, as traditional incomes (farm production and wages) are still an important source of total incomes, income inequality is low when the rural and urban populations are studied as two separate population classes. This latter point reinforces the significance of rural–urban separation in Sichuan and such a conclusion must also be true for most parts of China as well. Finally, it is worth noting that non-time wages, taxation and income transfers (remittances sent to relatives) helped reduce urban income inequality. This partially explains why urban Sichuan is still rather egalitarian after so many years of economic reforms.

## APPENDIX A

This appendix proves

$$G = 1 - \sum_{i=1}^{n} p_i (2Q_i - w_i), Q_i = \sum_{k=1}^{i} w_k \tag{A1}$$

Referring to Figure 5.1 in the main text where $p_i$, $w_i$ and $m_i$ respectively denote relative population frequency, income share and per capita mean income of group $i$ (a group may contain just one person, or one household, or many people, or many households). Although $m_i$ does not enter the formula, the arrangements of $p_i$ and $w_i$ are governed by an ascending order of $m_i$ such that $m_i < m_j$ if $i < j$ ($i, j = 1, 2, \ldots n$, $n$ is the number of groups). $Q_i$ is cumulative income share from the poorest group (first group) to the $i$-th group, or $Q_i = w_1 + w_2 + \ldots + w_i$, and $Q_n = 1$. Let $u$ be the weighted mean income for the whole population, then $w_i = p_i m_i / \sum p_i m_i = p_i m_i / u$. The area 2B in Figure 5.1 is the sum of 2 times $n$ tetrahedron areas, or

$$2B = p_1(2w_1 - w_1) + p_2(2w_1 + 2w_2 - w_2) + \ldots\ldots + p_i(2w_1 + 2w_2 + \ldots + 2w_i - w_i)$$
$$+ p_n(2w_1 + 2w_2 + \ldots + 2w_i \ldots + 2w_n - w_n)$$

$$= p_1(2\sum_{k=1}^{1} w_k - w_1) + p_2(2\sum_{k=1}^{2} w_k - w_2) + \ldots\ldots + p_n(2\sum_{k=1}^{n} w_k - w_n)$$

$$= p_1(2Q_1 - w_1) + p_2(2Q_2 - w_2) + \ldots\ldots + p_n(2Q_n - w_n), \text{ setting } Q_i = \sum_{k=1}^{i} Q_k$$

$$= \sum_{i=1}^{n} p_i (2Q_i - w_i), \text{ hence}$$

$$G = 1 - \sum_{i=1}^{n} p_i (2Q_i - w_i). \hspace{4cm} \text{q.e.d.}$$

By setting $p_i = p_j$, Pyatt *et al.*'s (1980) covariance formula can be obtained,

$$G = 2cov(m_i, r_i)/nu \qquad (A2)$$

where $r_i$ is the rank of group $i$ in an ascending order of $m_i$. This is the most popular covariance formula used in the literature (see Pyatt *et al.*, 1980; Lerman and Yitzhaki, 1984 and 1989). If $p_i = p_j$, $cov(m_i, r_i)$ is easily obtained by running an OLS regression between $m_i$ and $r_i$ to obtain $R^2$ then take the squared root and multiply the resulting correlation coefficient by the standard deviations of $m_i$ and $r_i$.

*Table A1*  Different estimates of Gini for rural Sichuan and its inter-regional component

| Equations | (A1) | (A4) | (A2) |
|---|---|---|---|
| (1)  Rural Sichuan ($n = 1,890$, $N = 8,055$, or 1,890 households and 8,055 people) | | | |
| | $G = 0.27456$ | $G = 0.27456$ | $G = 0.27368$ |
| | (0.000) | (0.000) | (−0.318) |
| (2)  Rural Sichuan inter-regional ($n = 13$, $N = 8,055$, or 13 regions and 8,055 people) | | | |
| | $G_B = 0.11984$ | $G_B = 0.11988$ | $G_B = 0.13111$ |
| | (0.000) | (0.033) | (9.403) |

Notes: The figures in parentheses are percentage errors from the true estimate of the respective Gini coefficients which are based on Pyatt's matrices (Pyatt, 1976) and identical to the results generated by (A1).

If $p_i \neq p_j$, (A2) is an incorrect estimator of the Gini. However, if $n$ is large, and the average frequency, $N/n$, is small ($N$ is total frequency), the error can be negligible (see Table A1), but $cov(m_i, r_i)$ cannot be obtained by running a simple OLS regression because it has to be generated through expression (A3).

$$cov(m_i, r_i) = \sum_{i=1}^{n} p_i(m_i - u)(r_i - \bar{r}) \qquad (A3)$$

Therefore, if $p_i \neq p_j$, using equation (A2) to derive $G$ is not only tedious, but also conditional on a large $n$ and a small $N/n$ in order to obtain a good estimate of $G$. To overcome the potential bias of equation (A2), Lerman and Yitzhaki (1989) propose the following modified covariance formula for $G$.

$$G = 2\sum_{i=1}^{n} p_i(m_i - u)(F_i - \bar{F}), F_i = \sum_{k=1}^{i} p_k - \left(\frac{p_i}{2}\right) \qquad (A4)$$

Mathematically, equation (A4) is not identical to equation (A1) but the estimated results from these two expressions are almost identical if $n$ is large and ($N/n$) is small (Table A1, part (1)). Their difference is negligible even for highly aggregated data (Table A1, part (2)). Table A1 shows different estimates of the Gini coefficient for rural Sichuan and its inter-regional component, which is effectively another Gini when the data is highly aggregated into a very small number of groups. Although (A4) is a better estimator of $G$ than (A2), it cannot be obtained through a simple OLS regression. It is also clear that the computation of (A4) is more tedious than that of (A1), especially when it is used for decomposition.

## APPENDIX B

This proves

$$G = G_A + G_B + G_O$$

This appendix uses Pyatt's game theory matrix (Pyatt, 1976) to prove that the Gini coefficient is exactly decomposed into three components when the total population is separated into a limited number of classes (population groups). It also proves that my four-step approach of decomposing the Gini coefficient in section 5.2.2 in the main text is identical to Pyatt's matrix but is much easier to apply in empirical analyses.

### B.1 The decomposition of Pyatt's matrix

Let the total population be divided into $S$ classes, $p_I$ the population share of class $I$ in total population ($I = 1, 2, \ldots S$), $m_I$ and $u$ denote respectively the mean income of class I and the mean income of total population. The Gini coefficient of the total population $G$ is defined in equation (B1).

$$G = \frac{P'EP}{u} = \frac{P'EP}{P'M}$$

$$\text{where } P' = (p_1, \ldots p_I, \ldots p_S), M = \begin{pmatrix} m_1 \\ \cdot \\ m_I \\ \cdot \\ m_S \end{pmatrix}, \sum_{I=1}^{S} p_I = 1. \tag{B1}$$

Pyatt suggests that the Gini coefficient is the ratio of the expected gain $P'EP$ to the population mean income $u = P'M$. $E$ is a squared matrix of $(S \times S)$, or

$$E = [E_{IJ}] = \begin{bmatrix} E_{11} & E_{12} & \ldots & E_{1S} \\ E_{21} & E_{22} & \ldots & E_{2S} \\ \ldots & \ldots & & \ldots \\ E_{S1} & E_{S2} & \ldots & E_{SS} \end{bmatrix} \tag{B2}$$

$E_{IJ}$ is the expected gain of a randomly selected individual moving from a lower to a higher income level within the same class when $I = J$, or the expected gain of a randomly selected individual moving from class $I$ to class $J$ when $I \neq J$.

If the population of class $I$ is divided into $S_I$ number of households, or household groups, let $p_{Ii}$ be the population share of group $i$ ($i = 1, 2, \ldots S_I$) in the population of class $I$, $m_{Ii}$ the mean income of group $i$ in class $I$. Also let $p_{Jj}$ be the population share of group $j$ ($j = 1, 2, \ldots S_J$) in the population of class $J$ which is divided into $S_J$ household groups, $m_{Jj}$ the mean income of group $j$ in class $J$ (different population classes may have different numbers of household groups).

$$E_{IJ} = \sum_{i=1}^{S_I} \sum_{j=1}^{S_J} \max \, [0,(m_{Ii}m_{Jj})] \, p_{Ii} \, p_{Jj,} \, \text{for all } I \text{ and } J, \, I, J = 1,2\ldots S. \quad (B3)$$

Then $E_{IJ}$ can be easily transformed into a $(S_I \times S_J)$ matrix. It is obvious that in order to derive $G$, one has to derive $S^2$ number of matrices. However, once it is established, matrix $E$ can be decomposed into three sub-matrices as shown in equation (B4).

$$E = E_A + E_B + E_O$$

$$E_A = \begin{bmatrix} E_{11} & & 0 \\ \ldots & E_{II} & \ldots \\ 0 & & E_{SS} \end{bmatrix}, E_B = \begin{bmatrix} & 0 & & \max\left[0,\left(E_{IJ} - E_{JI}\right)\right] \\ & & 0 & \\ \max\left[0,\left(E_{JI} - E_{IJ}\right)\right] & & 0 \end{bmatrix},$$

$$E_O = \begin{bmatrix} 0 & & \min(E_{IJ},E_{JI}) \\ & 0 & \\ \min(E_{JI},E_{IJ}) & & 0 \end{bmatrix} \quad (B4)$$

$E_B$ and $E_O$ can be simplified by Lemma B1 below:

*Lemma B1*

If matrix $E$ is derived based on an ascending order of class mean incomes so that $m_1 \leq m_2 \ldots \leq m_I \ldots \leq m_S$ (or $m_I \leq m_J$, if $I \neq J$), then the expected gain of a randomly selected individual moving from a low income class $I$ to a high income class $J$ ($E_{IJ}$) cannot be smaller than the expected gain of a randomly selected individual moving from $J$ to $I$ ($E_{JI}$), or $E_{IJ} \geq E_{JI}$. The difference between $E_{IJ}$ and $E_{JI}$ is exactly equal to the difference between the mean incomes of classes $J$ and $I$, or $E_{IJ} - E_{JI} = m_J - m_I \geq 0$.

With Lemma B1, $E_B$ and $E_O$ can be simplified as:

$$E_B = \begin{bmatrix} 0 & (E_{IJ} - E_{JI}) \\ & 0 & \\ 0 & 0 \end{bmatrix} = \begin{bmatrix} 0 & (m_J - m_I) \\ & 0 & \\ 0 & 0 \end{bmatrix}, E_O = \begin{bmatrix} 0 & E_{JI} \\ & 0 & \\ E_{JI} & 0 \end{bmatrix}$$

As matrix $E$ is now decomposed into three sub-matrices, the Gini coefficient in equation (B1) can be decomposed into three components as illustrated in equation (B5).

$$G = G_A + G_B + G_O = \frac{P'E_A P}{P'M} + \frac{P'E_B P}{P'M} + \frac{P'E_O P}{P'M} \tag{B5}$$

$G_A$ is the intra-class component of $G$. If there is no income inequality within each of all the classes, $G_A = 0$. $G_B$ is the inter-class component of $G$. If the mean incomes of all classes are identical, $G_B$ disappears. $G_O$ is the overlapped component of $G$. If the richest person in any low income class $I$ is not better off than the poorest person in any high income class $J$, $G_O$ vanishes.

## B.2 How the four-step approach matches equation (B5)

First, equation (5.1) in section 5.2.1 of the main text is equivalent to equation (B1) because both equations calculate exactly the same coefficient although they take different forms.

Second, if we recall that $E_A$ is a diagonal matrix where each element $E_{II}$ is the expected gain within population class $I$, then it is easy to know that $G_I = m_I E_{II}$ based on the same principle attached to equation (B1). Let us also recall that $w_I = p_I m_I / u = p_I m_I / P'M$ is the income share of class $I$ in the total population, then the first term in equation (B5) can be rearranged as follows:

$$G_A = \frac{P'E_A P}{P'M} = \frac{1}{u}\sum_{I=1}^{S} p_I^2 E_{II} = \frac{1}{u}\sum_{I=1}^{S} p_I^2 G_I m_I = \sum_{I=1}^{S} w_I p_I G_I \tag{B6}$$

As a result, it is only necessary to derive the class Gini coefficients, or $G_I$, in order to calculate $G_A$. The formula for $G_I$ is similar to equation (5.1) as explained in section 5.2.2 of the main text.

Third, the second term of equation (B5) is the inter-class component of the Gini coefficient but it can be represented by equation (5.3) of the main text just as equation (B1) can be represented by equation (5.1). The essence of this component is that the expected gain is the potential benefits moving from a lower class mean income to a higher class mean income. The expected gain of movements of individuals within classes is excluded in the calculation.

Lastly, unlike $G_A$ and $G_B$, I cannot find an equivalent non-matrix formula for the overlapped term $G_O$ in equation (B5). However, this is not important as the residual between $G$ and the sum of $G_A$ and $G_B$ will give the value of $G_O$. Alternatively, by use of equation (5.1) in section 5.2.1 in the main text, it is possible to derive $G$ and $G'$ according to different ordering principles (see explanation in sub-section 5.2.2), $G_O$ can be obtained as $G–G'$. Because $G_O$ can be derived in two different ways, there exists a build-in checking mechanism in the four-step approach discussed in sub-section 5.2.2.

## APPENDIX C

This appendix proves that

$$G = \sum_{f=1}^{F} w_f C_f. \tag{B6}$$

$G$ is the Gini coefficient for per capita total income which is defined in equation (5.1) of the main text. $w_f$ is the income share of income source $f$ in total income assuming that total income is divided into $F$ number of source incomes ($f = 1, 2, \ldots F$). In the main text, $w_f = u_f/u$. $u_f$ is the average source income $f$ of the whole population. $u$ is the average total income of the whole population. The sum of $w_f$ for all $f$ ($f = 1, \ldots F$) is equal to unity. The sum of all $u_f$s is equal to $u$. $C_f$ is the concentration coefficient of source income $f$.

Recall that

$$Q_{fi} = \sum_{k=1}^{i} w_{fk}$$

is the cumulative income share in total source income $f$ from the first household (or household group) up to the $i$-th household (or group), the right hand side of the above relationship can be expressed as follows according to equation (5.5) in the main text.

$$\sum_{f=1}^{F} w_f C_f = \sum_{f=1}^{F} \frac{u_f}{u}\left(1 - \sum_{i=1}^{n} p_i\left(2\sum_{k=1}^{i} w_{fk} - w_{fi}\right)\right) =$$

$$\sum_{f=1}^{F} \frac{u_f}{u} - \sum_{f=1}^{F} \frac{u_f}{u}\sum_{i=1}^{n} p_i\left(2\sum_{k=1}^{i} w_{fk} - w_{fi}\right) = 1 - Q \text{ where}$$

$$Q = \sum_{f=1}^{F} \frac{u_f}{u}\sum_{i=1}^{n} p_i\left(2\sum_{k=1}^{i} w_{fk} - w_{fi}\right) = \sum_{i=1}^{n} p_i\left(2\sum_{f=1}^{F} \frac{u_f}{u}\sum_{k=1}^{i} w_{fk} - \sum_{f=1}^{F} \frac{u_f}{u}w_{fi}\right) =$$

$$\sum_{i=1}^{n} p_i\left(2\sum_{k=1}^{i}\sum_{f=1}^{F} \frac{u_f}{u}w_{fk} - \sum_{f=1}^{F} \frac{u_f}{u}w_{fi}\right)$$

$$\text{use } w_{fk} = \frac{p_k m_{fk}}{u_f}, w_{fi} = \frac{p_i m_{fi}}{u_f}$$

where $w_{fk}$ (or $w_{fi}$) is the income share of income group $k$ (or $i$) in total factor income $f$, $p_k$ (or $p_i$) is the population share of income group $k$ (or $i$) in total population ($i, k = 1, \ldots n$), $m_{fk}$ (or $m_{fi}$) is the average per capita factor income $f$ of income group $k$ (or $i$) and $u_f$ is already defined above as the average per capita factor income f of the whole population. Then

$$Q = \sum_{i=1}^{n} p_i \left( 2 \sum_{k=1}^{i} \sum_{f=1}^{F} \frac{u_f}{u} \frac{p_k m_{fk}}{u_f} - \sum_{f=1}^{F} \frac{u_f}{u} \frac{p_i m_{fi}}{u_f} \right) = \sum_{i=1}^{n} p_i \left( 2 \sum_{k=1}^{i} \frac{p_k}{u} \sum_{f=1}^{F} m_{fk} - \frac{p_i}{u} \sum_{f=1}^{F} m_{fi} \right)$$

$$\sum_{f=1}^{F} m_{fk} = m_k \left( \sum_{f=1}^{F} m_{fi} = m_i \right), w_k = \frac{p_k m_k}{u} \left( w_i = \frac{p_i m_i}{u} \right)$$

Use all of the following relationships, where $w_{fk}$ (or $w_{fi}$), $p_k$ (or $p_i$), $m_{fk}$ (or $m_{fi}$) and $u_f$ are already defined above; $m_k$ (or $m_i$) is the average total income of income group $k$ (or $i$), $i, k = 1, \ldots n$; $w_k$ (or $w_i$) is the income share of income group $k$ (or $i$) in total income and $u$ is the average per capita income of the whole population. Then

$$Q = \sum_{i=1}^{n} p_i \left( 2 \sum_{k=1}^{i} \frac{p_k m_k}{u} - \frac{p_i m_i}{u} \right) = \sum_{i=1}^{n} p_i \left( 2 \sum_{k=1}^{i} w_k - w_i \right), \text{ hence}$$

$$1 - Q = 1 - \sum_{i=1}^{n} p_i \left( 2 \sum_{k=1}^{i} w_k - w_i \right) = 1 - \sum_{i=1}^{n} p_i (2Q_i - w_i) = G, \text{ thus}$$

$$G = \sum_{f=1}^{F} w_f C_f. \hspace{4cm} \text{q.e.d.}$$

# 6 Rural–urban and regional inequality in output, income and consumption under reforms

## 6.1 Introduction

China has registered over 25 years of rapid economic growth. However, the growth has been achieved at a high price, that is, an uncontrollable rise in inequality. The most important dimension of inequality is urban–rural inequality. The World Bank (1997) reports that urban–rural inequality explains over one-third of China's total inequality and over half of inequality growth from the late 1980s to the mid-1990s. In recent years, there are numerous studies on the issues of rising inequality, especially urban–rural inequality. This chapter uses provincial level data for the reform period of 1978–95 to study the evolution of urban–rural inequality over time.

## 6.2 Rapid growth but a more divided nation

### 6.2.1 Economic performance and income growth

A recent publication by the National Bureau of Statistics (NBS, 1996) provides time series data for many major economic indicators for all 30 provinces. We extracted data from this publication on four important economic variables: GDP, income, total expenditure and food expenditure. The income and expenditure data are available for both the rural and urban population. The GDP data is available for total GDP and its sectoral sources from agriculture, industry (including manufacturing and construction) and services (transportation, telecommunications and commerce). All variables are calculated in 1990 prices. Provincial GDP deflators are used to deflate GDP data. Provincial urban and rural consumer price indices are used to deflate income and expenditure data. Estimated results based on current prices can be quite different from those presented in this chapter.

The provinces are divided into three geo-economic zones according to the official definition (Yao and Liu, 1998). The eastern zone includes Beijing, Tianjin, Hebei, Liaoning, Shanghai, Jiangsu, Zhejiang, Fujian, Shangdong, Guangdong, Guangxi and Hainan. The central zone includes Shanxi, Inner Mongolia, Jilin, Heilongjiang, Anhui, Jiangxi, Henan, Hubei and Hunan. The western zone includes Sichuan, Guizhou, Yunnan, Tibet, Shaanxi, Gansu, Qinghai, Ningxia and Xingjiang.

Over the data period, as China's population increased by over one quarter (Table 6.1), there was a dramatic change in the rural–urban population structure. The share of urban population in total population rose from 16.7 to 29 per cent. This increase was partly due to urbanisation, and partly due to a new definition of urban population, which included people living in suburban areas. The pace of urbanisation accelerated from the mid-1990s. By 2002, the share of urban population rose to 39.1 per cent, with an increase of more than 10 percentage points in seven years.

*Table 6.1* The change in population structure, 1978–95

| Year | Total population (million) | Rural–urban structure (%) | | Geo-economic zones (%) | | |
| --- | --- | --- | --- | --- | --- | --- |
| | | Rural | Urban | West | Central | East |
| 1978 | 962.6 | 83.3 | 16.7 | 23.2 | 35.7 | 41.0 |
| 1995 | 1211.2 | 71.0 | 29.0 | 22.9 | 35.9 | 41.2 |
| 2002 | 1284.5 | 60.9 | 39.1 | 23.0 | 35.7 | 41.3 |

Sources: NBS, 1996, 2003.

Over the data period of 1978–95, per capita GDP rose 9.22 per cent per year (total GDP by 10.5 per cent per year, Table 6.2), only the fastest growing regions in Southeast Asia match this rate of growth.[1] Although there were significant differences across regions, every province experienced substantial growth (Figure 6.1). It is interesting to note that there were significant structural changes in the national and regional economies. In general, agriculture's share in GDP contracted sharply, declining from about 40 per cent to 19 per cent.[2] The amount of reduction in agriculture's share was almost equally distributed to industry and services. The structural change suggests that China was moving fast away from an agrarian economy towards an industrial one, particularly in the eastern region whose economic structure in 1995 resembled a middle-income economy with an agriculture share in GDP of less than 15 per cent.

Economic growth had a profound effect on people's living standards as reflected by the substantial increases in personal disposable incomes and consumption (Table 6.3 and Figure 6.2). The rural population benefited greatly from agricultural reforms, particularly the household production responsibility system, in the late 1970s and early 1980s (Lin, 1988; Johnson, 1988). From 1978 to 1984, per capita rural incomes rose by almost 15 per cent per year. Even the most disadvantaged western region registered an annual growth rate of 11.6 per cent. As a result, the rural–urban per capita income ratio declined from 2.85 to 1.79. Yet, it was only in this period that the peasantry saw their incomes grow faster than their urban counterparts. Growth in agricultural incomes was almost stagnant in the late 1980s because the government failed to raise agricultural procurement prices and substantially cut back agricultural investments (Sicular, 1993; Yao, 1994). The situation improved in the 1990s, even though, rural per capita income still grew much slower than urban incomes. The 1984–95 period saw a significant divergence in income growth across the regions. Rural incomes in the western and central

*Table 6.2* GDP growth and structural changes, 1978–95

|  |  | All China | West | Central | East |
|---|---|---|---|---|---|
| A | *Real per capita GDP (yuan/head)* | | | | |
|  | 1978 | 657.4 | 472.9 | 586.7 | 823.4 |
|  | 1995 | 2942.9 | 1764.9 | 2223.8 | 4222.5 |
| B | *Annual growth rates of per capita GDP (%)* | | | | |
|  | Total | 9.2 | 8.1 | 8.2 | 10.1 |
|  | Agriculture | 4.5 | 4.0 | 4.2 | 5.0 |
|  | Industry | 10.7 | 9.8 | 9.6 | 11.3 |
|  | Services | 12.0 | 11.5 | 11.5 | 12.4 |
| C | *GDP structure in 1978 (% of total)* | | | | |
|  | Agriculture | 39.7 | 48.4 | 45.1 | 33.6 |
|  | Industry | 40.2 | 33.3 | 37.7 | 44.0 |
|  | Services | 20.0 | 18.3 | 17.2 | 22.4 |
| D | *GDP structure in 1995 (% of total)* | | | | |
|  | Agriculture | 18.7 | 25.1 | 23.8 | 14.9 |
|  | Industry | 50.4 | 43.8 | 47.4 | 53.2 |
|  | Services | 30.9 | 31.0 | 28.8 | 31.8 |

Source: NBS, 1996.

Notes: All values are measured in constant 1990 prices. The industry sector includes construction and manufacturing. The service sector includes transportation, telecommunications and commerce.

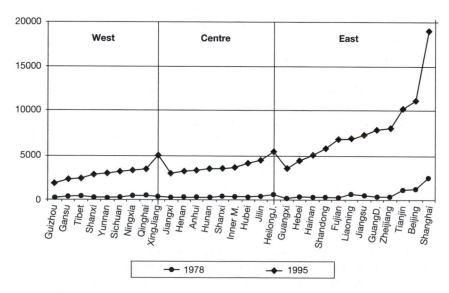

*Figure 6.1* Real per capita GDP by province, 1978 and 1995 (in yuan/head).

*Table 6.3* Real per capita income and consumption, 1978–95

| | China | | West | | Central | | East | |
|---|---|---|---|---|---|---|---|---|
| *Periods* | *Rural* | *Urban* | *Rural* | *Urban* | *Rural* | *Urban* | *Rural* | *Urban* |
| A  *Real per capita incomes (yuan/head)* | | | | | | | | |
| 1978 | 284.7 | 811.2 | 258.7 | 737.6 | 261.1 | 767.7 | 321.1 | 875.8 |
| 1984 | 645.6 | 1154.6 | 499.6 | 1085.6 | 620.3 | 994.8 | 759.1 | 1310.5 |
| 1995 | 908.9 | 2157.6 | 584.5 | 1978.3 | 776.9 | 1816.9 | 1232.3 | 2552.3 |
| *Annual growth (%)* | | | | | | | | |
| 1978–84 | 14.6 | 6.1 | 11.6 | 6.7 | 15.5 | 4.4 | 15.4 | 6.9 |
| 1984–95 | 5.9 | 11.0 | 2.7 | 10.5 | 3.8 | 10.6 | 8.4 | 11.8 |
| 1978–95 | 7.1 | 5.9 | 4.9 | 6.0 | 6.6 | 5.2 | 8.2 | 6.5 |
| B  *Real per capita total expenditures (yuan/head)* | | | | | | | | |
| 1978 | 254.3 | 663.4 | 240.0 | 620.7 | 226.7 | 578.2 | 287.1 | 751.5 |
| 1984 | 502.8 | 976.4 | 419.0 | 918.3 | 465.3 | 851.0 | 588.4 | 1100.2 |
| 1995 | 751.1 | 1769.6 | 550.0 | 1605.5 | 655.5 | 1492.7 | 962.9 | 2098.3 |
| *Annual growth (%)* | | | | | | | | |
| 1978–84 | 12.0 | 6.7 | 9.7 | 6.7 | 12.7 | 6.7 | 12.7 | 6.6 |
| 1984–95 | 6.9 | 10.4 | 4.6 | 9.8 | 5.9 | 9.8 | 8.6 | 11.4 |
| 1978–95 | 6.6 | 5.9 | 5.0 | 5.7 | 6.4 | 5.7 | 7.4 | 6.2 |

Source: NBS, 1996.

Notes: All values are measured in 1990 prices.

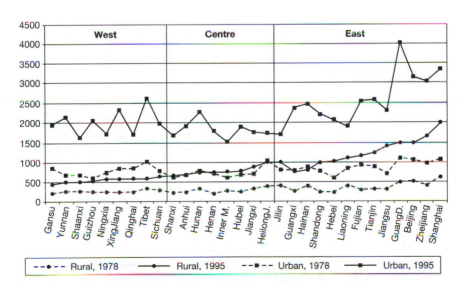

*Figure 6.2* Real per capita rural and urban incomes, 1978 and 1995 (yuan per capita, in ascending order of per capita rural incomes in 1995).

regions grew by only 2.7 and 3.8 per cent respectively, as opposed to 8.4 per cent in the east. Divergence was principally due to the slow progress of rural industrialisation in the former two regions, non-farm income becoming an important source of total income in the east after 1985 (Cheng, 1996; Yao and Liu, 1998).

Despite impressive growth in national output, income and consumption, the data in Tables 6.1 to 6.3 reveal two serious problems. First, regional inequality was large and increased over time. The eastern region became much more wealthy than the western and central areas. For example, the per capita GDP ratios between east–central–west changed from 1.00–0.71–0.57 in 1978 to 1.00–0.53–0.42 in 1995. The corresponding per capita income ratios changed from 1.00–0.83–0.75 to 1.00–0.70–0.59 for the whole population, and from 1.00–0.81–0.80 to 1.00–0.63–0.47 for the rural population. Second, rural–urban inequality increased after the initial phase of economic reforms, although it was not attributable to the productivity or efficiency gap between the rural–urban sectors. It was a direct result of government policy that was persistently urban biased. The rural–urban productivity difference was artificially created by government labour policy which prevented rural people from taking formal urban jobs while much of the urban production capacity was accumulated from resources transferred from the rural and agricultural sector over time (Knight, 1995). Despite significant improvement in SOE (a dominant force of the urban economy) performance after many years of reforms (Jefferson and Rawski, 1994; Perkins, 1994; Yao, 1997c), the SOE sector is still renowned for its inefficiency as the majority of firms are loss-making, depending on state subsidies (soft budget) for survival (Liu, 1999).

### 6.2.2 Regional growth divergence, not convergence

In the growth literature, if production (or income) inequality indicated by the coefficient of variation on per capita GDP (or income) declines over time, it is called convergence (Sala-i-Martin, 1996). Table 6.4 presents the coefficients of variations on real per capita rural–urban incomes, total expenditures, food expenditures, and real per capita total GDP and its source components of agriculture, industry and services.

There was a clear trend of divergence in per capita rural and urban incomes and total expenditures across provinces, but no evidence of divergence (or convergence) in food expenditure. The trend of per capita GDP distribution was unclear. The variation coefficient declined from 1978 to 1991 but rose slightly from 1992.[3] It is surprising to note that per capita agricultural GDP diverged over time while per capita GDP in industry and services converged. It may imply that the relatively backward regions were able to catch up with the more advanced regions in the process of industrialisation and commercialisation. The explanation for the rising inequality in agriculture GDP requires further investigation (see below).

Convergence can alternatively be measured by regressing per capita GDP growth (or income growth) on the initial level of per capita GDP (or income) as defined in equation (1). If the initially poor regions grow faster than the initially rich ones in the data period, the estimated coefficient ($\beta$) will be significant and negative. In the growth literature, this is called unconditional $\beta$-convergence.

Table 6.4 Variation coefficients of real per capita income, expenditure and GDP by sector

| Year | Urban population | | | Rural population | | | GDP per capita in 1990 prices | | | |
|---|---|---|---|---|---|---|---|---|---|---|
| | Income | Total expense | Food expense | Income | Total expense | Food expense | Total | Agriculture | Industry | Services |
| 1978 | 0.19 | 0.25 | 0.26 | 0.33 | 0.32 | 0.32 | 0.69 | 0.21 | 1.16 | 0.83 |
| 1979 | 0.16 | 0.19 | 0.23 | 0.33 | 0.30 | 0.29 | 0.68 | 0.25 | 1.16 | 0.80 |
| 1980 | 0.16 | 0.19 | 0.20 | 0.32 | 0.30 | 0.28 | 0.69 | 0.28 | 1.13 | 0.83 |
| 1981 | 0.16 | 0.16 | 0.18 | 0.29 | 0.32 | 0.28 | 0.67 | 0.34 | 1.16 | 0.80 |
| 1982 | 0.17 | 0.16 | 0.19 | 0.30 | 0.32 | 0.26 | 0.64 | 0.28 | 1.13 | 0.77 |
| 1983 | 0.19 | 0.18 | 0.20 | 0.31 | 0.32 | 0.25 | 0.64 | 0.24 | 1.11 | 0.77 |
| 1984 | 0.19 | 0.19 | 0.22 | 0.36 | 0.35 | 0.27 | 0.63 | 0.23 | 1.07 | 0.75 |
| 1985 | 0.20 | 0.19 | 0.22 | 0.32 | 0.34 | 0.25 | 0.62 | 0.25 | 1.04 | 0.69 |
| 1986 | 0.18 | 0.18 | 0.21 | 0.34 | 0.37 | 0.28 | 0.61 | 0.25 | 1.02 | 0.68 |
| 1987 | 0.20 | 0.19 | 0.22 | 0.36 | 0.37 | 0.29 | 0.60 | 0.26 | 0.99 | 0.67 |
| 1988 | 0.21 | 0.19 | 0.22 | 0.37 | 0.40 | 0.29 | 0.61 | 0.26 | 0.94 | 0.65 |
| 1989 | 0.21 | 0.20 | 0.23 | 0.42 | 0.40 | 0.32 | 0.60 | 0.25 | 0.93 | 0.64 |
| 1990 | 0.19 | 0.19 | 0.23 | 0.37 | 0.35 | 0.27 | 0.60 | 0.25 | 0.93 | 0.67 |
| 1991 | 0.21 | 0.21 | 0.24 | 0.40 | 0.36 | 0.32 | 0.60 | 0.27 | 0.91 | 0.66 |
| 1992 | 0.22 | 0.22 | 0.23 | 0.40 | 0.40 | 0.30 | 0.61 | 0.29 | 0.90 | 0.65 |
| 1993 | 0.24 | 0.24 | 0.26 | 0.42 | 0.37 | 0.34 | 0.61 | 0.30 | 0.87 | 0.65 |
| 1994 | 0.26 | 0.26 | 0.26 | 0.41 | 0.37 | 0.30 | 0.62 | 0.32 | 0.85 | 0.67 |
| 1995 | 0.26 | 0.26 | 0.28 | 0.42 | 0.38 | 0.29 | 0.63 | 0.34 | 0.85 | 0.68 |

Sources: NBS, 1996.

Notes: The coefficients are derived from per capita mean values across 30 provinces. All the values are measured in constant 1990 prices. Price indices are province and indicator specific.

$$y_t - y_0 = \alpha + \beta y_0 \qquad (6.1)$$

where $\beta = 1 - e^{-\lambda t}$, and $\lambda$ is the speed of convergence, $y_t$, $y_0$ are respectively the logarithms of per capita GDP (or income) in time $t$ and the initial period. Although many studies use data for the end and initial periods, this is subject to exogenous shocks of business cycles (Islam, 1995). To avoid this problem, we use three-year moving average data to run the regression.

It is possible that fast growth in the initially poor regions may lead to their per capita incomes surpassing those of the initially rich ones. Consequently, income inequality may increase over time, not because the rich become richer and the poor poorer, but because some of the initially rich become poor by the end of the data period. In this case, the two convergence indicators ($\delta$ and $\beta$) may not point to the same direction.[4] As there is ample evidence in our data that some initially poor provinces (e.g. Fujian, Guangxi and Guangdong) became much better off than some of the initially rich regions (e.g. Liaoning and Hebei), it is useful to derive both indicators for convergence measurement.

The estimated results based on equation (6.1) are presented in Table 6.5. The model is estimated in two specifications: one with and one without the zone dummy variables. The first specification is consistent with the definition of unconditional convergence while the second is conditional on zone clustering. Apart from rural per capita food expenditure and per capita industry GDP, we cannot find any evidence of unconditional convergence for any of the other indicators. This means that output and income growth did not depend on the initial level of output and income, a conclusion supported by the very low values of $R^2$ in all the regressions except rural food expenditures and industry GDP.

*Table 6.5* Summary results of regressions (dependent variable: $y_t - y_0$)

| Dependent variable | Without zone dummies | | | With zone dummies | | |
|---|---|---|---|---|---|---|
| | $\beta$ | *t-value* | $R^2$ | $\beta$ | *t-value* | $R^2$ |
| Urban income | 0.064 | 0.348 | 0.004 | −0.063 | −0.321 | 0.086 |
| Urban expenditure | −0.197 | −1.327 | 0.095 | −0.328 | −2.087* | 0.173 |
| Urban food expenditure | −0.130 | −0.914 | 0.029 | −0.225 | −1.376 | 0.074 |
| Rural income | 0.082 | 0.570 | 0.011 | −0.321 | −2.859* | 0.606 |
| Rural expenditure | −0.051 | −0.393 | 0.005 | −0.329 | −2.698* | 0.396 |
| Rural food expenditure | −0.460 | −2.884* | 0.229 | −0.632 | −5.248* | 0.609 |
| Total GDP | −0.091 | −0.882 | 0.027 | −0.321 | −3.989* | 0.564 |
| Agriculture GDP | −0.177 | −1.077 | 0.039 | −0.211 | −1.284 | 0.095 |
| Industry GDP | −0.323 | −3.031* | 0.247 | −0.488 | −6.558* | 0.691 |
| Service GDP | −0.142 | −1.777 | 0.101 | −0.295 | −3.707* | 0.390 |

Source: NBS, 1996.

Notes: (1) Figures with a * sign are statistically significant at the 5 per cent or below significance level. (2) The estimated coefficients on zone dummies are not presented but they all indicate that the eastern zone is better off than the central zone for all indicators, the central zone is better off than the western zone except with respect to urban per capita income and expenditures. (3) The dependent variable is the log difference between the last and the first values of three-year moving averages over the data period 1978–95. All values are in constant 1990 prices.

Once the zone dummy variables are included, all the estimated $\beta$ values are negative. Apart from that for urban income, they are also significant at the usual 5 per cent and below significance level. These results have very important implications as they indicate that between zones there is a clear rise in inequality, but within each of the zones, there is no evidence of divergence. Referring back to the result on agricultural GDP in Table 6.1, the estimated $\beta$ for agricultural GDP in Table 6.2 implies that some initially less productive regions in agriculture had become more productive than some initially more advanced regions. The change in the relative positions of agricultural productivity was so significant that even if there was weak evidence of convergence, there was a trend of rising inequality in agricultural productivity.

Combined with the results in Tables 6.4 and 6.5, it can be concluded that inter-provincial inequality did not decline over time. Instead, it may have risen. In addition, there is evidence showing a clear divergence of inequality between the three geo-economic zones. However, the exact extent of inter-zone inequality has to be analysed further.

## 6.3 A decomposition analysis of production, income and consumption inequality

This section discusses the methodology of inequality decomposition through use of the Gini coefficient, focusing on rural–urban inequality and inter-zone inequality based on provincial level per capita GDP, income, total expenditure and food expenditure. The per capita GDP inequality is also decomposed by its source components of agriculture, industry and services. The decomposition process is complicated but can be summarised and illustrated in Figure 6.3.

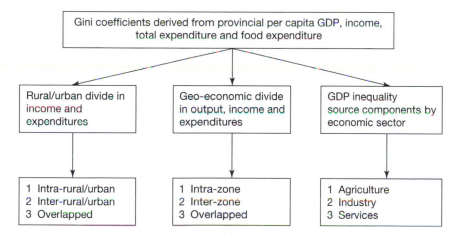

*Figure 6.3* Inequality decomposition structure.

### 6.3.1 Decomposition of the Gini coefficient by population class and income source

The Gini coefficient remains the most important and useful indicator of income inequality. Its usefulness is not only due to its popularity and simplicity, but also due to the fact that it can be decomposed by both population class and income source as detailed in Chapter 5.

Let $G$ denote the Gini coefficient for the entire population under concern, it can be decomposed into three components: intra-class, inter-class and overlapped as shown in equation (6.2).

$$G = G_A + G_B + G_O \tag{6.2}$$

$G_A$ is the intra-class component of $G$. If there is no income inequality within each of all classes, $G_A = 0$. $G_B$ is the inter-class component. If the mean incomes of all classes are identical, $G_B = 0$. $G_O$ is the overlapped component of $G$. If the richest person in any low income class is not better off than the poorest person in the next higher income class, $G_O = 0$. The relative contribution of $G_B$ to $G$ has important implications on inter-class income inequality. The larger is the ratio of $G_B/G$, the greater is the inter-class inequality. The contribution of $G_O$ to $G$ is also important. The smaller is the ratio of $G_O/G$, the more divided is between population classes.

If per capita income of the ith household, or group, $m_i$ ($i = 1,2, \ldots n$) is divided into $F$ number of income sources, the Gini coefficient ($G$) can be decomposed into $F$ number of components as shown in equation (6.3).

$$G = \sum_{f=1}^{F} w_f C_f \tag{6.3}$$

where $w_f$ is the share of source $f$ in total income and $C_f$ its concentration coefficient. In other words, the Gini coefficient that measures total income inequality is the weighted average of the concentration coefficients of all source incomes.

Intuitively, if $C_f > G$ and if total per capita income remains unchanged, an increase in the income share of source $f$ ($w_f$) will lead to more income inequality, or vice versa. Thus, the ratio $g_f = C_f/G$ has useful economic meaning. If $g_f > 1$, it means that source $f$ is inequality enhancing (Adams, 1994). As a result, the contribution of source $f$ to $G$ will be greater than its contribution to total income. It is useful to note that although $G$ can never be negative, $C_f$ can. If $C_f$ is negative, income source $f$ will reduce total income inequality irrespective of its share in total income. For example, if progressive income tax and transfer incomes are regarded as part of total income, they are most likely to have a negative concentration coefficient.

### 6.3.2 *Rural–urban divide and regional divide in income and expenditures*

#### (1)  *Rural–urban inequality*

The rural and urban samples are pooled together so that there are 60 population groups for each year. The Gini coefficients for per capita income, total expenditure and food expenditure are derived and decomposed into the intra-rural–urban, inter-rural–urban and overlapped components (Table 6.6).

*Table 6.6* Gini coefficients for per capita income, rural–urban combined

| Year | Per capita income | | | | Per capita total expenditure | | | | Per capita food expenditure | | | |
|------|------|--------|--------|--------|------|--------|--------|--------|------|--------|--------|--------|
| | $G$ | $G_B$ | $G_A$ | $G_O$ | $G$ | $G_B$ | $G_A$ | $G_O$ | $G$ | $G_B$ | $G_A$ | $G_O$ |
| 1978 | 28.5 | 69.1 | 30.9 | 0.0 | 28.0 | 63.0 | 36.7 | 0.2 | 27.0 | 63.6 | 36.4 | 0.0 |
| 1979 | 25.6 | 69.3 | 30.6 | 0.0 | 25.7 | 66.9 | 33.1 | 0.0 | 24.9 | 66.0 | 33.9 | 0.0 |
| 1980 | 24.4 | 69.0 | 31.0 | 0.0 | 24.7 | 69.8 | 30.2 | 0.0 | 23.9 | 68.0 | 32.0 | 0.0 |
| 1981 | 20.6 | 66.7 | 33.2 | 0.1 | 23.1 | 67.2 | 32.7 | 0.0 | 22.5 | 65.8 | 34.2 | 0.0 |
| 1982 | 19.7 | 62.2 | 37.6 | 0.2 | 21.4 | 63.5 | 36.4 | 0.1 | 21.0 | 62.9 | 37.1 | 0.0 |
| 1983 | 19.1 | 60.7 | 39.0 | 0.4 | 20.4 | 63.5 | 36.3 | 0.3 | 20.1 | 64.0 | 36.0 | 0.0 |
| 1984 | 19.7 | 64.0 | 35.1 | 0.9 | 21.4 | 68.3 | 31.2 | 0.5 | 20.8 | 67.7 | 32.2 | 0.2 |
| 1985 | 21.0 | 71.4 | 28.1 | 0.5 | 22.9 | 73.9 | 25.7 | 0.4 | 20.4 | 71.7 | 28.1 | 0.1 |
| 1986 | 24.0 | 74.7 | 25.1 | 0.2 | 24.1 | 75.0 | 24.6 | 0.4 | 22.1 | 73.6 | 26.3 | 0.1 |
| 1987 | 24.0 | 74.1 | 25.6 | 0.3 | 24.3 | 74.1 | 25.5 | 0.3 | 23.0 | 74.1 | 25.8 | 0.1 |
| 1988 | 24.2 | 74.3 | 25.4 | 0.4 | 25.3 | 75.6 | 24.0 | 0.4 | 23.8 | 75.4 | 24.5 | 0.1 |
| 1989 | 25.8 | 76.0 | 23.6 | 0.4 | 25.2 | 75.2 | 24.5 | 0.3 | 25.0 | 75.4 | 24.5 | 0.1 |
| 1990 | 25.8 | 76.6 | 23.2 | 0.2 | 25.1 | 76.1 | 23.8 | 0.1 | 24.1 | 74.2 | 25.7 | 0.1 |
| 1991 | 27.0 | 75.6 | 24.1 | 0.3 | 25.7 | 76.0 | 23.9 | 0.1 | 24.3 | 73.4 | 26.5 | 0.1 |
| 1992 | 27.8 | 76.3 | 23.5 | 0.2 | 26.7 | 76.3 | 23.4 | 0.3 | 24.4 | 75.0 | 24.9 | 0.1 |
| 1993 | 29.5 | 76.4 | 23.5 | 0.1 | 28.1 | 77.7 | 22.3 | 0.1 | 25.0 | 73.8 | 26.1 | 0.1 |
| 1994 | 29.7 | 75.4 | 24.6 | 0.0 | 28.4 | 76.0 | 24.0 | 0.0 | 24.7 | 72.6 | 27.2 | 0.2 |
| 1995 | 28.3 | 73.9 | 26.1 | 0.0 | 27.8 | 74.8 | 25.2 | 0.0 | 24.2 | 71.9 | 28.0 | 0.1 |

Notes: The range of $G$ is set to be (0, 100), with 100 representing absolute inequality. $G_B$, $G_A$, $G_O$ are respectively the inter-rural–urban, intra-rural–urban and overlapped percentage shares in $G$.

The results are consistent with the previous analysis based on the coefficients of variations. In all three indicators, inequality declined from 1978 to 1984 but increased after 1985. The improvement on income distribution in the earlier period was due to a faster growth in rural income than in urban income, but the worsening of distribution after 1985 was caused by an opposite movement of relative rural and urban income growth (also see Table 6.3). There are two striking elements. One is the large share of the inter-rural–urban component ($G_B$) in the overall inter-provincial inequality ($G$). This share also increased over the data period despite a slight U-turn in the early 1980s. The other is the remarkably small contribution of the overlapped component ($G_O$) to $G$. In most years, its share is close to zero, implying that even the richest rural people are worse off than the poorest urban population at the provincial level. This is by far the most striking evidence of urban policy bias in China's income distribution system. Moreover, it needs to be stressed that our data has not included various direct and indirect subsidies (e.g. housing, healthcare, education and pension) exclusively provided to the urban population. The World Bank (1997) estimates that if these subsidies had been included, the urban per capita incomes would have increased by up to 80 per cent, a figure similar to that estimated by Lardy (1983).

## (2) Regional inequality in GDP

As shown in Table 6.7, the Gini coefficient measuring inter-provincial inequality in real per capita GDP remained almost constant at around 19–20 during the period 1978–85. After 1985, it rose from 19.2 to 25, largely due to the rapid growth in the industry and service sectors, whose shares in total GDP not only increased significantly over the data period but whose contribution to overall inequality was also disproportionately greater than their income shares. Agricultural output was much more equally distributed than the outputs of industry and services although it, too, became less equally distributed over time. The concentration coefficient of per capita agricultural GDP was less than one fifth of the Gini coefficient in 1978

*Table 6.7* Decomposition of GDP Gini coefficient by income source

| Year | GDP (yuan) | As % of GDP | | | Gini and concentration ratios | | | | As % of GDP Gini | | |
|------|------------|-------|-------|-------|------|-------|-------|-------|---------|---------|---------|
|      |            | $W_A$ | $W_I$ | $W_S$ | $G$  | $C_A$ | $C_I$ | $C_S$ | $C_A/G$ | $C_I/G$ | $C_S/G$ |
| 1978 | 657  | 39.7 | 40.2 | 20.0 | 20.2 | 3.6 | 34.9 | 23.4 | 7.1  | 69.7 | 23.3 |
| 1979 | 705  | 39.5 | 40.3 | 20.2 | 19.4 | 4.0 | 33.1 | 22.2 | 8.1  | 68.8 | 23.1 |
| 1980 | 758  | 37.3 | 41.4 | 21.4 | 20.0 | 4.9 | 32.1 | 22.8 | 9.1  | 66.5 | 24.3 |
| 1981 | 788  | 37.8 | 39.6 | 22.6 | 19.9 | 5.4 | 32.4 | 22.2 | 10.2 | 64.6 | 25.2 |
| 1982 | 852  | 38.5 | 38.1 | 23.4 | 19.6 | 6.0 | 31.6 | 22.2 | 11.9 | 61.6 | 26.5 |
| 1983 | 934  | 37.8 | 38.1 | 24.1 | 19.2 | 6.1 | 30.8 | 21.5 | 12.0 | 61.1 | 26.9 |
| 1984 | 1066 | 36.6 | 38.8 | 24.6 | 19.5 | 6.7 | 30.4 | 21.4 | 12.6 | 60.5 | 26.9 |
| 1985 | 1209 | 33.0 | 40.8 | 26.2 | 19.2 | 5.1 | 30.0 | 20.2 | 8.7  | 63.8 | 27.5 |
| 1986 | 1271 | 31.7 | 40.7 | 27.6 | 20.0 | 6.6 | 28.9 | 22.2 | 10.5 | 58.9 | 30.6 |
| 1987 | 1394 | 30.0 | 41.3 | 28.7 | 20.4 | 6.2 | 29.4 | 22.3 | 9.2  | 59.5 | 31.3 |
| 1988 | 1531 | 27.5 | 43.0 | 29.5 | 21.1 | 7.2 | 29.1 | 22.5 | 9.4  | 59.1 | 31.5 |
| 1989 | 1569 | 27.0 | 42.7 | 30.3 | 20.9 | 6.0 | 29.4 | 22.4 | 7.7  | 59.9 | 32.4 |
| 1990 | 1611 | 27.6 | 42.0 | 30.4 | 20.9 | 6.6 | 28.9 | 22.9 | 8.6  | 58.0 | 33.3 |
| 1991 | 1746 | 25.8 | 42.7 | 31.6 | 21.8 | 7.5 | 28.7 | 24.1 | 8.8  | 56.3 | 34.9 |
| 1992 | 2000 | 23.4 | 44.7 | 31.8 | 22.8 | 8.2 | 28.8 | 25.0 | 8.4  | 56.6 | 35.0 |
| 1993 | 2314 | 21.2 | 47.4 | 31.4 | 23.7 | 8.0 | 29.3 | 25.7 | 7.2  | 58.7 | 34.1 |
| 1994 | 2631 | 19.6 | 49.4 | 31.0 | 24.6 | 8.2 | 29.8 | 26.4 | 6.6  | 60.1 | 33.4 |
| 1995 | 2943 | 18.7 | 50.4 | 30.9 | 24.9 | 8.4 | 30.1 | 26.7 | 6.3  | 60.6 | 33.1 |

Notes: GDP is calculated in 1990 prices, with its percentage shares of agriculture, industry and services respectively denoted by $W_A$, $W_I$, and $W_S$. $G$ is the Gini coefficient measuring inter-provincial inequality in per capita GDP, with concentration coefficients of agriculture, industry and services respectively denoted by $C_A$, $C_I$ and $C_S$.

but rose to about one-third in 1995. In 1978, agriculture accounted for 40 per cent of total GDP ($W_A$) and only 6.3 per cent ($C_A/G$) of the overall inequality. By 1995, agriculture's share in total GDP was less than 20 per cent, but due to the rising value of the concentration coefficient, its contribution to overall inequality was slightly higher than in 1978.

Industrial output was the most unequally distributed among the three sources of GDP over the entire data period. Its effect on total inequality, however, declined sharply over the years. In 1978, industrial output accounted for 40.1 per cent of total GDP, but explained about 70 per cent of total inequality. By 1995, its share in total GDP rose by more than 10 percentage points, but its share in total inequality declined by more than 9 percentage points. The service sector was the only sector whose contribution to total GDP and overall inequality rose simultaneously over the data period, its share in overall inequality rising by almost 10 percentage points although its contribution to total GDP rose by just over 3 percentage points.

Each of the GDP Gini coefficients for total GDP and its sources in agriculture, industry and services is decomposed into three components: inter-zone, intra-zone and overlapped. The results are presented in Table 6.8. Over the data period, agricultural GDP became much less equally distributed although it still remained the most equally distributed sector by the end of the data period. In contrast, industrial output was the most unequally distributed, although the degree of inequality declined over the years. The distribution of service output remained fairly stable throughout the data period.

The decomposition results offer some useful insights into spatial inequality of production. Both the intra-zone and overlapped terms declined. The share of the inter-zone component ($G_B$) in the Gini coefficient ($G$) was high and increased steadily over time in all three economic sectors. In industry and services, it explained more than three-quarters of total inequality. The overlapped component was remarkably small and declined over time. By 1995, it explained only 1.2 per cent of the total inequality in industry and 3.8 per cent of the total inequality in services. In the literature, many analysts cannot find a clear explanation for $G_O$ and are puzzled by its existence (Lambert and Aronson, 1993). In this case study, however, its meaning could not be clearer. It implies that there were few rich provinces in the low-income zones (west to central) which were better off than the poorest provinces in the high-income zones (east to central). In other words, it explains the extent to which the geo-economic zones are divided.

### (3) Regional inequality in income, total expenditure and food expenditure

In China, the rural and urban populations are two essentially heterogeneous groups in terms of their income and living standards. Hence, it is necessary to separate the two sub-populations when we study regional inequality.

Because the Gini coefficients are based on provincial level data, they reflect inter-provincial inequality. From some recent publications, however, we are able to obtain the rural and urban Gini coefficients based on household level data

Table 6.8 Gini coefficients of GDP by sector and their zone components

| Year | Total GDP | | | | Agriculture GDP | | | | Industry GDP | | | | Services GDP | | | |
|------|-----|-------|-------|-------|-----|-------|-------|-------|-----|-------|-------|-------|-----|-------|-------|-------|
| | $G$ | $G_A$ | $G_B$ | $G_O$ | $G$ | $G_A$ | $G_B$ | $G_O$ | $G$ | $G_A$ | $G_B$ | $G_O$ | $G$ | $G_A$ | $G_B$ | $G_O$ |
| 1978 | 20.2 | 30.5 | 58.6 | 11.0 | 9.0 | 30.0 | 39.4 | 30.6 | 36.9 | 34.4 | 46.7 | 18.9 | 26.1 | 26.9 | 66.3 | 6.7 |
| 1979 | 19.4 | 31.1 | 58.1 | 10.7 | 11.0 | 31.5 | 36.0 | 32.5 | 35.6 | 34.8 | 45.9 | 19.3 | 24.4 | 28.6 | 63.8 | 7.6 |
| 1980 | 20.0 | 30.4 | 59.9 | 9.6 | 10.7 | 30.4 | 38.6 | 31.0 | 34.9 | 34.1 | 48.8 | 17.1 | 25.0 | 28.8 | 63.7 | 7.5 |
| 1981 | 19.9 | 29.2 | 62.7 | 8.2 | 11.0 | 29.6 | 40.9 | 29.5 | 34.6 | 33.3 | 51.3 | 15.4 | 25.2 | 27.5 | 65.6 | 6.9 |
| 1982 | 19.6 | 28.9 | 62.9 | 8.2 | 11.3 | 29.6 | 46.1 | 24.2 | 33.7 | 33.7 | 49.8 | 16.5 | 25.0 | 26.5 | 66.7 | 6.8 |
| 1983 | 19.2 | 28.9 | 63.0 | 8.1 | 9.6 | 26.4 | 53.7 | 19.9 | 32.6 | 34.1 | 49.4 | 16.6 | 24.4 | 26.0 | 67.9 | 6.1 |
| 1984 | 19.5 | 29.4 | 62.4 | 8.2 | 10.2 | 27.7 | 52.8 | 19.5 | 32.3 | 33.6 | 50.4 | 16.0 | 24.5 | 27.8 | 64.6 | 7.6 |
| 1985 | 19.2 | 29.1 | 63.9 | 7.0 | 11.0 | 29.7 | 41.8 | 28.5 | 31.7 | 33.3 | 52.2 | 14.5 | 23.3 | 27.9 | 65.6 | 6.6 |
| 1986 | 20.0 | 29.1 | 63.9 | 7.0 | 11.9 | 30.9 | 40.3 | 28.8 | 30.8 | 32.5 | 55.7 | 11.8 | 24.1 | 28.3 | 64.4 | 7.2 |
| 1987 | 20.4 | 28.3 | 65.6 | 6.1 | 11.7 | 30.1 | 42.2 | 27.7 | 31.0 | 31.7 | 57.4 | 10.9 | 24.0 | 27.9 | 65.7 | 6.5 |
| 1988 | 21.1 | 27.6 | 66.0 | 6.4 | 12.0 | 30.2 | 43.1 | 26.7 | 30.2 | 30.5 | 60.0 | 9.5 | 23.7 | 26.8 | 67.6 | 5.6 |
| 1989 | 20.9 | 27.4 | 66.3 | 6.3 | 11.7 | 30.6 | 43.2 | 26.2 | 30.4 | 30.2 | 59.8 | 10.0 | 23.4 | 27.1 | 67.0 | 6.0 |
| 1990 | 20.9 | 27.8 | 65.6 | 6.6 | 11.1 | 30.5 | 39.7 | 29.9 | 29.9 | 29.7 | 61.2 | 9.1 | 23.9 | 27.6 | 66.2 | 6.2 |
| 1991 | 21.8 | 26.5 | 67.7 | 5.8 | 12.6 | 30.3 | 41.0 | 28.6 | 29.7 | 28.7 | 63.1 | 8.2 | 24.8 | 25.8 | 69.2 | 5.0 |
| 1992 | 22.8 | 24.7 | 71.1 | 4.2 | 13.0 | 29.7 | 43.6 | 26.7 | 30.0 | 26.6 | 67.6 | 5.8 | 25.5 | 24.3 | 71.2 | 4.5 |
| 1993 | 23.7 | 22.9 | 74.3 | 2.9 | 13.0 | 29.4 | 47.6 | 23.0 | 30.0 | 24.7 | 72.1 | 3.2 | 26.2 | 22.8 | 72.9 | 4.3 |
| 1994 | 24.6 | 22.0 | 75.8 | 2.2 | 14.7 | 26.2 | 44.8 | 29.0 | 30.2 | 23.9 | 74.7 | 1.4 | 26.9 | 21.9 | 74.2 | 3.9 |
| 1995 | 24.9 | 21.3 | 77.0 | 1.6 | 14.3 | 26.2 | 50.0 | 23.8 | 30.4 | 23.6 | 75.2 | 1.2 | 27.3 | 21.1 | 75.2 | 3.8 |

Notes: The Gini coefficients ($G$) have a range of values as (0, 100). $G_A$, $G_B$, $G_O$ denote respectively the percentage shares of the intra-zone, inter-zone and overlapped components in the corresponding $G$. GDP values are in 1990 constant prices.

(Ministry of Agriculture, 1995; World Bank, 1997). Combining these two sets of Gini values, we can present a complete picture of rural and urban inequality for the data period (Table 6.9).

*Table 6.9* Gini coefficients of rural and urban incomes and their inter-provincial components

| Year | Rural income inequality | | | Urban income inequality | | |
| --- | --- | --- | --- | --- | --- | --- |
| | $G$ | $G_B$ | $G_B/G$ in % | $G$ | $G_B$ | $G_B/G$ in % |
| 1978 | 21.2 | 15.4 | 72.5 | n.a. | 10.5 | n.a. |
| 1979 | 22.5 | 13.7 | 60.8 | n.a. | 9.3 | n.a. |
| 1980 | 23.7 | 13.2 | 55.5 | n.a. | 9.1 | n.a. |
| 1981 | 23.9 | 11.4 | 47.9 | 18.2 | 8.9 | 49.0 |
| 1982 | 23.2 | 12.3 | 53.1 | 17.9 | 9.2 | 51.6 |
| 1983 | 23.9 | 12.4 | 52.0 | 18.0 | 11.2 | 62.3 |
| 1984 | 24.6 | 13.0 | 53.0 | 19.2 | 10.2 | 53.2 |
| 1985 | 25.8 | 11.7 | 45.3 | 20.1 | 9.7 | 48.2 |
| 1986 | 28.8 | 13.2 | 46.0 | 21.5 | 9.0 | 42.0 |
| 1987 | 29.2 | 13.9 | 47.8 | 23.3 | 9.3 | 39.9 |
| 1988 | 30.1 | 14.4 | 47.9 | 23.8 | 9.5 | 40.1 |
| 1989 | 31.0 | 15.0 | 48.5 | 23.2 | 9.1 | 39.2 |
| 1990 | 29.4 | 14.4 | 49.1 | 22.5 | 9.4 | 41.8 |
| 1991 | 30.3 | 16.2 | 53.3 | 21.5 | 10.2 | 47.5 |
| 1992 | 31.4 | 16.6 | 52.9 | 30.5 | 10.9 | 35.7 |
| 1993 | 33.0 | 18.1 | 54.8 | 27.1 | 11.9 | 43.9 |
| 1994 | 32.0 | 18.4 | 57.6 | 28.8 | 13.1 | 45.5 |
| 1995 | 34.8 | 19.8 | 57.0 | 27.5 | 12.4 | 45.3 |

Sources: The values of $G$ for the rural population are taken from Ministry of Agriculture (1995). The values of $G$ for the urban population are derived from Figure 2.3 in World Bank (1997). The values of $G_B$ are based on provincial level data described in Section 6.1.

Notes: $G$ denotes the Gini coefficient based on household level incomes in 1990 prices. $G_B$ denotes the Gini coefficient based on provincial level data described in this paper. $G_B$ is the inter-provincial component of $G$. We cannot derive the intra-provincial and the overlapped due to data restriction.

At the household level, income inequality among both the rural and urban populations rose significantly over time. The rural Gini coefficient increased from 21.2 in 1978 to almost 35 in 1995, while the urban Gini coefficient rose from 18.2 in 1981 to 27.5 in 1995. In the early 1980s, China could be regarded as a relatively egalitarian society. By 1995, the extent of its inequality is comparable to many Southeast Asian nations (Table 6.10).

In most years during the data period, inter-provincial inequality, as measured by $G_B$ in Table 6.9, explained more than half of the total rural inequality but less than half of the total urban inequality. This implies that there was more household level and provincial level income inequality among the rural population than among the urban residents. It also implies that there was an implicit state policy to subsidise urban residents living in the less advantaged regions more than those living in the more prosperous areas. This was possible because the wage (and

*Table 6.10* Gini coefficients for some selected regions

| Regions | 1980s | 1990s |
|---|---|---|
| **China (1981 and 1995)** | **28.8** | **38.8** |
| Eastern Europe | 25.0 | 28.9 |
| High-income countries | 33.2 | 33.8 |
| South Asia | 35.0 | 31.8 |
| East Asia and the Pacific | 38.7 | 38.1 |
| Middle East and North Africa | 40.5 | 38.0 |
| Sub-Saharan Africa | 43.5 | 47.0 |
| Latin America and the Caribbean | 49.8 | 49.3 |

Source: World Bank, 1997: Table 1.

bonus) levels of state employees, including SOE workers, were regulated and manipulated by the central government. State wage policy was not consistent with the orthodox argument for efficiency, which requires wage levels to be determined by productivity. From the data, per capita GDP was about one-quarter higher in the central zone than in the west (Table 6.2) but per capita urban income was higher in the latter than in the former in 16 out of 18 years during the period 1978–95. In 1995, for example, per capita income in the central zone was 9 per cent less than in the west although per capita GDP was 26 per cent higher. One argument for the regional wage policy is that state employees need to be compensated for working in the more adverse areas of the western provinces. However, one may question why the state does not pay farmers more in the same regions. This question sounds naïve because the answer is so simple: farmers do not enjoy any protection from the state irrespective of where they live!

To understand the inter-zone inequality in income and expenditures, the rural and urban Gini coefficients representing inter-provincial inequality are respectively decomposed into their intra-zone, inter-zone and overlapped components (Table 6.11).

Consistent with the results in Table 6.9, income and expenditure inequality is more evident among the rural population than among urban residents. In both population groups, the inter-zone component was relatively small at the beginning of the data period but became a predominant factor of inter-provincial inequality by 1995. This phenomenon was particularly obvious in rural income and expenditures. In 1978, the inter-zone component accounted for just 8.5–34.0 per cent of inter-provincial inequality in food expenditures and incomes among the rural population, by 1995, it had risen to 63.8–81.7 per cent. Since rural income was unequally distributed, poor people in the poor regions have not benefited as much as their counterparts in the more prosperous regions. As a result, China still has a large number of rural people (70–170 million, depending on how a poverty line is drawn) living in absolute poverty despite the fact that national average per capita rural income has more than tripled over twenty years (Yao, 1999a).

*Table 6.11* Decomposition of the Gini coefficients of income and expenditure by zone

**For the rural population**

| Year | Income | | | | Total expenditures | | | | Food expenditures | | | |
|------|------|------|------|------|------|------|------|------|------|------|------|------|
| | $G$ | $G_B$ | $G_A$ | $G_O$ | $G$ | $G_B$ | $G_A$ | $G_O$ | $G$ | $G_B$ | $G_A$ | $G_O$ |
| 1978 | 15.4 | 34.0 | 33.0 | 33.0 | 17.2 | 27.6 | 33.2 | 39.2 | 16.3 | 8.5 | 34.0 | 57.5 |
| 1979 | 13.7 | 44.1 | 32.5 | 23.4 | 14.5 | 35.7 | 33.2 | 31.1 | 14.2 | 15.4 | 34.1 | 50.5 |
| 1980 | 13.2 | 52.7 | 30.9 | 16.4 | 12.7 | 48.0 | 31.9 | 20.1 | 13.0 | 24.2 | 33.6 | 42.2 |
| 1981 | 11.4 | 57.2 | 29.7 | 13.1 | 13.0 | 57.2 | 29.5 | 13.3 | 13.0 | 33.5 | 33.0 | 33.6 |
| 1982 | 12.3 | 58.9 | 28.6 | 12.6 | 13.2 | 53.5 | 30.0 | 16.5 | 13.1 | 27.1 | 33.6 | 39.3 |
| 1983 | 12.4 | 63.2 | 26.1 | 10.7 | 12.7 | 57.7 | 28.7 | 13.5 | 12.3 | 38.5 | 31.9 | 29.6 |
| 1984 | 13.0 | 66.1 | 25.4 | 8.5 | 12.8 | 59.2 | 28.0 | 12.8 | 12.4 | 36.5 | 31.9 | 31.6 |
| 1985 | 11.7 | 70.7 | 24.1 | 5.3 | 12.1 | 65.2 | 26.8 | 8.1 | 11.0 | 43.2 | 30.8 | 26.0 |
| 1986 | 13.2 | 69.2 | 24.4 | 6.4 | 13.1 | 65.1 | 26.9 | 8.0 | 11.7 | 42.4 | 30.6 | 27.0 |
| 1987 | 13.9 | 72.6 | 23.3 | 4.1 | 14.0 | 63.4 | 27.4 | 9.2 | 12.4 | 43.2 | 29.8 | 27.0 |
| 1988 | 14.4 | 72.5 | 22.9 | 4.6 | 14.5 | 65.5 | 26.6 | 7.9 | 12.3 | 44.0 | 29.0 | 27.0 |
| 1989 | 15.0 | 72.9 | 23.6 | 3.5 | 14.9 | 64.8 | 27.1 | 8.1 | 13.8 | 44.3 | 29.2 | 26.5 |
| 1990 | 14.4 | 71.2 | 24.6 | 4.2 | 14.0 | 66.6 | 26.6 | 6.7 | 13.3 | 48.0 | 29.5 | 22.4 |
| 1991 | 16.2 | 71.5 | 23.9 | 4.7 | 14.5 | 67.7 | 25.8 | 6.6 | 14.1 | 52.1 | 28.6 | 19.3 |
| 1992 | 16.6 | 71.9 | 24.9 | 3.2 | 15.6 | 69.2 | 26.0 | 4.9 | 13.9 | 54.6 | 28.3 | 17.1 |
| 1993 | 18.1 | 77.2 | 22.0 | 0.8 | 15.1 | 72.6 | 24.8 | 2.6 | 14.3 | 53.9 | 29.0 | 17.2 |
| 1994 | 18.4 | 77.6 | 21.0 | 1.3 | 16.2 | 67.5 | 26.2 | 6.3 | 14.4 | 55.8 | 28.7 | 15.5 |
| 1995 | 19.8 | 81.7 | 17.8 | 0.5 | 17.3 | 72.9 | 23.5 | 3.6 | 14.1 | 63.8 | 26.3 | 10.0 |

**For the urban population**

| Year | Income | | | | Total expenditures | | | | Food expenditures | | | |
|------|------|------|------|------|------|------|------|------|------|------|------|------|
| | $G$ | $G_B$ | $G_A$ | $G_O$ | $G$ | $G_B$ | $G_A$ | $G_O$ | $G$ | $G_B$ | $G_A$ | $G_O$ |
| 1978 | 10.5 | 36.5 | 34.8 | 28.7 | 15.6 | 41.1 | 31.8 | 27.1 | 15.1 | 46.3 | 34.3 | 19.3 |
| 1979 | 9.3 | 47.6 | 32.4 | 20.0 | 11.6 | 51.5 | 29.3 | 19.2 | 12.8 | 54.7 | 32.1 | 13.3 |
| 1980 | 9.1 | 62.3 | 27.4 | 10.4 | 11.5 | 66.1 | 26.3 | 7.6 | 11.2 | 61.7 | 29.8 | 8.5 |
| 1981 | 8.9 | 62.5 | 27.5 | 10.0 | 8.9 | 65.1 | 26.4 | 8.6 | 9.9 | 57.1 | 31.0 | 11.9 |
| 1982 | 9.2 | 65.9 | 26.8 | 7.3 | 9.3 | 65.5 | 27.5 | 7.0 | 10.1 | 60.7 | 29.7 | 9.6 |
| 1983 | 11.2 | 66.8 | 26.9 | 6.3 | 9.7 | 60.3 | 30.3 | 9.5 | 10.6 | 58.1 | 30.9 | 11.0 |
| 1984 | 10.2 | 65.1 | 28.0 | 6.9 | 10.1 | 61.4 | 30.5 | 8.1 | 11.6 | 61.8 | 29.8 | 8.4 |
| 1985 | 9.7 | 61.5 | 31.0 | 7.5 | 9.4 | 59.0 | 31.7 | 9.4 | 10.5 | 56.6 | 32.4 | 11.0 |
| 1986 | 9.0 | 63.0 | 30.7 | 6.3 | 8.9 | 60.8 | 31.4 | 7.7 | 10.7 | 57.2 | 32.0 | 10.8 |
| 1987 | 9.3 | 66.5 | 29.3 | 4.3 | 9.6 | 63.9 | 30.8 | 5.4 | 10.9 | 60.6 | 31.3 | 8.1 |
| 1988 | 9.5 | 72.0 | 26.0 | 2.0 | 9.4 | 70.2 | 27.0 | 2.8 | 11.1 | 66.0 | 28.6 | 5.4 |
| 1989 | 9.1 | 72.2 | 25.2 | 2.7 | 9.4 | 72.3 | 25.1 | 2.6 | 10.9 | 60.4 | 30.6 | 9.1 |
| 1990 | 9.4 | 73.2 | 25.1 | 1.8 | 9.7 | 71.2 | 25.8 | 2.9 | 11.8 | 66.5 | 28.1 | 5.5 |
| 1991 | 10.2 | 70.0 | 26.7 | 3.3 | 10.3 | 68.2 | 28.0 | 3.9 | 11.9 | 65.9 | 28.5 | 5.7 |
| 1992 | 10.9 | 69.8 | 26.2 | 4.0 | 10.6 | 70.5 | 26.5 | 3.0 | 11.3 | 65.4 | 28.1 | 6.5 |
| 1993 | 11.9 | 67.7 | 28.0 | 4.3 | 11.5 | 68.3 | 27.9 | 3.9 | 12.8 | 63.7 | 29.3 | 7.0 |
| 1994 | 13.1 | 65.7 | 28.0 | 6.3 | 12.8 | 66.2 | 28.4 | 5.4 | 13.4 | 61.4 | 29.4 | 9.2 |
| 1995 | 12.4 | 66.5 | 28.1 | 5.4 | 12.6 | 65.7 | 28.8 | 5.4 | 13.7 | 60.1 | 30.0 | 9.9 |

Notes: The Gini coefficients ($G$) measure inter-provincial inequality, with a range of values as (0, 100). $G_A$, $G_B$, $G_O$ denote respectively the percentage shares of the intra-zone, inter-zone and overlapped components in the corresponding $G$. Incomes and expenditures are in 1990 prices.

## 6.4 Conclusion

Economic growth in China over the last 25 years of reforms has been admirable. Due to this rapid growth, China has become an increasingly important power in the world economy, not only in terms of its economic strength, but also in terms of its strategic position as a political power in the Asian Pacific region. However, the ever rising inequality between the rural and urban populations, and across the provinces, has undermined the quality of economic development.

Although income growth has greatly changed China's image as one of the poorest nations in the world, dogged by a large proportion of people living in absolute poverty and sickness, the reduction in rural poverty would have been much faster had income growth not been so unequally distributed.

Inequality in China has two important features: a rural/urban divide and a regional divide. We have proved that rural–urban inequality accounts for over 70 per cent of inter-provincial inequality in expenditures and incomes. Inter-provincial inequality explains less than half of urban inequality but more than half of rural inequality. Inter-zone inequality explains up to over 80 per cent of inter-provincial inequality of rural income, and about two-thirds of inter-provincial inequality in urban income. Overall, rural inequality was more profound than urban inequality, due to a deliberate state policy to subsidise the urban residents living in the western region more than those living in other parts of the country. The state wage policy is not consistent with the orthodox argument for economic efficiency. However, since the same policy is not applied to the rural population living in the same adverse areas, the poorest people in rural China have not benefited much from the recent economic reforms. Consequently, rural poverty is highly concentrated in the western provinces where there is little prospect of sustainable economic growth (Riskin, 1994; Yao, 1999a).

The convergence analysis suggests that the Chinese regions were not converging over the data period in terms of production (GDP), incomes and expenditures. The lack of unconditional convergence implies that the provinces were diverging into three geo-economic zones. Increasing inter-zone inequality in output and income growths may have important economic, as well as political, implications. In economic terms, the poor in the western provinces will continue to be disadvantaged and the state has to spend billions of yuan each year on poverty alleviation. In political terms, the ever-rising regional divide has triggered massive inter-regional migration and periodic political riots in the poor areas, especially among the minority-nationality regions of Tibet, Xinjiang and Guizhou. This political tension may become a constant threat to China's long term economic growth.

In the literature, many authors argue that allowing inter-regional migration may be an effective solution to containing inter-regional inequality because emigrants can send money home once they find jobs in the prosperous areas. In our view, however, massive migration may have some serious negative effects on regional income distribution and social/political stability. First, because the people who migrate out of the poor areas are usually the young and educated development of the local economy (agricultural as well as industries) is greatly hampered because of labour and skill shortages. Second, some migrant workers may settle down permanently in the rich regions, reducing the possibility of sending money back home. Third, massive migration has created many social, economic, political and transportation problems for a country which still has a highly underdeveloped labour market and an utterly inadequate transportation system. Migrant workers face many disadvantages compared to their local counterparts, including low wages, loneliness and even physical abuse by their bosses. Fourth, migrant workers in recent years have imposed tremendous population pressures on the coastal areas where rapid industrialisation has resulted in severe environmental degradation.

In short, given the current situation in rural China, labour migration at best can only be regarded as a short-term solution to reduce spatial income inequality. At worst, it may even induce further inequality and other undesirable consequences which are as detrimental to the rich coastal areas as they are to the inland regions themselves. Instead, the long-term solution to inter-regional inequality in income and development should be through the encouragement of industrialisation in the western and central zones.

The rural–urban divide is a longstanding political and social issue. The state policy to exclude the rural populace from taking up formal urban jobs has created a capital-intensive (by Chinese standards) and highly inefficient urban economy. The recent SOE reforms have resulted in millions of people being laid off. In the short term, high unemployment may lead to urban unrest and destitution. It the long term, it may create a more competitive and efficient state sector and allow more people from the countryside to undertake formal employment in the cities. If this were to happen, rural–urban income inequality may be contained, or even reduced. However, it is difficult to imagine that Chinese peasants will enjoy a similar living standard to their urban counterparts in the next few decades. The struggle to eliminate rural–urban inequality is a long and painful process.

It appears that one possible way for the rural population to become prosperous is through the deepening of rural industrialisation. However, rural industrialisation has had its own problems. One is that as rural industries have developed highly unevenly across provinces, rural industrialisation itself has been a major factor responsible for ever rising regional inequality among the rural population (Chen and Fleisher, 1996; Rozelle, 1994). Another problem is that the rapid growth of rural industries has caused alarming environmental problems, particularly in the eastern region: fertile lands are being destroyed, air and water pollution is getting worse day by day.

All the above suggests that the state has a more important role to play. From a long-term point of view, more attention should be paid to preventing inequality from rising. Urban bias should be gradually reduced. Soft budgets should be replaced by a tighter financial discipline. Regional development policy should favour the least disadvantaged areas. More investments should be made in basic education, infrastructure, poverty alleviation, healthcare and the like in the western parts of the country. Finally, it needs to be stressed that creating a freer capital market may be more important than allowing inter-regional and rural–urban migration. The capital market in China is still heavily controlled by a few state banking and other financial institutions, which are renowned for their inefficiency, rent seeking and corrupt behaviour. This situation has to be changed. The deepening of financial sector reform should also allow collective and private financial institutions to compete with the state institutions. The state should pay more attention to removing the barriers on capital movement across regions.

# 7 Regional inequality and diverging clubs[1]

## 7.1 Introduction

Apart from the rising urban–rural inequality, another negative aspect of China's fast growth is the rising inequality between regions. In addition, it appears that provinces are clustered into different growth clubs, with the coastal regions becoming the growth engine and the western regions lagging behind with little chance of catching up despite recent efforts by the central government to support them. China's development experiences contradict the theoretical expectation of the neo-classical growth model which suggests that poor regions (countries) should be able to catch up with the rich regions (countries) over time due to the law of diminishing marginal returns on capital. This chapter uses a large panel data set to prove that the Chinese provinces are not only diverging, but they are also forming their own economic clubs under economic reforms. This phenomenon has important policy implications for income inequality and poverty reduction in China.

## 7.2 The theory of economic growth

One important feature of the neoclassical growth model is its implication for cross-country or regional convergence. A negative relationship between initial per capita incomes and rates of growth is considered to be evidence of absolute convergence. If such a negative relationship is dependent on some factors that control the steady state, e.g. physical and human capital, Mankiw *et al.* (1992), and Barro and Sala-i-Martin (1992) refer to it as conditional convergence. Interest in economic growth and the question of convergence was renewed in the critique of the neoclassical growth model by Romer (1986) and Lucas (1988). This criticism has led to many studies dedicated to applying cross-section and time-series techniques to both cross-country and cross-regional data.

From cross-sectional data, Barro (1991) and Mankiw *et al.* (1992) show no evidence of absolute convergence across most countries, but they do find evidence of conditional convergence among groups of countries with similar characteristics. In sharp contrast, time series analysis shows little evidence of convergence, even among those countries which are perceived to have similar characteristics (Quah, 1991, 1993 for a large set of capitalist economies; Campbell and Mankiw, 1989 and Bernard and Durlauf, 1995 for the OECD economies).

From cross-regional data, Barro and Sala-i-Martin (1992, 1995) find evidence of absolute convergence within the US and within Western Europe. Hsueh (1994), Chen and Fleisher (1996), Gundlach (1997) and Raiser (1998) find evidence of conditional convergence across the Chinese regions using different data samples. On the other hand, Brown *et al.* (1990) find no evidence of stochastic convergence across the US states using time series data. Stochastic convergence implies that per capita incomes converge to a common long-term state across the regions under concern. There do not seem to be any published studies on the Chinese regions using a time series technique, but a recent unpublished work by Yao *et al.* (2000) using a panel unit root test shows that the Chinese provinces diverged into two distinct clubs: namely coastal and interior regions. Their results are in sharp contrast to many previous cross-sectional studies on the Chinese regions.

The conflicting results from different studies indicate the need for further research on convergence analysis. This chapter focuses on the Chinese regions and uses the longest time series of GDP data in contemporary China from 1952 to 1997 (Hsueh and Li, 1999; NBS, 1997–8). Section 7.3 proposes a production model to explain why regions may diverge into different growth clubs within the same country. The hypothesis is that, in a developing economy where technology and capital are scarce, initial economic growth depends on the development of some growth centres, which will then lead the rest of the economy to expand. In China, the growth centres are concentrated along the eastern coast so that the nearby provinces benefit most from this development strategy. The spillover effects from growth centres to inland areas diminish as distance increases. Consequently, the further away a region is from the coast, the slower is its economic growth. This explains why the Chinese regions may diverge into different growth clubs with a clear geographical pattern.

To explore the existence of club divergence, it is assumed that China may have formed three different geo-economic clubs, corresponding to the three geo-economic zones specified by the government, i.e. east, central and west. This delineation of clubs is arbitrary but it fits with a popular perception by both policy makers and many researchers on China's regional economies.[2] The principal objective here is to test whether this popular perception can be supported by empirical evidence. Two conditions are defined for club divergence. First, per capita income converges to a long-term equilibrium level within each club. Second, per capita income diverges between clubs so that the rich become richer and the poor poorer.

Both parametric and non-parametric techniques are used to support the two conditions for club divergence. The parametric approach uses a simplified production function to test the effect of distance on economic growth using a cross-sectional data set for 30 provinces from 1978 to 1995. Another parametric approach relies on testing the existence of a unit root in the relative incomes of each club against national average incomes using a much longer panel data set from 1952 to 1997. The technique is proposed by Perron (1989) and applied by Carlino and Mills (1993) and Loewy and Papell (1996) for the US states. Carlino and Mills define two conditions for convergence: relative regional incomes should be stationary and initially poor regions should catch up, i.e. $\beta$ convergence. One limitation of their approach is that the tests for a unit root and for $\beta$ convergence are conducted in the same stochastic process. Consequently, conclusive results are not easy to obtain. To overcome this limitation, the unit root test is used to examine whether there is stochastic convergence, but the decomposition of an inequality index, i.e. the Gini coefficient, is also used to see whether there is $\beta$ convergence, i.e. whether the initially poor become relatively better off over the data period. If both parametric and non-parametric results are consistent, conclusions can be drawn with more confidence than those relying on a single technique. Different approaches lead to the same conclusion that there is no convergence among the Chinese provinces but there is convergence within each of the geo-economic regions.

## 7.3 A model of club divergence

In a large developing country where technology and capital are scarce, initial economic growth may have to be concentrated in a few cities or industrial bases, hereafter, the growth centres. The growth centres become the engines or examples of economic growth for the rest of the country. As a result, economic growth of a particular region is linked to the economic condition of its closest growth centre. In China, the most important urban and industrial centres are concentrated along the eastern coast, including the three largest metropolitan cities of Beijing, Tianjin and Shanghai, four special economic zones, 14 open cities, Hainan Island and the Pudong Development Zone. Beijing, Tianjin and Shanghai were the largest and strongest economic centres of the country. The special economic zones, the open cities, Hainan and the Pudong Development Zone were the fastest growing centres after economic reforms.[3]

The role of metropolitan cities as growth centres is discussed in great detail by Lucas (1988) and in World Bank (1999: 125–38). Large cities are found to have higher labour productivity than the suburban or rural areas because of the economies of agglomeration. According to the World Bank (1999: 127), agglomeration economies have two basic components. The first, localisation economies, refers to the benefits to firms from locating close to firms in the same industry. The second, urbanisation economies, refers to the benefits to firms from proximity to many different economic actors. Because China started the open policy in the east, many local and foreign firms flourished not only in the coastal cities themselves, but also in their suburban areas. Consequently, the coastal area had both the localization and urbanisation economies. The inland areas found themselves permanently disadvantaged even though the special status of the east was abolished long ago because economic development in the inland regions relied on the spillover effects from the coastal cities. However, spillover effects pass from the growth centres to their surrounding suburban areas first, then to other areas within the same province, then to the nearby provinces, and eventually to the most remote regions in the west. In general, the closer a particular region is to the growth centres, the faster will be its growth.

A theoretical model can be derived to explain the slow process of economic spillover from the east to the west. Let $y$ and $k$ denote output (GDP) and capital per labour respectively. Let $y$ be defined by a Cobb-Douglas production function (7.1).

$$y = Ak^{\alpha}e^{\varepsilon}, \quad A = \begin{cases} e^{\beta_0 - \beta_1 D_{min} - \beta_2 (D - D_{min})^2} & \text{if} \quad D > D_{min} \\ e^{\beta_0 - \beta_1 D} & \text{if} \quad 0 < D \leq D_{min} \\ e^{\beta_0} & \text{if} \quad D = 0 \end{cases} \tag{7.1}$$

$D$ denotes the total distance between a region and its closest growth centre. $D_{min}$ is a given length within which the effect of distance on labour productivity is log-linear, but beyond which the effect of distance on labour productivity is log-quadratic. $\varepsilon$ is a disturbance term.[4] Distance is assumed to have a negative effect on y so that $\beta_1$ and $\beta_2$ are two non-negative parameters.

For simplicity, consider one growth centre, denoted by C, and two neighbouring regions, denoted by A and B. The total distance between A and C is assumed to be not more than $D_{min}$. The total distance between B and C is greater than $D_{min}$ (Figure 7.1).

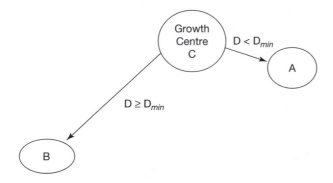

*Figure 7.1* Economic growth and linkage to a growth centre.

Taking logarithms on both sides of equation (7.1), the marginal products of distance for regions C, A and B, denoted respectively by $MPD_C$, $MPD_A$ and $MPD_B$, are derived below.[5]

$$MPD_C = \frac{\partial y}{\partial D} = 0, \quad MPD_A = \frac{\partial y}{\partial D} = -\beta_1 y_A, \quad MPD_B = \frac{\partial y}{\partial D}$$

$$= -(\beta_1 + 2\beta_2 (D - D_{min})) y_B$$

where $y_A$ and $y_B$ are GDP per labour of regions A and B respectively in any year. If all the other production conditions apart from distance are held unchanged, the differences of labour productivity between C and A, denoted by $\Delta MPD_{CA}$, and between C and B, denoted by $\Delta MPD_{CB}$, can be expressed as:

$$\Delta MPD_{CA} = MPD_C - MPD_A = \beta_1 y_A \tag{7.2}$$

$$\Delta MPD_{CB} = MPD_C - MPD_B = (\beta_1 + 2\beta_2(D - D_{min}))y_B \tag{7.3}$$

Due to the distance effect, C grows faster than A, and A grows faster than B, *ceteris paribus*.[6] However, because C is a growth centre, its economy is likely to be more capital intensive than A or B. Let $k_C$, $k_A$ and $k_B$ denote the capital/labour ratios in C, A and B respectively. It is likely that $k_C > k_A$, and $k_C > k_B$. Due to the law of diminishing marginal returns to capital implied by the neo-classical growth model, the marginal product of capital in C is likely to be smaller than that in A or in B.[7]

Let $MPK_C$, $MPK_A$ and $MPK_B$ be the marginal products of capital in C, A and B, respectively. If $MPK_C < MPK_A$, and $MPK_C < MPK_B$, the differences in the marginal products of capital will have a converging effect on economic growth between C and the other two regions. This converging effect may be cancelled out by the diverging effect of distance expressed in (7.2) and (7.3). Consequently, whether or not A or B can catch up with C will depend on the net effects of these two counteractive forces. Regarding convergence, there are three possible cases.

*Case 1* $(MPK_A - MPK_C) < \beta_1 y_A$, $(MPK_B - MPK_C) < (\beta_1 + 2\beta_2 (D - D_{min}))y_B$

In this case, the converging effect of capital is smaller than the diverging effect of distance. Both A and B can never catch up with C.

*Case 2* $(MPK_A - MPK_C) > \beta_1 y_A$, $(MPK_B - MPK_C) < (\beta_1 + 2\beta_2 (D - D_{min}))y_B$

In this situation, the converging effect is greater than the diverging effect in A but smaller than the diverging effect in B. Region A will gradually catch up with C, but region B can not.

*Case 3* $(MPK_A - MPK_C) > \beta_1 y_A$, $(MPK_B - MPK_C) > (\beta_1 + 2\beta_2 (D - D_{min}))y_B$

In case 3, the convergence effect is greater than the diverging effect in both A and B. As a result, both A and B will catch up with C, but the pace of convergence may be quite different from A to C than from B to C.

Because the distance from B to C is greater than $D_{min}$, it is far more difficult for B to catch up with C than A. In China, the east is similar to region C, the central is similar to region A, and the west is similar to region B. Since the East is home to the majority of China's growth centres, the diverging effect of distance on labour productivity is minimal within the eastern provinces. As the provinces become further away from the east, i.e. the central region, the distance effect becomes more significant. The west has the greatest distance so that the negative effect of distance will be the greatest for these provinces.

## 7.4 An empirical model and results

Equation (7.1) can be translated into a growth equation based on an augmented Solow growth model derived from a Cobb-Douglas production function as:[8]

$$\ln y_{ti} = \alpha + \beta_1 \ln(s)_i - \beta_2 \ln(n + g + \delta)_i + \varepsilon_i \tag{7.4}$$

where $i$ denotes the $i$th province, $y_{ti}$ denotes real per capita GDP in year $t$ (1995), $s$ is the investment/GDP ratio, $n$ is the population growth rate, $g$ is a rate of technological progress, $\delta$ is a rate of capital depreciation, and $\varepsilon$ is an error term.

The constant term $\alpha$ should be time invariant but distance-variant. In theory, it is possible to measure the distance of each province to the growth centres. In practice, it is quite complicated to do so because there are many growth centres.[9] For simplicity, let us assume that the entire east region is one large growth centre. The distance from the central to the growth centre, denoted by (east to central), is the same for all provinces in that region. The distance from the west to the central, denoted by (central to west), is the same for all provinces in the west. The total distance from the west to the growth centre, denoted by (east to west), is then equal to (east to central) + (central to west). We further assume that (east to central) = 1, (central to west) = 1, so that (east to west) = 2. With these assumptions, $\alpha$ can be expressed as:

$$\alpha = \alpha_0 - \theta_1 \text{ (east to central)} - \theta_2 \text{ (central to west)} \tag{7.4A}$$

where $\alpha_0$ is a constant term for the growth centre, i.e. the east, (east to central) takes the value of one if a province is either in the central or in the west and zero otherwise, and (central to west) takes the value of one if a province is in the west and zero otherwise.[10] By incorporating (7.4A) into (7.4) and use partial adjustment, the augmented growth model is given by:

$$\ln y_{ti} - \ln y_{0i} = \alpha_0 + \rho \ln y_{0i} + \beta_1 \ln(s)_i - \beta_2 \ln(n + g + \delta)_i \tag{7.4B}$$

$$+ \beta_3 \ln(\text{Export} / \text{GDP})_i - \theta_1 \text{ (east to central)} - \theta_2 \text{ (central to west)} + \varepsilon_i$$

where $y_{ti}$ and $y_{0i}$ are real per capita GDP in the end and beginning years respectively of the data period, and $s$ and $n$ are the average investment/GDP ratio and population growth rate respectively over the data period. Export/GDP is the exports/GDP ratio.[11]

The data used to estimate (7.4B) are taken from NBS (1996) for the period 1978 to 1995. All of the values, i.e. GDP, exports and investments, are measured in constant 1990 prices using provincial price deflators. Exports in US dollars are converted to values in Chinese yuan, using a real effective exchange rate derived by Yao and Zhang (2001b). Earlier data cannot be used because one cannot derive the investment/GDP ratio or measure exports before 1978. However, this data period corresponds to the most rapid growth years of the Chinese economy so it is the one most relevant for testing the effect of distance on regional growth. As in most other studies on regional growth (Mankiw *et al.*, 1992; Sala-i-Martin, 1996), it is assumed here that the sum of capital depreciation and technological growth rates $(g + \delta)$ equals 0.05.

The estimated coefficients on the distance variables are used to test the distance effect on regional growth. If both estimated coefficients are negative and significant, distance has a negative effect on growth and, the longer the distance, the stronger its effect. If the estimated coefficient on the first variable is insignificant but the second coefficient is significant and negative, distance has no effect when it is within the boundary of the central region. If both estimated coefficients are insignificant, distance has no effect in all regions. Equation (7.4B) is estimated with ordinary least squares using different specifications. The estimated results are presented in Table 7.1 and explained below.

The first model includes only $ln(y_0)$. If the estimated coefficient on $ln(y_0)$ would have been negative and significant, this would be evidence of absolute convergence of per capita GDP across all the provinces. The actual results show no such

*Table 7.1* Test for conditional convergence and distance effect on growth

*Dependent variable: $ln(y_t)$-$ln(y_0)$, sample 30 Chinese provinces, 1978–95*

| Variables | Model 1 | Model 2 | Model 3 | Model 4 |
|---|---|---|---|---|
| Intercept | 2.25 | 3.45 | 7.94 | 8.87 |
| | (2.93) | (1.09) | (3.49) | (4.13) |
| $ln(y_0)$ | −0.12 | −0.13 | −0.49 | −0.57 |
| | (−1.09) | (−0.94) | (−4.46) | (−5.27) |
| $ln(s)$ | – | −0.08 | 0.40 | 0.42 |
| | – | (−0.25) | (1.57) | (1.75) |
| $ln(n+g+\delta)$ | – | −0.70 | −1.35 | −1.36 |
| | – | (−0.53) | (−1.51) | (−1.64) |
| Distance (east to central) | – | – | −0.35 | −0.17 |
| | – | – | (−3.43) | (−1.66) |
| Distance (central to west) | – | – | −0.30 | −0.26 |
| | – | – | (−2.53) | (−2.32) |
| $ln(\text{export/GDP})$ | – | – | – | 0.20 |
| | – | – | – | (2.23) |
| Adjusted-$R^2$ | 0.04 | 0.07 | 0.61 | 0.82 |

Source: NBS, 1996.

Notes: *t*-values are in parentheses. $y_t$ and $y_0$ are real GDP per working-age person in 1995 and 1978, respectively.
$ln(s)=ln(\text{investment/GDP})$, $(n+g+\delta)=0.05$ reflect the average growth rates of population, technological progress and capital depreciation, respectively.

evidence because the estimated coefficient is insignificant. The second model includes $ln(y_0)$, $ln(s)$ and $ln(n+g+\delta)$. If the estimated coefficient on $ln(y_0)$ would have been negative and significant, this would be evidence of conditional convergence. In other words, different provinces converge towards their own steady states. The differences in provincial steady states are explained only by the variations in investments and population growth. The actual results show no evidence of conditional convergence. The effects of investment/GDP ratio and population growth are insignificant. The estimated coefficient on the investment/GDP ratio even has the wrong sign. We expect investment to have a positive effect and population growth a negative effect from the model.

Models 1 and 2 may be misspecified because the values of $R^2$ are small, i.e. 0.04 and 0.07. The third model adds two distance variables to the second model. The results become fundamentally different from those of the previous models and the value of $R^2$ increases to 0.61. The estimated coefficients on investment/GDP ratio and population growth rate have the expected signs and become much more significant than in the previous models. The estimated coefficients on two distance variables are negative and significant, supporting the hypothesis that distance has a negative effect on economic growth and that the longer the distance, the stronger its negative effect. The estimated coefficients imply that, after controlling for the differences in investment and population growth, per capita GDP grew 35 per cent more in the east than in the central region and 30 per cent more in the central region than in the west over the data period. The total difference between the east and the west is 65 per cent. Finally, it is interesting to note that the estimated coefficient on $ln(y_0)$ is now negative and significant. However, this does not mean that there is evidence of convergence across all provinces, instead, it provides evidence of convergence among provinces only in each of the three regions.

Model 3 may be missing out some important variables, e.g. human capital, infrastructure, policy and openness that are responsible for economic growth. We have tried a number of different variables in the model but found that only the export/GDP ratio is significant. Model 4 includes the average export/GDP ratio over the data period by province. This variable may represent the effect of openness on economic growth, but it also has a strong policy and geographical feature, particularly in the reform period. Since the late 1970s, China has adopted a far more open policy than before, featuring export promotion, foreign direct investments (FDI) and free market competition.

The results in Model 4 show that the export/GDP ratio, representing an export-promotion development strategy, has a significant and positive effect on economic growth. Our results are consistent with the conclusions of some recent studies, such as Wu (2001) for China, and Sengupta and Espana (1994) for the Asian newly industrialised economies. It is striking to note that even after the export/GDP ratio is included, the estimated coefficients on the distance variables are still negative and significant, although the estimated coefficient on the first distance variable becomes smaller.

In summary, the overall results presented in Table 7.1 show that distance has a significant and negative effect on economic growth. They support our hypothesis that the effects of economic spillover from the growth centres diminish as distance rises. This explains why inter-regional inequality increased rather than declined over the data period. However, we stress that the above model is simple, involves many assumptions, and ignores many factors responsible for growth convergence. In particular, the distance variable may reflect something more than just physical distance. Rather, it may include the pace of spillover of production technology and managerial skills from the growth centres to their neighbouring regions. This variable may also reflect the inter-regional barriers on the movement of labour and capital, and differences in the ability to adopt new technology and modern organ-isational practices between the rich and the poor regions. In the long run, the problems posed by physical distance could be reduced if the transportation and telecommunication infrastructures were improved. Other influences can be affected if human capital in the disadvantaged areas is improved. The real problem is that it may take a long time for the low-income regions, especially the west, to improve their production environment and human capital before the diverging effect of distance is overtaken by the converging effect of capital.

## 7.5 Alternative tests for club divergence

This section provides two alternative tests to demonstrate that China's provinces diverged into the different geo-economic clubs specified in the previous section. The first approach is a unit root test to investigate whether there is stochastic convergence among the provinces. The second approach is the decomposition of the Gini coefficient to investigate whether the movement of regional inequality has resulted in club formation. Data in this section are derived from Hsueh and Li (1999) for the period 1952 to 1995 and NBS (1997, 1998) for 1996 and 1997. Per capita GDP is calculated at 1990 prices using provincial GDP deflators for thirty provinces. The values of regional and national per capita GDP are weighted averages by provincial populations.

### 7.5.1 Unit root test

Let $x_{It}$ denote logged per capita income of region $I$ relative to per capita income in the nation at time $t$. The Dickey-Fuller test for the presence of a unit root can be expressed in two versions:

$$\Delta x_{It} = \alpha + \sum_{k=1}^{p} \beta_k \Delta x_{It-1} + \rho x_{It-1} + \varepsilon_{It} \quad \text{and} \tag{7.5}$$

$$\Delta x_{It} = \alpha + \beta_0 t + \sum_{k=1}^{p} \beta_k \Delta x_{It-1} + \rho x_{It-1} + \varepsilon_{It} \tag{7.6}$$

The only difference between (7.5) and (7.6) is the addition of a time trend in (7.6). $\Delta x_{It}$ is the first difference of $x_{It}$. $\varepsilon_{It}$ is a serially uncorrelated random shock with mean zero and a constant deviation.

In equation (7.5), if $\rho < 0$, shocks to relative incomes are temporary. Club relative incomes will converge to a long-run steady state. On the other hand, if $\rho = 0$, shocks to relative incomes may be permanent and club incomes may not converge. After adding a time trend, the results in equation (7.6) have different implications from those obtained from equation (7.5). If $\rho$ is smaller than zero in equation (7.5), it will still be smaller than zero in equation (7.6). However, if $\rho$ is equal to zero in equation (7.5), it may or may not be equal to zero in equation (7.6).

From equation (7.5), if $\rho = 0$, club relative incomes may not converge to their steady states. If $\rho < 0$, there are two possibilities depending on the estimated coefficients on the time trends for different clubs. If the coefficients are negative for the initially rich clubs but positive for the initially poor ones, there is conditional convergence. On the other hand, if the coefficients are positive for the initially rich clubs but negative for the initially poor ones, there is no conditional convergence. The relative incomes for the three regions are logged and plotted in Figure 7.2.

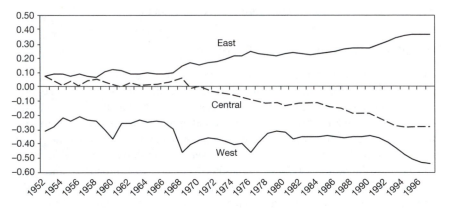

*Figure 7.2* Logged regional relative per capita GDP at 1990 constant prices.

Source: Hsueh and Li, 1999.

A close examination of Figure 7.2 suggests that per capita GDP in the west was much lower than the national average. Relative income frustrated around a mean level until the late 1980s but suffered a sharp decline in the 1990s. Per capita GDP in the central region was slightly higher than the national average until the late 1960s but experienced a gradual decline from 1970. By the end of the data period, it was much lower than the national average although still higher than in the west. Per capita GDP in the east was initially higher than that in the central region but the difference disappeared by 1958. Since then, it surpassed the level in the central region and continued to grow faster. At the end of the data period, it was substantially higher than the national average. Clearly the east is a different club from the rest of the country, but the distinction between the central region and the west is less significant.

We first perform standard unit root tests for the three regional log relative per capita GDP series using equations (7.5) and (7.6). Following the 't-sig' method suggested by Campbell and Perron (1991) and Perron (1994, 1997), we start with an upper bound, $p_{max}$, on $p$, or the number of terms on

$$\left( \sum_{k=1}^{p} \beta_k \Delta x_{It-k} \right),$$

which is determined a priori. If the last included lag is significant, choose $p = p_{max}$. If not, reduce $p$ by one until the last lag becomes significant. We set $p_{max} = 8$ and use the two-sided 10 per cent value of the asymptotic normal distribution to assess the significance of the lag.

The final results are reported in Table 7.2. Without a time trend, the null hypothesis of a unit root cannot be rejected in all cases. With a time trend, it is rejected for the relative incomes of the East and the West but cannot be rejected for the relative income of the central region.

*Table 7.2* Augmented Dickey-Fuller tests, $p_{max} = 8$

|  | *Coefficients* | *East* | | *Central* | | *West* | |
| --- | --- | --- | --- | --- | --- | --- | --- |
| *Without time trend* | p (no. of lags) | 1 | | 5 | | 4 | |
| | Intercept | 0.008 | (0.759) | −0.014 | (−1.670) | −0.006 | (−0.250) |
| | $\rho$ | −0.013 | (−0.394) | −0.048 | (−1.250) | 0.005 | (0.070) |
| *With time trend* | p (no. of lags) | 5 | | 5 | | 6 | |
| | Intercept | 0.032 | (3.00)** | 0.010 | (0.82) | −0.100 | (−3.65)** |
| | $\beta_0$ | 0.002 | (3.60)** | −0.003 | (−2.43)** | −0.005 | (4.41)** |
| | $\rho$ | −0.336 | (−3.71)** | −0.332 | (−2.72) | −0.666 | (−4.25)** |

Notes: (1) For the model without time trend, the critical values for $\rho$ are −3.75 for 1%, −3.0 for 5% and −2.73 for 10% (Harris, 1995). (2) For the model with time trend, the corresponding critical values are −4.38, −3.60 and −3.24. (3) '**' signifies significance at 5% level.

The estimated coefficient of the time trend is significant in all cases, which has important implications. Relative incomes in the east and the west are trend-stationary. Any shocks to these income series should be temporary. However, the east's relative income moved upward over time. In sharp contrast, the west's relative income moved downward. As for the central region, the situation is more complicated. On the one hand, its relative income shows a long-term declining trend. On the other hand, it does not have a clear long-run steady state, implying that shocks to its relative income are permanent. A possible explanation is that the east is pulling it up while the west is pulling it down, resulting in its movement in no clear direction. From the results in Table 7.2, it can be concluded that the east and the west belong to two different clubs, but the position of the central region is unclear and needs further testing.

## 7.5.2 Decomposition of the Gini coefficient

We use the Gini coefficient method and its decomposition to analyse the income clubs of China's provinces. This method has been used by many recent studies (Yang, 1999; Yao, 2000) to study regional inequality. The Gini coefficient is the most popularly used inequality index since its decomposition is easy to understand although its has an overlapping term that may cause some misunderstanding. In this chapter, the decomposition results are explained and a specific explanation of the overlapping term is provided. There are other decomposition methods, such as the generalised entropy class, notably Theil's index and the square of the coefficient of variation. If a decomposition of the Theil index is undertaken it will be seen that the results are strikingly similar to those of the decomposition of the Gini coefficient which is why the results based on Theil's index are not reported here.

For convergence analysis, the two conditions that must be satisfied to form geo-economic clubs are that first, the Gini coefficient within a region declines, and second, that the coefficient rises between regions at the same time.

In this section, we follow the decomposition procedure on the Gini coefficient using population class.[12] Let $G$ denote the Gini coefficient measuring inter-provincial income inequality. It can be decomposed into the following three components if the provinces are classified into three regions, east, central and west:

$$G + G_B + G_A + G_O$$

where $G_B$ is the between regional component, measuring the inequality of mean incomes among the three regions, $G_A$ is the intra-regional component, arising from inequality between provinces in the three regions, and $G_O$ is an overlapping term arising from the effect of rich provinces in poor regions being richer than poor provinces in rich regions. The percentage shares of $G_B$ and $G_O$ in $G$ have important implications on inter-regional inequality. A greater share of $G_B$ in $G$ signifies more inter-regional inequality. On the other hand, a smaller share of $G_O$ in $G$ means that provinces are separated more into rich and poor regions.

The decomposition results based on equation (7.7) are presented in Figure 7.3. Before 1967, the three components of the Gini coefficient measuring inter-provincial inequality were more or less equally distributed. Since then, the share of $G_B$ increased, largely at the expense of $G_O$ but with some reduction in $G_A$. The share of $G_B$ in $G$ rose from about 30 per cent in the 1950s and 1960s to almost 80 per cent in the 1990s. The share of $G_O$ in $G$ declined from almost 40 per cent in the 1960s to less than 2 per cent by the end of the data period. The share of $G_B$ declined from over 35 per cent to 20 per cent over the same period.

Figure 7.3 shows that the provinces diverged into different clubs because they satisfied the two conditions that, first, inter-regional inequality rises, and second, intra-regional inequality declines over the data period.

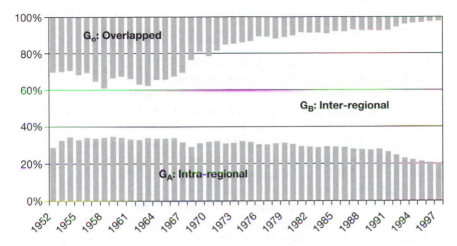

*Figure 7.3* Distribution of inter-provincial inequality by club components.

## 7.6 Conclusion

Empirical evidence suggests that China's provinces can be divided into three different geo-economic clubs corresponding to three regions, east, central and west. The east was initially rich and became richer over time. The central and west regions were initially poor and became poorer. The divergence of regional incomes became more apparent in the reform period than in the pre-reform period. In particular, the richest provinces are clustered in the east, and the poorest in the west. Hence, a clear three-tiered geographical pattern, with per capita income descending from the east to the central region, and then to the west.

This chapter tests the hypothesis that club divergence is due to the spillover from the growth centres, which are highly concentrated in the east, declines as provinces are further away from the centres. Regression results using a simplified augmented production function show that distance has a significant and negative effect on regional economic growth, even after controlling for the regional differences in investments, population growth, and exports in the reform period 1978 to 1995.

Previous studies have drawn some controversial conclusions as to whether per capita incomes have converged across the Chinese regions, or whether they have converged differently before and after the reform sub-periods. These studies provide important insights into our understanding of the real situation, but none of them uses a multi-techniques approach to establish their argument. Many studies also use data for a much shorter period. This paper uses the largest possible data set in contemporary China and different tests to demonstrate the same hypotheses on club divergence. The empirical results from this paper offer the following additional contributions to our understanding of regional economic development in China.

First, club divergence is due to the slow process of economic spillover from the growth centres to the remote provinces. Second, contrary to some previous studies, we find that the Chinese regions did not converge in the reform period. Third, club divergence has been caused by Deng's development strategy adopted from the beginning of economic reforms.

China's economic performance has been impressive by international standards for more than two decades after economic reforms, but the rising trend in regional inequality has become a crucial concern of the government. The recent efforts to boost economic development in the west are encouraging, but due to the distance effect and adverse production environment in some of the most remote provinces, i.e. Guizhou, Qinghai, Gansu, Ninxia and Yunnan, reducing regional inequality is by no means an easy task. Moreover, the fact that the Central region is not catching up with the east implies that China's regional development problem is not really only related to the west, it is a problem for the entire inland areas. Consequently, the lesson learned from the east should be applied to all the non-coastal provinces.

Government policy may play an important role in regional development through directing resources from the east to the rest of the country and creating a more flexible environment to reduce barriers on inter-regional movements of labour and capital. However, resource re-allocation may undermine future growth in the east. The real question is how to achieve high growth and reduce regional inequality at the same time. Unfortunately, development experiences in the past suggest that whatever action is taken by the government, regional inequality will remain a serious issue into the foreseeable future. If this problem cannot be resolved or mitigated, it may well become a critical impediment to future prosperity and a dangerous factor affecting political stability.

# 8 Understanding income inequality in China

## A multi-angle perspective

### 8.1 Introduction

In the previous two chapters, we look at the issues of urban–rural inequality and regional inequality. This chapter uses some household survey data to facilitate a more detailed study on the inequality issue through a multi-dimensional approach. In other words, inequality is examined through analysing urban–rural inequality, regional inequality and inequality within the urban and rural sub-populations.

Inequality can be attributed by different income sources. In the rural sector, income can be divided into farm and non-farm incomes. In the urban sector, income can be divided into wages, bonus, capital income and income transfers, etc. As income inequality can be decomposed by income factors, we examine how different sources of income have contributed to inequality for both the rural and urban sub-populations.

### 8.2 Background of inequality

When Deng Xiaoping started to reform the Chinese economy after the downfall of the Gang of Four in 1978, he had two principal objectives in mind. One was to transform China into a strong and powerful nation not only in terms of its size but also in terms of people's living standards. Another objective was to break away from the traditional egalitarian distribution system so that people's incomes were linked to their work efforts. Deng's policy was to allow some people to get rich first and other people to follow, and to allow some regions to develop quickly first and other regions to follow.

This was the ideological, political and policy background for implementing the household responsibility system in the countryside, and setting up the special economic zones, opening up the coastal cities, encouraging foreign direct investments (FDI), and allowing private ownership in the cities (McMillan and Naughton, 1992; Lin, 1995). Such policies have produced spectacular growth and vast improvements of people's living standards over the last 25 years. China's gross domestic product (GDP) rose six-fold, and people's living standards, measured in real per capita disposable income, increased in a similar order. China's economic success has attracted tremendous interest from both academic researchers and policy makers. Many studies have been conducted to explain why China has been so successful. Most of them have focused on analysing the effects of institutional reforms and productivity growth. There are relatively fewer studies on income distribution and as far as I am aware there has been no study on the linkage between economic growth and poverty except for a recent report by the World Bank (1997).

There are, however, many serious social and economic problems behind the apparent success of high growth. Among them are cronyism and the pervasive corruption of party and government officials, unbalanced regional economic growth, and rising income inequality. All of these contribute to the difficulty in eliminating poverty throughout the country. Income inequality within a region is partially explained by the implementation of Deng's policies that encouraged some people to get rich first, as well as the breaking-down of the traditional, communalised egalitarian income distribution system. Inter-regional income inequality is due to a number of factors, including preferential policies granted to the more prosperous coastal provinces and cities (Yao, 1997a) and the different natural and economic conditions between the coastal and inland areas. Cronyism, bribery and other forms of corruption, tax evasion and market distortions all contribute to rising inequality. Finally, the most obvious element of income inequality in China is the urban–rural divide. Even in the pre-reform era, almost all the urban citizens were guaranteed a job and subsidies and privileges that were not available to the rural population. After the reforms, the urban–rural divide has been maintained by the strict population registration system. As a result, almost all the poor people are either concentrated in the countryside, or live in the cities without an urban residency.

However, the nature of economic growth has brought about two fundamental problems in the economic system. One is unbalanced development among the regional economies. The other is the worsening of income distribution. As a result, poverty is still a major social, economic and political problem after 25 years of fast growth. Moreover, income inequality and poverty have a clear rural–urban and regional pattern. Due to historical reasons, the Chinese population has been separated into two relatively heterogeneous sub-populations, that is, the rural and the urban. Rural–urban inequality has been a key component in overall income inequality. The income sources and their relative importance in overall inequality are also different between the two populations. Hence, to study income inequality in China, one needs to understand the nature and development of rural–urban inequality, and to understand the nature and development of inequality among the separate rural and urban populations.

In the countryside, the production responsibility system and later the household contract responsibility system allowed some farmers to become rich first as their efforts were directly linked to production performance. Farm production growth slowed down considerably after 1984, and more efforts were made to develop non-farm enterprises, or township and village enterprises (TVEs). Fast development of TVEs has produced an unprecedentedly powerful impact on the rural economy (Yao, 1997a). Millions of farm workers have been transferred out of agriculture. TVEs have also become a major source of rural income, state tax revenues and exports. The share of TVE income as a proportion of rural per capita income grew from 7 per cent in 1978 to almost 40 per cent by 1992. However, uneven development of TVEs between regions has contributed to the ever-widening income gaps among the rural population.

In the cities, two major reforms have had a powerful impact on income growth and distribution. The first reform was the introduction of enterprise autonomy in state-owned enterprises, or SOEs. As early as 1980, some experiments were conducted to reform SOEs through the profit-sharing and bonus system (Hay *et al.*, 1994). Firms could retain a certain proportion of realised profits. This was in sharp contrast with the old system where they were not responsible for any losses or profits, rather they fulfilled a pre-set production plan given by the authorities. With profit-sharing, firms had more responsibility for their performance, and their successful survival depended on their ability to produce and retain profits. Workers also had more incentives to work hard because the amount of bonus depended on how much profit the firms were able to retain.

The second reform in the cities was the diversification of ownership. Under the old economic system, Mao Zedong did not allow private ownership and foreign investments. Hence, SOEs and urban collective units were the only possible employment outlets for urban citizens. Because of low efficiency and lack of flexibility, SOEs (and urban collective units) were unable to effectively employ all the urban labour force. This created widespread problems of over-staffing and under-utilisation of labour in the cities because most work units were forced to employ many unproductive or unwanted workers. As a result, the survival of SOEs heavily depended on state subsidies which had to come from severe exploitation of the politically powerless peasantry. By allowing non-state ownership and FDI since economic reforms, China has managed to create a much more competitive and diversified labour market. SOEs have become less and less dominant over the years both in terms of their contribution to the national economy and to employment (Jefferson and Rawski, 1994; Perkins, 1994). Fast development of non-state sectors has been a principal factor in the unprecedented success of the Chinese economy over the last two decades. Moreover, the creation of a diversified labour market has made it possible for China to launch a massive privatization programme in order to solve the loss-making problems of the SOEs in recent years. Without a diversified labour market, it would have been unthinkable for millions of state employees to have been made redundant during the latest reform programme.

Enterprise reform and ownership diversification have brought about profound effects on income growth and inequality in the cities. Before the reforms, almost all the city workers had only one income source, that is basic wages paid by their work units. Today, not only has the wages system been radically transformed, but the source of income has also been diversified. In the state sector, the former uniform wages have been replaced by timed wages, non-timed wages and bonuses. Timed wages are paid to permanent and regular employees. Non-timed wages are paid to contract workers whose jobs are no longer guaranteed on a permanent basis. Bonuses paid to both permanent and contract workers are generally linked to individual efforts and enterprise performance (Groves *et al.*, 1994; and Yao, 1997b).

As sources of income became increasingly diversified, leading to the appearance of a high-income group, the central government introduced an income tax system in 1985 on earners of over 800 yuan per month. At the beginning, few people earned more than the threshold of tax-free allowances. Nowadays, personal income taxes have become an important source of state revenue. Some urban people regularly send monies to their relatives living in the poor rural areas and these remittances are regarded as income transfers. Income taxes and income transfers are a dynamic source that reduces income inequality among the urban population.

Many available studies on inequality only focus on a particular subset of the entire population, e.g. the rural population, or the urban population (e.g. Hussain *et al.*, 1994; Knight and Song, 1993a; Yao, 1997a). As a result, the extent of rural–urban inequality has not been fully analysed. Regarding the sources of income inequality for the urban population, the importance of income taxes and income transfers has not been fully recognised. For rural inequality, little work has been done at the household level to examine the relative contribution of agricultural and non-agricultural incomes.

To wholly understand the extent of inequality in different aspects, it is impossible to rely on one simple set of data. To overcome the data problem, we first use some top-down information to present a general picture of overall income inequality for the whole country. We then use bottom-up data (subsets of household survey data) to study the detailed attributes of income distribution. More specifically, to understand the extent of rural–urban inequality, household survey data from Liaoning and Sichuan for the period 1988–90 is used. In addition, to understand the relative importance that farm and non-farm incomes plays in relation to rural inequality, rural household survey data is used from Sichuan, Liaoning and Jiangsu from 1988–90. To understand the relative importance that timed wages, non-timed wages, non-wages, tax and transfer incomes play in relation to urban inequality, urban household survey data is used from Sichuan and Liaoning from 1986–93.

The principal methodology is the calculation of Gini coefficients and their decomposition by population class and income sources as shown in Chapter 5.

## 8.3   Overall income inequality and the urban–rural divide

Economic reforms have brought about unprecedented growth in personal incomes. Real per capita incomes rose by 450 per cent in the rural areas and by 426 per cent in the cities from 1978 to 2003 (Table 8.1).

Rapid income growth has been accompanied by rising inequality. The Gini coefficient rose from 0.288 in 1981 to 0.388 in 1995 (World Bank, 1997).

In China, income inequality and the growth of inequality under economic reforms have been explained by two major factors: urban–rural inequality and inter-provincial inequality. Urban–rural inequality is a common feature in all provinces, rich or poor, inland or coastal, but inter-provincial inequality is more a rural phenomenon than an urban one (see next section). A recent World Bank study (1997) concludes that the urban–rural income gap was responsible for one third of total inequality in 1995 and one-half of the increase in inequality since 1985.

Table 8.1 Income growth and urban–rural inequality, 1978–96

| | Rural per capita income | | | Urban per capita income | | | Urban–rural income ratio | | |
|---|---|---|---|---|---|---|---|---|---|
| Year | Current price | 1990 price | Adjust 1990 price | Current price | 1990 price | Adjust 1990 price | Current price | 1990 price | Adjust 1990 price |
| 1978 | 134 | 220 | 287 | 343 | 762 | 1372 | 2.56 | 3.46 | 4.79 |
| 1980 | 191 | 306 | 398 | 478 | 968 | 1742 | 2.50 | 3.16 | 4.37 |
| 1985 | 398 | 593 | 771 | 739 | 1223 | 2078 | 1.86 | 2.06 | 2.70 |
| 1986 | 424 | 612 | 796 | 900 | 1391 | 2365 | 2.12 | 2.27 | 2.97 |
| 1987 | 463 | 644 | 837 | 1002 | 1425 | 2422 | 2.16 | 2.21 | 2.89 |
| 1988 | 545 | 685 | 890 | 1181 | 1391 | 2365 | 2.17 | 2.03 | 2.66 |
| 1989 | 602 | 674 | 876 | 1376 | 1393 | 2369 | 2.29 | 2.07 | 2.70 |
| 1990 | 686 | 686 | 892 | 1510 | 1510 | 2416 | 2.20 | 2.20 | 2.71 |
| 1991 | 709 | 700 | 910 | 1701 | 1619 | 2590 | 2.40 | 2.31 | 2.85 |
| 1992 | 784 | 741 | 963 | 2027 | 1775 | 2840 | 2.59 | 2.40 | 2.95 |
| 1993 | 922 | 765 | 994 | 2577 | 1944 | 3111 | 2.80 | 2.54 | 3.13 |
| 1994 | 1221 | 803 | 1044 | 3496 | 2110 | 3376 | 2.86 | 2.63 | 3.23 |
| 1995 | 1578 | 846 | 1100 | 4283 | 2213 | 3540 | 2.71 | 2.62 | 3.22 |
| 1996 | 1926 | 922 | 1198 | 4839 | 2299 | 3678 | 2.51 | 2.49 | 3.07 |
| 1997 | 2090 | 964 | 1253 | 5160 | 2377 | 3804 | 2.47 | 2.47 | 3.03 |
| 1998 | 2162 | 1006 | 1307 | 5425 | 2515 | 4023 | 2.51 | 2.50 | 3.08 |
| 1999 | 2210 | 1044 | 1357 | 5854 | 2749 | 4398 | 2.65 | 2.63 | 3.24 |
| 2000 | 2253 | 1066 | 1386 | 6280 | 2925 | 4680 | 2.79 | 2.74 | 3.38 |
| 2001 | 2366 | 1111 | 1444 | 6860 | 3173 | 5077 | 2.90 | 2.86 | 3.52 |
| 2002 | 2476 | 1164 | 1513 | 7703 | 3599 | 5758 | 3.11 | 3.09 | 3.81 |
| 2003 | 2644 | 1214 | 1578 | 8500 | 3933 | 6293 | 3.21 | 3.24 | 3.99 |
| Average annual growth rates (geometric averages in %) | | | | | | | | | |
| 1978–85 | – | 15.18 | 15.18 | – | 6.98 | 6.11 | –4.48 | –7.12 | –7.87 |
| 1985–2003 | – | 4.06 | 4.06 | – | 6.71 | 6.35 | 3.10 | 2.54 | 2.20 |

Sources: NBS, 1997–2003 (CSYB); People's Daily, 15 January 2004 for 2003.

Notes: Incomes at 1990 prices are deflated respectively by rural and urban living price indices. Rural income are net incomes, urban income are disposable incomes. Adjusted incomes: rural incomes are adjusted up by 30 per cent (15 per cent is due to price differentials between urban and rural areas, and 15 per cent is due to imputed housing rents which are not included in official statistics. Urban incomes are adjusted up, by 80 per cent for 1978–80, 70 per cent for 1981–89 and 60 per cent for 1990–2003 because of state subsidies in pensions, healthcare, housing and education.

Rural incomes grew rapidly at a rate of over 15 per cent per year in the earlier years of reforms from 1978–85 but began to lose ground after the increases in urban incomes in the following two decades (Table 8.1). China's rural–urban income inequality is large by international standards. Even the high ratios of urban–rural per capita incomes in the official statistics fail to capture the full extent of urban–rural inequality. If urban subsidies in housing, pensions, health, education and other elements are taken into account, urban incomes would have been higher by an average of up to 80 per cent (a figure estimated by the World Bank). On the other hand, rural prices may be lower. In addition, official statistics do not include rural housing rents as a source of income. However, even the most optimistic upward adjustment of rural incomes would not raise the official statistics by 30 per cent (the World Bank gives a 15 per cent premium). If the official statistics of urban incomes were raised by 80 per cent in 1978–80 (before urban price reform), 70 per cent in 1981–89 (with gradual urban price reform) and 60 per cent after 1990 (with further reforms on health, housing and education), and the official statistics of rural incomes by 30 per cent (15 per cent for low cost of living in the countryside and 15 per cent for imputed housing rents), the urban–rural income ratio would have been as high as 4.79 in 1978, but dropped to 2.7 in 1985 (the lowest during economic reforms), but it rose again to 3.99 in 2003 (Table 8.1 and Figure 8.1). Even in nominal terms, excluding the various state subsidies and benefits to the urban population, per capita urban–rural income ratio was 3.21 in 2003. Income per capita was only 2,644 yuan for the rural population, compared to 8,500 yuan for the urban population. Per capita incomes in the three richest cities, Guangzhou, Shanghai and Beijing, were respectively 15,200, 14,900 and 13,000 yuan, which are ten times as much as the per capita rural incomes of the poorest provinces of Gansu and Qinghai (*People's Daily*, 15 January 2004; *Sina News*, 6 February

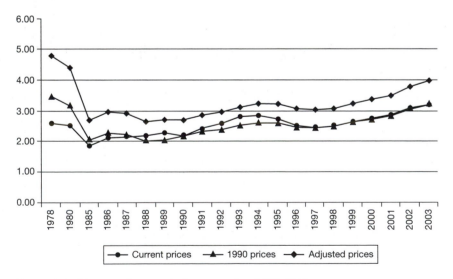

*Figure 8.1* Urban–rural per capita income ratios, 1978–2003.

2004). Many visitors to China are impressed by the high living standards of the prosperous cities, but how many people realise that the high buildings, motorways and luxury cars they see in Guangzhou, Shanghai and Beijing disguise the primitive living conditions in the poor rural areas where the vast majority of Chinese reside?

Another important dimension of inequality is inter-provincial. The World Bank estimates that almost one quarter of total inequality in 1995 and one third of the increase of inequality since 1985 was explained by inter-provincial inequality. A recent study by Yao on the rural population also draws a similar conclusion (Yao, 1997a).

To understand in more detail the extent of urban–rural divide, we can use some household survey data for Liaoning and Sichuan. Both provinces have a large population and they represent two different types of regional economies. Liaoning is a highly urbanised and high income province, whereas Sichuan is a much less urbanised and low income province. Hence the results for these two provinces will provide a good representation for the whole country. The data period was 1988–90 when China experienced a downturn in the growth of personal incomes and a reduction of inequality.

Measured in constant terms, per capita incomes declined in both provinces for both the rural and urban populations. When both rural and urban samples are merged together, the provincial Gini coefficient can be derived and decomposed into three components (inter-urban–rural, intra-rural–urban, and overlapped). Our decomposition results indicate that urban–rural income inequality accounts for 47–51 per cent of overall inequality (Table 8.2). These results are higher than the World Bank estimates using national data.

*Table 8.2* Decomposition of Gini coefficients by population class

| Components | Sichuan 1988–90 | | | Liaoning 1988–90 | | |
|---|---|---|---|---|---|---|
| | *1988* | *1989* | *1990* | *1988* | *1989* | *1990* |
| $G$ | 0.311 | 0.313 | 0.308 | 0.281 | 0.298 | 0.274 |
| $G_A$ | 0.158 | 0.155 | 0.146 | 0.117 | 0.121 | 0.109 |
| $G_B$ | 0.146 | 0.152 | 0.158 | 0.131 | 0.145 | 0.139 |
| $G_O$ | 0.007 | 0.005 | 0.004 | 0.033 | 0.033 | 0.025 |
| *As % of G* | | | | | | |
| $G$ | 100.0 | 100.0 | 100.0 | 100.0 | 100.0 | 100.0 |
| $G_A$ | 50.8 | 49.5 | 47.4 | 41.6 | 40.6 | 39.8 |
| $G_B$ | 46.9 | 48.6 | 51.3 | 46.6 | 48.7 | 50.7 |
| $G_O$ | 2.3 | 1.6 | 1.3 | 11.7 | 11.1 | 9.1 |
| *Urban–rural per capita incomes at 1990 prices (official data)* | | | | | | |
| Rural | 635 | 589 | 559 | 984 | 895 | 836 |
| Urban | 1530 | 1458 | 1424 | 1669 | 1605 | 1466 |
| Urban/rural | 2.41 | 2.48 | 2.55 | 1.70 | 1.79 | 1.75 |

Source: NBS, *Household Survey Data*.

Notes: $G_A$, $G_B$ and $G_O$ are inter-rural–urban, intra-rural–urban and overlapped terms of $G$, the Gini coefficient. All incomes are measured at 1990 prices.

If no household in a poor sub-population (rural) is better off than the poorest household in the higher income group (urban), the overlapped term $G_O$ is equal to zero. Hence the share of $G_O$ in $G$ is another useful indicator reflecting the extent of urban–rural division. In Sichuan, $G_O$ accounts for only 1.3 to 2.6 per cent of the overall provincial inequality, implying a near total urban–rural segmentation. The urban–rural income ratio is as high as 2.55. An urban–rural divide is also sharp in Liaoning but the extent of inequality is less severe than in Sichuan. Comparing the decomposition results of these two provinces suggests that there is more urban–rural inequality in a low income and less industrialised province than in a high income and more industrialised one. This suggests that urbanisation and industrialisation are important in reducing urban–rural inequality.

## 8.4  Rural income inequality and income sources

Income distribution in rural China over the last two decades has three main features. First, overall inequality rose significantly. The rural Gini coefficient rose from 0.212 in 1978, to 0.320 in 1994, and to 0.45 by 1998. Second, much of the rural income inequality is explained by interprovincial inequality, which in turn is mainly explained by inter-zonal inequality.[1] Over 50 per cent of the rural Gini coefficient was explained by inter-provincial inequality and over 70 per cent of inter-provincial inequality was explained by inter-zonal inequality (Table 8.3). Not only has inter-provincial inequality been a large component in overall rural inequality, but the rural economy has also drifted apart into three distinctive geographical zones. The coastal zone is much better off than the central zone, which in turn, is much better off than the western zone. In 1992, for example, per capita net income was 895 yuan in the east, 606 yuan in the central and only 484 yuan in the west. Third, off-farm income has been rising rapidly. In 1978, the share of off-farm income in total rural income was only 7 per cent. By 1992, it rose to almost 40 per cent. Off-farm

*Table 8.3* Rural Gini coefficients and inter-provincial and inter-zonal inequality

| Year | Rural Gini coefficient | Share of inter-provincial component (%) | Share of inter-zonal as a proportion of inter-provincial inequality |
|------|------|------|------|
| (1) | (2) | (3) | (4) |
| 1978 | 21.2 | – | – |
| 1980 | 23.7 | – | – |
| 1986 | 28.8 | 54.2 | 71.8 |
| 1987 | 29.2 | 54.1 | 75.3 |
| 1988 | 30.1 | 53.5 | 76.4 |
| 1989 | 31.0 | 50.6 | 77.1 |
| 1990 | 29.4 | 51.7 | 75.7 |
| 1991 | 30.3 | 55.1 | 73.7 |
| 1992 | 31.4 | 55.4 | 76.4 |

Source: Yao and Liu, 1998: Tables 5–7.

incomes are generated by production activities of the so-called township and village enterprises, or TVEs (MOA, *Chinese TVE Yearbook*, various years).

The greatest achievement of China's economic reforms is probably the successful development of TVEs. In 1978, the total number of TVEs was just 1.6 million, by 1993, it rose to 24.5 million. The real gross output value of TVEs rose by 25.6 per cent per year over 1978–93. In 1978, TVEs employed only 9.2 per cent of the rural labour force. In 1993, they employed 28 per cent. Fast growth in production has enabled TVEs to make a significant contribution to the state revenue. The share of TVE taxes as a proportion of total state tax revenue rose from 2.2 per cent in 1978 to 23.1 per cent in 1993. TVEs have also become a powerful and dynamic force of international trade. In the early years, the majority of TVEs produced only low-technology and low-valued products for the domestic market. Over the years, many TVEs began to produce a variety of export products. By 1993, about one-third of the national exports was accounted for by TVEs and this share continues to rise (MOA, various years). In less than 20 years, TVEs have grown from a negligible production sector to one that is comparable to SOEs and agriculture.

Fast development of TVEs has helped raise rural incomes substantially. However, due to uneven development across the country, the distribution of TVE outputs has a distinct spatial pattern. The eastern regions are much more developed than the central regions, which in turn, are more developed than the western provinces. In 1992, for example, the proportion of TVE employment was 30 per cent of the total rural labour force in the east, but it was only 24 per cent in the central and 15 per cent in the west. Per capita TVE gross output value was 1,798 yuan in the east, compared to 734 yuan in the central and 413 in the west (Yao and Liu, 1998).

Uneven development of TVE across regions is also reflected by the uneven contribution of TVE incomes to total rural incomes. Figure 8.2 shows the average per capita rural incomes and their TVE and agricultural components. It is clear that rural income inequality is largely due to the fact that rich provinces are much better off than the poor ones. It is also interesting to note that the distribution of agricultural incomes is far more equal than that of TVE incomes.

The per capita income ratio between the richest and the poorest provinces was 4.5 in total incomes, only 2.0 in agricultural incomes, but 13.4 in TVE incomes. When the Gini coefficient for total incomes and the respective concentration ratios for TVE and agricultural incomes are calculated based on provincial per capita incomes for the period 1990–92, it reveals that TVE income is disequalising while agricultural income is equalising. The share of TVE incomes in total rural incomes was 34 to 39 per cent but its share in the rural Gini coefficient was 55 to 64 per cent (Table 8.4).

At the provincial level, rural household survey data for Sichuan, Liaoning and Jiangsu for the period 1988–90 is used. A decomposition analysis on the Gini coefficient for each province reveals some further insights into the relative contribution of agricultural and non-agricultural incomes to the overall rural inequality. The summary results are presented in Table 8.5. There are significant differences between the three provinces in terms of the relative importance of non-farm

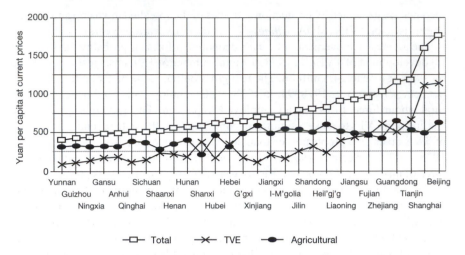

*Figure 8.2* Agriculture and TVE per capita incomes in rural China, 1992.
Source: MOA, 1992.

*Table 8.4* Decomposition of Gini coefficients by source, 1990–2 (at current prices)

| Year | Source | $m_f$ | $w_f$ | $C_f$ | $S_f$ |
|------|--------|-------|-------|-------|-------|
| 1990 | Agriculture | 370.2 | 65.99 | 8.35 | 36.18 |
|      | TVE | 190.8 | 34.01 | 28.62 | 63.91 |
|      | Total | 561.0 | 100.00 | 15.23 | 100.00 |
| 1991 | Agriculture | 381.2 | 63.36 | 11.93 | 45.37 |
|      | TVE | 220.4 | 36.64 | 24.84 | 54.62 |
|      | Total | 601.6 | 100.00 | 16.66 | 100.00 |
| 1992 | Agriculture | 419.8 | 60.58 | 11.10 | 38.64 |
|      | TVE | 273.2 | 39.42 | 27.00 | 61.17 |
|      | Total | 693.0 | 100.00 | 17.40 | 100.00 |

Sources: Data are derived from MOA, 1989–93, *Chinese Agricultural Statistical Data* (various issues, 1989–93); and MOA, 1989–93 *Chinese TVE Yearbook* (various issues). The results are extracted from Yao and Liu, 1998: Table 5.

Notes: $m_f$= national per capita average income for source $f$, $w_f$= share of source $f$ in total income, $C_f$= source concentration ratio, or Gini coefficient for Total income, calculated based on provincial average per capita incomes, $S_f$= source share in total Gini.

incomes in total incomes. In the sample period, the proportion of non-farm income (mostly TVE income) in total income was about 30 per cent in Jiangsu, 22 per cent in Liaoning and about 13 per cent in Sichuan. In all provinces over the period, the share of non-farm income in the Gini coefficient was greater than its share in total income, pointing to the same conclusion that non-farm income was dis-equalising while agricultural income was equalising. In Jiangsu, for example,

Table 8.5 Decomposition of rural Gini coefficients for selected provinces, 1988–90

| | Rural Liaoning | | | Rural Sichuan | | | Rural Jiangsu | | |
|---|---|---|---|---|---|---|---|---|---|
| | Total income | Farm income | Non-farm income | Total income | Farm income | Non-farm income | Total income | Farm income | Non-farm income |
| **1988** | | | | | | | | | |
| $C_f$ | 30.2 | 27.6 | 39.3 | 24.8 | 21.9 | 43.3 | 30.5 | 22.1 | 50.5 |
| $M_f$ | 984 | 765 | 219 | 635 | 549 | 86 | 1152 | 810 | 342 |
| $W_f$ | 100.0 | 77.7 | 22.3 | 100.0 | 86.5 | 13.5 | 100.0 | 70.3 | 29.7 |
| $S_f$ | 100.0 | 71.1 | 29.0 | 100.0 | 76.4 | 23.6 | 100.0 | 50.8 | 49.2 |
| **1989** | | | | | | | | | |
| $C_f$ | 31.9 | 29.4 | 40.0 | 24.5 | 21.2 | 45.3 | 31.2 | 22.6 | 51.5 |
| $M_f$ | 895 | 686 | 209 | 589 | 507 | 82 | 1024 | 719 | 305 |
| $W_f$ | 100.0 | 76.6 | 23.4 | 100.0 | 86.1 | 13.9 | 100.0 | 70.2 | 29.8 |
| $S_f$ | 100.0 | 70.7 | 29.3 | 100.0 | 74.4 | 25.7 | 100.0 | 50.9 | 49.2 |
| **1990** | | | | | | | | | |
| $C_f$ | 27.5 | 23.8 | 39.7 | 23.2 | 19.9 | 46.3 | 30.9 | 21.6 | 53.7 |
| $M_f$ | 836 | 646 | 190 | 560 | 489 | 71 | 955 | 676 | 279 |
| $W_f$ | 100.0 | 77.3 | 22.7 | 100.0 | 87.3 | 12.7 | 100.0 | 70.8 | 29.2 |
| $S_f$ | 100.0 | 67.1 | 32.9 | 100.0 | 74.7 | 25.3 | 100.0 | 49.3 | 50.7 |

Source: NBS, 1988–90 *Rural Household Survey Data*.

Notes: Total incomes are net incomes in 1990 prices. $C_f$ = concentration ratios for farm and non-farm incomes, Gini coefficient for total incomes; $M_f$ = average incomes; $W_f$ = income shares in total incomes; $S_f$ = shares in Gini coefficients.

non-farm income accounted for about 30 per cent of total income and almost one half of the overall inequality. In Sichuan, the inequality share accounted for by non-farm income was almost twice its share in total income.

## 8.5 Urban inequality and income sources

Before economic reform, there was little inequality among the Chinese urban residents. The urban Gini coefficient was as low as 0.18 in 1981. Economic reforms have allowed some people to earn more wages, bonuses and other sources of income. As a result, inequality started to grow. However, given the large size of the urban population and the extent of geographical diversity, inequality within the urban population is still low by international standards. The urban Gini coefficient reached a peak of 28 in 1994 but dropped to 26 in 1995 (World Bank, 1997). Our latest estimate of the urban Gini coefficient was 0.30 in 1998 (Yao *et al.*, 2004). Urban inequality has been significantly lower than rural inequality, especially when various urban subsidies are taken into account. This is not only reflected by the sizeable differences between the rural and urban Gini coefficients, but also by the per capita income ratios between the richest and the poorest provinces. In 1996, for example, the urban ratio was only 2.5 (7,721 yuan in Shanghai versus 3,102 in Inner Mongolia) but the rural ratio was 4.4 (4,846 yuan in Shanghai versus 1,101 in Gansu). In addition, the variations of per capita incomes by province were much more evident for the rural population than for the urban population (Figure 8.3). The difference in 2002 remained about the same. The urban ratio was 2.36 (14,296 yuan in Shanghai and 6,107 yuan in Guizhou) and the rural ratio was 4.17 (6,223.5 yuan in Shanghai and 1,489.9 yuan in Guizhou) (NBS, 2003).

Apart from Tibet, there are no significant differences between the western and central zones in the urban sector. Only in the three metropolitan cities (Beijing,

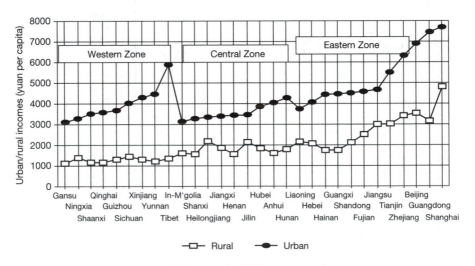

*Figure 8.3* Urban–rural per capita incomes in 1996 at current prices.

Shanghai and Tianjin), Zhejiang and Guangdong, do the urban residents have a much higher income than their counterparts in other provinces. Peasant households in the western provinces are significantly worse off than those in the other two zones.

Using household survey data for Sichuan and Liaoning for the period 1986–93, we can examine income inequality trends over time and the relative importance of various income sources. In each year for each province, total per capita income by household is decomposed into five different parts: timed-wages, non-timed wages (or piecemeal wages), non-wage income (including bonus and income from private and collective enterprises where payments are not in the form of fixed wages), and taxation and transfer incomes. Taxes and transfer incomes are defined by the National Bureau of Statistics (NBS) as the difference between gross household incomes minus household living incomes. As living incomes are regarded as the actual total incomes in this chapter, taxation and transfer incomes are negative in sign. Hence, they help reduce inequality, or they have a negative effect on the value of the Gini coefficient (see decomposition results in Table 8.6). During the data period, the Gini coefficient rose from 0.157 to 0.198 in Liaoning and from 0.177 to 0.237 in Sichuan (Columns 2 and 7 in Table 8.6). The upward movement of provincial Gini coefficients followed the national Gini coefficient which increased from 0.210 to about 0.250 over the same period (World Bank, 1997: Figure 2.3). In both provinces, timed-wages and non-wage incomes are two principal sources of urban total living incomes. However, timed wages are generally equalising while non-wage incomes are disequalising. The concentration coefficient of non-wage income was much higher than that of wage income in all years. In 1993, for example, the concentration coefficient of timed-wages was 0.139 in Liaoning and 0.158 in Sichuan, but the concentration coefficient of non-wage income (including bonuses) was respectively 0.230 and 0.273. Over the years, the importance of timed wages had declined but that of non-wage incomes had risen. Because the former was equalising and the latter disequalising, the Gini coefficient for total incomes had increased over time. Hence, it can be concluded that rising income inequality has been explained by the deepening of economic reforms in the urban economy, especially the reform of the wage system and the introduction of ownership diversification. Non-timed wages, or piecemeal wages, had little effect on the change of inequality. On the other hand, income taxes and income transfers out of the urban sectors (mainly as a result of remittances of urban residents to their rural relatives) had helped reduce urban inequality in absolute terms (Columns 6 and 11, Table 8.6).

## 8.6 Income inequality and poverty under economic reforms

### *8.6.1 The current situation of poverty in China*

China's record on poverty alleviation is admirable. Based on official figures, more than 200 million people have been lifted out of absolute poverty since 1978 (unofficial estimates differ greatly as will be seen in the following chapters). By 1995,

Table 8.6 Decomposition of Gini coefficients by income source for urban Sichuan and Liaoning, 1986–93 (yuan per capita at 1990 prices)

| | Urban Liaoning | | | | | Urban Sichuan | | | | |
| | Total income | Time wages | N-timed wages | Non wages | Tax & transfer | Total income | Time wages | N-time wages | Non wages | Tax & transfer |
| Years (1) | (2) | (3) | (4) | (5) | (6) | (7) | (8) | (9) | (10) | (11) |
|---|---|---|---|---|---|---|---|---|---|---|
| **1986** | | | | | | | | | | |
| $C_f$ | 15.7 | 11.3 | 22.9 | 21.0 | 13.8 | 17.7 | 14.3 | -17.3 | 21.3 | 11.2 |
| $M_f$ | 1337 | 824 | 8 | 629 | -124 | 1372 | 792 | 23 | 705 | -149 |
| $W_f$ | 100.0 | 61.6 | 0.6 | 47.0 | -9.3 | 100.0 | 57.7 | 1.7 | 51.4 | -10.9 |
| $S_f$ | 100.0 | 44.3 | 0.9 | 62.9 | -8.1 | 100.0 | 46.7 | -1.6 | 61.8 | -6.9 |
| **1987** | | | | | | | | | | |
| $C_f$ | 15.6 | 10.2 | 17.7 | 19.7 | 8.7 | 18.1 | 15.2 | -11.1 | 20.4 | 12.4 |
| $M_f$ | 1492 | 844 | 13 | 804 | -169 | 1403 | 795 | 15 | 766 | -173 |
| $W_f$ | 100.0 | 56.6 | 0.9 | 53.9 | -11.3 | 100.0 | 56.7 | 1.1 | 54.6 | -12.3 |
| $S_f$ | 100.0 | 37.1 | 1.0 | 68.2 | -6.3 | 100.0 | 47.5 | -0.7 | 61.5 | -8.4 |
| **1988** | | | | | | | | | | |
| $C_f$ | 16.3 | 8.9 | 17.8 | 20.1 | 2.7 | 20.1 | 15.5 | 1.8 | 23.3 | 17.2 |
| $M_f$ | 1669 | 822 | 25 | 989 | -167 | 1530 | 715 | 12 | 962 | -159 |
| $W_f$ | 100.0 | 49.3 | 1.5 | 59.3 | -10.0 | 100.0 | 46.7 | 0.8 | 62.9 | -10.4 |
| $S_f$ | 100.0 | 27.0 | 1.6 | 73.1 | -1.6 | 100.0 | 36.0 | 0.1 | 72.7 | -8.9 |
| **1989** | | | | | | | | | | |
| $C_f$ | 16.9 | 11.7 | 26.4 | 18.8 | 7.3 | 19.9 | 14.7 | -7.4 | 23.0 | 16.2 |
| $M_f$ | 1605 | 750 | 46 | 981 | -171 | 1458 | 627 | 10 | 969 | -148 |
| $W_f$ | 100.0 | 46.7 | 2.9 | 61.1 | -10.7 | 100.0 | 43.0 | 0.7 | 66.5 | -10.2 |
| $S_f$ | 100.0 | 32.4 | 4.5 | 67.8 | -4.6 | 100.0 | 31.8 | -0.3 | 76.7 | -8.2 |

| | | | | | | | | | | |
|---|---|---|---|---|---|---|---|---|---|---|
| **1990** | | | | | | | | | | |
| $C_f$ | 16.3 | 10.7 | 31.3 | 18.6 | 6.8 | 19.6 | 16.6 | -25.0 | 21.3 | 14.4 |
| $M_f$ | 1466 | 730 | 44 | 853 | -162 | 1424 | 641 | 10 | 918 | -145 |
| $W_f$ | 100.0 | 49.8 | 3.0 | 58.2 | -11.1 | 100.0 | 45.0 | 0.7 | 64.5 | -10.2 |
| $S_f$ | 100.0 | 32.6 | 5.8 | 66.2 | -4.6 | 100.0 | 38.2 | -0.9 | 70.2 | -7.5 |
| **1991** | | | | | | | | | | |
| $C_f$ | 17.4 | 10.1 | 23.8 | 21.8 | 12.5 | 20.4 | 15.0 | 4.7 | 23.1 | 12.9 |
| $M_f$ | 1543 | 707 | 44 | 945 | -153 | 1517 | 702 | 7 | 978 | -170 |
| $W_f$ | 100.0 | 45.8 | 2.9 | 61.2 | -9.9 | 100.0 | 46.3 | 0.5 | 64.5 | -11.2 |
| $S_f$ | 100.0 | 26.5 | 3.9 | 76.7 | -7.1 | 100.0 | 34.0 | 0.1 | 73.0 | -7.1 |
| **1992** | | | | | | | | | | |
| $C_f$ | 17.6 | 10.6 | 2.8 | 21.4 | 7.7 | 21.0 | 15.1 | -21.3 | 24.4 | 13.9 |
| $M_f$ | 1621 | 744 | 19 | 1021 | -163 | 1648 | 697 | 20 | 1104 | -174 |
| $W_f$ | 100.0 | 45.9 | 1.2 | 63.0 | -10.1 | 100.0 | 42.3 | 1.2 | 67.0 | -10.6 |
| $S_f$ | 100.0 | 27.7 | 0.2 | 76.5 | -4.4 | 100.0 | 30.5 | -1.2 | 77.7 | -7.0 |
| **1993** | | | | | | | | | | |
| $C_f$ | 19.8 | 13.9 | -9.5 | 23.0 | 9.7 | 23.7 | 15.8 | 0.1 | 27.3 | 15.3 |
| $M_f$ | 1684 | 702 | 41 | 1116 | -175 | 1771 | 642 | 38 | 1272 | -181 |
| $W_f$ | 100.0 | 41.7 | 2.4 | 66.3 | -10.4 | 100.0 | 36.3 | 2.1 | 71.8 | -10.2 |
| $S_f$ | 100.0 | 29.3 | -1.2 | 76.9 | -5.1 | 100.0 | 24.1 | 0.0 | 82.5 | -6.6 |

Source: NBS, 1986–93 *Urban Household Survey Data*.

Notes: Total incomes are living incomes in 1990 prices. $C_f$ = concentration ratios of source $f$, and Gini coefficient for total incomes; $M_f$ = per capita mean incomes of source $f$; $W_f$ = shares of source $f$ in total incomes; $S_f$ = shares of source $f$ in Gini coefficients.

the number of absolute poor was about 70 million. In the official statistics, the absolute poverty line is an annual per capita income of 318 yuan in 1990 prices. A higher line of poverty is 454 yuan at 1990 prices. When translated into a material context, absolute poverty in China means that a household does not have enough staple food to eat, cannot afford to buy enough warm clothing, and is unable to have all the children in that household educated up to primary school level. These households usually live in very poor housing conditions, with many people crowded into the same house without clean water and electricity.

According to official statistics, only 0.3 per cent of the urban population lived below the lower poverty line in 1981 and no people lived below that by 1995. Even if we use the higher poverty line, there were few urban people living in poverty. Based on the survey data of urban Liaoning and Sichuan, the incidence of urban poverty (percentage of urban population) was very low in the data period 1986–93 (Table 8.7).

*Table 8.7* Incidence of urban poverty, per capita income <454 yuan in 1990 prices

| Regions | 1986 | 1987 | 1988 | 1989 | 1990 | 1991 | 1992 | 1993 |
|---------|------|------|------|------|------|------|------|------|
| Liaoning | 0.00 | 0.00 | 0.25 | 0.33 | 0.26 | 0.00 | 0.10 | 0.25 |
| Sichuan | 0.80 | 0.66 | 0.67 | 0.71 | 0.77 | 0.71 | 0.52 | 0.43 |

Source: NBS, *Urban Household Survey Data for Liaoning and Sichuan, 1986–93.*

The official urban survey data has some limitations as it does not include rural people working in the cities. If these people were included, the incidence of urban poverty could be higher. Moreover, recent reforms of state-owned enterprises have laid off millions of factory workers. Some of them have found alternative employment shortly after leaving the factories, but many of them have not and may have ended up living in poverty, especially those households where both husbands and wives are made redundant at the same time. Our survey data does not cover the period when urban unemployment is a big problem. Therefore, the extent of poverty may have increased in recent years as will be sown in the following chapters. However, even if the level of urban poverty had doubled, it would still have been negligible compared to the level of rural poverty in percentage terms.

Hence it is clear that poverty in China is almost exclusively a rural phenomenon, unlike many other developing countries where urban poverty is pervasive. If the incidence of poverty in all Chinese cities were similar to urban Liaoning and Sichuan, there would have been fewer than one million urban residents for the whole country living below the higher official poverty line in 1993 and almost no people living under the lower poverty line. This number is negligible when it is compared to 70 million rural people living below the lower poverty line and 170 million living below the higher poverty line in 1995 (Table 8.8).

In Table 8.8, the incidence of poverty (percentage of rural population) for rural China is estimated as the weighted average of rural Jiangsu, Liaoning and Sichuan.

*Table 8.8* Incidence of rural poverty, 1988–95

| Region | Year | Percentage of population | | Number of the poor ('000) | |
|---|---|---|---|---|---|
| | | ≤ (318/p.c.) | ≤ (454/p.c.) | ≤ (318/p.c.) | ≤ (454/p.c.) |
| Jiangsu | 1988 | 1.92 | 7.70 | 990 | 3,971 |
| | 1989 | 3.20 | 11.79 | 1,652 | 6,086 |
| | 1990 | 4.83 | 14.72 | 2,546 | 7,759 |
| Liaoning | 1988 | 5.01 | 12.80 | 1,118 | 2,857 |
| | 1989 | 8.70 | 18.41 | 1,958 | 4,144 |
| | 1990 | 5.07 | 15.13 | 1,152 | 3,438 |
| Sichuan | 1988 | 8.75 | 29.57 | 7,909 | 26,728 |
| | 1989 | 11.37 | 35.79 | 10,372 | 32,648 |
| | 1990 | 11.72 | 38.81 | 10,805 | 35,779 |
| Rural China | 1988 | 6.10 | 20.43 | 52,702 | 176,538 |
| | 1989 | 8.46 | 25.93 | 73,825 | 226,395 |
| | 1990 | 8.65 | 28.02 | 77,338 | 250,506 |
| | 1995 | 7.77 | 18.88 | 70,000 | 170,000 |

Sources: NBS, 1988–90 *Rural Household Survey Data*; World Bank, 1997.

The percentage shares of rural people living in poverty for these three provinces are estimated using rural household survey data. The incomes are calculated in 1990 prices.

If we use the lower poverty line, the incidence of rural poverty ranged from 2 per cent in Jiangsu to about 12 per cent in Sichuan. An economic recession and high inflation in 1989 and 1990 resulted in a much higher incidence of poverty across the whole country. The estimated total number of absolute poor rose from 52.7 million in 1988 to over 77.3 million in 1990. This implies that the incidence of poverty is highly sensitive to income changes. By 1995, the total number of absolute poor was reduced to 70 million, compared favourably to the 270 million in 1978.

Despite China's great success in reducing poverty over the data period, the task to further reduce and eventually eradicate it is still tremendous. If we use the higher poverty line, which is equivalent to $1 per person per day at constant 1985 US dollar purchasing power, there were still about 170 million rural people living in poverty in 1995. To lift all of these people out of poverty is clearly problematic. The difficulty in eliminating poverty is compounded by dispersal of the poor over the country and the fact that rapid income growth has bypassed those pockets that have little prospect of growth without government support.

Rural income growth and the change of inequality have opposite effects on poverty alleviation. Running a log-linear regression of poverty incidence against per capita mean incomes and the provincial Gini coefficients for Jiangsu, Liaoning and Sichuan over the period 1988–90, we can estimate the elasticities of poverty incidence with respect to mean incomes and the Gini coefficients. The estimated results and related statistical tests are presented in equations (8.1) and (8.2) below.

$ln$(Poverty I) $=$ 13.16 + 5.77 $ln$(Gini coefficient) – 4.57 $ln$(mean income)

   ($t$-values)       (6.50) (4.91)                         (–8.32)

   $R2 = 0.96, n = 9$.                                                                                    (8.1)

$ln$(Poverty II) $=$   15.64 + 2.41 $ln$(Gini coefficient) – 3.10 $ln$(mean income)

   ($t$-values)       (10.50) (7.21)                        (–19.87)

   $R2 = 0.96, n = 9$.                                                                                   (8.2)

'Poverty I' and 'Poverty II' denote respectively the percentages of rural population living below the lower and higher poverty lines. The incidence of poverty measured by a higher line is less elastic to mean income and inequality changes than that by a lower line. The elasticities of poverty incidence at a lower line are 5.77 and –4.57 with respect to the Gini coefficient and mean income. This implies that, *ceteris paribus*, a 10 per cent rise in per capita mean income would reduce poverty incidence by 45.7 per cent, but a 10 per cent rise in the Gini coefficient would raise poverty incidence by more than 57.7 per cent. When poverty is measured by a higher line, a 10 per cent rise in mean income can only reduce poverty by 31 per cent, but a 10 per cent increase in the Gini coefficient would raise poverty by 24.1 per cent. The results in equations (8.1) and (8.2) suggest that although income growth is important in reducing poverty, rising inequality has a critical counter effect.

### 8.6.2  When can China eradicate poverty?

This sub-section presents three different scenarios to examine when poverty in China can more or less be eliminated. A number of assumptions are required for the projection of poverty. First, the projections are based on the rural population and only focus on type II poverty. This is because urban poverty is almost negligible compared to rural poverty and because type I poverty is too low a line for poverty definition. If the government wants to eliminate poverty, it should aim to eliminate type II poverty which is the poverty line defined by the World Bank at $1 per day per person in 1985 US$ purchasing power. Second, it is assumed that the growth in inequality, or the Gini coefficient, is determined by the growth of per capita mean income, with the latter following the historical trend of 1978–94. Third, the growth rate of type II rural poverty incidence is determined by the growth of per capita mean income and the growth of the rural Gini coefficient as shown in equation (8.3).

$$R_P = E_{PG} R_G + E_{PI} R_I$$                                                                        (8.3)

Where $R_P$, $R_G$, $R_I$ denote respectively the annual growth rates of poverty, Gini coefficient and per capita mean income. $E_{PG}$ and $E_{PI}$ denote respectively the elasticities of poverty incidence with respect to the Gini coefficient and per capita mean income. These two elasticities are derived from the results in equation (8.2). To estimate the annual growth rates of per capita mean income and the Gini coefficient, two more regressions are required. Equation (8.4) estimates the elasticity of the Gini coefficient with respect to per capita mean income, whilst equation (8.5) estimates the growth rate of per capita mean income. The Gini coefficients and real per capita incomes in rural China are taken for the period 1978–94. The OLS results indicate that for every 10 per cent rise in per capita mean income, the Gini coefficient increases by about 4.2 per cent. Over the data period, the average annual growth rate of per capita mean income rose by 5.26 per cent.[2]

$ln$(Gini) = 0.6402 + 0.4174 $ln$(mean income)
          (7.85)       (6.27)
$R^2 = 0.724, n = 17.$ (8.4)

$ln$(mean income) = −95.5 + 0.0513(time period)
                  (−7.31)   (7.51)
$R^2 = 0.790, n = 17.$ (8.5)

Assuming the income elasticity of the Gini coefficient and the average annual growth rate of per capita income remain the same as those estimated from equations (8.4) and (8.5), it is possible to predict the level of type II poverty by the year 2010 when the Chinese government aims for a *Xiaokang* living standard for all the people. A Xiaokang living standard means that absolute poverty should be more or less eliminated and the average per capita income should be around US$1,000 in 1980 prices.

The basic projected results are presented in the third and fourth columns under Scenario I in Table 8.9. With an average annual growth rate of 1.5 per cent, the total rural population will be 1.126 billion, and 2.68 per cent or 30.2 million people will still live below the type II poverty line. As 1978–94 was a very fast growing period for the Chinese economy, in the next 10 to 15 years, China may not be able to maintain the same high growth rate. Hence, Scenario II assumes that rural per capita income will grow half as fast during 1997–2010 as in 1978–94, or by just 2.63 per cent per annum. In the meantime, the growth of inequality will also be slower. As a result, the poverty incidence will be 6.21 per cent, or almost 70 million people. Scenario III predicts poverty incidence under the most optimistic assumptions. It assumes that per capita income will grow as fast as in the data period but the Gini coefficient is fixed at its 1996 level of 0.36. In other words, high growth in the future would be proportionally distributed among the population. The results of this scenario are astonishing. The incidence of poverty would be reduced down to just 1.14 per cent, or 12.8 million people.

The simulation results in Table 8.9 have a few important implications regarding poverty reduction in rural China. First, poverty alleviation is a long-term and painstaking process. It is almost impossible to totally eradicate rural poverty in the next 15 years even under the most optimistic scenario. Second, continuous rapid income growth is a necessary condition for poverty reduction but not a sufficient condition. A more effective way of poverty reduction is high income growth coupled with a fairer distribution system. If income inequality could be controlled to a certain level, poverty reduction would be more effective as income grows.

*Table 8.9* Predictions of rural poverty to the year 2010

| Year | Predicted total rural population | Scenario I poverty incidence | | Scenario II poverty incidence | | Scenario III poverty incidence | |
|---|---|---|---|---|---|---|---|
| | (million) | (%) | (number) | (%) | (number) | (%) | (number) |
| 1995 | 900.4 | 18.88 | 170.0 | 18.88 | 170.0 | 18.88 | 170.0 |
| 1996 | 913.9 | 13.74 | 125.6 | 13.74 | 125.6 | 13.74 | 125.6 |
| 1997 | 927.6 | 12.22 | 113.4 | 12.98 | 120.4 | 11.50 | 106.7 |
| 1998 | 941.5 | 10.88 | 102.4 | 12.27 | 115.5 | 9.62 | 90.6 |
| 1999 | 955.7 | 9.68 | 92.5 | 11.59 | 110.8 | 8.05 | 77.0 |
| 2000 | 970.0 | 8.61 | 83.5 | 10.95 | 106.2 | 6.74 | 65.4 |
| 2001 | 984.5 | 7.66 | 75.4 | 10.35 | 101.9 | 5.64 | 55.5 |
| 2002 | 999.3 | 6.82 | 68.1 | 9.78 | 97.7 | 4.72 | 47.2 |
| 2003 | 1014.3 | 6.07 | 61.5 | 9.24 | 93.7 | 3.95 | 40.1 |
| 2004 | 1029.5 | 5.40 | 55.6 | 8.73 | 89.9 | 3.31 | 34.0 |
| 2005 | 1045.0 | 4.80 | 50.2 | 8.25 | 86.2 | 2.77 | 28.9 |
| 2006 | 1060.6 | 4.27 | 45.3 | 7.79 | 82.7 | 2.32 | 24.6 |
| 2007 | 1076.5 | 3.80 | 40.9 | 7.36 | 79.3 | 1.94 | 20.9 |
| 2008 | 1092.7 | 3.38 | 37.0 | 6.96 | 76.0 | 1.62 | 17.7 |
| 2009 | 1109.1 | 3.01 | 33.4 | 6.58 | 72.9 | 1.36 | 15.1 |
| 2010 | 1125.7 | 2.68 | 30.2 | 6.21 | 69.9 | 1.14 | 12.8 |

Notes: (1) Scenario I assumes the following: average income growth follows the trend of 1978–94, which is 5.26 per cent per annum. The growth of Gini coefficient is the growth rate of mean income times the income elasticity of Gini coefficient, which is 0.417. The growth rate of poverty incidence is calculated by equation (8.3). (2) Scenario II assumes that mean income growth is half of the trend in 1978–94, or 2.63 per cent per annum. Other assumptions are the same as in scenario I. (3) Scenario III assumes mean income growth follows the trend in 1978–94 but the Gini coefficient is fixed at its 1996 level of 0.36.

## 8.7 Conclusion

Economic growth in China since 1978 has been spectacular. The improvements of people's living standards are significant. Rising incomes, however, have been unfairly shared among the population. As a result, China has been transformed from a highly egalitarian society into one that is comparable with the United States and the East Asian economies.

This chapter examines different aspects of income inequality in China. At the national level, inequality and its growth have been explained by the urban–rural divide and regional segmentation. Among the rural population, rising inequality is mainly explained by inter-regional disparity, which in turn, is largely explained by uneven development of TVEs. In the urban areas, it is the diversification of ownership and wage system reform that explain the worsening of income distribution. Finally, unlike other less developed countries, poverty is primarily a rural phenomenon in China even though massive rural–urban migration has taken place. However, it is important to note that some rural migrants living in the cities (without urban citizenship) and some urban citizens who are recently laid off from SOEs may have become or will become the urban poor. As official data on the urban population does not include rural migrants living in the cities and as massive unemployed SOEs workers (*xiagang zigong*) are a recent phenomenon, we have not been able to measure correctly the exact level of urban poverty but it is an important area of further research. In the following chapters, some additional data will be used to study the latest situation of poverty based on some more recent survey data. This chapter is useful in the sense that it provides a foundation for understanding the poverty issue in China.

The analysis in this chapter is based on a limited set of data. The results could be biased and have to be interpreted with caution. However, the methodologies presented in this chapter provide a basic analytical framework for studying poverty in China. In the following chapters, more analysis on poverty will be conducted using some newer and larger data sets.

# 9 Further study on inequality and poverty reduction

## 9.1 Introduction

Chapter 8 used some survey data from a few selected provinces to examine the various aspects of inequality and its relation to poverty. This chapter uses some more recent and larger data samples to study the same issue: how inequality affects poverty reduction.

We first study the income distribution and poverty situation in urban China and then study similar issues for rural China. The issue of urban poverty is linked to two main factors: rural migrants and urban unemployment. However, both rural migrants and urban unemployed workers are not included in the official statistics to be covered in this chapter. The issues of unemployed SOE workers and rural migrants will be left to the following two chapters.

Based on official statistics, the total number of rural poor was reduced from 270 millions in 1978 to 26 millions by 2000 (*People's Daily*, 2000b), but the official figures may be questionable. This chapter estimates that there are up to 5.5–15 million urban poor and 103–87 million rural poor in 1998. The battle against poverty is far from over in China and new groups of poor population are emerging, making poverty reduction more difficult in the future than before. However, China could meet the international target of poverty reduction by half from 1990 to 2015, with modest growth in both income and inequality. If China is able to fulfil its economic development plan and contain inequality in the next 15 years, poverty reduction will be much faster. China has one-fifth of the world population and one-sixth of the world poor. Its ability to reduce poverty will have an important impact on global poverty.

Some more objective estimates show that poverty reduction was even more substantive than suggested by the official statistics. In the previous chapter, we estimated that the total number of poor in the rural areas was reduced from about 600 millions in 1978 to 57–114 millions in 1996. The most recent estimates by DFID indicate that there are 65 to 270 mullions of people living below the low and high poverty lines ($0.6 and $1 per person per day). There is no up-to-date independent estimate on the poverty incidence in rural China, but we have obtained the latest household survey data in 1998 for the urban sector, and 1995 and 1998 for the rural sector. The data sets enable us to derive systematic estimates of urban and rural poverty up to 1998.

Until very recently, poverty has been considered to be primarily a rural phenomenon. Recent research, however, indicates that urban poverty exists to a significant degree. The following two factors have contributed to rising urban poverty: massive unemployment, 17.5 million unemployed workers by the end of 1998 (Meng, 2001) caused by the radical restructuring of the state-owned enterprises (SOEs) and the rising urban floating population. The estimated incidence of urban poverty ranges from 1.75 per cent (5.5 million) to 4.73 per cent (14.8 million) of the total urban population in 1998. These figures are substantially less than the estimated incidence of rural poverty despite the fact that we use much higher poverty lines for the urban population than for the rural population. The rural poverty head count rates range from 11 per cent to 20 per cent (103 to 187 million) of the rural population. As a result, we can conclude that poverty in China is still predominantly a rural phenomenon although urban poverty should not be neglected.

The incidence of poverty varies widely between regions in both the rural and urban sectors. In general, the eastern regions have much less poverty than other regions. The western provinces have the highest incidence of poverty. They also have the highest concentration of the minority population. In the urban sector, the east region accounts for 47 per cent of the total urban population but less than 30 per cent of the urban poor. The west region has only 18 per cent of the urban population but 23–28 per cent of the urban poor. Ningxia, Shaaxi and Tibet have the highest level of poverty, where the incidence of poverty is over 11 per cent compared to just 4.73 per cent for the national average measured by the high poverty line. By contrast, Beijing Guangdong, Jiangsu and Zhejiang have the lowest incidence of urban poverty, where the level of poverty is less than 1.5 per cent of the local urban population. In the rural sector, the incidence of poverty also has a clear regional pattern. In 1998, for example, the west region has only 25 per cent of the total rural population but 40 per cent of the total rural poor. The east region has about 39 per cent of the total rural population but less than 20 per cent of the rural poor. Gansu, Shaanxi, Yunnan and Guizhou have the highest incidence of rural poverty, where the head count rates of poverty are close to or more than 30 per cent of the local rural population measured by the high poverty line. All these provinces are located in the west. Beijing, Zhejiang, Jiangsu, Shandong, Guangdong and Liaoning have the lowest incidence of rural poverty, where the poverty head count rates are less than 10 per cent measured by the high poverty line.

The incidence of poverty is associated with or affected by many factors. These include income growth, inequality, openness, economic structure, infrastructure, education, location, topography, gender and rural industrialisation. Multivariate regressions, however, fail to identify more than two factors that are statistically significant in the same regression. The two most important factors are per capita mean income and the Gini coefficient measuring inequality. In both the rural and urban sectors, per capita income and the Gini coefficients explain 90 per cent or more of the variations in regional poverty head count rates. It is found that the incidence of poverty is highly responsive to income growth and the level of inequality. In the urban sector, a 1 per cent rise in per capita mean income can lead to a reduction of poverty by 1.5–1.7 per cent, but a 1 per cent rise in the level of inequality can lead to an increase in poverty by 1.5–3 per cent.

The incidence of poverty is even more sensitive to income and inequality growth in the rural sector than in the urban sector. A 1 per cent rise in per capita mean income can lead to a reduction of rural poverty by 2.6–2.8 per cent. A 1 per cent rise in the Gini coefficient, however, will cause poverty to increase by 2.13–3.5 per cent.

The sensitive response of poverty to income means that a significant income growth can easily lead to a total elimination of poverty in a relative short period of time (e.g. 15–20 years of consecutive growth). However, due to rising inequality, poverty reduction has been much slower than anticipated by both policy makers and economic analysts. In China, the slow process of poverty reduction has not been due to the lack of income growth, but to an unanticipated rise in inequality.

Inequality in China is multi-dimensional. The most important aspects of inequality include urban–rural inequality, inter-regional inequality, gender inequality, racial inequality, inequality of access to capital, education and health care. If the cost of living is not taken into account, the urban–rural inequality can explain more than two-thirds of the total inequality in China. In addition, the extent of urban–rural inequality was higher in the post-reform than in the pre-reform period except in 1979–84, when economic reforms started from the rural areas. The urban–rural per capita consumption ratio is well over 2.5 from 1952 to 1994 except in 1979–84, when the ratio was less than 2.5. Within the rural or the urban sector, inter-provincial inequality explains a large proportion (41–50 per cent) of total inequality.

Education is another important factor affecting income and poverty. In the urban sector, as the level of education of household head rises, per capita income increases. The higher is the level of education, the higher is the level of income. An urban worker with primary school education earns 38–58 per cent more than an urban worker without primary education. An urban worker with university education or more earns 54–83 per cent more than an urban worker with only primary education. In the rural sector, education matters only at the primary education level. People with or without primary education can have a household income gap of 5 per cent. There is no significant difference of household incomes between households whose heads have primary education or more. This means that education is less important in the rural areas than in the urban areas, particularly beyond the primary level. It explains why educated rural youth have to move to the cities and seek jobs with higher pay, because the rural areas are still engaged in low-skilled and low-return production activities.

Continuous reduction of poverty requires two basic conditions:

• sustainable economic growth and the improvement of average living standards
• constrained growth in inequality.

Sustainable economic growth is a pre-condition for the general improvement of people's living standards, and hence the reduction of poverty. However, the positive effect of income growth on poverty reduction may be totally negated by rising income inequality. Therefore, containing inequality is another important aspect for reducing poverty.

## 9.2 A brief literature review on economic growth, income inequality and poverty reduction in China

The Chinese economy has grown rapidly since the founding of the People's Republic (PRC hereafter). This is shown by the fact that GDP increased 36 times during 1952–99 in constant prices, and per capita GDP increased over 16 times during the same period. It is generally agreed that economic growth was much faster during the reform period (1978 to date) than during the pre-reform period (1952–77). The economic success of China (especially during the reform period) has attracted tremendous interest from academic researchers as well as policy makers. Studies on Chinese inequality are abundant (Hussain *et al.*, 1994; Knight and Song, 1993b; Tsui, 1991, 1993, 1996, 1998a, 1998b; Yao, 1997a, 1997b, 1999a, 1999b), but few present a comprehensive spatial and intertemporal picture for the 50-year period.

Regional development policies have featured prominently in the debates on China's economic development strategy. However, there are very few studies that have attempted to measure the relative contribution of intra-regional, inter-regional, urban, rural, and rural–urban inequalities to overall inequality in China.

Past studies on Chinese inequality have concentrated mainly on the persistence of rural–urban inequality. It has often been argued that the heavy-industry bias in economic development and restrictive rural-to-urban migration policies aggravated rural–urban disparities in China (Knight and Song, 1993b; Kueh, 1989; Perkins and Yusuf, 1984). Comparing rural–urban disparities in India and China, Bhalla (1990) analysed these in the light of such indicators as income and consumption, deposit-to-credit ratios (financial disparities), agricultural and industrial productivity and access to health services.

Tsui (1993) conducts a detailed decomposition of rural–urban and inland–coastal inequality with county-level data, using the inequality index of generalised entropy by Theil (1967) and three attributes of well-being: per capita gross value of industrial and agricultural output, infant mortality rate, and illiteracy and semi-illiteracy rate. However, his study is a snapshot for a single year (1982). Similar decompositions by Hussain *et al.* (1994) are only for 1986. Knight and Song (1993b), based on the output data of 2,400 counties of China in 1987, analysed the spatial influence on rural income inequality. Yao (1999c) made some headway in this direction on the basis of survey data in two selected provinces. However, his study was seriously hampered by the lack of statistical information. Dennis Tao Yang (2000) explained very well the causes for rising inequality in China but based his explanations on only two provinces in the period 1986–94. Morduch and Sicular (1998) suggested a new approach to decompose the inequality in a county covering 16 villages from 1990–3. Although Kanbur and Zhang (1999) provide an excellent framework for describing the relative contribution of rural–urban and inland–coastal inequality to overall regional inequality in China, their work covers only the 1983–95 period. Bhalla, Yao and Zhang (2002), employing newly released data covering 30 provinces from 1952–99, presented a comprehensive picture of the evolution of China's regional and rural–urban inequalities. They compared, for the first time, the inequalities before and since the economic reforms. By decomposing the inequality index into intra-regional and inter-regional components, or into urban and rural components, they explained the main causes for the persistence of inequalities.

Anti-poverty is a highly political task for the central and local governments in China. The huge poor population of this country attracted the attention of the United Nations, foreign governments and academic organisations. Researchers at the World Bank are currently engaged in analysing the development of Chinese poverty using micro-data for some provinces. Based on the Rural Household Survey carried out by the Rural Investigation Team of the National Bureau of Statistics, Ravallion and Jalan (1996) constructed a panel data set for the four southern provinces, Guangdong, Guangxi, Yunnan, and Guizhou, over the period 1985–90. A series of adjustments was made, targeted to eliminate the biases related mainly with the planning prices of non-marketed home production of grain. They find a higher incidence of poverty, but a lower severity of poverty: those near the poverty line are worse off than had previously been thought but the poorest are better off. They also confirmed the results in the literature, that is, notably rising rural inequality and regional divergence with little gain to the poor in the lagging rural inland regions.

Employing this data set, Jalan and Ravallion (1998a) assess the impact of China's poor-area development programmes. They find households in the targeted poor areas have significant higher rates of consumption growth than one would have expected, though still not enough to reverse their longer-term divergence from other areas. Without controlling for spatial externalities, the growth process entails a sizable underestimation of the welfare gain from the programme.

Jalan and Ravallion (1998b) further investigate the issue of transient poverty in rural China. They find considerable transient poverty in that region from 1985–90. One-half of the mean squared poverty gap and over one-third of the mean poverty gap is accounted for by year-to-year fluctuations in consumption. Transient poverty is likely to be a significant constraint on the effectiveness of targeted anti-poverty policies contingent on current levels of living for reaching the long-term poor. Jalan and Ravallion (1998b) and Ravallion and Jalan (1999) also explore the impact of neighbourhood endowments of physical and human capital on poverty. They find robust evidence of geographic poverty traps in southern rural China. The prospects for growth in poor areas will depend on the ability of governments and community organisations to overcome the tendency for under-investment that such geographic externalities are likely to generate.

Based on the assumption of subsistence intake and income data from the National Bureau of Statistics, the World Bank (1997) produced a time series on poverty in China, indicating a very low poverty ratio and a sharp decline of rural poverty from the end of 1970s to the middle of 1980s. Since then, the incidence of poverty hardly changed and became sensitive as to how incomes are estimated. Riskin (1993, 1994, 1996) reviewed the change of rural poverty in China. He uses rural household income survey data from the China Household Income Project carried out by a Sino-US team of social scientists in 1988. There is little difference in the estimates of the proportion of the poor in the above two studies, however, conclusions vary widely. The World Bank (1997: 5) wrote: 'most of China's remaining absolute poverty is now concentrated in a number of resource-poor rural areas, primarily in the northern, northwestern, and southwestern provinces'. In contrast, Riskin (1994: 282) wrote: 'a new, individualized kind of poverty may be developing within the core regions of agricultural China'. He also pointed out that (1996: 78): 'government anti-poverty efforts are regionally defined. If the findings presented are accurate, most rural poor reside outside officially designated poor regions and anti-poverty measures do not reach most of them'.

Following Riskin (1994) and employing the same survey data, Gustafsson and Li (1998) studied both the rural and urban poverty in China. They reached the similar conclusion of Riskin (1994, 1996).

Rozelle *et al.* (1998) employed county-level data to examine the sources and the effectiveness of targeted poverty investments in 43 poor counties of Shaanxi Province during the years 1986–91. Their overall objective is to analyse the effectiveness of Chinese poor area policy. For their sample, overall funding increased in the early years of the programme and then fell significantly in real terms after 1990. There was also a major policy change in the middle of the sample period, characterised by a redirection of spending after 1989 away from households and toward economic 'entities' and TVE and county-run enterprises. According to their results, targeted investment funds allocated directly to households for agricultural activity have a significant and positive effect on growth, while investments in township and village enterprises or county state-owned enterprises do not have a discernible effect on growth. Investments in agricultural infrastructure do not positively affect growth rates in agricultural output, suggesting that other types of basic investments (e.g. roads and education) should receive higher priority. These results suggest that the problem's initial emphasis on household lending was most appropriate for funding economic growth in poor areas.

Specifically, they seek to meet three objectives. First, they want to understand the evolution of poor area policy since the mid-1980s, trying to deduce the true goals of central and regional poor area officials, as well as how these policies have been implemented in the provinces. Next, they want to understand the magnitude and scope of investment into poor areas, and examine if changes in these policies have affected the uses of the investment funds. Finally, they want to determine the effectiveness of the investment of poor area funds, analysing which types of investments have generated growth, and which ones have not.

In spite of the huge success in the poverty reduction in rural China, there have been few studies on the causes of the success. Most of these studies have focused on the measures of rural poverty and its changes. The determinants of poverty reduction, however, have in large been ignored. Fan *et al.* (2000), using provincial level data over 1970–97, develop a simultaneous equation model to estimate the direct and indirect effects of different types of government expenditure on rural poverty and productivity growth in rural China. Their results show that government spending on production enhancing investments, such as agricultural research and development, irrigation, education and infrastructure have all contributed to agricultural production growth and to reduction in rural poverty. But different types of investments yield different poverty and production effects, and these impacts vary greatly across regions. Rozelle *et al.* (1997) studied the environmental degradation in China. They examined the association between environmental improvement and efforts to both alleviate poverty and control population growth.

Available studies on income inequality and poverty in China provide useful insights for our study, but most studies have not used the large data sets that are used in this chapter. Both urban and rural data from the National Bureau of Statistics and the Ministry of Agriculture for 1995 and 1998 are combined, covering more than two thirds of all the Chinese provinces. The data sets used are probably by far the largest among all the studies and should, therefore, produce more useful results than others.

## 9.3  Poverty and its determinants in urban China

### 9.3.1  Calculation of poverty lines

Considering the advantages and limitations of various methods used by NBS to evaluate the poverty lines for urban China, a recent ADB study adopts a similar approach to that suggested by Ravallion (1994) to derive the poverty lines for each individual province.

The estimation of the poverty line starts from the definition of a food poverty line. It then considers the evaluation of the basic non-food component. Depending on how the basic non-food component is evaluated, two poverty lines (low and high) are estimated for each region.

When deriving the food poverty line, the first important issue of consideration is the selection of an appropriate welfare indicator. This chapter uses per capita disposable income because we only have income data for the rural households.

Another important issue is the selection of households when a basic-need basket of food items is defined to evaluate the cost of food consumption. The poorest 20 per cent of households ranked by per capita expenditure are considered to be the relevant group whose consumption pattern is close to that of the households who may live in poverty. As a result, all the food items with complete price and quantity information from this group of households are listed. The food quantities are converted into calorie equivalents using a nutritional conversion table provided by the National Nutritional Society. The unit cost of calories consumed is then computed. This unit cost multiplied by 2,100 (minimum requirement of calorie per capita per day) and 365 (number of days in a year) yield the value of a food poverty line. At the national level, the food poverty line in 1998 was estimated as 1,390 yuan per capita per year, which was 23.63 per cent of the national average per capita income. The values of poverty lines for all the provinces are presented in Table 9.1.

The values of food poverty lines vary substantially across provinces, ranging from 941 yuan in Qinghai to 2,361 yuan in Shanghai. This implies that the same amount of food energy costs 2.5 times as much in Shanghai as in Qinghai. The differences in the values of food poverty lines reflect the extent to which food prices differ spatially.

Given a food poverty line, denoted by $Z_F$ for any particular region, the low and high poverty lines for that region can be derived from running the following regression suggested by Ravallion (1994).

$$S_j = \alpha + \beta \, ln\left(\frac{x_j}{Z_F}\right) + \gamma \, ln(n_j) \qquad (9.1)$$

Once the parameters in equation (9.1) are estimated, the low and high poverty lines can be evaluated by the following formulae.

The low line (denoted by $Z_L$) is:       $Z_L = Z_F \, (2-\alpha-\lambda \, ln(n))$

The high line (denoted by ZU) is:       $Z_U = Z_F \, (1+\beta)/(\alpha+\lambda \, ln(n)+\beta)$

where $ln(n)$ is the logarithm of average household size. The same regression is repeated for all provinces. The national poverty lines are the weighted averages of the provincial lines by provincial populations (not the survey sample populations).

In 1998, the total urban population was 312.4 million people. The average per capita disposable income was 5,633 yuan per year. The low and high poverty lines are respectively 1,869 yuan and 2,316 yuan. These are respectively 32 per cent and 39 per cent of per capita income. The results for individual provinces are presented in Table 9.1. Like the food poverty lines, the values of low and high poverty lines vary significantly across provinces. The evaluations of food poverty lines reflect consumers' tastes and consumption patterns as suggested by Ravallion (1994) and Deaton (1997). Since the food poverty lines are derived from the consumption information obtained from the poorest 20 per cent of households in each province, it can be said that they are the minimum costs necessary to buy the required amounts of nutrition in different locations. The substantial variations across different provinces suggest that it is important not to use the same line for the whole country.

### 9.3.2 *Estimated results on poverty incidence and poverty pattern*

The poverty head count rates by province derived from the survey results are presented in Table 9.2.

Table 9.1 Poverty lines evaluated by per capita expenditure in 1988 (yuan/year)

| Provinces | Population '000 | Per capita income | Poverty lines | | | As % of per capita income | | |
|---|---|---|---|---|---|---|---|---|
| | | | $Z_F$ | $Z_L$ | $Z_H$ | $Z_F$ | $Z_L$ | $Z_H$ |
| Beijing | 7,495 | 8,472 | 1,983 | 2,565 | 3,118 | 23.41 | 30.28 | 36.80 |
| Tianjin | 5,313 | 6,693 | 1,728 | 2,371 | 2,993 | 25.82 | 35.42 | 44.71 |
| Hebei | 12,532 | 5,392 | 1,336 | 1,886 | 2,509 | 24.78 | 34.97 | 46.53 |
| Shanxi | 8,312 | 4,277 | 960 | 1,297 | 1,616 | 22.45 | 30.32 | 37.78 |
| Neimenggu | 7,973 | 4,277 | 1,008 | 1,395 | 1,824 | 23.57 | 32.60 | 42.65 |
| Liaoning | 18,769 | 4,930 | 1,259 | 1,746 | 2,203 | 25.53 | 35.42 | 44.69 |
| Jilin | 11,319 | 4,525 | 1,051 | 1,447 | 1,831 | 23.23 | 31.98 | 40.46 |
| Heilongjiang | 16,663 | 4,430 | 1,071 | 1,475 | 1,878 | 24.17 | 33.29 | 42.39 |
| Shanghai | 9,696 | 8,767 | 2,361 | 3,086 | 3,636 | 26.93 | 35.20 | 41.48 |
| Jiangsu | 20,295 | 6,462 | 1,448 | 1,880 | 2,228 | 22.41 | 29.10 | 34.48 |
| Zhejiang | 9,477 | 8,396 | 1,824 | 2,438 | 2,989 | 21.72 | 29.04 | 35.61 |
| Anhui | 12,043 | 4,932 | 1,319 | 1,758 | 2,138 | 26.75 | 35.64 | 43.34 |
| Fujian | 6,670 | 7,192 | 1,554 | 2,046 | 2,416 | 21.61 | 28.45 | 33.60 |
| Jiangxi | 9,065 | 4,033 | 1,164 | 1,506 | 1,809 | 28.85 | 37.34 | 44.85 |
| Shandong | 23,218 | 5,315 | 1,308 | 1,902 | 2,566 | 24.61 | 35.78 | 48.28 |
| Henan | 16,804 | 4,040 | 1,076 | 1,496 | 1,904 | 26.62 | 37.02 | 47.14 |
| Hubei | 16,458 | 5,121 | 1,354 | 1,828 | 2,283 | 26.44 | 35.70 | 44.58 |
| Hunan | 12,793 | 5,348 | 1,277 | 1,723 | 2,146 | 23.88 | 32.22 | 40.13 |
| Guangdong | 22,764 | 11,975 | 2,083 | 2,636 | 3,061 | 17.39 | 22.01 | 25.56 |
| Guangxi | 8,168 | 5,920 | 1,572 | 2,077 | 2,507 | 26.56 | 35.08 | 42.35 |

| | | | | | | | | |
|---|---|---|---|---|---|---|---|---|
| Hainan | 1,891 | 5,367 | 1,693 | 2,132 | 2,465 | 31.54 | 39.73 | 45.93 |
| Sichuan | 15,077 | 5,333 | 1,259 | 1,658 | 2,004 | 23.61 | 31.08 | 37.58 |
| Guizhou | 5,188 | 4,542 | 1,341 | 1,760 | 2,137 | 29.51 | 38.75 | 47.06 |
| Yunnan | 6,111 | 5,852 | 1,484 | 1,944 | 2,359 | 25.37 | 33.22 | 40.32 |
| Tibet | 342 | 6,262 | 1,456 | 1,915 | 2,237 | 23.26 | 30.58 | 35.73 |
| Chongqing | 6,352 | 5,230 | 1,355 | 1,809 | 2,214 | 25.92 | 34.59 | 42.34 |
| Shaanxi | 7,804 | 4,362 | 1,080 | 1,524 | 2,014 | 24.77 | 34.93 | 46.18 |
| Gansu | 4,720 | 4,046 | 1,127 | 1,495 | 1,819 | 27.85 | 36.94 | 44.94 |
| Qinghai | 1,342 | 3,417 | 941 | 1,229 | 1,484 | 27.55 | 35.95 | 43.42 |
| Ningxia | 1,554 | 4,234 | 1,085 | 1,561 | 2,093 | 25.62 | 36.86 | 49.42 |
| Xinjiang | 6,213 | 4,795 | 1,117 | 1,452 | 1,772 | 23.29 | 30.27 | 36.96 |
| **All China** | **312,421** | **5,633** | **1,390** | **1,869** | **2,316** | **23.63** | **31.77** | **39.37** |

Notes: National averages are weighted averages using provincial populations as weights. $Z_F$, $Z_L$, and $Z_H$ are respectively the food, low and high poverty lines.

*Table 9.2* Poverty incidence by province in urban China ('000 people and per cent)

| Region | By low poverty lines | | By high poverty lines | | Gini coefficients |
|---|---|---|---|---|---|
| | '000 | % | '000 | % | |
| Beijing | 20 | 0.26 | 54 | 0.73 | 0.2142 |
| Tianjin | 99 | 1.87 | 360 | 6.77 | 0.2579 |
| Hebei | 288 | 2.30 | 651 | 5.20 | 0.2351 |
| Shanxi | 332 | 3.99 | 596 | 7.17 | 0.2985 |
| Neimenggu | 161 | 2.02 | 510 | 6.40 | 0.2646 |
| Liaoning | 431 | 2.29 | 1150 | 6.13 | 0.2534 |
| Jilin | 455 | 4.02 | 853 | 7.54 | 0.2615 |
| Heilongjiang | 348 | 2.09 | 1154 | 6.92 | 0.2786 |
| Shanghai | 126 | 1.29 | 314 | 3.24 | 0.2158 |
| Jiangsu | 138 | 0.68 | 244 | 1.20 | 0.2395 |
| Zhejiang | 23 | 0.24 | 153 | 1.62 | 0.2330 |
| Anhui | 135 | 1.12 | 348 | 2.89 | 0.2265 |
| Fujian | 8 | 0.11 | 145 | 2.18 | 0.2623 |
| Jiangxi | 53 | 0.59 | 310 | 3.42 | 0.2225 |
| Shandong | 192 | 0.82 | 1172 | 5.05 | 0.2327 |
| Henan | 545 | 3.24 | 1410 | 8.39 | 0.2415 |
| Hubei | 223 | 1.35 | 934 | 5.67 | 0.2437 |
| Hunan | 123 | 0.96 | 462 | 3.61 | 0.2542 |
| Guangdong | 44 | 0.19 | 154 | 0.68 | 0.2963 |
| Guangxi | 92 | 1.13 | 246 | 3.01 | 0.2393 |
| Hainan | 88 | 4.63 | 150 | 7.94 | 0.2668 |
| Sichuan | 459 | 3.04 | 711 | 4.72 | 0.2738 |
| Guizhou | 163 | 3.15 | 260 | 5.00 | 0.2405 |
| Yunnan | 98 | 1.61 | 225 | 3.69 | 0.2344 |
| Tibet | 30 | 8.63 | 39 | 11.31 | 0.2863 |
| Chongqing | 57 | 0.89 | 260 | 4.09 | 0.2142 |
| Shaanxi | 346 | 4.43 | 932 | 11.95 | 0.2870 |
| Gansu | 113 | 2.38 | 304 | 6.44 | 0.2582 |
| Qinghai | 46 | 3.44 | 76 | 5.63 | 0.2284 |
| Ningxia | 69 | 4.45 | 210 | 13.51 | 0.2701 |
| Xinjiang | 164 | 2.64 | 383 | 6.16 | 0.2847 |
| East | 1548 | 1.06 | 4795 | 3.28 | – |
| Central | 2375 | 2.13 | 6577 | 5.90 | – |
| West | 1545 | 2.82 | 3399 | 6.21 | – |
| **Urban China** | **5467** | **1.75** | **14772** | **4.73** | **0.2955** |

Source: NBS, 1998 *Urban Household Survey Data*.

Notes: Poverty lines are derived from per capita expenditure. The capability measurement is per capita disposable income.

The poverty incidences in the central and west regions are significantly higher than in the eastern region. The east region accounts for 46.8 per cent of the total urban population but only 28–30 per cent of the total number of poor. The west region accounts for 17.5 per cent of the total urban population but 23–28 per cent of the total number of poor.

### 9.3.3 Sensitivity of poverty incidence with respect to income

Sensitivity analysis on poverty incidence can be conducted using a parametric approach. Poverty incidence is primarily determined by two counteractive forces: income and income distribution. A higher per capita income tends to reduce poverty holding income distribution unchanged. On the other hand, a more unequal distribution tends to raise poverty holding per capita income constant. The quantitative effects of income and income distribution can be evaluated through running a multivariate regression. The dependent variable is a specified poverty rate. The independent variables will be per capita mean income and the Gini coefficient, which is used to measure income distribution.

Since there are 31 provinces in the data set, it is possible to derive 31 data points to support a cross-section regression. The regression models are specified below.

$$ln(\text{poverty incidence}) = \text{Intercept} + \alpha\ ln(\text{mean income}) + \beta\ ln(\text{Gini coefficient}) \tag{9.2}$$

Per capita mean income, poverty rates and Gini coefficients by province are given in Tables 9.1 and 9.2 in the previous section.

Because poverty incidences for each province are measured by both low and high poverty lines, the regression model can be run in two different versions. The first uses poverty incidences measured by the low poverty lines. The second uses poverty incidences measured by the high poverty lines. The regression results are reported in Table 9.3.

All the estimated coefficients are statistically significant below the 5 per cent critical level. The incidences of poverty, either measured by the low or high poverty line, are highly sensitive to the mean incomes and income inequality. Since the model is specified in a double-log form, the estimated coefficients are the corresponding elasticity of poverty incidence with respect to the independent variables. For example, the elasticity of poverty measured by the low poverty line with respect to mean income is −1.572. This means that if mean income rises by 10 per cent, poverty incidence will increase by about 16 per cent, holding income

*Table 9.3* Effects of income and income distribution on poverty incidences

| Dependent variable | Intercept | *ln(income)* | *ln(Gini)* | *Adj-R²* | *Observation* |
|---|---|---|---|---|---|
| | *Estimates of coefficients on the independent variables* | | | | |
| *ln*(Poverty I) | 18.37 | −1.572 | 3.069 | 0.51 | 31 |
| | (5.41) | (−4.19) | (3.52) | | |
| *ln*(Poverty II) | 18.74 | −1.733 | 1.469 | 0.54 | 31 |
| | (6.59) | (−5.51) | (2.01) | | |

Sources: NBS and the research team.

Notes: (1) Poverty I and poverty II respectively denote poverty incidences measured by low and high poverty lines. (2) Figures in parentheses are *t*-statistics. Income is per capita mean income by province. Gini is the Gini coefficient.

distribution unchanged. The results show that poverty incidence is slightly more sensitive to mean income if it is measured by the high poverty line than if it is measured by the low poverty line.

Poverty incidence is very sensitive to income distribution. For example, if the Gini coefficient increases by 10 per cent, the poverty incidence measured by the high poverty line will rise by almost 15 per cent if per capita mean income is unchanged. The results also show that poverty incidence is far more sensitive to income distribution if it is measured by the low poverty line than if it is measured by the high poverty line. If the Gini coefficient rises by 10 per cent, the poverty incidence measured by the low poverty line will increase by over 30 per cent.

### 9.3.4 Some special features of income and poverty distribution

*(1) Household income equation*

Household incomes are determined by various factors. This sub-section runs some partial regressions to identify the main characteristic variables on household incomes.

The multivariate regression models are illustrated by equation (9.3).

$$ln(y_i) = F(\text{sex, education, age, location}) \tag{9.3}$$

where $y_i$ is defined as per capita income of household $i$, sex is the sex of the household head, education is the education level of the household head, location is a geographical location of the household. In actual regressions, sex is a dummy variable, taking a value of 1 if the household head is male, and 0 for female. Education is a set of dummy variables, taking the value of 1 if the household head belongs to the respective education category, and 0 otherwise. Age is also a set of dummy variables taking the values of 1 and 0. Location is a dummy variable, taking a value of 1 if the household belongs to the eastern region, and 0 otherwise. Provincial dummy variables have been used in various regressions but their estimated coefficients provide little information useful for this study.

In Table 9.4, the dependent variable is log per capita income by household. The estimated results show the following information. First, per capita income in male-headed households is 12.7 per cent lower than that in female-headed ones if age, education and location are controlled. Second, there are significant differences in per capita incomes among different aged groups. Households headed by young people (aged below 30) have the lowest per capita income. The highest income group is those with heads at the age range of 45–60. On average, average per capita income in this group is almost 14 per cent higher than for the age group below 30.

Third, education has a substantial impact on per capita income. The highest income group is families whose heads have received higher education. On average per capita income in this group is almost 40 per cent higher than the base group whose heads have received only primary education. The most disadvantaged group is those households whose heads have received education below the primary school level. In other words, the heads of these households are either illiterate or semi-illiterate. The estimated coefficients on the education variables show a clear hierarchical structure of per capita income. As the level of education rises, per capita income increases. Finally, location has an important effect on per capita income. Other things being equal, per capita income in the eastern region is 35 per cent higher than the rest of the country.

*Table 9.4* Per capita income and characteristics of household head, dependent variable = *ln*(per capita income)

| Independent variables | Coefficient | t-value |
|---|---|---|
| Constant | 7.361 | 28.30 |
| Male | −0.127 | −16.10 |
| Aged 30–45 | 0.110 | 6.72 |
| Aged 45–60 | 0.138 | 8.09 |
| Aged > 60 | 0.131 | 6.86 |
| > BA degree | 0.483 | 24.80 |
| University education or more | 0.367 | 21.80 |
| Technical school | 0.297 | 17.70 |
| Senior high school | 0.212 | 13.40 |
| Junior high school | 0.116 | 7.68 |
| < primary school | −0.151 | −3.13 |
| Eastern region | 0.350 | 46.70 |
| Adj-R$^2$ | | 0.29 |
| Number of observations | | 16,550 |

Source: NBS, 1998 *Urban Household Survey Data* for all provinces.
Note: The base person comparison is male, aged 30 or less, primary education living in the inland area.

*(2) Wage equations of household heads and their spouses*

Because the characteristics of household heads have an important effect on family income, it is useful to study the relationship between wage income of household heads and their characteristics.

The wage equation can be defined by a multivariate regression model illustrated by equation (9.4). The dependent variable is log total income earned by household heads. The explanatory variables are the personal characteristics of household heads and location.

$$ln(w_i) = F(\text{sex, education, age, location}) \tag{9.4}$$

Equation (9.4) is estimated in two versions: with and without education. The regression results are presented in Table 9.5. Without considering education, there is a significant difference between male and female heads of households. On average, male household heads earn 11.8 per cent more than female household heads. If education is controlled, the male–female earning gap is only 8.9 per cent. This implies that 2.9 per cent of gross male–female earning gap is due to education difference.

Education has a substantive effect on earnings. Household heads without a primary education earn less than half that of household heads with primary education. Per capita earning descends monotonically from the highest to the lowest education level. People with higher education earn twice as much as people without primary education. The location factor is also important. It explains 28.5 per cent of earning differences.

The results in Table 9.4 show that female-headed households attain a higher income than male-headed households, but the results in Table 9.5 show that male household heads earn more than female household heads. There are two possible explanations for the controversial results. One is that the average number of people in female-headed household may be smaller than that of male-headed ones. From the data, the average household sizes are 3.37 and 3.27 respectively for male- and female-headed households, implying that the former is 2.7 per cent larger than the latter. From the sample of 17,000 households, 34 per cent were headed by females while 66 per cent by males. However, the per capita income difference between the two types of household is 12.6 per cent (Table 9.4), which is much larger than the difference in family sizes.

*Table 9.5*  Wage equation for the household heads, dependent variable = *ln*(earning of household head)

| Independent variables | Without education | | With education | |
|---|---|---|---|---|
| | Coefficient | t-value | Coefficient | t-value |
| Constant | 8.640 | 41.58 | 8.330 | 31.32 |
| Male | 0.118 | 11.70 | 0.089 | 9.15 |
| Aged 30–45 | 0.121 | 5.76 | 0.162 | 7.96 |
| Aged 45–60 | 0.137 | 6.35 | 0.223 | 10.56 |
| Aged > 60 | 0.018 | 0.76 | 0.163 | 6.93 |
| > BA degree | – | – | 0.544 | 22.48 |
| Higher education | – | – | 0.432 | 20.61 |
| Technical school | – | – | 0.371 | 17.75 |
| Senior high school | – | – | 0.258 | 13.05 |
| Junior high school | – | – | 0.147 | 7.80 |
| < primary school | – | – | –0.577 | –9.32 |
| Eastern region | 0.288 | 30.00 | 0.285 | 30.61 |
| Adj-$R^2$ | | 0.063 | | 0.13 |
| Number of observations | | 16,550 | | 16,550 |

Note: In the first model, the base person for comparison is male, aged 30 or less, living in the inland area. In the second model, the base person for comparison is male, aged 30 or less, primary education living in the inland area.

The second explanation may be the difference between the earnings of the second or third wage earners between the male- and female-headed households. Since the majority of Chinese urban households have two wage earners (the head and spouse), we only consider the earning differences of the spouses. The same wage equation for household heads is estimated for their spouses. The results are shown in Table 9.6.

*Table 9.6* Wage equation of the spouses of household heads, dependent variable = *ln*(earning of spouses of household heads)

| Independent variables | Without education | | With education | |
|---|---|---|---|---|
| | Coefficient | t-value | Coefficient | t-value |
| Constant | 8.290 | 35.68 | 7.100 | 26.04 |
| Male | 0.418 | 32.41 | 0.292 | 22.91 |
| Aged 30–45 | 0.081 | 3.34 | 0.149 | 6.43 |
| Aged 45–60 | 0.013 | 0.50 | 0.169 | 6.93 |
| Aged > 60 | –0.138 | –4.54 | 0.127 | 4.24 |
| > BA degree | – | – | 0.834 | 26.49 |
| Higher education | – | – | 0.730 | 27.47 |
| Technical school | – | – | 0.671 | 26.45 |
| Senior high school | – | – | 0.425 | 18.10 |
| Junior high school | – | – | 0.261 | 11.85 |
| < primary school | – | – | –0.383 | –6.57 |
| Eastern region | 0.394 | 31.99 | 0.399 | 34.08 |
| Adj-$R^2$ | 0.13 | | 0.21 | |
| Number of observations | | 16,550 | | 16,550 |

Source: NBS, 1998, *Urban Household Survey Data* for all provinces.

Note: In the first model, the base person for comparison is male, aged 30 or less, living in the inland area. In the second model, the base person for comparison is male, aged 30 or less, primary education living in the inland area.

Without considering education, the male–female earning gap is 41.8 per cent, which is substantially higher than the earning gap of male–female household heads. After controlling for education differences, the earning gap of male–female spouses is 29.2 per cent, which is also substantially greater than the corresponding earning gap of male–female household heads. The earning differentials between different education groups are also large. The highest earning group (with the highest education level) earns 120 per cent more than the lowest earning group (the least educated).

Comparing the results in Tables 9.4 to 9.6, we can now solve the puzzle of gender and income inequality. The fact that female-headed households are better off than male-headed households is not really explained by the difference in household size as suggested by the World Bank for Vietnam (World Bank, 1999a), neither does it mean that there is no gender inequality in income. Gender inequality is revealed by the significant difference between male–female earnings, not by the difference of per capita incomes between male- and female-headed households. In our data set, the male–female earning differential is about 9 per cent between the household heads, but it is as high as 29 per cent between the spouses.

The results lead to two important conclusions. First, one cannot use the income difference between female- and male-headed households to infer gender inequality. Second, why female-headed households are better off than male-headed households is explained by the fact that female household heads have spouses who earn substantially more than those of male household heads.

### 9.3.5 Determinants of urban poverty

*(1)  Characteristics of poor versus non-poor households*

Poor households tend to have bigger family size and more children than non-poor households. They also tend to have less living space. An average poor household has 3.78 people, 1.48 children and 9.8 m² of living space per capita, compared to 3.32 people, 1.13 children and 11.96 m² of living space per capita for the non-poor households (Table 9.7).

Because the poor households have less income and more people, they tend to consume less than the non-poor households. On a per capita basis, total expenditure of poor households is only 36.71 per cent of that of the non-poor households. Even for necessity goods (foods, clothing, housing and medication), the poor households consume less than half the level of the non-poor ones (Table 9.7). Per capita expenditures on 'daily goods, services and durable goods' and 'transportation/ communication' for the poor households were less than one-fifth the levels of the non-poor.

*Table 9.7* Comparison of poor and non-poor household characteristics

|  | Non-poor household (1) | Poor household (2) | Poor/ non-poor (2)/(1) | All households |
| --- | --- | --- | --- | --- |
| Household size | 3.32 | 3.78 | 113.86 | 3.34 |
| Children/household | 1.13 | 1.48 | 130.97 | 1.14 |
| Living area (m²/head) | 11.96 | 9.80 | 81.94 | 11.86 |
| Living expenses (yuan/head) | 4915.79 | 1804.35 | 36.71 | 4768.67 |
| Of which: |  |  |  |  |
|   Food | 2163.10 | 1006.78 | 46.54 | 2108.43 |
|   Clothing | 519.35 | 141.50 | 27.25 | 501.49 |
|   Daily goods/services/durable | 423.26 | 56.70 | 13.40 | 405.93 |
|   Health & medication | 221.83 | 100.46 | 45.29 | 216.09 |
|   Transport/communication | 303.64 | 56.52 | 18.61 | 291.96 |
|   Leisure/education/culture | 569.66 | 158.85 | 27.89 | 550.24 |
|   Housing | 483.09 | 235.93 | 48.84 | 471.41 |
|   Miscellaneous goods & service | 231.93 | 47.87 | 20.64 | 223.23 |

Source: NBS, 1998 *Urban Household Survey Data.*

*(2)  Household characteristics and poverty*

If we run a probit model for the determination of poverty, it is possible to identify key variables responsible for poverty at the household level. As shown in equation (9.5), the dependent variable takes the value of 1 if the household is poor, and 0 otherwise. Because sex, age, education, location have found to have important effects on family income, they should also have an important effect on poverty. Apart from these variables, equation (9.5) also includes the dependency ratio, which is defined as the number of household members divided by the number of working persons in a given household.

Pr(poverty) = *F*(sex, age, education, location and dependency ratio)    (9.5)

The estimated coefficients are all statistically significant (Table 9.8). This means that all the included variables are important factors affecting poverty at the household level. For example, male-headed households are 2.1 per cent more likely than female-headed households to be in poverty. Households headed by older people are less likely to be poor than those headed by younger people. As household heads receive more education, their households will become less vulnerable to poverty. Households headed by the least educated are the most likely to live in poverty. Location is also an important factor for poverty. Households living in the east are less likely to be poor than those in the inland areas. Finally, the dependency ratio is also important. The higher the dependency ratio, the more likely the family will live in poverty.

*Table 9.8* A probit model of poverty determination by some key variables

| Independent variables | Marginal effect on poverty | t-value |
|---|---|---|
| Constant | 0.337 | 26.60 |
| Male | 0.021 | 5.42 |
| Aged 30–45 | −0.030 | −3.70 |
| Aged 45–60 | −0.017 | −2.10 |
| Aged > 60 | −0.019 | −2.02 |
| > BA degree | −0.110 | −11.60 |
| College | −0.099 | −12.00 |
| Technical school | −0.088 | −10.80 |
| Senior high school | −0.063 | −8.19 |
| Junior high school | −0.041 | −5.61 |
| < primary school | 0.048 | 2.03 |
| Eastern region | −0.015 | −4.21 |
| Dependent ratio | 0.120 | 30.10 |
| Adj-$R^2$ | | 0.06 |
| Number of observations | | 16,550 |

Source: NBS, 1998, *Urban Household Survey Data*.

Notes: The dependent variable has a value of one if the household's per capita income is less than the poverty line, and zero otherwise. The poverty lines are province-specific.

## 9.4 Poverty and poverty determinants in rural China

### 9.4.1 Calculations of poverty lines

There are no data on food and non-food consumption at the household level to derive rural poverty lines in the same way as we have done for the urban sector. As a result, we have to rely on estimates provided by the statistical authority, the World Bank and some other independent researchers. The starting point is to use the estimates provided by the Chinese government. The official poverty line for 1990 was set at 318 yuan per capita per year.

The official poverty line has been criticised for being too low. Hence it tends to underestimate the extent of poverty, although it is a useful benchmark for poverty analysis. The World Bank used a higher line at 454 yuan per capita per year in 1990 (World Bank, 1997). It was based on the $1 per day per capita standards at purchasing power parity (PPP). The imputed PPP exchange rate was 1.24 yuan per dollar but the official exchange rate was 4.83 yuan per dollar in 1990.

Poverty lines for other years have been derived based on the above values adjusted by the consumer price index (CPI) for the rural population, or the rural CPI. Table 9.9 provides estimates of rural poverty lines for the period 1990–9 based on the poverty lines in 1990 and the rural CPI for the whole country.

*Table 9.9* Estimates of rural poverty lines

| Year | Rural CPI | Low poverty line | High poverty line |
| --- | --- | --- | --- |
| 1990 | 100.0 | 318 | 454 |
| 1991 | 102.3 | 325 | 464 |
| 1992 | 107.1 | 341 | 486 |
| 1993 | 121.7 | 387 | 553 |
| 1994 | 150.2 | 478 | 682 |
| 1995 | 176.5 | 561 | 801 |
| 1996 | 190.4 | 606 | 865 |
| 1997 | 195.2 | 621 | 886 |
| 1998 | 193.3 | 615 | 877 |
| 1999 | 190.4 | 605 | 864 |

Sources: NBS, 1999, *Statistical Yearbook of China*, p. 291; World Bank, 1997, for the poverty lines in 1990.

There are three potential limitations on the estimated poverty lines. First, it does not take into account the regional differences in prices, tastes and consumption patterns. In theory, poverty lines should not be the same for all regions due to the spatial variations in purchasing power parity. For example, 100 yuan in rich regions may not buy the same amount of consumer goods as does 100 yuan in poor provinces. Second, using a national CPI to estimate poverty lines over time may not reflect the real changes in regional prices. Third, the rural CPI may not be the appropriate price index for adjusting the poverty lines over time.

Despite these caveats, there are advantages to using the estimates of these poverty lines. The first advantage is consistency, because the poverty lines are estimated with the same approach in different years. As a result, poverty comparisons over time can be easily understood and interpreted. The second advantage is simplicity. Once the poverty lines are known for one year, the poverty lines can be derived for several years.

It is important to note that the rural poverty lines are substantially lower than the urban ones. In 1998, the low and high urban poverty lines are respectively 1,869 and 2,316 yuan per capita per year (the official urban poverty line is 1,800 yuan). The corresponding rural poverty lines are only 615 and 877 yuan. The rural–urban poverty lines ratios are respectively 33 per cent and 38 per cent. In the same year, per capita urban income was 5,633 but per capita rural income was 2,447 yuan, with a per capita rural–urban income ratio of 43 per cent.

It is well recognised that the rural and urban populations are highly hetero-geneous, not only because of the large urban–rural income disparity, but also because of the large differences in the cost of living between the cities and the countryside. However, the significant differences of poverty lines are unlikely to be explained by the differences in the cost of living. It is likely that in comparison with the rural poverty lines, the urban poverty lines are overestimated. Alternatively, one may argue that the rural poverty lines are underestimated in comparison with the urban poverty lines.

Because the urban poverty lines were estimated by the ADB using an inter-nationally acceptable approach, there is no obvious reason to dispute that the urban poverty lines have been overestimated. In particular, if the urban poverty lines were too high, the estimated incidence of urban poverty would be high as well. The results in the previous section show that the urban poverty head count rates are only 1.75–4.73 per cent, which are very low by international standards.

Another possibility is that the estimates of rural poverty lines are too low. Different studies (World Bank, 1997; Yao, 2000) have suggested that the official rural poverty line is too low as it is set with some political consideration. In contrast, the high rural poverty line is estimated by the World Bank and there is no obvious reason to suggest that it is too low. However, the comparison of the urban and rural poverty lines at least indicates that we should use the high poverty line as the preferred measurement for rural poverty.

If the high rural poverty line is not too low, and if there were no differences in the costs of living between the cities and the countryside, then the same poverty line used for the rural population should be used for the urban population. If the high rural poverty line were used to measure urban poverty, the urban poverty head count rate in 1998 would be just 0.1 per cent. The majority of provinces in the east and central regions would have no urban people living below the poverty line (877 yuan per capita per year). On the other hand, if we used the urban poverty lines to measure rural poverty, the rural poverty head count rates would be 55.3 per cent by the low poverty line (1,869 yuan per capita per year) and 66.1 per cent by the high poverty (2,316 yuan per capita per year). The estimated poverty rates are certainly unreal and would never be accepted by the government or any independent researchers.

The above discussion suggests that the definition of an appropriate poverty line can be difficult and controversial. As a result, whatever poverty lines are used, the results must be interpreted with caution. Moreover, it is important to use more than one poverty line and to conduct some sensitivity analyses so that we can examine the changes in poverty rates with respect to alternative definitions of poverty lines.

### 9.4.2  *Data and estimated results on rural poverty incidence in 1995 and 1998*

*(1) Household survey data*

We are unable to obtain household survey data from the NBS. However, we have obtained data from two alternative sources: the Chinese Academy of Social Sciences (CASS) for 1995 and the Ministry of Agriculture (MOA) for 1998. The data set for 1995 contains about 8,000 households from 19 provinces. The households were randomly selected using the national household survey framework. In other words, the design of the sample was intended to represent the whole country. The data set for 1998 contains about 15,000 households from 19 provinces. The households were randomly selected in 1986. The same households were surveyed every year.

Although the data sets come from different sources, they have similar characteristics and contain household level income and population information for the same provinces. To make the two data sets comparable, we use provincial level rural CPI to convert the values in 1995 into comparable values in 1998. In other words, the income levels are all measured in 1998 prices. One important difference between the two data sets is that the data in 1998 contain more households than in 1995. Consequently, the computation results are more stable using the 1998 data than using the 1995 data. The following presentation will be mainly focused on the 1998 data. The 1995 data is used only when regressions require a sufficient number of observations. The summary statistics and the Gini coefficients derived from the 1998 data are presented in Table 9.10 by the selected provinces.

The sample provinces had a total rural population of 777 million people in 1998. They represent about 83 per cent of the national rural population. From the sample data, per capita income was 2,377 yuan. The national average rural income was 2,163 yuan per capita (NBS, 2000), which was 25 per cent higher than in 1995 (1,727 yuan/head).

The Gini coefficient for the whole sample is 0.4606, which is 22 per cent higher than the Gini coefficient derived from the 1995 data (0.3773).

The Gini coefficient varies widely across provinces, ranging from 0.30 in Hubei to 0.52 in Yunnan. Except Zhejiang, Guangdong and Yunnan, all the provinces have a Gini coefficient smaller than the national Gini coefficient. This is an indirect indication of large inter-provincial income inequality. Per capita income ranges from 1,226 yuan in Gansu to 4,378 yuan in Beijing. Most provinces in the east have a per capita income much higher than the national average. These include Beijing, Liaoning (2,930), Jiangsu (2,789), Zhejiang (3,815), and Guangdong (4,283). The lowest income provinces are concentrated in the west, including Shaanxi (1,619) and Gansu.

*(2) Estimated poverty head count rates*

The poverty head count rates by province are presented in Table 9.11. They are measured by the low and high poverty lines in 1995 and 1998 for all the sample

*Table 9.10* Rural population, income and Gini coefficients in 1998

| Province | Population ('000) | Income (yuan/head) | Gini coefficients |
|---|---|---|---|
| Beijing | 3,617 | 4,378 | 0.4231 |
| Tianjin | 53,331 | 2,067 | 0.3891 |
| Shanxi | 23,059 | 1,893 | 0.4191 |
| Liaoning | 22,272 | 2,930 | 0.3984 |
| Jilin | 14,804 | 1,899 | 0.4749 |
| Jiangsu | 51,063 | 2,789 | 0.3649 |
| Zhejiang | 35,398 | 3,815* | 0.4935 |
| Anhui | 49,999 | 2,115 | 0.3966 |
| Jiangxi | 31,829 | 1,810 | 0.3992 |
| Shangdong | 65,755 | 2,441 | 0.3386 |
| Henan | 77,300 | 1,802 | 0.4399 |
| Hubei | 42,696 | 1,868 | 0.2995 |
| Hunan | 52,378 | 2,102 | 0.3666 |
| Guangdong | 48,966 | 4,283 | 0.4809 |
| Sichuan | 93,011 | 1,982 | 0.3481 |
| Guizhou | 30,325 | 1,842 | 0.4398 |
| Yunnan | 34,011 | 2,054 | 0.5203 |
| Shaanxi | 27,375 | 1,619 | 0.4392 |
| Gansu | 20,202 | 1,226 | 0.4167 |
| Sample provinces | 777,389 | 2,377 | 0.4606 |
| **All China** | **940,250** | **2,163** | |
| Conversion factor | 1.21 | | |

Sources: NBS, 1999a: 404. NBS, 1999b: 22, *Fifty Years of Statistical Data of New China* for per capita rural incomes of the whole country, p. 414 for the per capita income of Zhejiang. NBS, 1998, *Rural Household Survey Data*.

Note: * Per capita income of Zhejiang from the survey sample was substantially higher than the value published by NBS. As a result, the mean income is taken from NBS, 2000.

provinces. The low and high poverty lines in 1995 are respectively 561 and 801 yuan per capita per year. The corresponding values for 1998 are 615 and 877 yuan per capita per year (Table 9).

Regional and national poverty rates are weighted by provincial populations (not by sample populations). At the national level, the incidence of poverty increased by 2.36 percentage points from 1995 to 1998 if it is measured by the low poverty lines, but declined by 1.37 percentage point if it is measured by the high poverty lines. This reversed change in poverty rates using different poverty lines suggests that poor people are highly concentrated around the low poverty lines. As a result, the incidence of poverty is highly sensitive to alternative poverty lines.

The increase in poverty measured by the low poverty lines is particularly worrying, not because of the rise in poverty incidence, but because of the implied difficulty in poverty reduction in rural China. As discussed previously, national average per capita income actually rose by about 25 per cent, which is an impressive growth. National income growth did not benefit the poor who lived around the poverty lines. In other words, rising rural income must have been accompanied with rising inequality, an issue to be discussed below.

The changes in poverty head count rates at the provincial level are far more complicated than at the national level. If we focus on the change in poverty rates measured by the high poverty lines, although most provinces experienced a significant reduction in poverty, some provinces experienced an increase. The largest reduction in poverty was found in the following provinces: Liaoning, Jilin, Zhejiang and Hubei. Most provinces experiencing a rise of poverty were highly concentrated in the central regions, including Anhui, Jiangxi and Henan. One obvious explanation was that there was a prolonged and severe flooding in central China in 1998, which must have had a detrimental impact on agricultural production and farm incomes. The estimated results suggest that the poor households are highly susceptible to natural disasters.

*Table 9.11* Rural poverty head count rate in 1995 and 1998

| | 1995 | | 1998 | | Change 1998 minus 1995 | |
|---|---|---|---|---|---|---|
| | *Low* | *High* | *Low* | *High* | *Low* | *High* |
| Beijing | n.a. | n.a. | 5.12 | 8.37 | 5.12 | 8.37 |
| Hebei | 11.71 | 25.96 | 11.71 | 21.47 | 0.00 | −4.49 |
| Shanxi | 14.36 | 32.53 | 16.03 | 26.35 | 1.67 | −6.18 |
| Liaoning | 15.63 | 27.10 | 5.62 | 12.07 | −10.01 | −15.03 |
| Jilin | 24.85 | 36.19 | 20.03 | 28.09 | −4.82 | −8.10 |
| Jiangsu | 0.97 | 1.99 | 4.93 | 10.07 | 3.96 | 8.08 |
| Zhejiang | 8.14 | 14.18 | 3.21 | 5.30 | −4.93 | −8.88 |
| Anhui | 2.33 | 13.55 | 11.07 | 19.01 | 8.74 | 5.46 |
| Jiangxi | 1.63 | 8.19 | 14.50 | 25.49 | 12.87 | 17.30 |
| Shandong | n.a. | n.a. | 3.13 | 9.20 | n.a. | n.a. |
| Henan | 3.73 | 11.70 | 16.75 | 29.11 | 13.02 | 17.41 |
| Hubei | 16.55 | 29.29 | 6.34 | 13.93 | −10.21 | −15.36 |
| Hunan | 5.79 | 17.57 | 5.83 | 14.72 | 0.04 | −2.85 |
| Guangdong | 0.53 | 1.35 | 3.57 | 6.70 | 3.04 | 5.35 |
| Sichuan | 9.79 | 27.90 | 10.62 | 21.05 | 0.83 | −6.85 |
| Guizhou | 12.16 | 39.11 | 15.09 | 28.50 | 2.93 | −10.61 |
| Yunnan | 15.99 | 39.79 | 26.09 | 36.52 | 10.10 | −3.27 |
| Shaanxi | 10.68 | 36.70 | 18.06 | 34.14 | 7.38 | −2.56 |
| Gansu | 25.15 | 52.37 | 31.19 | 48.72 | 6.04 | −3.65 |
| *By region* | | | | | | |
| East | 6.24 | 12.41 | 5.40 | 10.98 | −0.84 | −1.43 |
| Central | 7.43 | 18.16 | 12.16 | 21.92 | 4.73 | 3.76 |
| West | 12.77 | 35.05 | 16.87 | 29.20 | 4.10 | −5.85 |
| **All China** | **8.60** | **21.26** | **10.96** | **19.89** | **2.36** | **−1.37** |

Using the estimated poverty head count rates, it is possible to estimate the poverty head counts for the sample provinces and for rural China. Poverty head count is the product of the head count rate by the rural population. Table 9.12 presents the poverty head counts for three large regions and for rural China.

*Table 9.12* Numbers of poor in rural China and regional distribution in 1995 and 1998

| Year | 1995 | | 1998 | |
|---|---|---|---|---|
| | *Low* | *High* | *Low* | *High* |
| Number of poor in rural China | | | | |
| China ('000) | 79,610 | 196,836 | 103,054 | 186,950 |
| *As % of total* | | | | |
| East | 22.1 | 17.7 | 17.8 | 19.9 |
| Central | 35.4 | 35.0 | 41.7 | 41.4 |
| West | 42.6 | 47.3 | 40.6 | 38.7 |

Notes: There are 18 provinces in the sample for 1995 and 19 provinces in 1998. The total numbers of national poor people are inflated by a factor of 1.279 for 1995 and 1.71 for 1998 to reflect the ratio of total rural people to the total rural population in the samples. The rural population shares in 1998 are 39.27 per cent for east, 35.73 per cent for central and 25 per cent for west.

The total number of poor for rural China ranged from 79.6 million to 196.8 million in 1995, and from 103.1 million to 187.0 million in 1998.

To have a better understanding of rural poverty, Table 9.13 presents various estimates of the number of rural poor and the incidence of poverty as percentage of the rural population.

*Table 9.13* Comparisons of alternative estimates of rural poverty

| *Estimates according to* | *Number of rural poor (million)* | *As % of total population* |
|---|---|---|
| This chapter (1998) | 103–187 | 11.0–19.9 |
| Yao for 1996 | 57–114 (62–123) | 6.7–13.3 |
| DFID for 1998 | 65–270 (51–214) | 5.4–23.0 |

Sources: Table 9.12, Yao, 2000, DIFD, 1998.

Notes: (1) In this chapter, the rural population in 1998 is 940 million. The total population used by Yao to derive the number of poor is the agricultural population, which is 864 million in 1996, but the total rural population is 929 million. The total population used by DFID to derive the number of poor is 1.2 billion in 1998. (2) The numbers in parentheses are adjusted estimates using the rural population as total population. (3) The low numbers are derived from the low poverty lines, the high numbers are derived from high poverty lines.

The poverty head count rates in this chapter are substantially higher than the estimated by Yao (2000). Yao and this chapter use the same real poverty lines for two different years, so the huge discrepancy must be due to one or two of the following reasons. First, Yao uses data for three provinces to estimate the national poverty rate. If per capita incomes in the three provinces are higher than the national mean income, and/or income distribution in these provinces are more equal than the national income distribution, the incidence of poverty would have been underestimated. Second, if inequality has increased much faster than income in the period 1996–8, the incidence of poverty would have increased from 1996 to 1998.

The incidence of poverty in this chapter is higher (by 5.6 per cent points) than the estimated provided by DFID if poverty is estimated by a low poverty line, but lower (by 3 per cent points) if poverty is measured by a high poverty line. Both sets of estimates are for the same year, hence the discrepancy may be explained by one or two of the following reasons. First, the two sources may have used different measures for the low and high poverty lines. Compared with the results in this report, the estimates made by DFID may have used a lower measure for the low poverty line and a higher measure for the high poverty line. Second, both sources may use different data samples. Even the lowest estimates of rural poverty in China presented in Table 9.13 are much higher than the official figure of 42 million (*People's Daily*, 2000b).

The large discrepancy between the estimates in this chapter (and other sources) and the official figures may be due to sample biases, but it may also be due to some other reasons. The government may have used a very different approach to estimate poverty, or it may have deliberately underestimated the incidence of poverty for political reasons. However, without knowing the exact causes for such a huge discrepancy, one has to be cautious on the interpretation of the estimated results. Nevertheless, we are certain that poverty must still be a big problem in rural China, given the high sensitivity of different estimates with respect to different poverty lines. In addition, if the estimates presented here reflect the true picture of poverty in rural China, the large number of rural poor implies that the task to reduce poverty is far from being ended by the year 2000 as often claimed by many government statements. In fact, rural poverty is so susceptible to the changing economic environment, to all kinds of human and natural uncertainties and risks that it should be taken as a very serious policy issue not just for the next few years, but for the future decades to come.

Another difficult issue on rural poverty is related to the skewed distribution of income between regions. The western region accounts for about 25 per cent of the total rural population but explains about 40 per cent of the total poor. The eastern region accounts for over 39 per cent of the rural population but explains less than 20 per cent of the total poor. This spatial pattern implies that the western provinces are more susceptible to poverty than the rest of the country. However, this does not mean that the other provinces have no serious poverty. In fact, even the most prosperous provinces, including Beijing, Tianjin, Shangdong, Guangdong, Zhejiang and Jiangsu have large numbers of poor people, and they are highly vulnerable to short term fluctuations in production and incomes.

## (3) Sensitivity of poverty incidence with respect to income

Rural poverty may be determined by many factors. Two important determinants are per capita income and the Gini coefficient, which represents the distribution of income. There are other variables that may affect poverty. We have considered the following variables in the poverty equation:

- per capita income
- Gini coefficients
- trade/GDP ratio
- TVE/agricultural output ratio

- transportation
- expenditure on education
- adult illiteracy rate.

We use the poverty rates measured by the low and high poverty lines for both 1995 and 1998 to run various regressions. The model is expressed in equation (9.6) below:

$$\text{Poverty incidence} = F(\text{income, Gini, } Z) \tag{9.6}$$

Where $Z$ is a set of different variables including the trade/GDP ratio, TVE/ agricultural output ratio, expenditure on education, transportation and adult illiteracy rate. All the variables are measured at the provincial level. Since we have 19 provinces in each of the two years, we have 38 observations. All the values are measured in constant 1998 prices. With various estimations, it is found that apart from per capita income and the Gini coefficient, none of the other variables has an estimated coefficient with statistical significance. As a result, we only report the regression results, which contain only two explanatory variables for poverty, that is, per capita income and the Gini coefficients.

The estimated results are presented in Table 9.14. The dependent variable is the *ln*(poverty incidence), the two explanatory variables are *ln*(per capita income) and *ln*(Gini coefficient). The estimated coefficients have the expected signs and are highly significant. The model explains 87 per cent of the variations in poverty incidence, implying that these two variables are the dominant factors of rural poverty.

On the whole, the incidence of rural poverty is highly sensitive to the change in per capita average income and income distribution. Based on the high poverty line, if per capita mean income rises by 10 per cent, the poverty incidence will decline by almost 27 per cent if income distribution is held unchanged. On the

*Table 9.14* Effects of income and inequality on rural poverty

| Dependent variable | Estimates of coefficients on the independent variables | | | Adj-$R^2$ | Observation |
| | Intercept | ln(income) | ln(Gini) | | |
| --- | --- | --- | --- | --- | --- |
| *ln*(Poverty I) | 10.83 | −2.82 | 3.51 | 0.88 | 32 |
| | (7.36) | (−13.27) | (11.50) | | |
| *ln*(Poverty II) | 16.04 | −2.68 | 2.13 | 0.87 | 32 |
| | (10.20) | (−13.30) | (7.72) | | |

Sources: CASS, 1995 and MOA, 1998, rural survey data.

Notes: (1) Poverty I and poverty II respectively denote poverty incidences measured by low and high poverty lines. (2) Figures in parentheses are *t*-statistics. Income is per capita mean income by province. Gini is the Gini coefficient. (3) In the regression, Beijing in 1995 and 1998, Shangdong in 1995 and Zhejiang in 1998 were excluded from the regression.

other hand, if per capita mean income is held unchanged, a 10 per cent rise in the Gini coefficient will lead to a 21 per cent increase in poverty. The incidence of poverty measured by the low poverty line is more sensitive to the changes in income and inequality. It implies that more people are located towards to the low poverty line than towards to the high poverty line.

### (3) Household income, external environment and characteristics of household heads

The rural survey data in 1995 have a few important external factors that may be used to explain income inequality. They include the following characteristic variables in the villages where households reside:

- topography (plain, hilly and mountainous)
- telephone services (with or without)
- remote or not from the urban districts or towns
- minority region or not
- designated poor county or not
- water supplied by fountain, wells or other sources.

We defined a household income equation and use a set of dummy variables to represent the above variables. For example, if a household lives in a village with telephone services, the dummy variable 'telephone' will take the value of 1, and 0 otherwise. We also include a location variable to represent the location effect on household incomes. It is represented by three regional dummy variables: east, central and west. They also take the values of 1s and 0s.

The estimated results are presented in Table 9.15. The dependent variable is *ln*(per capita household income). The estimated coefficients roughly represent the percentage difference of per capita incomes between the specified household group and its comparison counterpart. For example, the estimated coefficients on two included topography dummy variables imply that on average, per capita household income in the hilly and mountainous areas are about 11 per cent less than that in a plains area. All the included dummy variables, except the remote regional dummy variable, are statistically significant, implying that there are significant differences of per capita incomes between the included household groups.

Households residing in a village with telephone services are better off than those residing in a village without telephone. This means that telecommunication is associated with higher incomes.

Households in minority areas are substantially poorer than in the non-minority areas. The estimated coefficient on 'poor county' suggests that average income in designated poor counties are about 30 per cent less than in non-poor counties. Households in the central region are 14 per cent better off than their counterparts in the west region, but 15 per cent worse off than their counterparts in the east region. Households living in an area with a good water supply (fountain or well) are better off than those living in areas without a good water supply.

*Table 9.15* Household income and external environment in rural areas, 1995: dependent variable = *ln*(per capita income)

| Variable | Coefficients | t-value |
|---|---|---|
| Intercept | 6.701 | 80.4 |
| *Topography (comparison: plain)* | | |
| Hilly | −0.106 | −5.87 |
| Mountainous | −0.113 | −5.11 |
| Telephone | 0.124 | 7.04 |
| Remote areas | −0.062 | −0.89 |
| Minority areas | −0.162 | −5.16 |
| Defined as poor county | −0.291 | −16.16 |
| *Water supply (comparison: fountain water)* | | |
| Water supplied by wells | −0.104 | −5.82 |
| Water supplied by other means | −0.104 | −4.4 |
| *Region (comparison: central)* | | |
| East | 0.145 | 7.84 |
| West | −0.141 | −6.61 |
| $R^2$ | | 0.15 |
| Number of observations | | 7965 |

Source: CASS, 1995, *Rural Household Survey Data.*

The regression results have important policy implications on the targeting of poverty reduction. One such implication is already reflected by the government policy to designate poor counties for poverty alleviation. As Carl Riskin (1994) has pointed out that poverty is not just prevalent in the adverse and isolated regions, but can also prevail in the relatively more prosperous areas due to the so-called marginalisation effect of economic growth. The government should make every effort to improve the production and living environment. For example, providing telephone services, water supply, and regional specific subsidy schemes may be effective means of reducing rural poverty.

Like the analysis for the urban households, per capita household income can be affected by the characteristics of household heads in rural China. Age, education, farm type and the number of dependants are important characteristics of household heads. The 1998 survey data included the following variables about household heads:

- age
- farm type
- village cadres or not
- education attainment
- dependency ratio (total household members/working persons)
- location (east, central and west).

A similar regression was run to include all the above-listed variables as explanatory variables for the dependent variable *ln*(per capita household income). Apart from the dependency ratio, all the variables took binary values of 1s and 0s as in the previous regression. The results are reported in Table 9.16. For the age variables, the relationship between age and income is not clear, although per capita income in the age group (41–50) tends to be significantly lower than other age groups.

Farm type has a significant effect on household income. Pure agricultural households have the lowest income. As households move away from agriculture to non-agricultural activities, their incomes increase. The highest income group is that of households engaging in pure non-agricultural production, followed by 'other farm type' and 'mainly non-agriculture with other activities'. If a household head happens to be a village cadre, there is a tendency to have higher income, but this is not a significant factor.

The effect of education attainment on rural income is interesting. From the urban data, education has a monotonic rising effect on family incomes as education attainment of household heads improves. From the rural data, education does not have a monotonic effect on household incomes. It has the largest effect when household heads have completed primary education, but no effect when household heads have more than primary education.

If the estimated results are correct (i.e. not subject to sample biases), then it can be concluded that education in rural China beyond the primary level will not have any significant effect on household income. It implies that rural production

*Table 9.16* Rural household income and characteristics of household heads, 1998: dependent variable = *ln*(per capita income)

|  | Coefficient | t-value |
| --- | --- | --- |
| Intercept | 7.472 | 255.48 |
| *Age (comparison aged< 30)* | | |
| Aged 31–40 | −0.025 | −0.99 |
| Aged 41–50 | −0.050 | −1.99 |
| Aged 51–60 | 0.003 | 0.10 |
| Aged more than 60 | 0.177 | 4.99 |
| *Farm type (comparison: pure agriculture)* | | |
| Main agriculture with others | 0.055 | 3.55 |
| Main non-agriculture with others | 0.385 | 19.16 |
| Pure non-agriculture | 0.685 | 20.27 |
| Other farm types | 0.497 | 10.18 |
| Village cadre | 0.041 | 1.22 |
| *Education (comparison: primary school)* | | |
| Illiterate and semi-illiterate | −0.048 | −1.94 |
| Junior high school | −0.003 | −0.20 |
| Senior high school or more | −0.036 | −1.46 |
| *Region (comparison: central)* | | |
| East region | 0.476 | 30.45 |
| West region | −0.059 | −3.45 |
| *ln*(dependency ratio) | −0.463 | −22.32 |
| $R^2$ | | 0.17 |
| Number of observations | | 15,050 |

Source: MOA, 1998, rural household survey data.

may be still focused on low skills and low education techniques. Hence, return to education beyond the primary level is close to zero. This also explains why educated rural youth have to migrate to the cities because they cannot find skill-intensive and high-return employment in their local areas. The location effect is also obvious in the 1998 rural survey data. The east is better off than the central, which, in turn, is better off than the west.

Finally, the estimated coefficient on the dependency ratio indicates that labour participation and/or family size has an important effect on rural income. If the dependency ratio rises by 10 per cent, per capita mean income declines by almost 5 per cent. Hence, households with more young children or elderly dependents tend to be significantly poorer than those with less non-working family members. It implies that households with more dependants will fall into poverty more easily. This is not only because per capita income is low, but also because young children and elderly are more likely to spend on education and healthcare, rendering the households substantially more vulnerable to unexpected illness and the rising cost of education and health.

## 9.5 Conclusion and policy implications

Compared to any other studies on poverty in China, this chapter uses by far the largest household survey data sets. The urban data cover all the provinces in 1998. The rural data cover 19 provinces for two different years. Hence the results should be more comprehensive and reliable than any previous estimates on poverty in China.

Before we draw any conclusions, however, it is necessary to point out a few limitations on the data and the approaches adopted to analyse and estimate poverty. The first limitation is that we are unable to derive comparable poverty lines for both the urban and rural sectors. Hence, a direct comparison of urban and rural poverty incidences is inconclusive, although it is possible to prove that rural poverty is far more serious than urban poverty.

Another limitation is that we are unable to derive regional poverty lines for the rural population. As a result, the estimated incidence of poverty may have been understated in the high-income provinces, but overstated in the low-income regions. If more data are available, one should try to estimate and use regional poverty lines, rather than use a single poverty line for the whole nation to measure poverty.

A third limitation is that there is no information on the gender differences of poverty between the male and female sub-populations in the rural data. Due to out-migration from the poor to the rich regions, there is a tendency that the weak, the old and the females are more likely to be left behind in the poor regions. Consequently, poverty among women may be much more severe than among men.

Despite all these limitations, this report provides a lot of useful information unavailable from any previous studies on the poverty situation in China. A few important conclusions can be drawn.

First, the incidence of poverty in China is far greater than the most recent government estimates. The government aimed to eliminate absolute poverty by the year 2000 in the late 1980s. The estimates in this chapter suggest that the rural sector alone had a poor population of between 103 to 187 million people. The lower estimate is four times the official figure and the higher estimate is six times. The huge discrepancy between the estimates in this chapter and the official figures implied that poverty in China was far from being eliminated by the year 2000. Despite a significant increase in per capita average income, the incidence of rural poverty rose by over 2 percentage points from 1995 to 1998 if it is measured by a low poverty line, but declined by over 2 percentage points if it is measured by a high poverty line. The fluctuation in the rate of poverty reduction has a number of serious implications. It indicates that poverty reduction is not guaranteed by income growth alone. The benefits of increased income may be over offset by the negative effects of more inequality. It also implies that a large proportion of low-income people are clustered near the defined poverty line so that some people may be considered non-poor in one year but fall into poverty in another. This is the so-called transient poverty in the literature. Transient poverty is mainly caused by the fluctuation in per capita income. Rural incomes are influenced by a variety of factors. For example, a flood, a drought, or illness of family members, can have such a detrimental effect on household incomes that non-poor households can become poor in a short period of time. The vulnerable people are usually in the low-income groups who have little capital assets (or savings) to withstand any short-term reduction in incomes without falling into poverty. Women who rely mainly on one particular income source (e.g. cropping) are the most vulnerable to being trapped in poverty if they do not have any male adult family members working off-farm.

Second, the slow process of poverty reduction in China is not due to the lack of income growth, but due to rising income inequality. China used to be a rather egalitarian society in both the urban and rural sectors before economic reforms. Since economic reforms, inequality increases almost continuously over time. Rising inequality may be an inevitable outcome of high economic growth in the early stages of development, but international experiences suggest that inequality is not a necessary condition for successful economic performance. In fact, too much inequality may become an obstacle to sustainable growth in the long term. One may argue that without allowing for some degree of inequality, China may not have been able to achieve such a high growth rate in the past 20 years. However, one may equally argue that had China not evolved into a highly inequal society, economic performance might have been even better. Moreover, even if rising inequality were a necessary condition for high growth, the quality of growth was poor because it did not benefit the poor sector of the society.

Third, inequality in China has some features different from those of other developing countries:

- unusually high urban–rural income inequality
- unusually high inter-regional inequality
- non-agricultural income dominates rural income inequality.

Although most developing countries have a clear urban–rural income divide, urban–rural income inequality in China is much more serious than in other countries. In addition, urban-income inequality has been induced by government policies that have been persistently urban-biased.

Inter-regional inequality is caused by a number of factors, the most important one being location. The richest provinces are concentrated along the eastern coast. The poorest provinces are clustered in the northwest. The location factor matters greatly because the coastal regions have a much better agricultural production environment and more water. They are close to foreign markets, especially Hong Kong, Taiwan, Japan and Korea. They also have much better infrastructure and human resources.

Apart from location, government policies were also responsible for inter-regional inequality. In the early years of economic reforms, government policies were particularly favourable to the special economic zones and the open cities. These cities and zones are all located along the eastern coast. Massive investments poured into these development areas, putting the inland areas in a permanently disadvantaged position.

Thanks to the rapid development of rural non-farm enterprises, non-agricultural income has become an increasingly important source of rural income. It has also become a dominant source of income inequality due to the uneven development of non-farm enterprises across regions. Although China has the second largest land territory in the world, it has an acute shortage of land compared to the majority of the developing countries. As a result, rural income cannot depend just on land and agriculture, but the strict policy on rural to urban migration means that there has been a rising population pressure on land. Consequently, whether a rural area can prosper depends largely on its ability to diversify out of agriculture. In the past twenty years, the prosperous regions in the east were able to develop rural industries rapidly, but the poor western regions are left behind, resulting in a sharp increase in regional income inequality.

Fourth, the incidence of poverty is greatly influenced by education. In both the urban and rural sectors, education plays an important role in poverty reduction. In the urban sector, in particular, the higher the level of education of the household head, the less likely a household is subject to poverty. The average earning of household heads increases significantly step by step as the education level moves from below primary schooling to higher education. In the rural area, per capita income (hence the likelihood of the household falling into poverty) is significantly higher in households whose heads have achieved at least primary education than in those whose heads have attained less than primary education. However, per capita incomes are no greater when household heads have been educated beyond the primary level. It implies that the rural areas are still dominated by the low-skilled and low-return farm or non-farm enterprises. It explains why the educated youth, particularly the young males, have to move to cities and seek jobs with higher pay.

Fifth, rural-to-urban and rural-to-rural migration has important implications on poverty reduction and the welfare of poor women. In the literature, there is a hectic debate on whether migration is beneficial to poverty reduction. Some people argue that migration is an effective way of reducing poverty in the poor regions. This is because migrants can earn more in the cities or in the rich rural regions than in the local areas. Other people argue that migration has a number of undesirable effects on the poor regions. First of all, once the younger and more educated males move out of the poor regions, local production suffers due to the shortage of skills and labour. In addition, if the migrants do not send, or are unable to send, money back home, the people left behind will suffer. This is particularly true if the people left behind are women and the elderly, who are usually much more vulnerable to poverty than any other groups of people. Some empirical studies show that the elderly women are among the poorest group of the population in the poor and remote regions due to the out-migration of males.

Sixth, although we cannot have data to show income inequality between men and women from the rural data, we are able to find significant differences between average male and female earnings from the urban data. In the urban areas, average per capita incomes are higher in the female-headed households than in the male-headed households, but this does not mean that females earn more than males. On the contrary, male workers earn much more than female workers. From the urban data, it is found that the difference of earnings between male and female household heads is much smaller than the difference of earnings between male and female household spouses. This explains why female-headed households are better off than male-headed ones despite the existence of male–female earning inequality. The analysis in this chapter suggests that studies on male–female earning disparity should be focused on an individual rather than a household basis.

Seventh, inequality in China is multi-dimensional, apart from urban–rural inequality, inter-regional inequality, gender inequality, there is still a racial inequality. Racial inequality has not been studied in great detail in the literature, but the rural data for 1995 does show a clear racial divide. The average per capita income of the minority group is significantly lower, and the incidence of poverty higher, than the rest of the population. Racial inequality has both economic and political implications. The remote (and inland) areas are the most disadvantaged regions. They also have the highest concentration of the minority nationalities. These regions include Guizhou, Tibet and Xingjiang. The ever-rising inter-regional inequality means that there is also a widening income gap between the minority groups and the *hans*. In recent years, there are periodic riots and protests again the main nationality government by the minority people. The political unrest may be just a reflection of discontent on the rising inequality of incomes.

These conclusions have important policy implications for poverty reduction in China in the future. One of our conclusions is that poverty in China is still predominantly a rural phenomenon although the extent of urban poverty should not be ignored. In particular, the massive number of unemployed SOE workers and the floating urban population from the rural areas indicates that urban poverty will become increasingly more evident in the foreseeable future.

Nonetheless, the number of urban poor is still substantially less than the number of rural poor even if we apply a much higher poverty line to the urban sector than to the rural sector. Due to this consideration, it is suggested that the fight against poverty will still be focused on the rural population. Another conclusion is that the fight against rural poverty is far from over.

To reduce inequality, China needs to have a clear regional development strategy that favours the disadvantaged areas. The recent efforts to strengthen economic development in the western region show that the government is aware of the inequality problem and is moving in the right direction to tackle this issue.

Apart from reducing inter-regional inequality, it is also important to contain urban–rural inequality and to allow free movement of both labour and capital between the two sectors. It is also important to open up the inland areas for more international trade and investment. Production in the poor rural areas needs to be diversified out of pure agricultural activities. Special attention should be paid to reduce female poverty. To do that, more education and training and more employment opportunities should be created for women. Special policies should also be granted to the remote and minority areas.

Only when China is serious in tackling every aspect of inequality can it be possible to develop a sustainable basis for continuing reduction of poverty. The government can do a lot of things to help the poor. Apart from allocating extra resources to the poverty alleviation programme, it is more important to use these funds effectively. Some funds can be used for short-term purposes, but the majority of funds should be used to invest in long-term projects, such as education, healthcare, micro finance, transportation and telecommunications. Compared to many other developing countries, China has achieved a great deal in all kinds of poverty reduction efforts, but there is still a great deal of room for improvement. What is crucial is that the government should not be complacent about the seriousness of poverty and the difficulty in reducing it.

# 10 Unemployment and urban poverty

## 10.1 Introduction

China launched a radical reform from 1996 to resolve the problem of state-owned enterprises (SOEs). The state allowed SOEs to lay off workers in large numbers. By the end of 2000, more than 20 million workers were retrenched, making the most profound impact on the livelihood of at least one-fifth of the urban households throughout the country. By 2003, the total number of retrenched workers rose to more than 40 million in urban China. With more and more rural migrants moving to the towns and cities, laid-off workers struggle to find alternative employment in the non-state sector. Consequently, a significant proportion of the households with laid-off workers has been trapped in poverty, a phenomenon unthinkable in urban China even before the economic reforms started in the late 1970s (Fan, 2000).

The redundancy programme has been implemented in the backdrop of rapid economic growth for a period of over two decades. China's real GDP per capita rose about six-fold from 1978 to 2002. Real income per capita in both the rural and urban areas grew in a similar order (Yao and Zhang, 2001). China's economic miracle originated in the agricultural sector, and made possible by the household responsibility system, or HRS (Johnson, 1988). Later reforms were focused on the urban sector, starting from the early 1980s. Initially, the government aimed to imitate the rural HRS in SOEs through the introduction of a bonus payment system, the contract responsibility, the director's responsibility, and the replacement of profit delivery by taxation (Chen *et al.*, 1988; Jefferson, 1989; Lau and Brada, 1990; Lee, 1990; Hay *et al.*, 1994). Such reforms were considered to have a positive impact on productivity and efficiency (Groves *et al.*, 1994; Jefferson and Rawski, 1994; Jefferson *et al.*, 1992; Yao, 1997c; Perkins, 1994; McMillan and Naughton, 1992). However, previous reforms have failed to prevent SOEs from making accumulated losses. In 1995–6, for example, around 50 per cent of SOEs were making losses (Meng, 1999, 2000). Before 1996, any losses would be written off by the state and loss-making firms continued to receive subsidised credits for investments. Such a 'soft budget', however, was changed to a 'hard budget' under the new reform regime. Firms were given a limited period of time (1997–2002) to reduce or eliminate losses, but the only way to do so was either to shut down completely, or to significantly downsize the workforce (Appleton *et al.*, 2001).

In this chapter, we propose a theoretical model to explain the mechanism of redundancy. Our model assumes that SOEs are paying workers more than their marginal product so they are less competitive than the non-SOE firms. The reason why SOEs have to pay high wages is that they have to provide various subsidies to their employees. The non-SOE firms do not have any obligation to do so. Hence, their wage rates are lower than the wage rate of SOE workers. Before the redundancy programme was implemented, an SOE's losses could be written off by the state, obviating the need to cut wages or to lay workers off. Only with the introduction of the redundancy programme were SOEs allowed to lay workers off. In the meantime, the state ceased to provide huge subsidies to the firms who consequently have to reduce their workforce in order to maintain the same wage rates.

Unemployment has a significant impact on the welfare of urban households. A household may fall into poverty if its working members who are laid off cannot find alternative employment in the non-state sector. Below is a simple model to explain why an urban household may fall into poverty. The model implies that the probability of a household falling into poverty depends on the probability that a household member is laid off and the probability that the laid-off workers can find alternative employment in the non-state sector. As the probability that a laid-off worker can find alternative employment depends on the structure of the local economy, a region with a more developed non-state sector will provide more opportunities for alternative employment for the laid-off workers. Further more, the more working members are laid off, the more likely that a household will become trapped in poverty.

To test our hypotheses, both first-hand household survey data and official survey data for Tianjin and Guangzhou in 1998 are used to quantify the effect of redundancy on poverty.[1] There are a number of interesting findings. First, it is the poor households that are more subject to redundancy. Hence, the effect of redundancy on poverty is greater than generally expected. Second, redundancy before 1996 was mainly restricted to female workers. Hence, the effect of redundancy on poverty was modest because male household heads kept their jobs if their wives lost theirs. After 1996 redundancy affected both males and females, unskilled and skilled. As a result, the effect of redundancy on poverty became more severe than before. Third, the effect of redundancy on poverty is less severe in cities with a prosperous non-state sector than in cities without such a sector. Fourth, households with both male and female heads losing jobs are the most vulnerable to poverty. Fifth, children's education and healthcare were hit hardest as a result of redundancy. Finally, although the government had tried a few measures to help laid-off workers cope with poverty, the measures were believed to be ineffective. Hence, the problem of urban poverty will become a permanent feature in China, a feature that was considered unthinkable before economic reforms.

## 10.2  Why SOEs have to lay off workers and how redundancy affects poverty

### 10.2.1  An SOE redundancy model

Assume that an SOE aims to minimise the cost of production given a certain output or revenue, which follows the Cobb-Douglas technology, it is possible to set up an optimisation model for the firm.

$$\text{Minimise} \quad wL + rK = C \tag{10.1}$$

$$\text{Subject to} \quad Q = AK^\alpha L^\beta \tag{10.2}$$

where $w$ is the wage rate, $r$ the cost of capital, $Q$ output, $K$ capital, $L$ labour, $\alpha$ output elasticity of labour, and $\beta$ output elasticity of capital.

The Lagrangean equation with cost minimisation is,

$$\pi = wL + rK + \lambda(Q - AK^\alpha L^\beta) \tag{10.3}$$

Taking partial derivatives of (10.3) with respect to $w$, $r$ and $\lambda$, and setting them equal to zero, we can solve for a conditional demand function of labour.[2]

$$L = \frac{\beta r}{\alpha w} K \tag{10.4}$$

Equation (10.4) states that labour demand is a function of capital and labour elasticities, wage rate, capital cost and the level of capital input.

Given the levels of $w$, $r$ and $K$, let us assume that the firm is not overstaffed, which has a labour force $L$. In other words, if the firm were to pay workers at the wage rate of $w$ and capital at $r$, it would not have to lay off workers. However, if the firm has to pay higher wages than $w$, say, $\bar{w}$, then the demand for labour has to decline if the firm still wants to minimise the cost of production. With $\bar{w}$ and to maintain the same level of employment, the firm has to make less profit or even a loss.

In the Chinese SOE sector, workers are usually paid at $\bar{w}$, which is higher than $w$, a theoretical wage rate equal to the marginal product of labour. A recent study by Appleton *et al.* (2001) indicates that SOE workers were paid about one-third more than the wages if they were to work in the non-state sector. Knight and Song (1991, 1993b) also have a detailed study on the urban wage differential between the state and non-state sectors. A more comprehensive study by Dong and Putterman shows that for the 556 SOEs surveyed during the period 1990–4 the average wage rate was 4,510 yuan, which was 13.2 per cent higher than the average estimated marginal product of labour (Dong and Putterman, 2003). One explanation for the significant difference between the actual wage rate and the marginal product of labour is because SOEs have to provide housing benefit, pension and medical care for their employees. As a result, firms are unable to maximise profits, or minimise cost. Many of them even make huge losses. In the past, the losses were usually written off by the state. Loss-making firms were also allowed to expand through capital investments (Groves *et al.*, 1994; Hay *et al.*, 1994). This is the so-called soft budget constraint. The soft budget has been responsible for the inefficiency and mounting losses of SOEs. From 1996, the State Council started to implement radical reforms to reduce SOE losses. Consequently, firms have been closed down if they have accumulated excessive losses, or they have to reduce their size of operation. In either way, most firms have to lay off workers and reduce the scale of investment projects.

The scale of redundancy by any firm can be calculated in equation (10.5).

$$U = L - \overline{L} = \frac{\beta r}{\alpha w} \overline{K} - \frac{\beta r}{\alpha \overline{w}} \overline{K}, \tag{10.5}$$

$$U = \left( \frac{\overline{w} - w}{w \overline{w}} \right) \left( \frac{\beta}{\alpha} \right) r \overline{K}$$

where $U$ is the scale of redundancy.[3] Assuming that capital is fixed at $\overline{K}$, the redundancy model has the following properties, which provide important explanations as to why SOEs have to lay off workers.

*Property 1*   $U$ is a positive function of the difference between the actual wage rate and a market competitive rate, or $(\overline{w} - w)$.

Over time, $w$ is under tremendous pressure as the development of the non-state sectors has made the labour market far more competitive in the reform period than before. Although firms and the state have been trying to reduce $\overline{w}$, through reforming the welfare system, including the reduction in housing benefit and other subsidies, the wage difference $(\overline{w} - w)$ remains high (Appleton *et al.*, 2001).

*Property 2*   $U$ is a positive function of the cost of capital, $r$. In the past, capital cost was kept low because of the soft budget. The introduction of a hard budget under reforms implies that firms have to pay for their capital at a competitive market rate.

### 10.2.2 How does redundancy affect poverty?

Poverty in China was largely confined to the rural sector until the recent radical reform in SOEs. Hence previous studies on poverty have been focused on the rural population. Some useful studies on rural poverty can be found in Ahmad and Wang, 1991; Riskin, 1994; World Bank, 1997; Ravallion and Jalan, 1999; Gustafsson and Zhong, 2000; Yao, 2000 and others.

Urban poverty is a recent phenomenon but it has attracted significant attention of researchers, policy makers and international organisations. The World Bank, the Asian Development Bank and the Department for International Development in the UK have commissioned a number of research projects to study the situation of SOE redundancy and its effect on urban poverty. Some recent studies on urban poverty are also related to the urban floating population, or the rural migrants working in the cities. In this sub-section, we do not intend to have a detailed review on the literature. Instead, we develop a simple model to explain why SOE redundancy can affect urban poverty.

Let us consider an urban household whose adult members only worked in the SOE sector before the redundancy programme was introduced. With the redundancy programme, some working members were laid off. We use $N$ to denote the total number of the household members, $L$ the total number of workers. Out of $L$, $L_s$ remain in the SOE sector and the rest are laid off. Among the laid off, $L_o$ find alternative employment in the non-SOE sector, but the rest, denoted by $L_u$, cannot find any employment and become unemployed.

Assume the wages rates in the SOE and non-SOE sectors are fixed at $\bar{w}$ and $w$, the income for unemployed SOE workers is $B$, which is the unemployment benefit paid by SOE and the state. Let $q_s$, $q_o$ and $q_u$ respectively denote the probabilities that an SOE worker is not laid off, is laid off but finds employment in the non-SOE sector, and is laid off but cannot find any alternative employment.

With the above notation, it is easy to derive the expected income per capita of the household with redundancy.

$$Z = \frac{L}{N}(q_s\,\bar{w} + q_o w + q_u B) \tag{10.6}$$

where $Z$ is expected income per capita.

If the expected income per capita is less than the poverty line, denoted by $F$, the household will be trapped in poverty. Hence, the probability function that a household will become poor after some of its working members are laid off can be expressed below.

$$P = g\left(F - \frac{L}{N}(q_s\bar{w} + q_o w + q_u B)\right) \tag{10.7}$$

Assume $\bar{w} > w >> B$, and $\bar{w}D > wD \geq F$, but $BD << F$, where $D = L/N$ is the dependency ratio of the household, then the poverty probability function has the following properties.

*Property 1*   The probability of an urban household falling into poverty is a negative function of the probability that its working members can remain employed in the SOE sector, or

$$\frac{\partial P}{\partial q_s} < 0.$$

*Property 2* The probability of an urban household falling into poverty is a negative function of the probability that its laid-off members can find alternative employment in the non-SOE sector, or

$$\frac{\partial P}{\partial q_o} < 0.$$

*Property 3* The probability of an urban household falling into poverty is a positive function of the probability that its laid-off members cannot find alternative employment in the non-SOE sector, or

$$\frac{\partial P}{\partial q_u} > 0.$$

The above properties suggest that whether an urban household becomes poor depends not only on how many working members of the household are laid off, but also on how many of the laid-off members can find alternative employment in the non-SOE sector. In a region where the non-SOE sector is prosperous (e.g. Guangzhou, see the following survey results), the likelihood for a laid-off worker to find alternative employment is high. Hence, the probability that a household falls into poverty will be low after some of its members are laid off. In a region where the local economy is more dominated by the SOE sector (e.g. Tianjin, see the following survey results), the effect of firing SOE workers on poverty will be greater.

## 10.3 Household survey data and definition of poverty lines

### 10.3.1 First-hand household survey

To understand how redundancy can affect urban poverty, a first-hand household survey was conducted in June 2000. The survey focused on Tianjin and Guangzhou. Tianjin had a lot of laid-off workers from SOEs, which were the backbone of the local economy. It had a good representation of China's ongoing SOE reforms. Tianjin faced a rather difficult situation of employment as laid-off SOE workers were struggling to find jobs after they had been made redundant. This was due in part to the lack of employment opportunities in the non-state sector. By contrast, Guangzhou had a more prosperous non-state sector economy than Tianjin. Hence, its unemployment situation was relatively better, although it also had a great number of laid-off SOE workers. These two cities had distinct differences in their economic conditions. Hence, a comparative study between them will present a good picture of SOE reforms and the effects of redundancy on poverty.

In Guangzhou, 100 households were selected from ten large and medium size SOEs. In Tianjin, 200 households were selected, also from ten large and medium size enterprises. The samples were so selected that all households had at least one laid-off member, either the household head, or the spouse of the household head.

The enterprises in each city were randomly selected from a list of large and medium sized enterprises, which had experienced more than 20 per cent of workforce reduction after 1996. The city labour bureaux provided the list of enterprises. Once an enterprise was selected, the enterprise manager provided a list of retrenched workers' households. Ten households were randomly selected from each enterprise in Guangzhou and twenty were randomly selected from each enterprise in Tianjin.

To compare this sample with official household survey data, the official household survey data for 1998 for the urban population in the two cities was also obtained. The official household survey data are available from the National Bureau of Statistics (NBS) every year for every province and sample cities. The official data is so collected that they will represent the overall situation of entire cities. The data used for this survey are biased towards those households with retrenched SOE workers.

### 10.3.2  Definition of poverty

The incidence of poverty can be estimated in various ways, including the head count index, poverty gap and poverty severity indices. This chapter considers only the poverty head count index, which is defined as the proportion of people with per capita income equal or less than a pre-defined poverty line in the total sample population.

The first important question on the measurement of poverty is the definition of poverty lines. There are numerous ways to calculate the poverty lines. This chapter follows the procedure defined in the previous chapter. The general poverty line is regarded as the sum of two components: basic food expenditure (the food poverty line) and basic non-food expenditure. The basic non-food expenditure can be calibrated in two ways, hence the division of the general poverty line into 'lower' and 'higher'.

Using the urban household survey data in 1998 (NBS, 1998), the poverty lines for Guangdong, Tianjin and urban China are presented in Table 10.1.

*Table 10.1* Poverty lines for Guangzhou, Tianjin and urban China in 1998 (yuan per capita)

| Region | Food poverty line | Lower poverty line | Higher poverty line |
| --- | --- | --- | --- |
| Tianjin | 1728 | 2329 | 2986 |
| Guangzhou | 2515 | 3175 | 3704 |
| **Urban China** | **1390** | **1847** | **2296** |

Source: NBS, 1998, *Urban Household Survey Data.*

Note: Urban China is for the urban population of the whole country.

## 10.4 Data analysis

### 10.4.1 Summary results from the survey data

Analyses from the survey data are conducted according to the structure laid out in the questionnaires. The results include the following aspects.

*(1) Demographic structure and main characteristics of household heads*

The data cover 100 households in Guangzhou and 200 households in Tianjin. The average family size of the sample is 3.24 with a dependency ratio of 0.49.[4] The average age of the male household heads is 44 and that of female household head is 42. The average years of employment before redundancy are 24 for male household heads and 22 for female household heads.

About half of the surveyed households have their male and female heads both retrenched. About one quarter of the households have their male heads and the other quarter their female heads retrenched. The severity of redundancy varies significantly between Guangzhou and Tianjin. Tianjin has a much higher proportion of households with two laid-off household heads than Guangzhou, i.e. 53 per cent versus 37 per cent (Table 10.2).

*Table 10.2* Composition of sampled households by the number of unemployed (%)

| Household type | Guangzhou | Tianjin | All |
| --- | --- | --- | --- |
| Both male and female heads lost jobs | 36.7 | 53.1 | 47.6 |
| Only male household head lost job | 29.6 | 22.4 | 24.8 |
| Only female household head lost job | 33.7 | 24.5 | 27.6 |
| **All** | **100** | **100** | **100** |

Source: Survey data.

In both cities, about one-third of the male household heads lost their jobs before 1996 and the other two-thirds lost their jobs in and after 1996. There is also a clear regional pattern of difference between the two cities. Guangzhou appeared to have laid off workers earlier than Tianjin. About 47 per cent of workers were laid off before 1996 in Guangzhou, compared to 30 per cent in Tianjin.

Over half of the laid-off SOE workers are in the age group of 41–50, a prime age group. Compared to the older people, they have more family burden. Compared to the younger people, they find it more difficult to enter alternative employment. Hence, the effect of unemployment in this age group is particularly severe.

*(2) The effect of unemployment on household income and expenditures*

For any particular household, if one or more than one of its members is laid off, there is an adverse effect on household income, and hence expenditure. To measure the effect of unemployment on income and expenditure, we collect income and expenditure data for the 12 month period before and the 12 month period after at least one household member becomes redundant. All household incomes are converted into comparable values in 1998 prices using the consumer price indices of the two cities.

The adverse effect of redundancy on income and expenditure varies significantly between the two cities and different types of household group. At the aggregate level, average income per capita declined from 5,336 to 4,404 yuan, or by 16 per cent. If households are classified by the number of laid-off members, then those with two laid-off household heads suffer most. Their average income per capita declined by 23.4 per cent. This is compared to a reduction of 16.4 per cent for those households with laid-off male heads and to 5.9 per cent for those households with laid-off female heads (Table 10.3).

*Table 10.3* Effects of redundancy on household incomes (yuan per capita in 1998 prices)

| | Income per capita before redundancy (1) | Income per capita after redundancy (2) | Difference (3)=(2)–(1) | Difference in % (3)/(1)*100 |
|---|---|---|---|---|
| *Household type* | | | | |
| Male and female heads lost jobs | 4558.9 | 3488.6 | −1070.3 | −23.5 |
| Only male household head lost job | 5428.7 | 4536.4 | −892.3 | −16.4 |
| Only female household head lost job | 6230.5 | 5864.3 | −366.1 | −5.9 |
| *By city* | | | | |
| Guangzhou | 7711.4 | 6399.5 | −1312.0 | −17.0 |
| Tianjin | 3972.4 | 3385.6 | −586.8 | −14.8 |
| ALL | 5235.9 | 4404.1 | −831.9 | −15.9 |
| *By date of unemployed* | | | | |
| Before 1996 | 5910.2 | 5796.4 | −113.9 | −1.9 |
| From 1996 | 4858.9 | 3625.6 | −1233.3 | −25.4 |

Source: Survey data.

The timing of redundancy also has important implication on household income. If a household member was laid off before 1996, the effect on income would be much smaller than if the member was laid off after 1996. The average income per capita declined by only 2 per cent if the household heads were laid off before 1996, but by 25 per cent if they were laid off after 1996. There are some possible explanations for this. First, people who lost jobs earlier may have found alternative employment in the non-state sector. Second, people who lost their jobs from 1996 are less likely to find alternative employment in the non-state sector. Third, redundancy in the post-1996 era was carried out more compulsorily than before. The radical reform laid off people irrespective of whether the households had already had a laid-off member or not. In other words, the redundancy programme since 1996 has brought about more households with both male and female heads retrenched. In addition, the post-1996 reform has shed more male jobs than female ones. Since male earnings are generally much higher than female earnings, the effect of more male redundancy after 1996 on income is more than before 1996. The surveyed data shows that 85 per cent of the households with two laid-off members, and 95 per cent of the households with laid-off male heads were registered from 1996. Female household heads dominated job losses before 1996, but no households are found to have only female heads laid off after 1996.

The structure of household incomes has changed dramatically for the SOE households with laid-off workers. Before any household member became redundant, wage and bonus income accounted for 93 per cent of total household incomes. This share declined to 60 per cent after at least one member was retrenched. The proportions of benefit, pension and other incomes increased after the household head(s) was made redundant. On average, benefit and pension accounts for 22 per cent of total household incomes after redundancy. Other income sources, including self-employment, accounts for only 18 per cent (Table 10.4). This means that laid-off workers have limited opportunities to earn incomes from the non-state sector.

*Table 10.4* Effect of unemployment on household income structure

|  | Before unemployment | | | After unemployment | | |
|---|---|---|---|---|---|---|
|  | Wage & bonus | Benefit & pension | Other income | Wage & bonus | Benefit & pension | Other income |
| Guangzhou | 88.57 | 1.23 | 10.2 | 40.5 | 38.31 | 21.19 |
| Tianjin | 95.68 | 1.25 | 3.07 | 70.2 | 13.68 | 16.12 |
| **All** | **93.28** | **1.24** | **5.48** | **60.09** | **22.06** | **17.85** |

Source: Survey data.

There are significant differences between the two cities. Wages and bonuses account for a much smaller proportion of total income in Guangzhou than in Tianjin. Correspondingly, benefit, pension and other income sources account for a much larger share of total income in the former than they do in the latter. Compared to Tinijin, Guangzhou is more open, prosperous and less dominated by SOEs, and hence has more job opportunities in the non-state sector.

### (3) Results from qualitative questions

The survey asks laid-off workers a number of qualitative questions. These questions concern workers' occupations, the reasons for redundancy, the effects of redundancy on their quality of life, the difficulty in finding alternative jobs, their attitudes towards SOE reforms, and their opinions on the government and the future prospects of the country.

OCCUPATION OF LAID-OFF SOE WORKERS AND REASONS FOR REDUNDANCY

In a normal situation, enterprises tend to lay off more unskilled workers than skilled ones. The survey data shows that this is not the case here. In fact, the large majority of the laid-off workers are either classified as skilled (49 per cent), professional (12 per cent), or managerial (15 per cent). It is clear that the redundancy programme has targeted all types of personnel. This must be due to the poor financial situation of the enterprises. There are a number of reasons for SOEs to fire workers. About 45 per cent of the respondents indicated that their enterprises needed to reduce costs. About one-third of the correspondents said that their firms were taken over or had to close down. Only one-fifth of them said that their firms wanted to increase profits. This suggests that four-fifths of the firms were loss-makers.

EFFECT OF REDUNDANCY ON THE QUALITY OF LIVES

This question asks correspondents to rank from 1 (most seriously) to 5 (least seriously) the degree of severity of the effects of redundancy on their lives. Over one-third of the households ranked 1, more than one-third ranked 2, and one-quarter ranked 3. The proportion of households considering redundancy to have little effect on their lives (ranking 4 or 5) is only 3.4 per cent (Table 10.5).

*Table 10.5* Effects of unemployment on the quality of lives

| City | 1 Most seriously | 2 | 3 | 4 | 5 Least seriously | |
|------|------|------|------|------|------|------|
| Guangzhou | 25.97 | 31.17 | 37.66 | 2.6 | 2.6 | 100 |
| Tianjin | 36.51 | 40.21 | 20.63 | 1.06 | 1.59 | 100 |
| **All** | **33.46** | **37.59** | **25.56** | **1.5** | **1.88** | **100** |

Source: Survey data.

The quality of life comprises the following elements: income, expenditure, healthcare, child education and the psychiatric effect of redundancy. One serious effect was on education. About 45 per cent of the households indicated that education of their children was most seriously affected as a result of redundancy. The situation in Tianjin was more serious than in Guangzhou as Tianjin was more badly hit by the redundancy programme. About 53 per cent of the surveyed households in Tianjin suggested that the education of children was most seriously affected. This compared to only 25 per cent of households in Guangzhou. The effect on healthcare was even more obvious, particularly in Tianjin, where 59 per cent of households said that healthcare was most seriously undermined.

The surveyed households were also asked to evaluate their comparative wealth position among the population within the local city. Before redundancy, about one-third of the households considered themselves to be among the poorest quartile of

*Table 10.6* Self-ranking in household groups before and after redundancy (%)

| City | Richest quarter | Second richest quarter | Third richest quarter | Poorest quarter | All households |
|------|------|------|------|------|------|
| *Before redundancy* | | | | | |
| Guangzhou | 0.01 | 15.58 | 57.14 | 27.27 | 100 |
| Tianjin | 0.53 | 6.35 | 54.50 | 38.62 | 100 |
| **All** | **0.38** | **9.02** | **55.26** | **35.34** | **100** |
| *After redundancy* | | | | | |
| Guangzhou | 0.00 | 2.6 | 38.96 | 58.44 | 100 |
| Tianjin | 0.53 | 3.17 | 31.75 | 64.55 | 100 |
| **All** | **0.38** | **3.01** | **33.83** | **62.78** | **100** |

Source: Survey data.

households in the city. After redundancy, this proportion rose to almost two-thirds (Table 10.6).

About half of the households in the third richest quarter before redundancy moved to the last quarter. Over 80 per cent of the households in the second quarter before redundancy moved to the third and last quarters. Few households reported an improvement of living standards after redundancy.

The sharp deterioration of living standards is due to the difficulty in finding alternative employment. Households were asked to rank from 1 (most difficult) to 5 (least difficult) regarding the difficulty in finding new jobs. About 40 per cent of households ranked 1, 39 per cent ranked 2, 17 per cent ranked 3, and only 4 per cent ranked 4 or 5. This means that four-fifths of laid-off workers found it almost impossible to find alternative employment. The job market in Tianjin is more difficult than in Guangzhou. However, even in Guangzhou, more than two-thirds of laid-off workers found it almost impossible to enter new employment. The survey results are consistent with Appleton *et al.* (2001), who found that only 38 per cent of laid-off workers were able to find alternative employment. Their study was based on a much larger household survey data set with over 8,000 urban households in six provinces in 1998.

ATTITUDES OF LAID-OFF WORKERS TOWARDS SOE REFORMS

The direct effect of redundancy is obvious, but how did the laid-off workers respond to the reforms?

It is surprising to note that about one-quarter of the households considered the reforms to be correct and believed that their difficulty would be temporary. More than half of the households considered the reform to be right for the state, but not right for the workers. Only 15 per cent of the households considered the reforms and job losses to be wrong (Table 10.7).

Only a small proportion of laid-off workers considered the ongoing reform to be wrong for both the state and the workers. The majority of laid-off workers

*Table 10.7* Attitudes of unemployed workers on SOE reforms

| City | Reform right, difficulty temporary | Reform wrong, job losses wrong | Right for state, not for workers | Other explanation | All |
|------|------|------|------|------|------|
| Guangzhou | 24.68 | 10.39 | 59.74 | 5.19 | 100 |
| Tianjin | 23.81 | 17.46 | 49.74 | 8.99 | 100 |
| **All** | **24.06** | **15.41** | **52.63** | **7.89** | **100** |

Source: Survey data.

appeared to support the reform programme although they were hurt badly. This poses an important policy challenge to the government on how to deal with the problems associated with massive redundancy. The central government has implemented a few programmes, including training, redeployment and unemployment benefits to help laid-off workers cope with short-term hardship.

How well *has* the government supported the laid-off workers? One question is designed to ask the opinion of household heads. The results are highly disappointing regarding government's performance in this regard. Less than 2 per cent of the correspondents thought that the government had done a lot to help them. Over half of the households indicated that the government had done a lot but that the results were poor. Another 46 per cent of the households suggested that the government had not done enough to help them.

If the government has not done enough, or it has done something but it was not helpful to laid-off workers, what should the government do to improve the situation? One question asks how best can the government help. One-third of the households indicated that they need more benefits. Over half of the households suggested that the government should try to find jobs for them. Only 5 per cent of the households considered training to be important. The government emphasises training to be one of the most important initiatives to help laid-off workers, but the survey results gave little support for such an initiative. This probably explains why most laid-off workers were not happy with what the government had done for them. Lack of financial support and lack of job opportunities were the most important concerns.

The most useful information that policy makers and economic researchers need to know is probably the perception of laid-off workers on their own future. Surprisingly, only 1 per cent of the households had an optimistic view, and 14 per cent a moderately optimistic view. About 45 per cent of the households were indifferent and 40 per cent were either pessimistic or relatively pessimistic. On the whole, the households in Guangzhou were less pessimistic than in Tianjin, reflecting a location difference in job opportunities and incomes (Table 10.8). In Tianjin, almost half of the households were pessimistic or relatively pessimistic. In Guangzhou, only 20 per cent of the households had the same view.

*Table 10.8* Perception of unemployed workers on their future

| City | Optimistic | Moderate optimistic | Indifferent | Moderate pessimistic | Pessimistic | All |
|------|-----------|--------------------|-------------|---------------------|-------------|-----|
| Guangzhou | 2.6 | 18.2 | 59.7 | 18.2 | 1.3 | 100 |
| Tianjin | 0.5 | 11.6 | 39.7 | 31.8 | 16.4 | 100 |
| **All** | **1.1** | **13.5** | **45.5** | **27.8** | **12.0** | **100** |

Source: Survey data.

### 10.4.2 The effect of redundancy on poverty

This sub-section focuses on the analysis of poverty and the effect of redundancy on poverty using the poverty lines in Table 10.1. The effect of redundancy on poverty can be studied in the following way. We first derive and compare the poverty head count rates using incomes per head before and after at least one household member is laid off. We then derive and compare the poverty head count rates for three groups of households, those with two laid-off heads, those with laid-off male heads only and those with laid-off female heads only. Finally, we derive and compare the poverty head count rates using official urban household survey data provided by NBS (1998) with the poverty head count rates derived from our own survey data.

Let us compare our own survey data with official household survey data. The poverty head count rates derived from the official data are low. In Guangzhou, few people had incomes at or below the defined poverty lines. In Tianjin, the poverty head count rates ranged from 1.6 per cent to 6.7 per cent. The poverty head count rates derived from our survey data are much higher even before any household member was laid off. This suggests that the households in our survey were much more vulnerable to poverty than the average household in the local cities before the redundancy programme was implemented. In other words, before any household members were made redundant, the surveyed households were already disadvantaged. Redundancy made them even more vulnerable to poverty. For the two cities concerned, the poverty head count rates range from 9.1 per cent to 25 per cent before any household member was laid off. These rates ranged from 34.5 per cent to 46.4 per cent after at least one household member was laid off. Obviously, the effect of redundancy on poverty is devastating.

Even for the households with laid-off workers, there were substantial differences in poverty. Households with both laid-off male and female heads suffered most. Over half to two-thirds of these households were trapped in poverty after redundancy. This result provides strong evidence to support the theoretical model that relates redundancy with poverty. The model implies that poverty is not necessarily caused by redundancy itself, but by the probability of a retrenched worker finding alternative employment. If a household has two retrenched workers, the probability of both of them finding alternative employment is significantly lower than if there were only one retrenched worker in the household.

The second hardest-hit group were those households with laid-off male heads only. The poverty head count rates for this group ranged from 29 per cent to 38 per cent after the male heads were laid off. The least affected group were those households with laid-off female heads only. However, even this group had a high incidence of poverty. The head count rates were from 13 per cent to 19 per cent.

*Table 10.9* Poverty incidence in survey sample and NBS household survey data in 1998 (poverty head count rates as % of population)

| | Poverty after unemployment | | Poverty before unemployment | | Poverty from official data | |
|---|---|---|---|---|---|---|
| | *Low* | *High* | *Low* | *High* | *Low* | *High* |
| Household type | | | | | | |
| Male and female heads lost jobs | 50.66 | 67.98 | 13.38 | 33.55 | – | – |
| Only male household head lost job | 28.57 | 37.70 | 6.35 | 25.79 | – | – |
| Only female household head lost job | 13.45 | 19.27 | 4.73 | 10.55 | – | – |
| *By city* | | | | | | |
| Guangzhou | 31.9 | 41.3 | 12.5 | 24.2 | 0.0 | 0.0 |
| Tianjin | 35.9 | 49.2 | 7.2 | 25.5 | 1.6 | 6.7 |
| **All** | **34.5** | **46.4** | **9.1** | **25.0** | **0.9** | **3.7** |

Source: Own household survey data. NSB, 1998, *Urban Household Survey Data*.

Notes: (1) 'Low' and 'High' mean that poverty head count rates are measured by the lower and higher poverty lines respectively. The poverty lines are provided in Table 10.1. (2) The first four columns of figures are derived from this survey data. The last two columns of figures are derived from the official household survey data.

## 10.5 Conclusion

This chapter develops two simple models to explain why SOEs have to lay off workers and why redundancy can cause poverty. No attempt is made to estimate the theoretical models. Instead, analyses are conducted based on first-hand and official household survey data to provide non-parametric evidence to support the hypotheses derived from them. Our first-hand survey data focused on 20 large and medium sized SOEs with more than 20 per cent of their workforce retrenched after 1996 in Guangzhou and Tianjin. Over fourth-fifths of these firms were loss-makers, supporting our first model, which suggests that low productivity and hard budget constraints are principal reasons for redundancy. The effects of redundancy on poverty vary significantly between the two sampled cities, across different household groups, and between different time periods of redundancy. The different effects reflect different probabilities of finding alternative employment by re-trenched workers, providing non-parametric evidence for our redundancy–poverty model, which implies that poverty is not necessarily caused by redundancy, but by the likelihood of retrenched workers finding alternative employment.

There are 300 households covered in the survey data and 800 households covered by the official household survey data. The official data represents the 'average' household of the concerned cities, but our own survey data represents only the households affected by the redundancy programme.

Despite the simplicity of our models, they provide a clear framework for understanding the mechanism of redundancy and its effect on urban poverty. SOEs have to lay off workers for the following reasons. First, the change of the soft budget to hard budget implies that losses can no longer be written off by the state and firms are asked to pay the market cost of capital investments. Second, SOEs usually pay their workers more than the so-called market or efficient wages. This is due to the obligation that they have to provide expensive subsidies to workers on housing, pension, healthcare and education.

The effect of redundancy on poverty depends not only on the probability of redundancy, but also on the probability that a laid-off worker can find alternative employment in the non-state sector. In other words, redundancy may not mean unemployment if the laid-off workers can easily find jobs elsewhere in the economy. The real problem is that only a small proportion of laid-off workers were able to find jobs in the non-state sector. The large majority of them ended up being unemployed and depended on state benefits for their living.

The radical reform to improve SOE efficiency involves massive compulsory redundancies. Before 1996, redundancy was probably carried out on a more voluntary and selective basis. In particular, the vast majority of redundancies were targeted at female household heads. This policy had a clear element of sexual discrimination, but it had the least impact on household incomes, as female household heads usually earned less than their male counterparts.

By contrast, the reforms after 1996 involved compulsory redundancies, targeting mainly the male household heads. Furthermore, redundancy was made irrespective of whether the same household had already lost one job or not. As a result, many households had both male and female heads retrenched. Hence, the effects of redundancy on household incomes and poverty proved to be far more devastating than before. Households with two retrenched heads are most vulnerable to poverty and deserve the greatest assistance from the government. About 50 per cent of our sampled households belong to this group whose poverty head count rate rose from as high as 34 per cent before redundancy to 68 per cent after redundancy. It is apparent that the effect of redundancy on poverty is detrimental.

However, the assistance programmes implemented by the government are disappointing. The biggest problems facing laid-off workers' households are job opportunities and financial support, for both of which the government is able to offer the least help.

In China, there are up to 20 million laid-off SOEs workers with about 30 million household members. Our survey data indicates that over one-third to almost one half of the population lives in poverty after redundancy, comparing to 9.1–25 per cent before redundancy. The net effect of redundancy on poverty is 15–19 per cent of the total population with laid-off household members. These are equivalent to 4.5 to 6.0 million people for the whole country. A recent study by the Asian Development Bank (2001) shows that the total number of urban poor ranged from 17 to 34 millions in 1998. If our sample is representative of the country, we can infer that about 18–26 per cent of China's urban poor are due to the recent SOE reforms and rising unemployment of SOE workers.

The effect of redundancy on poverty is significant, but what can the government do to reduce the hardship of the affected people? The answer is 'very little'. China needs to develop a strong non-state sector, including private, collective and foreign invested firms to absorb not only the expanding labour force, but also the large number of laid-off SOE workers. Economic reforms in the last 25 years have brought about a great success in the non-state sector, which has overtaken the state sector in terms of output and employment. However, the non-state sector has not become strong enough to absorb so many people. Hence, the future prospect of employment is unlikely to become better before it becomes worse than it is today. As a result, urban poverty is likely to rise before it declines. This means that the government needs to consider various options to mitigate the suffering of the unemployed and the poor. However, it seems that the best help from the government is a financial one. Since the initial intention of SOE reforms is to reduce the financial burden of loss-making firms on the state coffers, asking the government to provide more financial support to the unemployed will violate the initial objective of the reforms.

So, China has a dilemma here. If the government wants to reduce its financial burden, the country has to tolerate more unemployment and poverty. If the government does not want unemployment and poverty to rise, the country has to tolerate a certain extent of SOE inefficiency and loss-making. The 'win–win' situation of China's economic reforms has gone. A new situation has arrived, where there are winners and losers. It is up to the government to make a clear trade-off between efficiency and poverty. However, whatever the government will do in future, there are already some 30 million people suffering from job losses, reduced living standards, and above all, poverty.

# 11 Is migration a way of escaping poverty in China?

## 11.1 Introduction

Since economic reforms, the government has allowed free migration from the countryside to the cities. Most recent data suggests that there are up to 100 million farmers seeking jobs in every town and city throughout the country. Migration is a result of rising urban–rural inequality and the lack of employment opportunities in the countryside. Most economic analysts argue that migration is an effective way of reducing urban–rural income inequality, and hence of escaping poverty. Empirical evidence in China over the last two decades, however, does not support this argument. Although migration has increased tremendously, urban–rural inequality has not been reduced; instead it has been rising progressively over time. In addition, there is no evidence to support the contention that the incidence of rural poverty has been significantly reduced as a result of migration.

This chapter presents some theoretical and empirical models to study the determinants of rural–urban migration. The empirical results should be useful to understand the nature and reasons for massive rural–urban migration.

Our theoretical model is based on Harris and Todaro's two-sector migration model, but our empirical model is extended to include rural industries so that it can be regarded as an extended model to Harris and Todaro.

In Harris and Todaro's (1970) pioneering study on rural–urban migration in Africa, they developed a rural–urban migration model based on a two-sector economy, in which migration decision is centred on equating the expected earnings between the rural and urban sectors. This model is influenced by Arthur Lewis's two-sector development model (1954). In essence, the economy is divided into a modern industrial sector and a primitive agricultural sector. Later literature on migration has extended Harris and Todaro's model (Gary, 1975; Corden and Findlay, 1975; Yap, 1977; Cole and Sanders, 1985). More recently, Bhattacharya (1993) provides a review of literature on rural–urban migration in contemporary less developed countries. In particular, Ghatak *et al.* (1996) show that migration does not flow automatically in response to wage differentials.

In short, Harris and Todaro's model provides a clear theoretical framework for understanding the motivation of rural–urban migration. In practice, however, the model has some limitations in explaining the real migratory behaviour of peasants in the developing countries. For example, it does not consider the effects of changes in industrial structure and the existence of rural non-farm employment on migratory decision. In China, the change of development strategy from being capital intensive before economic reforms, to being labour intensive under economic reforms after 1978, has enabled the urban economy to create many more jobs. Coupled with the relaxation of the regulation on rural–urban migration, the urban economy has been able to absorb tens of millions of rural migrants. In the meantime, rapid development of rural non-farm industries has created many employment opportunities for rural workers to migrate out of agriculture without moving to the cities. This explains why there are fewer peasants moving to the cities than there should have been if Harris and Todaro's model were to prevail in China. In the literature, many studies show that rural migrants working in the cities are more educated than those left behind in the countryside. However, Zhao (1999) shows that the rural industrial sector tends to attract the best educated rural workers in Sichuan, which is China's most populous province supplying the largest number of out-migrants to other provinces. Song (2002) suggests that rural non-farm employment is an important outlet for peasants to diversify their risk of labour allocation before they make a decision on migration. Without the rural industries, there should have been more rural workers moving into cities than there are today. This means that we cannot directly apply Harris and Todaro's model to fully understand rural–urban migration in contemporary China.

In China, economic reforms and uneven regional economic development have created an environment for massive rural–urban migration in the past decades. Wu and Li (1996) survey the literature on China's rural-to-urban labour migration. Liang and White (1997) examine how economic conditions, foreign capital investment, and the presence of rural enterprises influence inter-provincial migration. Wang and Zuo (1999) point out that China's widened urban–rural divide arises from a socialist industrialisation process, which created a hastened heavy industry base at the expense of its rural population. The huge urban–rural income gap and a massive reservoir of rural surplus labour were the main explanations for the rapid increase of rural migrants in the cities.

The existing literature provides an important insight into understanding the actual situation of migration in China, but there is no study that provides a clear theoretical framework of analysis with empirical testing. This chapter proposes an alternative migration model, assuming that migration is demand-driven, rather than the exact equilibrium of supply and demand.[1] This is because the number of migrants depends on the ability of the urban economy as well as the employment capacity of the rural non-farm sector. The model assumes that the supply of rural migrants is unlimited given the special circumstances of contemporary China. As a result, we do not start from the general equilibrium model proposed by Harris and Todaro, which could be considered as inadequate for China. In other words, our model disagrees with the argument that the urban–rural wages differential is the only variable that equilibrates the demand and supply of migration, although it is an important factor of migratory decision. Other factors, such as the development of the rural non-farm economy and urban industrial structure, are also important.

We start with a basic CES production function and then incorporate the migratory decision variable into the model. We deliberately focus on the following determinants of rural–urban migration: the rural and urban wages rates, urban labour force and the cost of migration.

In the empirical model, we test the effects of the following variables on rural–urban migration: real urban wages, real rural wages, rural non-farm employment and urban unemployment. We also use two sets of panel data for the model. The first set of data is about in-migration from other provinces. The second set of data is about in-migration from other counties in the same provinces. The data sets cover 29 provinces for a four-year period, 1995–8. Data on migration are obtained from *China Labour Statistical Yearbook* (NBS, 1997–9). Data on other variables are obtained from *Statistical Yearbook of China* (NBS, 1995–9).

## 11.2 Development strategy and rural–urban migration

Before economic reforms started in 1978, rural–urban migration was strictly controlled in China. In the literature, many studies attribute the lack of migration to government policy (Knight and Song, 1999; Zhao, 1999; Yao and Zhang 2001a). However, few authors have provided an economic explanation as to why China had to impose a strict policy on migration. One possible explanation is that the government wanted to protect the interests of urban citizens, but a better explanation lies in the development strategy adopted in the pre-reform period.

Before the People's Republic was founded in 1949, China had gone through a period of civil wars, imperialist invasions, especially the Japanese occupation during the Second World War of 1937–45 and the Civil War between the Communist and the Nationalist Parties between 1946 and 1949. Decades of continuous wars reduced China into a nation full of poverty and destitution. Hence, the biggest task of the Communist Party was to rebuild China and lift its population out of extreme poverty and hunger.

After three years of land reforms in 1949–52, the Communist Party was to develop a modern urban industrial sector. There were two alternative development strategies faced by the leadership. One was to develop low-tech and labour-intensive industries based on processing agricultural products and consumer goods. The other was to develop capital-intensive heavy industries. China opted for the second strategy. The leadership believed that without the development of heavy industries, China would never be able to catch up with the advanced capitalist countries like the US and the UK. Such a strategy was naïve if it were evaluated with modern development theory, as China did not exploit its comparative advantage by using its abundant labour resources.

The consequence of this development strategy is as follows. The heavy industrial sector accounted for over 50 per cent of total investments in the period 1953–78 although its share in total employment was initially less than 3 per cent of the national labour force. The agricultural sector accounted for less than 12 per cent of total investments but employed about 80 per cent of the total labour force. Massive investments led to a rapid growth in industrial output. Industry's share in national income rose from 22 per cent in 1953 to 49 per cent in 1978. However, rapid growth in industrial output did not create sufficient employment opportunities for the urban sector to absorb rural workers. The share of industrial employment in total employment increased from 8 per cent to only 18 per cent over a twenty-five year period from 1953 to 1978 (Yao, 1994).

The increase in industrial employment hardly matched the growth of the urban labour force. As a result, it was not possible to allow rural–urban migration without causing significant urban unemployment. On the contrary, the government had to send millions of educated urban youth to the countryside during the Cultural Revolution in order to keep urban unemployment under control.

Hence, the tight control on rural–urban migration in the pre-reform period could only be explained by the development strategy focusing on capital-intensive industries. Economic reforms after 1978 changed the development strategy from being capital intensive to being labour intensive. This new strategy and its effect on employment can be demonstrated in Figure 11.1.

Since China was short of capital investments in the initial stage of economic development, it is reasonable to assume that capital resources are fixed at $\bar{K}$ but labour resources are unlimited. A capital-intensive development strategy will follow an expansion path $OA$, which is typical of the pre-reform era. A labour-intensive development strategy will follow an expansion path $OB$, which is typical of the reform period.

Following the labour intensive expansion path, with the same capital, more output can be produced and more labour can be employed. The difference of output is $(Q_B - Q_A)$, and the difference of employment is $(L_B - L_A)$. Assuming full employment in the urban sector and the urban labour force is $L_A$, the pre-reform strategy was able to ensure full employment for the urban population but unable

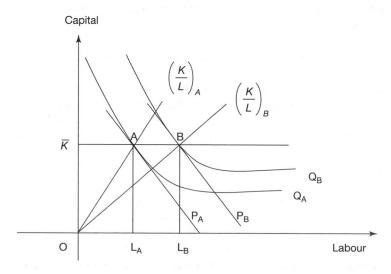

*Figure 11.1* Effect of industrial structure on employment with fixed capital.

to absorb any rural migrants. By contrast, given the same capital resources, the post-reform strategy was able to increase output and employment so that the urban sector could absorb rural migrants. Hence, the relaxation of regulation on rural–urban migration was possible because of the adoption of the new development strategy.

The change of development strategy is reflected by the shift in the national industrial output structure. In 1949, for example, the heavy industrial sector (capital intensive) accounted for only 26 per cent of the total industrial output. Its share increased rapidly before economic reforms. By 1978, it was about 57 per cent. The share of light industry (labour intensive) declined correspondingly from 74 per cent to 43 per cent over the same period. From 1979, due to the new industrial development strategy, the share of heavy industrial output was gradually reduced. By 1998, it was only 49 per cent, while the share of light industrial output rose to 51 per cent (NBS, 1999c: 38).

With more output, the urban sector is able to make more investments. The assumption of fixed capital can be relaxed. If we increase capital investment and follow a similar expansion path like *OB*, more and more employment will be created in the urban economy. The development experiences in the past decades show that this is exactly what has happened in China. There has been a fast growth in the numbers of cities and the sizes of the cities have also been expanding rapidly. Part of the growth in the urban economy was due to the growth of the original urban population, but much of the growth has been due to the transformation of suburban areas into proper urban areas and massive rural–urban migration (Figure 11.2).

In 1997, for example, among the 7.10 million new urban employees, only 36.6 per cent were urban residents, and the rest are rural migrants (26 per cent), graduates (31.7 per cent) and others.[2]

Apart from the new development strategy, the Chinese government also allowed farmers to set up rural non-farm enterprises, or township and village enterprises (TVEs). The development of TVEs was rapid in the prosperous coastal areas right from the inception of rural reforms in the late 1970s. It then spread into the inland

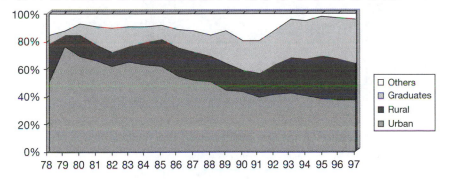

*Figure 11.2* Sources of new urban employees, 1978–98 (%).

Data Source: NSB, 1998, *China Labour Statistical Yearbook*

areas from the mid-1980s. Over the last few decades, the TVE sector has provided a substantial outlet for absorbing agricultural surplus labour. It has also made a huge contribution to the growth of the Chinese economy as a whole. Although TVE development is also important in other developing countries, its role in the Chinese economy has been fundamental in the following distinct aspects. First, TVEs have become one of the most important economic sectors (along with the state-owned enterprises and agriculture) in the Chinese economy in terms of their contribution to GDP. Second, unlike the state-owned industries, the development of TVEs does not require investment from the government. Third, TVEs are the most important employers of surplus agricultural workers. Fourth, TVEs have become an increasingly important source of rural incomes and national exports (Yao and Liu, 1996).

In rural China, rapid growth of agricultural productivity and rural population resulted in hundreds of millions of surplus farm workers looking for jobs outside agriculture. The total rural labour force increased from 306 million in 1978 to 493 million by 1998. Due to land shortage, it is estimated that a significant proportion of the rural labour force is not required for agricultural production, which is generally arduous and low-paid. Hence, without the development of TVEs, all the surplus labour would either have to move to the cities or have to stay in agriculture with low productivity.

From 1978 to 1998, TVE employment increased from 28.27 million to 125.37 million, or by 343.5 per cent. In addition, the rural private and self-employed non-farm enterprises created another 16.04 million jobs by 1990, rising to 45.92 millions in 1998. Figure 11.3 shows that the total rural non-farm employment in 1998 was more or less on a par with the employment of the entire urban economy, which includes state-owned industries, urban collective and private enterprises, and foreign-owned firms and joint ventures.

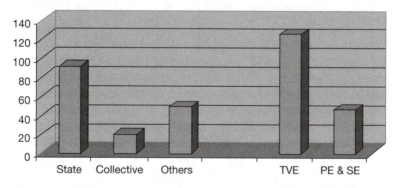

*Figure 11.3*  Urban and rural non-farm employment in 1998 (millions)

Data Source: NSB, 1999, *China Statistical Yearbook*

## 11.3 A theoretical model of migration

In the previous section, we discuss that only when the urban economy creates enough employment opportunities does the government allow peasants to work in the cities. However, what makes the cities so attractive to rural migrants? This section develops a theoretical model to answer this question. We use a CES production function to prove that urban–rural wage differential is an important determinant of rural–urban migration. It is also shown that other factors, including urban unemployment, rural wages and migration cost, are also important. For simplicity, we focus on a two-sector economy, rural and urban, and deliberately leave out the TVE sector, which will be considered in the next section when we discuss the empirical model of migration.

Let us consider a labour market with many urban areas and one identical rural area. There are a lot of rural to urban migrants. The household registration system of China keeps the urban labour force separate from rural migrants. Each urban area is assumed to have only one production unit called the firm, whose objective is to maximise profit. Profit maximisation means that there is no other way to produce the same output at a lower cost so that cost minimisation is a necessary condition for profit maximisation. Hence, a cost minimisation problem (CMP) is equivalent to a profit maximisation problem (PMP). In addition, as pointed out by Mas-Colell *et al.* (1995), the CMP has an advantage over the PMP if the firm is not a price taker in the output market. Since our model assumes that output is fixed, the CMP is particularly appropriate.

In the following CMP model, labour demand $E_i$, capital demand $K_i$, and migration $M_i$ are endogenous variables, whereas rural wages $W_0$, urban wages $W_i$, and the price of capital $P_i$ are exogenous variables. Central and local governments determine urban wages $W_i$. Agricultural productivity determines rural wages $W_0$.

It is further assumed that the firm in province $i$ has the following CES production function.

$$\left[(a_i E_i)^\rho + (b_i K_i)^\rho\right]^{\frac{1}{\rho}}$$

with $\rho < 1 \quad a_i > 0 \quad b_i > 0$

If output is fixed, the CMP can be expressed in (11.1),

$$\min \quad W_i E_i + P_i K_i = C_i$$

$$\text{s.t.} \left[(a_i E_i)^\rho + (b_i K_i)^\rho\right]^{\frac{1}{\rho}} = Y_i \tag{11.1}$$

$$E_i, K_i > 0$$

where $C_i$ and $Y_i$ are respectively the cost of production and the fixed output level of the firm in province $i$.

The corresponding Lagrangean equation of the CMP can be expressed in (11.2).

$$L = W_i E_i + P_i K_i - \lambda \left[ (a_i E_i)^\rho + (b_i K_i)^\rho - Y_i^\rho \right] \tag{11.2}$$

Taking the first-order conditions with appropriate manipulation, the conditional demand functions of labour ($E_i$) and capital ($K_i$) are given in (11.3) and (11.4).[3]

$$E_i = \frac{Y_i \left( \dfrac{W_i}{a_i} \right)^{\frac{1}{\rho-1}}}{a_i \left[ \left( \dfrac{W_i}{a_i} \right)^{\frac{\rho}{\rho-1}} + \left( \dfrac{P_i}{b_i} \right)^{\frac{\rho}{\rho-1}} \right]^{\frac{1}{\rho}}} \tag{11.3}$$

$$K_i = \frac{Y_i \left( \dfrac{P_i}{b_i} \right)^{\frac{1}{\rho-1}}}{b_i \left[ \left( \dfrac{W_i}{a_i} \right)^{\frac{\rho}{\rho-1}} + \left( \dfrac{P_i}{b_i} \right)^{\frac{\rho}{\rho-1}} \right]^{\frac{1}{\rho}}} \tag{11.4}$$

In a two-sector economy, the Harris and Todaro model implies that rural–urban migration is driven by expected incomes. In general, migrants move from the countryside of poor regions to the cities of prosperous areas. When migrants in China were asked what was the key factor for them in choosing a vocation, 65 per cent of them answered higher income (Zhang *et al.*, 1995).

Let $M_i$ be the number of rural to urban migrants and $F_i$ the local urban labour force in province $i$. The total urban labour force in that province is $M_i + F_i$ and the total urban employment is $E_i$. If migrants cannot get a job in urban areas, they will be paid nothing.

Let $W_0$ be peasants' wages in the rural areas. $T_i$ is a migration-related cost, which may include fees for a permit to live and work in the urban areas, transportation, other pecuniary expenses, and even the invisible cost of loneliness and separation from home and relatives.

The probability that a migrant can get a job in urban areas is

$$\frac{E_i}{(M_i + F_i)}$$

and the probability that a migrant cannot get a job in urban areas is

$$\frac{M_i + F_i - E_i}{(M_i + F_i)}.$$

The migrants' expected income in urban areas is

$$\frac{E_i}{(M_i + F_i)} W_i + \frac{M_i + F_i - E_i}{(M_i + F_i)} 0 - T_i.^4$$

The rural–urban expected income equilibrium condition is

$$W_0 = \frac{E_i}{(M_i + F_i)} W_i + \frac{M_i + F_i - E_i}{(M_i + F_i)} 0 - T_i$$

So $W_0 = \dfrac{E_i}{(M_i + F_i)} W_i - T_i$ \hfill (11.5)

Substituting (11.3) into (11.5) with manipulation, the migration equation can be expressed in equation (11.6).

$$M_i = \frac{Y_i \left(\dfrac{W_i}{a_i}\right)^{\frac{\rho}{\rho-1}}}{(W_0 + T_i) \left[\left(\dfrac{W_i}{a_i}\right)^{\frac{\rho}{\rho-1}} + \left(\dfrac{P_i}{b_i}\right)^{\frac{\rho}{\rho-1}}\right]^{\frac{1}{\rho}}} - F_i \hfill (11.6)$$

where the stock of rural-to-urban migrants is expressed as a function of exogenous variables: urban wages $W_i$, rural wages $W_0$, capital price $P_i$, migration cost $T_i$, urban labour force $F_i$, and fixed output level $Y_i$.

Equation (11.6) is our simplified two-sector migration model, which has the following properties.

*Property 1* Migration is a negative function of urban labour force, including urban unemployment, because

$$\frac{dM_i}{dF_i} = -1$$

*Property 2* Migration is a negative function of expected rural incomes, because

$$\frac{dM_i}{dW_0} = \frac{-Y_i \left(\dfrac{W_i}{a_i}\right)^{\frac{\rho}{\rho-1}}}{(W_0 + T_i)^2 \left[\left(\dfrac{W_i}{a_i}\right)^{\frac{\rho}{\rho-1}} + \left(\dfrac{P_i}{b_i}\right)^{\frac{\rho}{\rho-1}}\right]^{\frac{1}{\rho}}} < 0$$

*Property 3*  Migration is a negative function of migration-related cost, because

$$\frac{dM_i}{dT_i} = \frac{-Y_i\left(\frac{W_i}{a_i}\right)^{\frac{\rho}{\rho-1}}}{(W_0+T_i)^2\left[\left(\frac{W_i}{a_i}\right)^{\frac{\rho}{\rho-1}}+\left(\frac{P_i}{b_i}\right)^{\frac{\rho}{\rho-1}}\right]^{\frac{1}{\rho}}}$$

*Property 4*  Migration is an increasing function of urban production, because

$$\frac{dM_i}{dY_i} = \frac{\left(\frac{W_i}{a_i}\right)^{\frac{\rho}{\rho-1}}}{(W_0+T_i)\left[\left(\frac{W_i}{a_i}\right)^{\frac{\rho}{\rho-1}}+\left(\frac{P_i}{b_i}\right)^{\frac{\rho}{\rho-1}}\right]^{\frac{1}{\rho}}} > 0$$

*Property 5*  Migration is an increasing function of the cost of capital, because

$$\frac{dM_i}{dP_i} = \frac{-Y_i\left(\frac{W_i}{a_i}\right)^{\frac{\rho}{\rho-1}}\frac{1}{\rho}\left[\left(\frac{W_i}{a_i}\right)^{\frac{\rho}{\rho-1}}+\left(\frac{P_i}{b_i}\right)^{\frac{\rho}{\rho-1}}\right]^{\frac{1-\rho}{\rho}}\frac{\rho}{\rho-1}\left(\frac{P_i}{b_i}\right)^{\frac{1}{\rho-1}}\frac{1}{b_i}}{(W_0+T_i)\left[\left(\frac{W_i}{a_i}\right)^{\frac{\rho}{\rho-1}}+\left(\frac{P_i}{b_i}\right)^{\frac{\rho}{\rho-1}}\right]^{\frac{2}{\rho}}}$$

$$= \frac{Y_i\left(\frac{W_i}{a_i}\right)^{\frac{\rho}{\rho-1}}\left(\frac{P_i}{b_i}\right)^{\frac{1}{\rho-1}}}{b_i(1-\rho)(W_0+T_i)\left[\left(\frac{W_i}{a_i}\right)^{\frac{\rho}{\rho-1}}+\left(\frac{P_i}{b_i}\right)^{\frac{\rho}{\rho-1}}\right]^{\frac{1+\rho}{\rho}}} > 0$$

*Property 6*  Migration is likely to be a positive function of urban wages, but this is not guaranteed. The extent to which migration responds to urban wages depends on the value of the elasticity of labour-capital substitution.

The derivative of migration to urban wages is the function of $\rho$.

$$\frac{dM_i}{dW_i} = \frac{Y_i \frac{\rho}{\rho-1}\left(\frac{W_i}{a_i}\right)^{\frac{1}{\rho-1}}\frac{1}{a_i}}{(W_0+T_i)\left[\left(\frac{W_i}{a_i}\right)^{\frac{\rho}{\rho-1}}+\left(\frac{P_i}{b_i}\right)^{\frac{\rho}{\rho-1}}\right]^{\frac{1}{\rho}}} - \frac{Y_i\left(\frac{W_i}{a_i}\right)^{\frac{\rho}{\rho-1}}\frac{1}{\rho-1}\left(\frac{W_i}{a_i}\right)^{\frac{1}{\rho-1}}\frac{1}{a_i}}{(W_0+T_i)\left[\left(\frac{W_i}{a_i}\right)^{\frac{\rho}{\rho-1}}+\left(\frac{P_i}{b_i}\right)^{\frac{\rho}{\rho-1}}\right]^{\frac{1+\rho}{\rho}}}$$

$$= \frac{Y_i\left(\frac{W_i}{a_i}\right)^{\frac{1}{\rho-1}}\left\{\left(\frac{W_i}{a_i}\right)^{\frac{\rho}{\rho-1}}+\frac{\rho}{\rho-1}\left(\frac{P_i}{b_i}\right)^{\frac{\rho}{\rho-1}}\right\}}{a_i(W_0+T_i)\left[\left(\frac{W_i}{a_i}\right)^{\frac{\rho}{\rho-1}}+\left(\frac{P_i}{b_i}\right)^{\frac{\rho}{\rho-1}}\right]^{\frac{1+\rho}{\rho}}}$$

The elasticity of substitution between labour and capital

$$\sigma = \frac{1}{1-\rho}$$

measures the curvature of an isoquant. For the value of $\sigma$, we consider two different cases regarding the relationship between urban wages and migration.

*Case 1* if $\rho \leq 0, 0 < \sigma \leq 1$, then $\frac{\rho}{\rho-1} \geq 0$, so $\frac{dM_i}{dW_i} > 0$

This means that if $(0 < \sigma \leq 1)$; higher urban wages always attracts more migration.[5]

*Case 2* if $0 < \rho < 1, \sigma > 1$, then $-\infty < \frac{\rho}{\rho-1} < 0$, so $\frac{dM_i}{dW_i}$ is undetermined.

Case 2 does not guarantee that migration can be attracted by high urban wages. This is a critical limitation of Harris and Todaro's model, which assumes a monotonic response of migration to urban wages. In case 2, however, the higher is the value of the elasticity of substitution, the less likely is the urban sector to create extra jobs for rural migrants.

## 11.4 An empirical model of migration for China

The migration model in equation (11.6) can be testified using empirical data.[6] For this purpose, we use a panel data set for 29 provinces in the period 1995–8. We use the so-called in-migration data. That is, for each province, migrants are from other provinces (inter-migration), and from other counties of the same province (intra-migration). The migration model in equation (11.6) has not considered the role of TVE employment. In the following empirical models, this variable will be included.

Based on the six properties of equation (11.6) and taking into account the effect of TVEs, we propose the following empirical models for analysis.

$$MP_{it} = (W_{it}, U_{it}, W_{0it}, TVE_{it}, Z_{it})$$ (11.7)

$$MC_{it} = (W_{it}, U_{it}, W_{0it}, TVE_{it}, Z_{it})$$ (11.8)

Where the subscripts $i$ and $t$ denote province $i$ in year $t$. $MP$ is the percentage share of in-migrants from other provinces in the local labour force, including both rural and urban. $MC$ is the percentage share of in-migrants from other counties within the same provinces in the local labour force. $TVE$ is the percentage share of TVE employment in the rural labour force. $W$ is average urban wages rate measured in constant prices. $W_0$ is average rural net income per capita measured in constant prices. It represents rural or agricultural wages rate. $Z$ is a set of dummy variables for years and/or for provinces.

Theoretically, urban wages and TVE employment should have a positive effect on in-migration from other provinces, and on in-migration from other counties within the same province. The role of urban wages in attracting migration is easy to explain as long as the urban industrial sector is not highly capital intensive. It was discussed earlier that China's urban industries have become more labour intensive since economic reforms than before. Hence, we should expect urban wages to have a significant and positive effect on rural–urban migration. The role of employment in TVEs needs some explanation. In theory, it reflects the level of rural industrialisation, which, in turn, reflects the extent of prosperity in a particular region. A region with high TVE employment means that it must be more prosperous than others. This has two possible implications on migration decision. First, it implies that peasants in that region are less likely to move out to other provinces or counties to look for non-farm or urban jobs. Second, it means that the region under concern is more likely to attract migrants from other provinces or counties into that region. Either way, TVE employment will have a positive relationship with in-migration.

Urban unemployment is expected to have a negative effect on in-migration from other provinces or other counties from the same province. Local rural wages should also have a negative effect on in-migration from other provinces. This is not because higher local rural wages do not attract people from other provinces. It is because people are more likely to move out to other provinces if the local rural wages are low. Consequently, local rural wages has a push effect on in-migration from other provinces to the cities. This is opposite to the pull effect of urban wages. Similarly, rural wages may also affect migrants from other counties within the same provinces and the effect is expected to be negative. This is because a region with high rural wages will attract peasants to stay at home and reduce the number of migrants coming to work in the local towns and cities.

Although migration in China has become more and more popular, it is difficult to obtain complete and accurate data for the whole country and every province. Hence, many previous studies on migration in China have had to use sample survey data, instead of aggregate regional or national data (Zhao, 1999; Song, 2002). This chapter attempts to use macro-level data for the empirical models. Macro-level migration data are available in *China Labour Statistical Yearbook* (NBS, 1997–9). The summary statistics as shown in Table 11.1, however, includes only migrants from other provinces or other counties to the local urban areas.

*Table 11.1* In-migration in China ('000 people)

|                                          | 1995    | 1996    | 1997    | 1998    |
|------------------------------------------|---------|---------|---------|---------|
| Total in migration                       | 13220.6 | 16764.3 | 16175.4 | 15893.3 |
| In-migration from other provinces        | 6963.9  | 8753.2  | 9473.6  | 9384.8  |
| In-migration from other counties of same provinces | 6256.8  | 8017.1  | 6685.2  | 6437.0  |

Source: NBS, 1997–9, *China Labour Statistical Yearbook.*

The total number of migrants increased from about 13 million in 1995 to about 16 million in 1998. Over half of the in-migrants come from other provinces. The rest are from other counties within the same province.

The figures in Table 11.1 may significantly understate the real scale of migration in China. They do not include migrants who work in the rural areas and who do not register with the local city or township governments. If such migrants were included, the total number would have been much greater. However, since we do not have reliable estimates of these migrants, we can only rely on the published data.

The data show that in-migration in China is highly concentrated in some eastern provinces, such as Guangdong, Zhejiang, Jiangsu, Fujian, Beijing, Shanghai and Tianjin. For instance, Guangdong alone accounted for over 30 per cent of the total in-migrants of China in 1998, followed by Zhejiang (9.6 per cent) and Fujian (6 per cent).

When migrants are measured as the percentage shares in the local labour force (the dependent variable in our models), Beijing has the highest concentration (14 per cent), followed by Tianjin (9.3 per cent).

As for the explanatory variables in the models, TVE employment, urban wages and rural wages are all available from the *China Labour Statistical Yearbook* (NBS, 1996–9). The average urban youth unemployment rate is 9 per cent, with a minimum 0.9 per cent in Beijing and a maximum 26 per cent in Qinghai. The rural–urban income gap is large. For the whole sample period, the average rural net income per capita is 1,500 yuan per year, with a minimum 700-yuan in Gansu and a maximum 4,000-yuan in Shanghai. The average urban wage is 4,700 yuan per year, with a minimum 3,400-yuan in Jiangxi and a maximum 8,600-yuan in Shanghai. The average urban–rural wage ratio is 3.13, offering tremendous incentives for migration if peasants were allowed to compete freely with urban workers for jobs.

The summary statistics and explanations of the dependent and independent variables are provided in Table 11.2.

*Table 11.2* Summary statistics of dependent and independent variables

|  |  | Mean | Std dev. | Min. | Max. |
|---|---|---|---|---|---|
| MP | (%) | 1.93 | 2.77 | 0.00 | 14.00 |
| MC | (%) | 1.09 | 1.38 | 0.00 | 9.30 |
| U(t–1) | (%) | 8.97 | 4.67 | 0.89 | 26.30 |
| Income (t–1) | (1000 yuan) | 1.53 | 0.68 | 0.72 | 3.96 |
| Wage (t–1) | (1000 yuan) | 4.71 | 1.16 | 3.37 | 8.57 |
| TVE (t–1) | (%) | 31.90 | 15.80 | 5.39 | 69.70 |

Sources: *MP* and *MC*, NBS, 1997–9, *China Labour Statistical Yearbook*, all the other variables, NBS, 1996–9, *China Statistical Yearbook*.

Notes: *MP* = migrants from other provinces as per cent share of the total labour force. *MC* = migrants from other counties in the same province as per cent share of the total labour force. TVE employment is defined as the percentage share of TVE employment in the rural labour force. Urban wages are measured in constant prices. Rural wages are measured in constant prices as per capita rural net income. (t–1) means data are lagged by one year.

Equations (11.7) and (11.8) are estimated in TSP with a panel data methodology. The explanatory variables are instrumented to avoid the problem of endogeneity. The instruments are the lagged values of the corresponding variables. The same model can be estimated in two different ways: the plain OLS with the random effect model which treats residuals as random errors, and the fixed effect model which treats the residuals as regional-specific errors. Using Hausman's test, we find that the random effect model is acceptable. It also performs better than the fixed effect model. Consequently, we report results of the random effect models in this section. The results are given in Table 11.3.

Both panels A and B in Table 11.3 show that the results are interesting and consistent with the theoretical expectations discussed above. TVE employment and urban wages have significant and positive effects on in-migration from other provinces or from other counties within the same provinces. This means that the rural–urban income differentials play an important role in attracting rural–urban migration. The development of TVEs in the local economies also has an important effect on migratory decision. Regions with more TVE employment are more attractive to migrants from other provinces or other counties. This is because local peasants are more likely to stay at home if they can find off-farm employment in the rural areas, leaving more opportunities for peasants from other regions to come to the local cities and towns.

Rural wages have a significant and negative impact on in-migration from other provinces and from other counties of the same provinces. This means that high

Table 11.3 Migration equations in China: panel data for 29 provinces in four years, 1995–8

A *Dependent variable = in-migrants from other provinces, as % of local total labour force*

| Variables | Without year dummy | | With year dummy | |
|---|---|---|---|---|
| | Coefficient | t-values | Coefficient | t-value |
| TVE employment (t–1) | 0.042 | (3.33) | 0.045 | (3.50) |
| Urban unemployment (t–1) | −0.111 | (−3.06) | −0.140 | (−3.42) |
| Rural wages (t–1) | −1.614 | (−3.16) | −2.001 | (−3.51) |
| Urban real wages (t–1) | 2.217 | (8.66) | 2.314 | (8.72) |
| Intercept | −6.396 | (−6.88) | −6.645 | (−7.29) |
| Adj-$R^2$ | 0.72 | | 0.73 | |
| LM test for heteroscedasticity | 33 | p=0.00 | 33 | p=0.00 |

B *Dependent variable = in-migrants from other counties in the same provinces, as % of local total labour force*

| Variables | Without year dummy | | With year dummy | |
|---|---|---|---|---|
| | Coefficient | t-values | Coefficient | t-value |
| TVE employment (t–1) | 0.022 | (2.31) | 0.023 | (2.24) |
| Urban unemployment rate (t–1) | −0.041 | (−1.96) | −0.052 | (−1.99) |
| Rural real wages (t–1) | −1.001 | (−1.93) | −1.165 | (−2.11) |
| Urban real wages (t–1) | 0.649 | (2.43) | 0.693 | (2.48) |
| Intercept | −0.771 | (−1.06) | −0.992 | (−1.25) |
| Adj-$R^2$ | 0.15 | | 0.15 | |
| LM test for heteroscedasticity | 11.80 | p=0.00 | 15.10 | p=0.00 |

Notes: TVE employment is defined as the percentage share of TVE employment in the rural labour force. Urban wages are in '000 yuan/head measured in constant prices. Rural wages are rural net incomes in '000 yuan per capita measured in constant prices.

rural wages tend to reduce inter- and intra-migration, as peasants are happier to stay in agriculture if they can earn higher incomes in that sector. On the other hand, if rural wages are low, peasants will look for alternative employment out of agriculture.

## 11.5 Conclusion

Over the past two and a half decades, China has experienced rapid economic growth and social changes. People's living standards have vastly improved. Millions of peasants have moved out of agriculture, either working in the cities and towns as migrants, or working in the TVEs.

In this chapter, it is argued that the relaxation of government policy on migration under economic reforms has been possible because of the change of industrial development strategy. As the pre-reform development strategy was focused on the development of heavy industries, industrial output growth failed to absorb a large number of employees so that it would be impossible to allow rural–urban migration without incurring massive urban unemployment and poverty. The new development strategy was focused on China's comparative advantage through the development of labour-intensive industries. As a result, the same investment or output was able to create more jobs than before, enabling the urban economy to expand rapidly not just in output, but also in employment.

In the literature, most studies consider that the urban–rural wage differential is the primary factor attracting migration. In the Chinese case, the migratory decision of peasants can be shown to be influenced by a whole set of factors due to the special characteristics of the Chinese institutions. The most important feature of the Chinese economy is the rapid growth of TVEs, which provide an important outlet of employment for surplus agricultural labour.

However, even if we account for the employment of TVEs, the urban economy is still unable to absorb all the peasants who wish to move out of agriculture. Thus, the classical migration model that focuses on the general equilibrium of supply and demand does not work for China. In this chapter, migration is deemed to be demand driven, rather than supply driven. On the supply side, there are far too many peasants who would be attracted by the large urban–rural income gap. On the demand side, however, the ability of the urban economy to absorb labour is limited despite the change of the industrial development strategy. Our demand-driven model is based on the assumption that there is an unlimited supply of migrants. Hence, the urban–rural wage differential is not the only determinant of migratory decisions. The cost of migration, urban unemployment and TVE employment are other important determinants. Using a CES production function, a theoretical model was developed to prove that migration is a negative function of rural wages, urban unemployment, the price of capital and migration costs. Migration is also proved here to be a positive function of urban output and wages.

The empirical results are robust for both inter-migration and intra-migration. Urban wages and TVE employment are found to have positive effects. Rural wages are found to have an opposite effect. The results support our hypothesis that the development of TVE must have played an important role in migration. They also support the argument that the urban–rural wages differential is an important pecuniary incentive of migration. However, population pressure and, therefore, the level of urban unemployment are significant and negative factors holding back rural migration into the cities.

The theoretical and empirical models explain why and how such large-scale rural–urban migration has taken place in China under economic reforms. However, the question of whether migration can help reduce poverty still remains a controversial issue. Based on the discussion in the previous chapters, we have presented clear evidence that poverty in rural China is still a difficult problem, which is exaggerated by the ever rising rural–urban income inequality.

Classical economic theories, including those presented in Harris and Todaro's model, imply that as long as rural people are allowed to work in the cities and earn higher incomes than they do in the countryside, the rural–urban income gap will be reduced as a result of migration. The problem in China is that migration may not be an effective way of reducing urban–rural inequality and or for the peasantry to escape poverty. One may argue that migration is a phenomenon of, instead of a solution to, poverty. Many informal estimates show that there is a floating population of more than 100 million people in China but not all of them are captured by official statistics. This number represents over 10 per cent of the rural population.

If migration were a solution to poverty, then we should expect two important outcomes from migration: urban–rural income inequality should decline, and within-rural inequality should also decline. This is because migrants should be able to earn more in the cities and send money back to the countryside, and there should be more migrants from the poorer regions than from the richer regions. Empirical evidence, however, has shown opposite outcomes: urban–rural inequality and within-rural inequality have risen sharply in the 1990s and has continued into the new century, a period corresponding to massive and rising migration. One may well argue, therefore, that migration is an outcome of polarisation and poverty, instead of a solution to escaping poverty, at least in the Chinese case over the last 10 to 20 years.

But how can one explain the paradox between the theoretical expectation and the empirical outcome? As has been mentioned and discussed in the previous chapters, we can summarise the main reasons why migration is not a solution to poverty reduction:

- Migrant workers do not enjoy the same employment opportunities as their urban counterparts.
- State policy still directly or indirectly discriminates against rural migrants.
- Rural migrants earn much less and have to support more people than do urban workers.
- Poor areas are deprived of able and young people so that local production is suffocated, leading to more rural–urban inequality.

In the long term, the most effective solution to reducing rural poverty is rural industrialisation and urbanisation, increased agricultural productivity, improved rural infrastructure and education. These require substantial investments and a sharp reversal of the government's urban biased policy. However, based on the development experiences of the last 55 years, one cannot be optimistic that this will happen. The fight against urban–rural inequality and poverty could become a permanent feature of economic development in China for many decades to come.

# Notes

### 3 Agricultural and rural development

1 'Three differences' refer to the difference between urban workers and rural peasants, the difference between urban and rural people and the difference between manual and mental workers (blue and white-collar workers).

### 4 Openness and economic performance

1 Hong Kong and Macao accounted for 54.31 per cent of China's accumulative FDI in 1984–95, Japan 8.2 per cent, Taiwan 7.82 per cent, USA 8.0 per cent, Singapore 3.81 per cent, Korea 2.85 per cent and UK 2.34 per cent (NBS, various issues, 1984–98).
2 Ding (1998) has a detailed study on the foreign exchange black market and exchange flight in China in this period.
3 A relevant study by Brada, *et al.* (1993) also shows that devaluation (change in the real exchange rate) had a positive effect on the balance of trade in China.
4 IMF signed emergency lending agreements with Thailand in August 1997 ($17 billion), with Indonesia in November 1997 ($35 billion) and with Korea in December 1997 ($57 billion). The actual amounts of disbursement were, however, much smaller. IMF also attached a number of conditions for the loans. Such conditions, including a drastic restructuring of the financial systems in the middle of a deep crisis, are blamed for aggravating, rather than easing the crisis (Radelet and Sachs, 1998).

### 5 Decomposition of Gini coefficients by population class and income source: a spreadsheet approach and application

1 Note that $m_i$'s do not enter equation (5.1) but the order of $w_i$ and $p_i$ are determined by $m_i$. In addition, $w_i$ is calculated from $m_i$ and $p_i$ with the relationship $w_i = p_i m_i / u$, $u$ is average per capita income of the total population.
2 The economic interpretation of $G_O$ is also referred to by Yitzhaki, 1994; Silber, 1989; Milanovic, 1994; and Lambert and Aronson, 1993.
3 I am grateful to Liwei Zhu who has generously given me the household survey data.

### 6 Rural–urban and regional inequality in output, income and consumption under reforms

1 The average annual growth rate of total GDP in South Korea was 9.6 per cent in the period 1970–91. It was 9.2 per cent in Hong Kong and 8.3 per cent in Singapore in the period 1970–80 (World Bank, 1993).
2 When measured in current prices, agriculture's share in GDP declined from 29 to 21 per cent, indicating a significant price effect on structural change over the data period.

3 Martin Raiser (1998, Table 1) presents a similar set coefficients of variation (CV) for per capita GDP. His estimates are very different from ours. We believe that he may have overestimated the CV for the earlier years and underestimated it for the later years because he does not use the same complete data as we do. He acknowledges that he has difficulty in understanding the Chinese data.

4 Unconditional $\beta$-convergence is a necessary but not a sufficient condition for $\delta$-convergence. As a result, $\delta$-convergence must imply unconditional $\beta$-convergence, but not vice versa.

## 7 Regional inequality and diverging clubs

1 This chapter is largely based on the paper by Yao and Zhang (2001b).

2 The classification of economic clubs does not need to be based on the official definition. Some authors may divide China into two regions: coastal and non-coastal (Chen and Fleisher, 1996). Some authors may not agree that Guangxi should belong to the Eastern region as it is still a relatively poor province. However, to make the results recorded here more relevant for policy making, this chapter retains the official definition. In addition, strong similarity has been found within each of the three economic clubs in terms of growth, per capita income and investments in the past twenty years of economic reforms. For example, Guangxi may be a relatively poor province measured by per capita income compared to other provinces in the east, but it has a higher growth rate and more foreign direct investments than most of the central and western provinces.

3 The eastern provinces are close to China's largest foreign investors, i.e. Hong Kong, Taiwan, Singapore and Japan. Foreign direct investment was an important factor in the phenomenal growth in the east after economics reforms (Wu, 2001).

4 The density and quality of growth centres are important for the growth of the neighbouring regions. For simplicity of discussion, only the distance factor is used here. Provinces in the central and west clubs also have their growth centres, i.e. large and medium-sized cities or industrial bases. However, these centres are sparsely located and their economic conditions are generally much poorer than their eastern counterparts for various reasons, including lack of foreign investments, high concentration of SOEs and poor institutions.

5 The distances for C, A and B are as follows: for C, $D = 0$; for A, $0 < D < D_{min}$; for B, $D > D_{min}$.

6 Although it is likely that $y_A$ [more] $y_B$, it is expected that $\beta_1 y_A << (\beta_1 + 2\beta_2 (D-D_{min})) y_B$.

7 It is also possible that the marginal product of capital in C is greater than that in A or in B. In such a case, A and B can not catch up with C even if the diverging effect of distance is ignored. For convenience of discussion, we assume that the marginal product of capital in C is smaller than that in A or in B.

8 See Mankiw *et al.*, 1992, for more discussion of the growth model.

9 As an alternative to measure the effect of distance, Beijing, Shanghai and Guangzhou were selected as three representative growth centres. The physical distances from each provincial capital to these cities was measured, with the shortest distance being used as the distance variable. Thirty distances were taken and scaled to a value range from 0 to 10. This continuous variable is used to replace the discrete distance variables in (4B). The results show strong support for the hypothesis, as the estimated coefficient is negative and significant. However, the results presented in this paper are easier to understand so that we do not present results using this alternative distance variable.

10 The distances (east to central), and (west to central) may take different values other than one. Different values do not affect $t$-statistics but change only the sizes of the estimated coefficients in (4B). However, by setting these distances equal to one, we can derive the differences of per capita GDP growth between the three geo-economic regions after controlling for other variables.

11  See Yao and Zhang, 2001b, for a more detailed explanation of the growth model for China.
12  Yao's method can also be used to decompose the Gini coefficient by income sources.

## 8  Understanding income inequality in China: a multi-angle perspective

1  The provinces and cities are classified into three economic zones: east, central and west. For detailed classification, see Yao and Liu (1998).
2  The average annual growth rate is the exponent of the estimated coefficient of time period in equation (8.5) minus one.

## 10  Unemployment and urban poverty

1  Redundancy is different from unemployment. A redundant, or laid-off, worker can find a job in the non-SOE sector, or can end up being unemployed. Hence, only when a laid-off worker cannot find another job can we say this worker is unemployed.
2  The conditional demand function of labour is the same whether the firm pursues cost minimisation or profit maximisation. In this section, we follow the cost minimisation model.
3  In estimating an empirical redundancy equation for the Chinese SOEs, apart from wages, Dong and Putterman also include some other variables such as the capital structure, capital/labour ratio and profitability of the firm. However, high wages is found to be the most important factor responsible for redundancy (Dong and Putterman, 2003).
4  The dependency ratio is the number of household members younger than 18 or older than 60 divided by the number of household members aged between 18–60.

## 11  Is migration a way of escaping poverty in China?

1  The supply side factors are certainly important but we can reasonably assume that there is unlimited supply of migrants, at least in the short and medium terms.
2  The share of graduates seems high but it actually includes those who are urban residents and work in the cities upon graduation.
3  Detailed mathematical proofs are not provided here but available from the author on request.
4  It is assumed that a rural migrant will have the same chance of being employed and earning the same urban wages as an urban resident. However, since a rural migrant has a migration cost $T_i$ and will paid nothing if she or he cannot get a job in an urban area, the expected income is less than the expected income of an urban resident by that amount.
5  This scenario corresponds to an industrial structure where labour cannot be easily substituted by capital. It is likely that a labour intensive industry will have such a property.
6  Due to data available, we do not test all the hypotheses of the theoretical model in the empirical model. Instead, we only focus on the main determinants of migration, including real urban and rural wages, urban unemployment and TVE.

# References

Adams, R. (1994), Non-farm income and inequality in rural Pakistan: a decomposition analysis, *Journal of Development Studies*, **31**(1): 110–133.

Ahmad, E. and Y. Wang (1991), Inequality and poverty in China: institutional change and public policy, 1978 to 1988, *World Bank Economic Review*, **5**(2): 231–57, May.

Ahuja, Vinod, Benu Bidani, Francisco Ferreira and Michael Walton (1997), *Everyone's Miracle? Revisiting Poverty Reduction and Inequality in East Asia*, Washington, DC: World Bank.

Alderman, H., P.A. Chiappori, L. Haddad, J. Hoddinot and R. Kanbur (1995), Unitary versus collective models of the household: is it time to shift the burden of proof? *The World Bank Research Observer*, **10**.

Appleton, S., J. Knight, L. Song and Q. Xia (2001), Towards a competitive labour market? Urban workers, rural–urban migrants, redundancies and hardship in urban China, paper presented at the American Economic Association Annual Conference, 2001, New Orleans.

Arellano, M. and R.S. Bond (1998), *Dynamic Panel Data Estimation Using DPD98 for Gauss*, mimeo, Institute for Fiscal Studies, London.

Asian Development Bank (2001), *Urban Poverty in China*, a technical report prepared for the Bank and the Chinese government.

Balassa, B. (1988), The interaction of factor and product market distortions in developing countries, *World Development*, **11**(2).

Barro, Robert J. (1991), Economic growth in a cross-section of countries, *Quarterly Journal of Economics*, **106**(2): 407–43, May.

Barro, Robert J. and Jong-Wha Lee (1993), International comparisons of educational attainment, *Journal of Monetary Economics*, **32**(3): 363–94.

Barro, Robert J. and Xavier X. Sala-i-Martin (1992), Convergence, *Journal of Political Economy*, **100**(2): 223–51, April.

Barro, Robert J. and Xavier X. Sala-i-Martin (1995), *Economic Growth*, New York: McGraw Hill.

Bernard, Andrew B. and Steven N. Durlauf (1995), Convergence in International Output, *Journal of Applied Econometrics*, **10**(2): 97–108, April–June.

Bhalla, A.S. (1990), Rural–urban disparities in India and China, *World Development*, **18**(8): 1097–110.

Bhalla, A.S. (1995), *Uneven Development in the Third World: A Study of China and India*, London: Macmillan Press.

Bhalla, Ajit, Shujie Yao and Zongyi Zhang (2002), Causes of inequalities in China, 1952 to 1999, *Economics of Transition*, **11**(1): 29–39.

Bhattacharya, N. and B. Mahalanobis (1967), Regional disparity in household consumption in India, *American Statistical Association Journal*, March: 143–62.

Bhattacharya, P.C. (1993), Rural–urban migration in economic development, *Journal of Economic Surveys* **7**(3): 243–62.

Bourguignon, F., M. Browning, P.A. Chiappori and V. Lechene (1993), Intrahousehold allocation of consumption: a model and some evidence from French data, *Annales d'Economie et de Statistics*, **29**: 137–56.

Brada, J., A.M. Kutan and S. Zhou (1993), China's exchange rate and the balance of trade, *Economics of Planning*, **26**: 229–42.

Brohman, John (1996), Postwar development in the Asian NICs: does the neoliberal model fit reality?, *Economic Geography*, **72**(2): 107–30.

Brown, Lester R. (1995), *Who Will Feed China? Wake-up Call for a Small Planet*, The Worldwatch Environmental Alert Series, New York: W.W. Norton and Company.

Brown, Scott J., N. Edward Coulson, and Robert F. Engle (1990), *Non-cointegration and Econometric Evaluation of Models of Regional Shift and Share*, National Bureau of Economic Research Working Paper: 3291, March.

Bruce, J. (1989), Homes divided, *World Development*, **17**(7).

Campbell, John Y. and N. Gregory Mankiw (1989), International evidence on the persistence of economic fluctuations, *Journal of Monetary Economics*, **23**(2): 319–33, March.

Campbell, John Y. and Pierre Perron (1991), Pitfalls and opportunities: what macroeconomists should know about unit roots, in O.J. Blanchard and S. Fisher, eds., *NBER Macroeconomics Annual 1991*, Cambridge, MA: MIT Press, pp. 141–201.

Carlino, Gerald A. and Leonard O. Mills (1993), Are US regional incomes converging? A time series analysis, *Journal of Monetary Economics*, **32**(2): 335–46, November.

Chang, Gene Hsin and Wen, James Guangzhong (1997), Communal dining and the Chinese famine of 1958–61, *Economic Development and Cultural Change*, **46**(1): 1–34.

Chen, Chung, Lawrence Change and Yiming Zhang (1995), The role of foreign direct investment in China's post-1978 economic development, *World Development*, **23**(4): 691–703.

Chen, Jian and Belton M. Fleisher (1996), Regional income inequality and economic growth in China, *Journal of Comparative Economics*, **22**: 141–64.

Chen, Kuan, Gary H. Jefferson, Thomas G. Rawski, Hongchang Wang and Yuxin Zheng (1988), New estimates of fixed investment and capital stock for Chinese state industry, *China Quarterly*, **114**: 243–66, June.

Cheng, Yuk-shing (1996), A decomposition analysis of income inequality of Chinese rural households, *China Economic Review*, **7**(2): 155–67.

Chinese Academy of Social Sciences (CASS) (1995) *Special Household Survey Data in 1995*, Beijing.

*China Economic Information* (2004), Issue 1 (Beijing).

*Chinese Economic Yearbook* (1982), Beijing: Statistical Press.

*Chinese Economic Yearbook* (1990), Beijing: Statistical Press.

Chou, W.L. and Y.C. Shih (1998), The equilibrium exchange rate of the Chinese Renminbi, *Journal of Comparative Economics*, **26**: 165–74.

Cole, William and Richard D. Sanders (1985), Internal migration and urban employment in the third world, *American Economic Review*, **75**: 481–494.

Corden, W.M. and R. Findlay (1975), Urban unemployment, intersectoral capital mobility and development policy, *Economica*, **42**: 59–78.

Cowell, Frank (1980), On the structure of additive inequality measures, *Review of Economics Studies*, **47**: 521–531.

Deaton, A. (1997), *The Analysis of Household Surveys: A Microeconometric Approach to Development Policy*, Baltimore, MD: Johns Hopkins University Press.

Deninger, Klaus and Lyn Squire (1996), A new data set measuring income inequality, *The World Bank Economic Review*, **10**(3): 565–91.

Department for International Development (DFID, UK) (1998), *Country Strategy Paper for China* London: DFID.

Ding, Jianping (1998), China's foreign exchange black market and exchange flight: analysis of exchange rate policy, *The Developing Economies*, **36**(1): 24–44.

Dollar, D. and R. Gatti (1999), Gender inequality, income, and growth: are good times good for women? Policy research report on gender and development, Working Paper Series No. 1, Washington, DC: World Bank, May.

Dong, F. (1980) China's economy undergoes a sharp change, *Chinese Economic Studies*, **14**(1): 19–37.

Dong, Xiaoyuan and L. Putterman (2003), Soft budget constraints, social burdens, and labour redundancy in China's state industry, *Journal of Comparative Economics*, **31**(1): 110–33.

Dowling, Peter (1997), Asia's economic miracle: a historical perspective, *Australian Economic Reiew*, **30**(1): 113–23.

*The Economist* (1997–9, various issues), Economic Indicators.

Edwards, Sebastian (1998), Openness, productivity and growth: what do we really know?, *The Economic Journal*, **108**: 383–98.

Erturk, K. and N. Cagatay (1995), Macroeconomic consequences of cyclical and secular changes in feminization: an experiment in gendered macro-modelling, *World Development*, **23**(11): 1969–77.

Fan, G. (2000), The dynamics of transition in China: Change of ownership structure and sustainability of growth, Paper presented at the International Conference of China Growth Sustainability in the 21st Century, Canberra, Australia.

Fan, Shenggen, Linxiu Zhang and Xiaobo Zhang (2000), How does public spending affect growth and poverty? The experience of China, The Second Annual Development Network Conference, Tokyo, Japan 11–13 December 2000.

Fei, J.C. and G. Ranis (1964), *Development of the Labour-supply Economy: Theory and Policy*, Homewood, IL: Irwin.

Fei, J., G. Ranis and Shirley Kuo (1978), Growth and the family distribution of income by factor components, *Quarterly Journal of Economics*, February, 17–53.

Fei, J., G. Ranis and Shirley Kuo (1979), *Growth with Equity: Taiwanese Case*, Oxford: Oxford University Press.

Fields, Gary S. (1975), Rural–urban migration, urban unemployment and underemployment, and job-search activity in LDCs, *Journal of Development Economics*, **2**: 165–87.

*Financial Times* (2003), Import–export data, China hits record $6 billion trade surplus (in October 2003), 14 November, p. 10.

Fleisher, B.M. and Jian Chen (1997), The coast–noncoast income gap, productivity, and regional economic policy in China, *Journal of Comparative Economics*, **25**: 220–36.

Gao, S. (1996), *China's Economic Reform*, London: Macmillan Press.

Gastwirth, J. (1972), The estimation of the Lorenz curve and Gini index, *Review of Economics and Statistics*, **54**: 306–316.

Ghatak, S. and K. Ingersent (1984), *Agriculture and Economic Development*, London: Wheatsheaf Books.

Ghatak, S., P. Levine and S. Wheatley Price (1996), Migration theories and evidence: an assessment, *Journal of Economic Surveys*, **10**(2): 159–98.

Greenaway, D. (1998), Does trade liberalisation promote economic development? *Scottish Journal of Political Economy*, **45**(5): 491–511.

Griffin, K. and Renwei Zhao (1993), *The Distribution of Income in China*, New York: St Martin's Press.

Groves, T., Y. Hong, J. McMillan and B. Naughton (1994), Autonomy and incentives in Chinese state enterprises, *Quarterly Journal of Economics*, **109**: 183–209.

Grown, Caren, Diane Elson and Nilufer Cagatay (2000), Introduction, *World Development*, **28**(7): 1145–56.

Gundlach, Erich (1997), Regional convergence of output per worker in China: a neoclassicalinterpretation, *Asian Economic Journal*, **11**(4): 423–42, December.

Gustafssion, B. and Li, S. (1998) The structure of Chinese poverty (1988), *The Developing Economies*, **36**: 387–406.

Gustafsson, B. and Wei Zhong (2000), How and why has poverty in China changed? A study based on microdata for 1988 and 1995, *The China Quarterly*, **164**: 983–1006.

Hanmer, Lucia and Felix Naschold (1999), Are the international development targets attainable? Working Paper, London: Overseas Development Institute.

Harris, Richard I.D. (1995), *Using Cointegration Analysis in Econometric Modelling*, London: Prentice Hall/Harvester Wheatsheaf.

Harris, John and Michael Todaro (1970), Migration, unemployment and development, *American Economic Review*, **60**: 126–42.

Harrold, Peter (1995), China: foreign trade reform: now for the hard part, *Oxford Review of Economic Policy*, **11**(4): 133–46.

Hay, D., D. Morris, Shaojia Liu and Shujie Yao (1994), *Economic Reform and State-owned Enterprises in China 1979–87*, Oxford: Oxford University Press.

Hazell, Peter B. R. and Alisa Roell (1983), *Rural Growth Linkages: Household Expenditure Patterns in Malaysia and Nigeria*, Research Report No. 41, Washington, DC: International Food Policy Research Institute.

Hirschman, A.O. (1958), *The Strategy of Economic Development,* New Haven, CT: Yale University Press.

Hoddinott, J. and L. Haddad (1995), Does female income share influence household expenditures? Evidence from Côte d'Ivoire, *Oxford Bulletin of Economics and Statistics*, **57**(1): 77–96.

Hsueh, Tien-tung (1994), Pattern of regional development in the People's Republic of China, *Asian Economic Journal*, **8**(1): 1–38, March.

Hsueh, Tien-tung and Qiang, Li (eds) (1999), *China's National Income*, Boulder and Oxford: Westview Press.

Hussain, A, P. Lanjouw and N. Stern (1994), Income inequalities in China: Evidence from household survey data, *World Development*, **22** (12): 1947–57.

Islam, Nazrull (1995), Growth empirics: a panel data approach, *Quarterly Journal of Economics*, **110**: 1127–70.

Jalan, Jyotsna and Martin Ravallion (1998a), Are there dynamic gains from a poor-area development program?, *Journal of Public Economics*, **67**: 65–8.

Jalan, Jyotsna and Martin Ravallion (1998b), Transient poverty in postreform rural China, *Journal of Comparative Economics*, **26**: 338–357.

Jalan, Jyotsna and Martin Ravallion (2000), Geographic poverty traps? A micro model of consumption growth in rural China, Working Paper, the World Bank.

Jefferson, Gary H. (1989), Potential sources of productivity growth within Chinese industry, *World Development*, **17**(1): 45–57, January.

Jefferson, Gary H. and Thomas G. Rawski (1994), Enterprise reform in Chinese industry, *Journal of Economic Perspectives*, **8** (2): 47–70.

Jefferson, Gary H., Thomas G. Rawski and Yuxin Zheng (1992), Growth, efficiency, and convergence in China's state and collective industry, *Economic Development and Cultural Change*, **40**(2): 239–66, January.

Johnson, D.G. (1988), Economic reforms in the People's Republic of China, *Economic Development and Cultural Change*, April: S225–45.

Kai-yuan, Tsui (1998), Factor decomposition of Chinese rural income inequality: new methodology, empirical findings, and policy implications, *Journal of Comparative Economics*, **26**: 502–28.

Kakwani, Nanak C. (1980), *Income Inequality and Poverty: Methods of Estimation and Policy Applications*, Oxford: Oxford University Press.

Kanbur, Ravi and Xiaobo Zhang (1999), Which regional inequality? The evolution of rural–urban and inland–coastal inequality in China from 1983 to 1995, *Journal of Comparative Economics*, **27**: 686–701.

Klasen, S. (1999), Does gender inequality reduce growth and development? Evidence from cross-country regressions, policy research report on gender and development, Washington DC: The World Bank, May.

Knight, J. (1995), Price scissors and inter-sectoral resource transfers: who paid for industrialization in China?, *Oxford Economic Papers*, **47**(1): 117–35.

Knight, J. and Shi Li (1993), The determinant of educational attainment, in K. Griffin and R. Zhao (eds), *The Distribution of Income in China*, New York: St Martin's Press.

Knight, John and Lina Song (1991), The determinants of urban income inequality in China, *Oxford Bulletin of Economics and Statistics*, **53**(2): 123–54.

Knight, John, and Lina Song (1993a), Why do urban wages differ in China?, in K. Griffin and R. Zhao (eds), *The Distribution of Income in China*, New York: St Martin's Press.

Knight, J.; and Lina Song (1993b), The spatial contribution to income inequality in rural China, *Cambridge Journal of Economics*, **17**: 195–213.

Knight, John and Lina Song (1999), Employment constraints and sub-optimality in Chinese enterprises, *Oxford Economic Papers*, **51**(2): 284–99.

Knight, John and Lina Song (2000), Differences in educational access in rural China, draft of working paper, Institute of Economics and Statistics, University of Oxford.

Krugman, P. (1998), Bubble, boom, crash: theoretical notes on Asia's crisis, mimeo, Cambridge, MA: MIT.

Kueh, Y.Y. (1989), The Maoist legacy and China's new industrialization strategy, *China Quarterly*, **119**: 420–47.

Kuznets, S. (1964), Economic growth and the contribution of agriculture, in C.K. Eicher and L.W. Witt (ed.), *Agriculture in Economic Development*, New York: McGraw-Hill.

Lambert, P.L. and J.R. Aronson (1993), Inequality decomposition analysis and the Gini coefficient revisited, *Economic Journal*, **103**: 1221–7, September.

Lardy, Nicholas R. (1980), Regional growth and income distribution in China, in Robert F. Denberger (ed.), *China's Development Experience in Comparative Perspective*, Cambridge, MA: Harvard University Press, pp. 153–90.

Lardy, N.R. (1983), *Agriculture in China's Modern Economic Development*, Cambridge: Cambridge University Press.

Lardy, N.R. (1992), Chinese foreign trade, *China Quarterly*, **131**: 691–720.

Lardy, Nicholas R. (1995), The role of foreign direct investment in China's economic transformation, *China Quarterly*, **143**: 1065–82.

Lau, Kam-Tin and Josef Brada (1990), Technological progress and technical efficiency in Chinese industrial growth: a frontier production function approach, *China Economic Review*, **1**(2): 113–24, Fall.

Lee, Keun (1990), The Chinese model of the socialist enterprises: an assessment of its organization and performance, *Journal of Comparative Economics*, **14**(3): 384–400, September.

Lerman, Robert I. and Shlomo Yitzhaki (1984), A note on the calculation and interpretation of the Gini index, *Economics Letters*, **19**: 363–8.

Lerman, Robert I. and Shlomo Yitzhaki (1985), Income inequality effects by income source: a new approach and applications to the United States, *Review of Economics and Statistics*, **67**, 151–6.

Lerman, Robert, I. and S. Yitzhaki (1989), Improving the accuracy of estimates of Gini coefficients, *Journal of Econometrics*, **42**: 43–7.

Lewis, W.A. (1954), Economic development with limited supplies of labour, *Manchester Schools*, **22**: 139–91.

Liang, Zai and Michael J. White (1997), Market transition, government policies, and interprovincial migration in China: 1983–1988, *Economic Development and Cultural Change* **45**(2): 321–39.

Lin, Cyril Z. (1995), The assessment: Chinese economic reform in retrospect and prospect, *Oxford Review of Economic Policy*, **11**(4): 1–23.

Lin, J.Y. (1988), The household responsibility system in China's agricultural reform: a theoretical and empirical study, *Economic Development and Cultural Change*, Supplement: 199–224, April.

Lin, Justin Yifu (1990), Collectivization and China's agricultural crisis in 1959–61, *Journal of Political Economy*, **98**(6): 1228–52, December.

Lin, J.Y. (1992), Rural reforms and agricultural growth in China, *American Economic Review*, **82**(1): 34–51.

Liou, K.T. (1998), *Managing Economic Reforms in Post-Mao China*, London: Praeger.

Liu, Minquan (1999), Capitalist firms, public enterprises: ownership reform and privatization of Chinese state-owned enterprises, in S. Cook, S. Yao and J. Zhuang (ed.) *The Chinese Economy under Transition*, London: Macmillan Press.

Liu, Xiaming, Haiyan Song, Yinqi Wei and Peter Romilly (1997), Country characteristics and foreign direct investment in China: a panel data analysis, *Weltwirtschaftliches Archiv*, **133**(2): 311–29.

Loewy, Michael B. and David H. Papell (1996), Are US regional incomes converging? Some further evidence, *Journal of Monetary Economics*, **38**(3): 587–98, December.

Lu, Xieyi (2003), The problem of peasant workers must be fundamentally resolved, *Xin Hua When Zhai*, December: 9–14.

Lucas, Robert E., Jr. (1988), On the mechanics of economic growth, *Journal of Monetary Economics*, **22**(1): 3–42, July.

Mankiw, N. Gregory, David Romer and David N. Weil (1992), A contribution to the empirics of economic growth, *Quarterly Journal of Economics*, **107**(2): 407–37, May.

Mas-Colell, A., M.D. Whinston and J.R. Green (1995), *Microeconomic Theory*, Oxford: Oxford University Press.

McMillan, John and Barry Naughton (1992), How to reform a planned economy: lessons from China, *Oxford Review of Economic Policy*, **18**(1): 130–43, Spring.

Mellor, J.W. (1976), *The Economics of Growth: A Strategy for India and the Developing World*, Ithaca, NY: Cornell University Press.

Mellor, J. and Uma J. Lele (1973), Growth linkages of the new food grain technologies, *Indian Journal of Agricultural Economics*, **18**(1): 35–55, January–March.

Meng, X. (1999), Urban unemployment and social security reform in China, Manuscript, Australian National University.

Meng, X. (2000), *Labour Market Reform in China*, Cambridge: Cambridge University Press.

Meng, Xin (2001), Unemployment, consumption smoothing and precautionary saving in urban China, paper presented to the ASSA annual conference in New Orleans, LA, USA.

Milanovic B. (1994), The Gini-type functions: an alternative deviation, *Bulletin of Economic Research*, **46**(1): 81–91.

Ministry of Agriculture (MOA) (Planning Bureau) (1989), *China Rural Statistical Compilation, 1949–86*, Beijing: Agricultural Publishing House.

Ministry of Agriculture (MOA) (various issues, 1986–99), *Statistical Data of Chinese Agriculture*, Beijing: Agricultural Publishing House.

Ministry of Agriculture (MOA) (Research Centre of Economic Policy) (1991), *Rural China: A Review of Policy Research, Volume II*, Beijing: Reform Publishing House.

Ministry of Agriculture (MOA) (1995), *China's Agricultural Development Report, 1995*, Beijing: Agriculture Press.

Ministry of Agriculture (MOA) (1998), *Rural Household Survey Data in 1998*, Beijing: Agriculture Press.

Ministry of Agriculture (MOA) (2002), *Household Survey Data*, Beijing: Agriculture Press.

Ministry of Agriculture (MOA) (1978–1987, 1988, 1989, 1990, 1991, 1992 and 1993), *Chinese TVE Yearbook*, Beijing: Agriculture Press.

Mookherjee, D. and Shorrocks, A.F. (1982), A decomposition analysis of the trend in UK income inequality, *Economic Journal*, **92**: 886–902.

Morduch, Jonathan and Terry Sicular (1998), Rethinking inequality decomposition, with evidence from rural China, Development Discussion Paper No. 636, Harvard Institute for International Development, Harvard University.

National Bureau of Statistics (NBS) (1960), *Ten Years of Great Success*, Beijing: Statistical Press.

National Bureau of Statistics (NBS) (1986–93), *Urban Household Survey Data for Liaoning and Sichuan, 1986–93*, Beijing: Statistical Press.

National Bureau of Statistics (NBS) (1988–90), *Rural Household Survey Data for Jiangsu, Liaoning and Sichuan, 1988–90*, Beijing: Statistical Press.

National Bureau of Statistics (NBS) (1990), Household surveys data, Beijing: Statistical Press.

National Bureau of Statistics (NBS) (various issues, 1980–2003), *Statistical Yearbook of China (CSYB)* Beijing: Statistical Press.

National Bureau of Statistical (NBS, 1996), *China Regional Economy: A Profile of 17 years of Reform and Open-up*, Beijing: Statistical Press.

National Bureau of Statistics (NBS) (1997–9), *China Labour Statistical Yearbook*, various issues, Beijing: Statistical Press of China.

National Bureau of Statistics (NBS) (1998), *Urban Household Survey Data,* Beijing: Statistical Press.

National Bureau of Statistics (NBS) (1999a), *Population Statistical Yearbook of China*, Beijing: Statistical Press.

National Bureau of Statistics (NBS) (1999b), *Fifty Years of Statistical Data of New China*, Beijing: Statistical Press, Beijing.

Nolan, P. (1991), Reforms and social development in China, mimeo, University of Cambridge.

Nolan, P. (1995), *China's Rise, Russia's Fall*, Basingstoke: Macmillan Press.

Nolan, P. (2003), China at the crossroads, unpublished manuscript, University of Cambridge.

Nolan, P. and F. Dong (1990), *The Chinese Economy and Its Future*, Cambridge: Polity Press.

Nolan, P. and R.F. Ash (1995), China's economy on the eve of reform, *China Quarterly*, **144**: 980–98.

Nolan, P. and X. Wang (2000), Reorganising amid turbulence: China's large-scale industry, in S. Cook, S. Yao and J. Zhuang (eds), *The Chinese Economy Under Transition*, Basingstoke: Macmillan Press.

Pan, Shaohua (1998), Asia Pacific economic cooperation and regionalism in the world of globalisation and regionalisation, unpublished PhD dissertation, University of Sheffield, UK.

*People's Daily* (2000a), China becomes the 9th largest exporting nation in the world, 14 March, p. 1.

*People's Daily* (2000b), There are further eight million people moving out of poverty in rural China, 26 December, p. 1.

*People's Daily* (2000c), China's GDP surpasses the landmark of one trillion US dollars, 31 December, p. 1.

*People's Daily* (2001), Shanghai's per capita GDP surpasses 4000 US dollars, 3 January, p. 1.

*People's Daily* (2003), 4 July.

*People's Daily* (2003a), International trade, 13 October, p. 1.

*People's Daily* (2003b), Urban and rural resident deposits break the 10 trillion yuan record, 18 October, p. 1.

*People's Daily* (2003c), Telephones: numbers reach 500 million, 24 October, p. 1.

*People's Daily* (2004), 12 January; 15 January; 20 January; 21 January; 10 February.

Perkins, D. (1988), Reforming China's economic system, *Journal of Economic Literature*, **26**(2): 601–45.

Perkins, Dwight (1994), Completing China's move to the market, *Journal of Economic Perspectives*, **8**(2): 23–46.

Perkins, D. and S. Yusuf (1984), *Rural Development in China*, Baltimore, MD: Johns Hopkins University Press.

Perron, Pierre (1989), The great crash, the oil price shock and the unit root hypothesis, *Econometrica*, **57**(6): 1361–401, November.

Perron, Pierre (1994), Trend, unit root and structural change in macroeconomic time series, in B.B. Rao (eds), *Cointegration for the Applied Economists*, London: Macmillan Press, pp. 113–46.

Perron, Pierre (1997), Further evidence on breaking trend functions in macroeconomic variables, *Journal of Econometrics*, **80**(2): 355–385, October.

Pomfret, R. (1997), Growth and transition: why has China's performance been so different?, *Journal of Comparative Economics*, **25**: 422–40.

Prybyla, J.S. (1985), Economic problem of communism: a case study of China, in *Comparative Economic Systems: Models and Cases*, Homewood, IL: Irwin.

Pyatt, G. (1976), On the interpretation and disaggregation of Gini coefficients, *Economic Journal*, **86**: 243–55.

Pyatt, G., C.-N. Chen; J. Fei (1980), The distribution of income by factor components, *Quarterly Journal of Economics*, 451–73, November.

Quah, Danny (1991), International patterns of growth: I. Persistence in cross-country disparities, working paper, Cambridge, MA: MIT.

Quah, Danny (1993), Empirical cross-section dynamics in economic growth, *European Economic Review*, **37**(2–3): 426–34, April.

Radelet, S. and D. Jeffrey Sachs (1998), The east Asian financial crisis: diagnosis, remedies, prospects, *Brooking Papers on Economic Activity*, 1: 1–90.

Raiser, Martin (1998), Subsidising inequality: economic reforms, fiscal transfers and convergence across Chinese provinces, *Journal of Development Studies*, **34**(3): 1–26.

Rao, V.M. (1969), Two decompositions of concentration ratio, *Journal of the Royal Statistical Society, Series A*, **132**: 418–25.

Ravallion, Martin (1994), *Poverty Comparisons*, Chur: Harwood Academic Publishers.

Ravallion, Martin and Jyotsna Jalan (1996), Growth divergence due to spatial externalities, *Economics Letters*, **53**: 227–32.

Ravallion, Martin and Jyotsna Jalan (1999), China's lagging poor areas, *American Economic Review*, **89**(2): 301–5.

Rawski, Thomas G. (2001), What is happening to China's GDP statistics? *China Economic Review*, **12**(4): 347–54.

Riskin, C. (1987), *China's Political Economy: The Quest for Development Since 1949*, Oxford: Oxford University Press.

Riskin, C. (1994), Chinese rural poverty: marginalised or dispersed?, *American Economic Review*, **84**(2): 281–4.

Riskin, Carl (1996), Rural poverty in post-reform China, in R. Garnaut, S. Guo and G. Ma (eds) *The Third Revolution in the Chinese Countryside*, Cambridge: Cambridge University Press.

Romer, P. (1986), Increasing returns and long-run growth, *Journal of Political Economy*, **94**(4): 1002–37.

Rozelle, S. (1994), Rural industrialisation and increasing inequality: emerging patterns in China's reforming economy, *Journal of Comparative Economics*, **19**: 362–91.

Rozelle, Scott, Jikun Huang and Linxiu Zhang (1997), Poverty, population and environmental degradation in China, *Food Policy*, **22**(3): 229–51.

Rozelle, Scott, Albert Park, Vincent Benziger and Changqing Ren (1998), Targeted poverty investments and economic growth in China, *World Development*, **26**(12): 2137–51.

Sala-i-Martin, Xavier X. (1996), The classical approach to convergence analysis, *Economic Journal*, **106**: 1019–36, July.

Seguino, Stephanie (2000), Gender inequality and economic growth: a cross-country analysis, *World Development*, **28**(7): 1211–30.

Sengupta, Jati K. and Espana, Juan R. (1994), Exports and economic growth in Asian NICs: an econometric analysis for Korea, *Applied Economics*, **26**: 342–57.

Shalit, Haim (1985), Calculating the Gini index for individual data, *Oxford Bulletin of Economics and Statistics*, **47**: 185–9.

Shorrocks, Anthony, F. (1982), Inequality decomposition by factor components, *Econometrica*, **50**: 193–211.

Shorrocks, Anthony, F. (1984), Inequality decomposition by population subgroups, *Econometrica*, **52**: 1369–85.

Sicular, T. (1993), The quest for sustained growth in Chinese agriculture, in A.J. Rayner and D. Colman (eds), *Current Issues in Agricultural Economics*, London: Macmillan Press.

Silber, J. (1989), Factor components, population subgroups and the computation of the Gini index of inequality, *Review of Economics and Statistics*, **71**: 107–15.

Song, Lina (1999), Gender effects on household resource allocation in rural China, working paper, Institute of Economics and Statistics, University of Oxford.

Song, Lina (2002), Income maximisation or risk-aversion? The motivation for rural–urban labour migration in China, unpublished manuscript, University of Nottingham.

Stiglitz, Joseph (2002), China takes own steps to leapfrog poverty, *The Times*, Monday 24 June, p. 41.

Theil, H. (1967), *Economics and Information Theory*, Amsterdam: North-Holland.

Tsui, Kai Yuen (1991), China's regional inequality, 1952–1985, *Journal of Comparative Economics*, **15**(1): 1–21.

Tsui, Kai Yuen (1993), Decomposition of China's regional inequalities, *Journal of Comparative Economics*, **17**: 600–27.

Tsui, Kai Yuen (1996), Economic reform and interprovincial inequalities in China, *Journal of Development Economics*, **50**(2): 353–68.

Tsui, Kai Yuen (1998a), Factor decomposition of Chinese rural income inequality: new methodology, empirical findings, and policy implications, *Journal of Comparative Economics*, **26**: 502–28.

Tsui, Kai Yuen (1998b), Trends and inequalities of rural welfare in China: evidence from rural households in Guangdong and Sichuan, *Journal of Comparative Economics*, **26**: 783–804.

The United Nations (1997), *Economic and Social Survey of Asia and the Pacific*, Economic and Social Commission for Asia and the Pacific, Bangkok: ESCAP.

US Department of Commerce, Economics and Statistics Administration, and Bureau of Census (1980–96), *Statistical Abstract of the United States*.

Walters, B. (1995), Engineering macroeconomics: a reconsideration of growth theory, *World Development*, **23**(11): 1869–80.

Wang, Feng and Xuejin Zuo (1999), Inside China's cities: institutional barriers and opportunities for urban migrants, *American Economic Review*, **89**(2): 276–80.

World Bank (1991), *China: Managing an Agricultural Transformation (Part I – Grain Sector Review), Working Papers, Volume I: Working Papers 1–3*, China Department, Agricultural Operations Division, Asia Regional Office, Washington, DC: World Bank.

World Bank (1993), *The East Asian Miracle*, Washington, DC: World Bank.

World Bank (1993, 1999, 2000, 2002), *World Development Report, Various Issues,* Oxford: Oxford University Press.

World Bank (1997), *Sharing Rising Incomes: Disparities in China*, Washington, DC: World Bank.

World Bank (1999a), Vietnam development report 2000: attacking poverty, *Joint Report of the Government–Donor–NGO Working Group for Vietnam*, Washington, DC: World Bank.

Wu, Harry X. and Zhou Li (1996), Rural-to-urban migration in China, *Asian-Pacific Economic Literature*, **11**: 54–67.

Wu, Zhongmin (2001), Regional unemployment, rural-to-urban migration and the economic reforms of China, PhD thesis, Department of Economics, University of Southampton.

Wu, Zhongmin and Shujie Yao (2003), Inter-migration and intra-migration in China, a theoretical and empirical analysis, *China Economic Review*, **14**: 371–85.

Yang, Dennis Tao and Hao Zhou (1996), Rural–urban disparity and sectoral labor allocation in China, paper presented at the annual meeting of the Association for Asian Studies, April, Honolulu, Hawaii.

Yang, D. Tao (2000), Urban-biased policies and rising income inequality in China, *American Economic Review*, **89**(2): 306–10.

Yao, Shujie (1994), *Agricultural Reforms and Grain Production in China*, London: Macmillan Press.

Yao, Shujie (1997a), Decomposition of Gini coefficients by income factors: a new approach and application, *Applied Economics Letters*, **4**: 27–31.

Yao, Shujie (1997b), Industrialization and spatial income inequality in rural China, 1986–92, *Economics of Transition*, **5**(1): 97–112.

Yao, Shujie (1997c), Profit sharing, bonus payment, and productivity: a case study of Chinese state-owned enterprises, *Journal of Comparative Economics*, **24**: 281–296.

Yao, Shujie (1999a), On the causal factors of the China's famine during 1959–61, *Journal of Political Economy*, **107**(6): 1365–72.

Yao, Shujie (1999b), On the decomposition of the Gini coefficient by population class and income source: a spreadsheet approach, *Applied Economics*, **34**: 1249–64.

Yao, Shujie (1999c), Economic growth, income inequality and poverty in China under economic reforms, *Journal of Development Studies*, **35**(6): 104–30, August.

Yao, Shujie (2000), Economic development and poverty alleviation in China under economic reforms, *Economic Development and Cultural Change*, **48**(3): 447–74.

Yao, Shujie (2002), China's rural economy in the first decade of the 21st century: problems and growth constraints, *China Economic Review*, **13**(4): 354–60.

Yao, Shujie (2004), Unemployment and urban poverty in China, a case study of Guangzhou and Tianjin, *Journal of International Development*, **16**: 171–88.

Yao, Shujie and D. Colman (1990), Chinese agricultural policy and the grain problem, *Oxford Agrarian Studies (Oxford Development Studies)*, **18**(1): 23–34.

Yao Shujie and Jirui Liu (1996), Decomposition of Gini coefficients by class: a new approach, *Applied Economics Letters*, **3**: 115–119.

Yao, Shujie and Jirui Liu (1998), Economic reforms and spatial income inequality in China, *Regional Studies*, **32**(8): 735–46.

Yao, Shujie and Zongyi Zhang (2001a), On regional inequality and diverging clubs: a case study of contemporary China, *Journal of Comparative Economics*, **29**: 466–84.

Yao, Shujie and Zongyi Zhang (2001b) Regional growth in China under economic reforms, *Journal of Development Studies*, **38**(2), 167–86, December.

Yao, Shujie and Zongyi Zhang (2003), Openness and economic performance, a comparative study of China and the East Asian newly industrialised economies, *Journal of Chinese Economic and Business Studies*, **1**(1): 71–96.

Yao, Shujie, Zongyi Zhang and Lucia Hanmer (2004), The implications of growing inequality on Poverty reduction in China, *China Economic Review*, **15**: 145–63.

Yao, Yudong, D. Newbery and P. Pedroni (2000), Have China's provinces formed an income divergence club since 1978?, mimeo, University of Cambridge.

Yap, Lorene Y.L. (1977), The attraction of cities: a review of the migration literature, *Journal of Development Economics*, **4**: 239–64.

Yitzhaki, S. (1994), Economic distance and overlapping of distributions, *Journal of Econometrics*, **61**: 147–59.

Yue, Chia Siow (1999), Trade, foreign direct investment and economic development of Southeast Asia, *The Pacific Review*, **12**(2): 249–70.

Zhang, Xiaohui, Changbao Zhao and Liangbiao Cheng (1995), 1994: the positive description on the inter-regional migration of rural labour force, *Strategy and Management*, **5**: 26–34.

Zhang, W.W. (2000), *Transforming China*, London: Macmillan Press.

Zhao, Yaohui (1999), Labour migration and earnings differences: the case of rural China, *Economic Development and Cultural Change*, **48**(4): 767–82.

# Index